THE COMPLETE BOOK OF AUSTRALIAN FISHING

THE COMPLETE BOOK OF AUSTRALIAN FISHING

STEVE STARLING

M

Acknowledgements

Among the many individuals and organisations who helped in some way with the production of this book several stand out. Most notable are Brett 'Booger' Deeney and his staff at *The Compleat Angler* tackle store, located in Dymock's Arcade, George Street, Sydney.

Thanks also go to *The Tackle Shop* in Waverley, and to Ian Muller at *Kiama Bait and Tackle*.

I would also like to express my appreciation to David Roche of *Studio 10* in Redfern, Sydney for the equipment photography and Jenny Muller for her help at the keyboard.

Above all, I'd like to thank my fellow anglers, here and throughout the world, for their combined wisdom passed to me freely over the past twenty five years. Fishing is truly a sport which recognises no boundaries of language, nationality or geography, and the exchange of information which occurs whenever anglers get together is surely the life blood of this wonderful undertaking we call recreational fishing.

First published 1991 by
PAN MACMILLAN PUBLISHERS AUSTRALIA,
a division of Pan Macmillan (Australia) Pty Limited
63-71 Balfour Street, Chippendale, Sydney NSW 2008
ACN: 001184014

Published by arrangement with Bacragas Pty Limited. Level 6, 8 Help Street,
Chatswood NSW 2067

Copyright © Steve Starling 1991
Illustrations copyright © Bacragas Pty Limited 1991

All rights reserved. No part of this book may be reproduced or transmitted in
any form or any means, electronic or mechanical, including photocopying,
recording or by any information storage and retrieval system, without prior
permission in writing from the publisher.

National Library of Australia
cataloguing in publication data

Starling, Stephen.
The complete book of Australian fishing.

Includes index.
ISBN 0 7329 0742 X.

1. Fishing — Australia. I. Title.

799.10994

Edited by Annabel Adair
Design and art by J. Harvey Hapi and Benjamin Mitchell
Illustrations by J. Harvey Hapi
Typeset in Janson
Produced in Hong Kong through Mandarin Offset

Contents

Introduction

Tackle 9

Baits and Lures 53

Fish Species 75

Techniques 129

Reading the Water 171

Fishing Locations 189

Index

Introduction

Surveys of our recreational habits consistently place fishing among the top three outdoor activities, with more than four million Australians 'wetting a line' every year. Swimming and tennis are the only other sports that can match those figures.

In the process of pursuing their piscatorial passions, this army of anglers spends well over two billion dollars per annum on hooks and sinkers, rods and reels, fishing line, petrol, bait, accommodation and all of the other essentials, accessories and peripherals of the sport.

Not even the threat of economic uncertainty can dull the enthusiasm of the avid angler. Indeed, during the recession of 1990/91, sales figures for low to mid-priced tackle jumped significantly, confirming the theory that tough times have little impact on certain forms of leisure spending.

So what has fishing got to offer that makes it so attractive to one in four Australians? Is it the chance it presents to escape the daily grind and soak up some of our great outdoors? Is it the comradeship and cameraderie of one's fellow anglers? Or the innate satisfaction that comes with hunting food for the family table? In truth, it is all of these things and more. It's also the mystery and uncertainty of the catch, the challenge of pitting intelligence against animal instincts and the satisfaction of occasionally winning.

I firmly believe that fishing touches a primal chord within us, and that it always has and always will. The earliest records of human civilisation mention recreational angling, and even before that, I am sure that more than a few cavemen fished on long after they'd fed the tribe — simply because they enjoyed it!

Despite its immense popularity — or perhaps even because of it — fishing remains cloaked in false mysteries. There is still a widely held notion that chance or luck plays a major role in angling results and that those gifted few who excel at the sport do so through some form of charmed good fortune verging on sorcery!

The truth is, consistently successful fishermen make their own luck. They do this through an understanding of their quarry, a close familiarity with their equipment, keen observation of their environment and, above all else, a willingness to invest a little extra time and effort to obtain a favourable result — in other words, exactly the same combination of attributes that characterises champions in any other sport. 'Luck' plays a tiny part, and its significance diminishes to zero over the longer run.

While it is no doubt true that some of these traits are inherited or develop in the angler while he or she is very young, it is also true that they can be learnt like other skills. Great anglers are both born and made!

The aim of this book is to provide, in one easily accessible source, the basic information about tackle, techniques, fish species, baits and rigs that the apprentice angler needs to make the quantum leap from luck to ability.

This is a leap that can be made at almost any age and any point along the recreational fishing road. For that reason, this is not only a text for the novice, but also for the more experienced angler who is ready to throw away the rabbit's feet and four-leaved clover and start making a little of his own good luck.

The bottom line is that fishing is like any other activity in life. The more you know, the more you enjoy and the better you become. This book can be one vital rung in that ladder. I sincerely hope it helps to bring you better fishing and the warm glow that comes with it!

Tackle

Since World War 2, the fishing tackle industry has consistently been among the first to make widespread use of new materials such as nylon, high-impact plastics, fibreglass, titanium and the 'space-age' composites — especially those based on graphite. These light, strong materials now form the basis of the lines, rods, reels and other items we use in our day-to-day angling. Indeed, it is rather easy to take them for granted, and to forget that our angling ancestors made do with much less 'user-friendly' equipment!

The performance of tackle made from these modern materials is generally so good that some observers are tempted to claim that there is little scope left for further development. Such people have existed throughout history; no doubt they also figured that the bone fish hook was such a quantum leap beyond its timber-and-twine predecessor that there was no room left for improvement!

As we approach the end of the twentieth Century, technology continues to evolve, albeit at a slower rate in some areas; and there is no reason to believe that this evolution will not continue to have an impact on the design and manufacture of fishing tackle. The past decade alone has brought us laser-sharpened hooks, multi-polymer lines, liquid crystal depth sounders, satellite position plotters, complex scent additives and affordable two-speed reels, to name just a few of the more significant innovations.

These technological advances beg an obvious question: Is fishing still a 'fair' sport, or have we weighted it too much in our favour? In other words, do the fish still stand a fighting chance? Anyone who fishes often cannot help but smile at that question. The number of times we return home empty-handed — with nothing more than a bag full of excuses or another 'one that got away' story — are all the answer that is needed.

The fact is, fish are becoming harder to catch. Many stocks have been reduced through over-harvesting and environmental degradation; others have simply become sensitized by man's activities, and 'wised-up' to traditional angling methods. In short, more anglers are pursuing less fish, and those fish are not as naive as their forebears. In many cases, our breathtaking technological tackle advances are doing little more than maintaining the status quo. In other areas, we are actually slipping behind.

To be consistently successful as fishermen, we must stay informed of the latest developments in tackle and technique, and be willing to try new ideas. On the other hand, it does not pay to become slavishly dependent on 'hardware' alone. As any computer buff will tell you, it's the 'software' that ultimately counts. In our case, that software is common sense, observation, know-how and commitment. An angler with his or her share of those assets will get by with the most basic of equipment.

Intelligent anglers keep an open mind on technological matters. They realise that not all the 'revolutionary breakthroughs' touted by manufacturers are necessarily steps forward along the evolutionary path of man-versus-fish. There is a certain degree of fashion and inbuilt obsolescence in the tackle industry, as in any other, and these factors present traps for the unwary or the gullible. In the long run, however, the angling community applies a kind of collective judgement to new items of equipment or styles of gear that come onto the market. Only the 'right stuff' survives for any appreciable period — the gimmicks and rip-offs fall aside and are relegated to history.

The tackle categories examined in this chapter cover most of the fishing gear used in Australia and New Zealand today. Brand names may change, model numbers come and go, and construction materials continue to evolve as they always have, but the basics of tackle remain largely unchanged. For that reason, the bulk of the information contained in this chapter will still be as applicable in the year 2001 as it was in 1991.

THE COMPLETE BOOK OF AUSTRALIAN FISHING

Ultra-Light and Light Spinning Reels

Spinning reels are also widely known as threadlines or fixed-spool reels, especially in European literature. Here in Australia and New Zealand, colloquial names such as 'eggbeater' and 'coffee grinder' are frequently applied to this style of fishing reel. These reels became widely available during the 1940s and '50s. Today, they are the most popular choice among anglers in Australasia, Europe and Canada, and come a close second behind closed-face or spincast reels in the United States.

Spinning, threadline or fixed-spool reels are characterised by the fact that their spools remain stationary when casting, with line spilling off over the lip of the spool. To retrieve line, a metal or ceramic bail arm is engaged. Driven by the reel's revolving rotor head, this bail arm wraps line around the stationary spool as the handle is cranked. The spool itself only rotates when line is pulled from the reel against the drag (slipping clutch), or via some form of pre-set 'bait-runner' device.

Spinning reels should always be located underneath the rod, although the distance from the butt to the reel seat varies with the size of the reel and the individual preferences of anglers. Light and ultra-light spinning reels of the type under discussion here are normally located between 10 and 35 centimetres from the butt end of the rod. Spinning reels are made in both right and left hand drive, although most modern types are ambidextrous, with the handle able to be moved from the right to the left side in a few minutes, using the most basic of tools.

There is considerable argument about which side of the reel the handle should be fitted to. Most experienced anglers agree that there are benefits for right handed operators in using a left hand wind spinning reel, particularly in the light and ultra-light tackle categories under discussion here.

When operating in this mode, the angler is able to execute a single-handed cast with his or her dominant arm, and commence the retrieve immediately, without swapping the outfit from one hand to another. Naturally, these advantages are less clear cut where double-handed casting is involved.

Light and ultra-light spinning reels are primarily used for freshwater and estuarine angling, although they have applications in other environments when fine lines are used. In fact, some sport fishermen take these small reels offshore and employ them to cast baits or lures at powerful pelagic species, including middle-weight

ABOVE: Light spinning tackle is a popular choice among estuary anglers. This lure caster has taken a fine flathead from a southern estuary.

kingfish, tuna and mackerel.

Regardless of the specific angling environment or target species pursued, light and ultra-light threadlines are best suited to lines with breaking strains between one and five kilos, and typically hold 150 to 250 metres of this light line. Most light and ultra-light spinning reels weigh between 180 and 280 grams, and have retrieve rates or gear ratios varying between about 4:1 and 6:1 (in other words, one turn of the handle results in four to six turns of the rotor head). Beyond these basic specifications, there is considerable variation between individual makes and models.

All modern spinning reels are fitted with a fighting drag or slipping clutch. This allows line to be pulled from the spool against a pre-set tension, helping to prevent break-offs when large or active fish are hooked. The two major drag or clutch configurations found on spinning reels are front drag and rear drag designs.

Front drag reels have a knob on

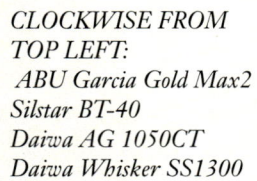

CLOCKWISE FROM TOP LEFT:
ABU Garcia Gold Max2
Silstar BT-40
Daiwa AG 1050CT
Daiwa Whisker SS1300

the face of the spool which is used to set and adjust the drag tension. This knob forces down on a series of metal and fibre washers inside the spool, thus controlling the drag's tension. In contrast, rear drag reels have a knurled dial or knob at the back, or on the underside, of the reel body. This acts upon a set of washers located within the body of the reel, applying tension to the main shaft that carries the spool.

Both drag styles have their advantages and disadvantages, primarily associated with the ease of making adjustments whilst playing a fish. Rear drag styles allow the tension to be adjusted quickly and conveniently, without risk of the angler's fingers touching or entangling the line. On the other hand, the front drag design is a time-proven and traditional configuration, and is generally agreed to be a more reliable and easily serviced system.

Other features found on some light and ultra-light spinning reels are 'bait runner' or free-spool mechanisms, 'fast-cast' bail tripping systems and 'long-spool' designs intended to assist in the casting of light lures and baits.

Bait-runner or free spool mechanisms are especially useful when presenting baits to relatively wary species in still or slow moving waters. They allow line to be pulled from the spool under very light tension, but facilitate the immediate engagement of the pre-set fighting drag at any point.

Long-spool designs are becoming increasingly popular among anglers who place great emphasis on making long casts with relatively light baits and lures. As well as a long, tapered spool, such reels usually feature a modified line-laying motion or oscillation, which also enhances the free flow of line when casting.

Fast-cast or bail triggering devices have less clear cut advantages and do not appear to be as popular today as they were a few years ago.

In summary, light and ultra-light spinning or threadline reels are much favoured by freshwater and estuarine anglers using light lines to pursue species such as trout, perch, bream, flathead, whiting and the like. They also have limited applications in the hands of more experienced anglers pursuing larger targets such as snapper, kingfish, tuna and mackerel.

Medium and Heavy Threadline Reels

Medium and heavy spinning or threadline reels are among the most popular reel styles used in Australia and New Zealand. They are particularly favoured by estuary and shore-based anglers fishing from beaches, jetties, breakwalls and the ocean rocks, as well as amongst offshore boat fishermen. Medium-sized spinning reels also have limited applications at the heavier end of the freshwater spectrum, and are popular with some barramundi anglers in northern Australia.

Spinning, threadline or fixed-spool reels of all sizes are characterised by the fact that their spools remain stationary when casting, with line spilling off over the lip of the spool. To retrieve line, a metal or ceramic bail arm is engaged. Driven by the revolving rotor head, this bail arm wraps line around the stationary spool as the handle is cranked. The spool itself only rotates when line is pulled from the reel against the drag (slipping clutch), or via a pre-set 'bait-runner' device.

Spinning reels should always be located underneath the rod, although the distance from the butt to the reel seat varies with the size of the reel and the individual preferences of anglers. Medium and heavy spinning reels are usually cast with a double-handed action, and for this reason, they should be located between 30 and 50 centimetres from the butt end of the rod.

Spinning reels of all sizes are made in both right and left hand drive, although most modern types are ambidextrous, with the handle able to be moved from the right to the left side in a few minutes.

LEFT TO RIGHT:
Mitchell 499 Pro
Silstar RXB-50
Shimano Bait Runner BTR 4500
Penn Spinfisher 850SS

LEFT: A pair of heavyweight giant trevally taken while casting surface lures off heavy spinning tackle.

There is disagreement about which side of the reel the handle should be fitted to. Many experienced anglers argue that there are benefits for right handed operators in using a left hand wind spinning reel, although these benefits are more clear cut in the light and ultra-light tackle categories discussed in the previous pages. When it comes to double-handed casting with medium and heavy threadlines, the choice between left and right hand cranking is less important, and is a matter of personal preference.

Medium and heavy spinning reels range in weight from about 280 to more than 500 grams. They are best suited to line gauges from four or five kilos right up to 12 or 15 kilos breaking strain. Lines heavier than 15 or 16 kilos are generally considered to be unsuitable for use with spinning reels of any size.

The medium and large spinning reels discussed here typically feature gear ratios varying between 3.5:1 and 6:1 (in other words, each turn of the handle results in three and a half to six turns of the rotor head and line pick-up). Gear ratios at the lower end of this range (3.5:1 up to about 4.8:1) are best when using heavier lines and targeting big, powerful fish.

Beyond these basic specifications, medium and heavy spinning reels share the same features as the light and ultra-light models discussed. Refer to those pages for descriptions of variations in drag (clutch) configurations and other systems.

Medium and heavy spinning reels offer an attractive combination of easy casting, high retrieve speed, structural integrity and line capacity in a reasonably-priced package. As such, they will always be immensely popular among anglers pursuing species such as snapper, salmon (kahawai), tailor, drummer, barramundi, trevally, middle-weight tuna and kingfish. In experienced hands, they are also effective tools on larger game fish including sharks, sailfish and small marlin.

It must be remembered, however, that no spinning reel — regardless of size — should be used as a 'winch', and that certain demanding tasks are better tackled by other reel styles such as overheads and sidecasts.

Closed-Face Reels

Closed-face reels are also known as spincast reels or 'spincasters' in some literature. They are small to medium reels generally used in freshwater or estuarine environments, although the largest models have some limited applications in general saltwater angling.

Closed-face or spincast reels are intended to be used on top of the rod, and are often coupled with special baitcaster or plug rods featuring a trigger or pistol-grip butt configuration. They may also be used with conventional, straight-butt rods.

Another closely-related group of reels known as semi-closed face reels are used underneath the rod in the manner of a spinning reel. Although popular with European freshwater anglers — particularly competition 'match' and 'coarse' fishermen — these semi-closed face models are not especially common in Australia and New Zealand, and are regarded as having only limited local application.

Standard closed-face reels are characterised by the conical or semi-spherical metal or plastic 'nose-cone' which covers the spool and line load. A hole in the centre of this cover permits the passage of the line, which is picked up and wrapped around the stationary spool via one or more spring-loaded pins mounted on the internal rotor head. Because of this configuration, closed-face reels fall into the same tackle 'family' as spinning reels: the fixed-spool reels. As with spinning reels, the spool of a closed face reel only rotates when line is pulled from the reel against the pre-set tension of the drag or slipping clutch.

Closed-face reels are made in both right and left hand drive, although some modern types are ambidextrous, the handle easily moving from the right to the left.

To cast a closed-face reel, a button or lever is depressed, usually with the angler's thumb. This retracts the pick-up pins and secures the line by pressing or pinching it between the inside of the spool cover and a rubber flange. Releasing the button or lever removes this pressure and allows line to flow freely over the lip of the spool and out through the hole in the spool cover. After the cast is completed, the angler turns the handle to re-engage the pick-up pins. Continuing to crank the handle will spin the rotor head and wrap line back onto the fixed spool.

The number and design of the pick-up pins in a closed-face reel are a good indicator of the reel's quality. Models with only one or two small, fixed, metal pins are generally inferior to those with a greater number of large diameter ceramic or polished pick-ups. In the very best and most expensive closed-face reels, the pick-ups will actually be fitted with rollers, which turn under load to reduce friction and wear on the line.

Drag systems on closed-face reels tend to be less sophisticated than those found on quality spinning reels. Most are adjusted via a star wheel on the handle shaft or a knurled dial atop the reel's body. These apply pressure to one or more washers, which in turn determine the tension of the slipping clutch. The majority of closed-face reels weigh between 200 and 400 grams and have comparatively limited line capacities. Most are suited to line strengths in the two to six kilo breaking strain range, and will hold from 70 to 150 metres of line, depending on the line's diameter. Unlike most other reel styles, many closed-face models are presented for sale already loaded with line by the manufacturer or importer.

The gear ratios of closed-face reels vary between about 3:1 and a little over 5:1, al-

TACKLE

LEFT: *A pair of beautiful trout from a high country stream. The brown on the right was taken on a closed-face reel.*

though most models retrieve line quite slowly, as a result of the relatively small diameter of their spools.

The greatest attributes of the closed-face reel are its ease of use and considerable casting accuracy over shorter distances. Even a novice can quickly master one of these reels and, with a little practice, become highly efficient at placing a bait or lure within a small target area at ranges up to 20 metres or so.

These features make the closed-face reel a handy tool for targeting bass, trout, perch, catfish and other light to middle-weight freshwater species, as well as bream, flathead, whiting and some other estuarine fish. Larger models will also cope with barramundi, saratoga, tailor, salmon (kahawai) and similar species, although great care must be exercised to prevent corrosion in these reels when using them around salt or brackish waters.

LEFT TO RIGHT:
Daiwa GC100
Kencor 310
Zebcoul 3 Classic
ABU Garcia ABU Matic Ultra Cast

Baitcaster Reels

Baitcasters or baitcasting reels are also known as plug reels or 'multipliers', although the latter term is mostly confined to British literature. Baitcasters are actually small to medium overhead reels with a revolving spool. They are most easily separated from the other overhead reels (featured on the next pages) by virtue of their smaller size, and also by means of the level-wind or line laying device fitted to the front of most baitcasters.

Baitcasters belong to the larger 'family' of fishing reels characterised by their revolving spools. The axle-mounted spool of a baitcaster turns to recover line as the handle is cranked, as well as to pay out line when a cast is made. The spool will also rotate to yield line against the tension of the drag (slipping clutch) when a fish is hooked.

Baitcasting reels are designed to be used on top of a rod, and are often coupled with specialist baitcaster or plug rods featuring a trigger or pistol-grip butt configuration. They may also be used with conventional, straight-butt rods. Smaller baitcasters are often cast with a single-handed action, while medium and large models may be used double-handed.

A button, lever or thumb-bar is used to disengage the gears prior to casting. This is called the free-spool lever or button. With the reel in free-spool, the angler uses his or her thumb to control the rotation of the spool, releasing pressure to allow line to flow, 'feathering' it lightly to prevent over-runs and backlashes, then clamping down once again to stop the spool from spinning at the completion of the cast. On most models, the

evenly across the spool. On older-style baitcasters, this level-wind was constantly engaged. More modern designs, however, incorporate a feature which allows the level-wind to disengage whenever the reel is placed in free spool or the drag yields line to a hooked fish. This allows for longer, easier casts and less friction on the line.

Nearly all of the baitcasters sold in Australia and New Zealand today have the handle on the right hand side and cannot be adapted for left-handed cranking. However, most manufacturers do feature at least a few left hand models in their catalogues, and these may be ordered if so desired.

The drag or slipping clutch on a baitcaster consists of one or more washers which nestle in a recess on the main drive gear and impose tension on the drive train. This tension is adjusted by means of a star wheel situated under the cross-bar of the handle. As a rule, the drag systems on baitcasters are superior in smoothness and reliability to those found in spinning and closed-face reels. Where applicable, the angler may also exert extra pressure against a hooked fish by clamping or squeezing down on the spool with his or her thumb.

Some baitcasters also feature a ratchet, clicker, or strike alarm which may be engaged when the reel is left unattended.

The majority of baitcasters on the market today weigh between 220 and 350 grams. Despite their relatively small size and light weight, they have generous line capacities, and most will accommodate anywhere from 180 to 350 metres of line in a gauge suited to their overall dimensions. Most baitcaster users choose lines with breaking strains between about two and eight kilos, although larger models will easily cope with the strains imposed by fishing with 10 to 15 kilo line. Gear ratios in baitcasters vary between about 4:1 and 7:1, although smaller models retrieve line relatively slowly, despite their high gear ratios. This is due to the small diameter of their spools.

Because the spool itself spins when a cast is made, over-runs and backlashes are always a possibility. These potential problems deter many newcomers from trying baitcasters, although with a reasonable amount of practice, most users soon achieve relatively trouble-free performance. Also, these days most quality baitcasters are fitted with anti-backlash devices of one type or another. These use friction, centrifugal force or magnetic field forces to control the spinning spool and slow it as the sinker or lure decelerates towards the end of a cast. A careful adjustment of these controls soon ensures smooth casts.

Despite their common name, these reels are used to cast lures more often than baits. In particular, they are popular with specialist lure casters targeting bass, barramundi, Murray cod and golden perch in freshwater; and flathead, mangrove jack, trevally, tailor and salmon (kahawai) in the salt. They are also well suited to light line work on offshore sport and game fish such as the smaller members of the tuna clan, snapper, mackerel and kingfish.

Although more expensive and somewhat more difficult to master than equivalent spinning and closed-face reels, baitcasters offer superior drag performance, line capacity, casting accuracy and control over hooked fish. For this reason, they are much favoured by more experienced anglers undertaking demanding styles of angling in fresh and saltwater environments.

ABOVE: This massive, 29 kilo giant trevally was taken on a surface popper cast from a large baitcaster or plug reel mated to a double-handed baitcaster rod and nine kilo breaking strain line. The fish was taken at Lizard Island, in far north Queensland.

ABOVE LEFT: A northern angler with a fine mangrove jack landed on double-handed baitcasting or plug tackle.

LEFT: These five baitcaster or plug reels are representative of the state-of-the-art equipment currently available to anglers in Australia and New Zealand.

gears are automatically re-engaged by partially turning the handle.

As well as a free spool control, almost all baitcasters are fitted with a level-wind device. This is a metal or ceramic line-guide mounted on an Archimedean screw. As the handle is turned to recover line, the level-wind moves slowly back and forth to lay the line

CLOCKWISE FROM TOP LEFT:
Shimano Coriolos CO-200
ABU Garcia 6500C Sprint
ABU Garcia 5000 Sprint
ABU Garcia 2500C
Shimano Citica CI-200

Overhead Casting Reels

Overhead reels are also called 'multipliers' or 'revolving drum' reels. They are almost identical in design to the baitcasting reels discussed on the previous pages, but are generally larger and do not feature a level-wind, line-laying device like that found on most baitcasters.

As their name implies, overhead reels sit atop the rod. They vary in size from the dimensions of a large baitcaster right up to giant, lever drag game reels capable of holding a kilometre or more of 60 kilo breaking strain line!

BELOW: Gaffing a yellowfin tuna taken on an overhead casting reel.

Game reels and some other special purpose overheads designated as trolling or deep sea models (discussed on the following pages) are not intended for casting, although skilled anglers may be able to deliver short casts with these reels when circumstances demand. However, another large class of overheads are specifically designed for casting.

Modern overhead casting reels generally weigh between 280 and 450 grams. Smaller models are suited to lines with breaking strains between about four and nine kilos, while larger models will easily cope with lines in the 10 to 20 kilo range.

Their capacities are generous, with spools that will typically accommodate between 200 and 600 metres of the chosen line gauge. Gear ratios in overhead casting reels range from 3:1 to at least 6:1. Slower ratios are preferred for heavy-duty tasks and applications demanding the use of very strong line, while faster retrieve rates are ideal when lure casting for speedy pelagic species such as tuna, kingfish and mackerel.

Nearly all the overhead reels sold in Australia and New Zealand today have the handle on the right hand side and cannot be adapted for left-handed cranking. However, most manufacturers do feature a few left hand models in their catalogues, and these may be ordered if so desired.

As with baitcasters, the spool of an overhead reel revolves to recover line, and also when casting. A free-spool button or lever disengages the gear train prior to casting and the angler's thumb controls the release and flow of the line. Casts with these reels are made with a double-handed action, and to facilitate this casting style, the reel is usually located between 40 and 60 centimetres above the butt end of the rod. Once the cast is completed, the gears are re-engaged by turning the handle

LEFT TO RIGHT:
ABU Garcia Ambassadeur 7C
ABU Garcia Ambassadeur 10
Daiwa Sealine 400H
Shimano Star Drag 4GT

ABOVE: A large yellowtail kingfish taken on a high speed overhead casting reel at Lord Howe Island.

or moving the free-spool lever.

Over-runs and backlashes are a potential problem when casting overhead reels, due to the revolving spool — particularly on larger models with relatively heavy spools. Modern cast controls featuring mechanical, centrifugal or magnetic spool brakes remove some of the risks, but in the long run there is no substitute for practice and an 'educated' casting thumb. Once mastered, overheads offer superb casting performance and are much favoured by anglers who regularly need to throw their baits or lures long distances from rocks, beaches, jetties or breakwalls.

Almost all overhead casting reels feature multi-washer drag or clutch systems controlled via a star wheel located underneath the cross-bar of the handle. This star wheel presses down on a spring or thrust washer which, in turn, regulates the tension on a series of metal and fibre washers nestled in a recess on the main gear cog. These drag systems are usually superior to those found on even the largest spinning reels. Where applicable, the angler may also exert extra pressure against a hooked fish by clamping or squeezing down on the spool of an overhead with his or her thumbs. Nearly all overhead casting reels are also fitted with a ratchet alarm or clicker, which may be activated when the reel is left unattended. This alarm is usually engaged via a sliding button on the end plate opposite the handle.

Overhead casting reels are not for everyone, but in demanding angling scenarios which call for the use of relatively heavy lines and the execution of long casts, they are hard to beat. In particular, they are favoured by shore-casters targeting snapper, kingfish, mulloway, sharks, tuna and mackerel, as well as boat anglers trolling, casting or bottom fishing for a variety of species.

Game and Trolling Reels

ABOVE: An aerobatic sailfish jumps just out of tagging range. Fast, powerful fish such as these demand the very best in tackle, and most anglers opt for light, lever drag game reels or high quality star drag models.

CLOCKWISE FROM TOP LEFT:
Penn Senator 40/ 113H
Penn International 50TW
Shimano Triton TLD 15
Daiwa Sealine 400H

Game and trolling reels are simply overheads which are not designed specifically for casting. Instead, they are intended for use from a boat, or a deep water shore location such as a jetty, where the line may be lowered directly into the water or lobbed a short distance.

Some reels in this category are no more than star-drag overheads without cast controls and with heavier spools than their casting counterparts. Others are sophisticated tools designed to accommodate the specific line classes recognised by the International Game Fish Association (IGFA) and its many world-wide affiliates. This latter group of reels are mostly fitted with lever drags rather than the conventional combination of washers and a star wheel found on overhead casting reels and simpler trolling models.

Game and trolling reels come in an array of sizes, from small models weighing 400 grams or so and suited to four or six kilo line, right up to giant models weighing several kilos and capable of holding a kilometre or more of 60 kilo breaking strain nylon or dacron line. (The 60 kilogram or 130 pound line class is the heaviest category recognised by the IGFA and its affiliates for the granting of records and merit certificates.) Apart from variations in size and weight, and the presence of sophisticated lever drag systems on more advanced models, the overall design and function of a game reel is almost identical to that of a baitcaster or overhead casting reel.

As with the other overhead reels described in this chapter, the spool of a game or trolling reel revolves to recover line, and also when paying it out. On star drag versions, a free-spool button or lever disengages the gear train to facilitate the paying out or casting of a bait or lure, while lever drag models require the lever to be pulled back towards its lightest setting. The gears remain meshed at all times in most lever drag reels, with 'free spool' being achieved through the relaxation of tension or pressure on the drag plates. In both cases, the angler's thumbs should help to control the release of line from the reel to prevent loose loops, over-runs and backlashes from occurring.

Lever drag systems were developed to provide the powerful, smooth clutch settings required to fight big fish on heavy line, although they have become increasingly popular with light line anglers pursuing active sport and game species. Instead of operating through relatively small washers nestled within the main gear cog, lever drags employ much larger pressure plates and brake surfaces. These are usually housed in the end plate opposite that carrying the handle (the left

hand end plate in a right hand wind reel).

As well as the main lever controlling the clutch, most lever drag game reels are also equipped with a pre-set dial, knob or lever. This controls the actual range of settings available through the main lever, and is vital in adjusting the tension settings to suit specific line classes. More fastidious game fishermen preset their drags with the help of a spring balance or weighing scales every time they venture out to pursue big fish. In most cases, they set their 'strike' or 'fighting' drag at about one third of the rated breaking strain of their line.

Gear ratios in game and trolling reels generally range between 1:1 and 4.5:1. These ratios are lower than those found in casting reels and are intended to provide maximum cranking and line recovering power when fighting big, powerful adversaries such as sharks, tuna and billfish. However, because of the relatively large spool diameters of these reels, line recovery is still quite rapid, despite the lower gear ratios.

Some of the most advanced lever drag game reels feature two or even three gear ratios, which may be selected at will by the angler and altered throughout a fight. High ratios are normally selected when recovering line quickly as the boat backs down or chases a fish, and lower gears engaged when a big fish sounds and must be pumped back towards the surface.

Nearly all the game and trolling reels sold in Australia and New Zealand have the crank handle and drag controls on the right hand end plate, and cannot be adapted for left-handed cranking. However, left hand models may be specially ordered from some manufacturers.

All game and trolling reels are fitted with a ratchet or strike alarm which may be set to sound a warning when line is pulled from the spool by a striking fish.

Game and trolling reels are among the most expensive items of tackle on the market today, with a top-line 60 kilo lever drag model costing several thousand dollars. However, they are unquestionably the best tools yet designed for battling big, active sport and game species in deep water.

Centrepin and Sidecast Reels

Centrepins are the most basic of all fishing reels. They consist of a line storage spool revolving on metal bushes or ball bearings attached to an axle, which is in turn mounted to a backing plate. Most are direct drive, with no gears whatsoever. Some have rudimentary drag systems, a ratchet or strike alarm, and perhaps a hardened metal or ceramic line guide, but the basic design remains the same. True centrepins are not widely used in Australia and New Zealand today, with the major exception of fly reels, which are discussed separately on the following pages.

The only group of local anglers who still rely on free-running centrepin reels to any great degree are the luderick or blackfish specialists of the Australian east coast, who find these simple but effective reels ideal when float fishing in moving water. Even among these diehards, centrepins are slowly giving way to lightweight sidecasts and spinning reels, although traditionalists rightfully lament the passing of the true 'knuckle-dusters', as centrepins were once known.

Sidecast reels are a fascinating variation on the centrepin theme. Although the concept originated in Britain late last century, the sidecast reel is today synonymous with Australian angling. Indeed, the world's only major manufacturer of sidecast reels — the Alvey company — is located in the suburbs of Brisbane, Queensland. From here, sidecast reels in a wide range of models and sizes are shipped all over Australia, New Zealand and, to an increasing extent, other parts of the world.

A sidecast is essentially a centrepin reel whose spool may be twisted or rotated through 90 degrees so that it can be cast in the manner of a fixed-spool reel — with the line flowing off over the lip of the spool. To recover line once a cast is completed, the spool is twisted back until it is once more aligned with the rod. This simple but innovative feature turns the sidecast into one of the most effective casting reels ever built, especially in the area of light and ultra-light baits and lures. In essence, sidecasts offer the powerful direct drive and sensitivity of a centrepin, combined with the easy casting capabilities of a spinning reel. They also require the minimum of care and maintenance. For these reasons, they have long been popular with Australian anglers, particularly those fishing from beaches, ocean rocks and jetties.

The disadvantages of sidecast reels are the potential line twist generated by the rotation and re-alignment of the spool every time a cast is made, the relatively slow retrieve speed of even the largest models, and the need to use a longer than normal rod with large diameter guides or runners. Furthermore, the reel seat on this rod should be located within 12 to 18 centimetres of the butt — much lower than normally found on double-handed casting rods. To prevent the problems caused by line twist, sidecast users should incorporate at least one, and ideally two, relatively small swivels into every rig they tie. One of these swivels should be tied in place well back up the line — above all other items of terminal tackle, be they sinkers, floats or lures.

Modest retrieve speeds and the necessity of using a long rod with large runners and a low reel mount are not seen as major drawbacks by regular sidecast users. Most of these anglers cast baits rather than lures, so retrieve speed is not critical, and long rods may actually be an advantage when distance casting from the shore, or even from a boat.

Sidecast reels are particularly well suited to scenarios where fish must be 'winched' up sheer cliff faces or onto high wharves and jetties. Few geared reels would cope with such abuse over a long period of time, but

the sturdy sidecasts take it in their stride.

Sidecasts are also ideal in situations where slack line needs to be fed quickly to a timidly biting fish. This is easily achieved by 'back-winding' a sidecast reel. The same slack can also be removed rapidly to set the hook if the need arises.

Although the most basic ('A' type) sidecasts must be 'palmed' like a centrepin when fighting a fish, more advanced types with drag systems and even non-reversing handles are also manufactured ('E' and 'C'

LEFT: The author with a 7.5 kilo blue groper taken on a large sidecast reel. These powerful, direct-drive reels are ideal for battling with stubborn, hard fighting fish such as groper, drummer, mulloway and sharks. They are also the ideal choice when fish need to be winched up cliff faces.

types). Most of these models are available in both right and left hand wind configuration. Similarly, sidecasts come in a wide range of sizes and line capacities, although in practical terms, spool diameters less than 12 or 15 centimetres negate many of the benefits and exaggerate the problems of the sidecast design. These reels are at their best and most useful in diameters of 15 to 20 centimetres. In those size ranges, they may be matched with lines as light as three or four kilos, or as heavy as 20 to 30 kilos!

In summary, sidecasts are well worth considering where there is an obvious need for a simple, robust reel to cast light and medium weight baits, and where rod length is not a major constraint. As such, they will remain a favourite reel style with a broad cross-section of the Australasian angling public.

LEFT TO RIGHT: Alvey 650-C5, Alvey 55-A5, Alvey 475-A52-FB, Steelite Centrepin.

Fly Reels

Fly reels are modified centre-pins designed specifically for fly fishing. Although constructed in a very similar manner to the general purpose centrepins described on the previous pages, fly reels do incorporate certain distinctive features.

Most fly reels are fitted with line guards, constantly engaged ratchets or 'clickers' and at least a rudimentary drag system. Most are also characterised by the holes drilled in their spools and back plates. These holes reduce the weight of the reel, as well as allowing the fly line and backing to dry more thoroughly after use. The vast majority of fly reels feature a direct drive — one turn of the handle resulting in one rotation of the spool. A few are geared, usually at a low ratio between about 1.5:1 and 3:1. The drag or clutch systems fitted to fly reels vary considerably, from simple clickers that impose a minimal amount of tension, through to multi-disc systems coupled with non-reversing handles. The latter are mostly employed in saltwater fly fishing.

Small numbers of so-called 'automatic' fly reels are still available, although they are not popular here in Australia and New Zealand. These quaint and somewhat old-fashioned reels

FAR RIGHT: A chunky rainbow trout taken on an Argentinian-made STH Neu Queen No.8 fly reel. Note the numerous ventilation holes in the reel's spool to help the line and backing dry out after use.
RIGHT: An estuary-dwelling flathead taken on light saltwater fly tackle and a streamer fly. Saltwater fishing places extra demands on fly tackle, especially reels. Those designed for trout and salmon may not be up to the task.

CLOCKWISE FROM TOP LEFT:
System Two 1011
Hardy Sovereign 7/8
Hardy Princess
Hardy Golden Prince 5/6
ABU Garcia Diplomat 256

rely on a clockwork mechanism which recovers loose line and backing at the squeeze of a trigger or press of a button. Most are small and intended for light-weight freshwater work. They have few obvious benefits.

In most styles of freshwater and light saltwater fly fishing, the reel serves as little more than a line storage device. During the casting and retrieval of the fly, and even when playing and landing small to medium-size fish, many experienced anglers prefer to strip the line in and pay it out by hand. Only when fishing is completed and line needs to be wound back onto the reel, or when a larger than average fish is hooked, does the reel come into play.

These light reels need only the most basic of drag systems — a clicker or simple calliper drag will normally suffice, backed up by an exposed spool rim which the angler may 'palm' or apply finger pressure to when fighting a larger adversary. Similarly, freshwater and light saltwater reels do not need large line capacities. So long as they can accommodate a full length fly line (usually about 30 metres) and an additional 40 or 50 metres of backing, they will easily handle any trout, bass, sooty grunter, flathead or bream hooked by a fly fisherman.

Heavy freshwater and medium weight saltwater targets such as barramundi, salmon (kahawai), large tailor, snapper, school kingfish, queenfish and small to medium tuna require a somewhat more sophisticated drag system and a more generous line capacity. Reels used in the pursuit of these targets should be fitted with a good calliper or disc drag with a reasonable range of tension settings, as well as an exposed spool rim for 'palming'. They should also be capable of storing a full length fly line and at least 100 metres of backing.

The most demanding of all fly fishing scenarios involves the targeting of medium to heavy-weight game and sport fish such as big trevally, tuna, kingfish, sailfish and even marlin. Reels for this purpose need to be robustly constructed. They should feature a very smooth disc drag system with a wide range of settings and be able to accommodate a full length fly line and at least 300 metres of backing. Such reels are sophisticated pieces of machinery, with a price tag to match!

An important consideration in the purchase of a fly reel is the fact that some light models and even a few medium-weight reels are not designed for salt and brackish water use. Extreme care must be exercised to prevent corrosion in these fly reels. Even fly reels built with saltwater angling in mind need careful attention and maintenance if they are to give long term, trouble free service. Water and salt tend to accumulate in the line load and can lead to damaging corrosion if not flushed clear with freshwater and thoroughly dried after use.

When selecting a fly reel, give consideration to the intended angling applications. Don't buy a more elaborate or expensive model than you need for the tasks at hand.

Ultra-Light and Light Spinning Rods

Ultra-light and light spinning rods or 'flick sticks' are intended for single-handed casting with small spinning (threadline) or semi-closed reels. Both of these reel styles are used underneath the rod. This type of rod is extremely popular among lure and bait fishermen targeting fresh and saltwater species such as trout, perch, sooty grunter, bream, flathead, whiting and even small snapper, tailor and salmon (kahawai).

Today, these light-weight rods are made almost exclusively from hollow, high-modulus fibreglass, kevlar, graphite fibres, boron, or a combination of those substances. These 'high-tech' materials offer an incredible strength-to-weight ratio and provide sensitivity, casting and fish-fighting performance undreamt of a decade or two ago.

Ultra-light and light spinning rods vary in length between about 1.5 and 2.5 metres, with most being in the 1.7 to 2.2 metre range. They typically carry between four and seven runners or line guides, and have their reel seats located 10 to 30 centimetres above the butt. The handles or grips are made from rubberised materials such as hypalon and duralon, or from cork. Cork handles are preferred by many expert anglers because of their extremely light weight and the way in which they transmit vibrations and delicate bites from the rod blank to the angler's hands. Most anglers choose to match these light rods with lines testing between one and five kilos, and casting weights from just a gram or two up to perhaps 25 or 30 grams.

The concept of balance is vitally important in light and ultra-light outfits built around these single-handed spinning rods. The rod, reel, line strength and casting weight should all be matched to provide optimum performance. When all of these factors are correctly balanced, a single-handed 'flick stick' becomes a virtual extension of the angler's arm and hand, and is a pleasure to use, hour after hour and day after day.

Many fine single-handed spinning rods are available 'off the rack' in better tackle stores, although some anglers still prefer to purchase a blank and construct their own rod, or have one custom built by a professional rod builder.

ABOVE: Trout anglers are one of the largest single user groups of ultra-light and light spinning rods. This handsome rainbow was taken on a custom rod.
TOP RIGHT: An estuary spin fisherman uses a light gaff to secure a flathead hooked on ultra-light spinning tackle and a diving lure.
RIGHT: From top to bottom — Ian Miller Ultimate Jig Flicker, Custom-built Sabre 1–2 kg rod, Shimano Aeroglas AR-2602, Daiwa Tele-lite GF-210L.

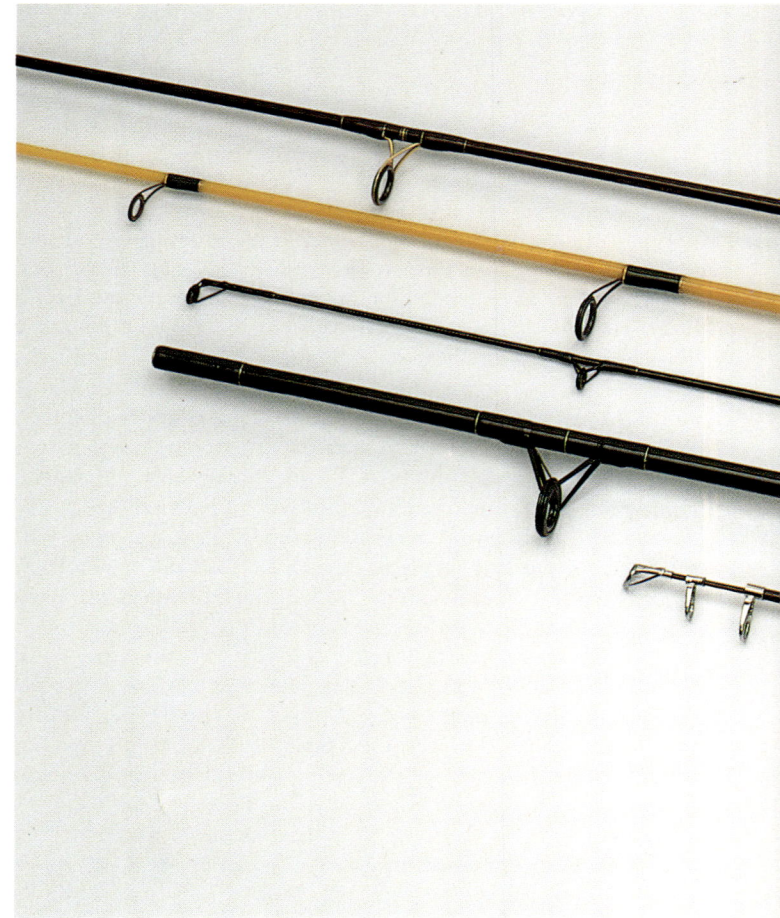

MODERN ROD MATERIALS

A revolution in rod making materials has occurred since the 1950s. Prior to that period, most fishing rods were made of bamboo, cane, timber or even metal. With the advent and widespread use of petroleum-based plastics, glassfibre or fibreglass soon emerged as the rod blank material of choice. Early fibreglass rod blanks were of solid construction. They were heavy and unresponsive. However, the development of hollow fibreglass blanks heralded a new era of strong, light-weight and affordable fishing rods.

Hollow fibreglass rods are manufactured by wrapping glass-fibre cloth around a metal jig or 'mandrel', then saturating the cloth with fibreglass resin. A catalyst mixed with the resin causes it to set, after which the mandrel may be removed and the blank trimmed and sanded as desired. This basic technique for manufacturing hollow fibreglass rods remains largely unchanged today, although there have been major advances in cloth and resin formulas, cloth cutting patterns and mandrel designs.

The next major step forward in rod construction was the use of carbon fibres or graphite. These materials were mixed with the glass fibres, or replaced them completely, to give a rod that was lighter and considerably more sensitive. Such materials are said to have a high 'modulus'; in other words, they return to their straight or unstressed state very rapidly after being flexed or bent. Graphite and graphite/glass composite rods are typically baked at high temperatures to assist in the setting and bonding of the resin and cloth.

Other materials such as kevlar and boron have also been used in rod manufacture with mixed results. Today, however, the bulk of rods and rod blanks on the market are made of hollow fibreglass, graphite or fibreglass/graphite composites.

Double-Handed Spinning Rods

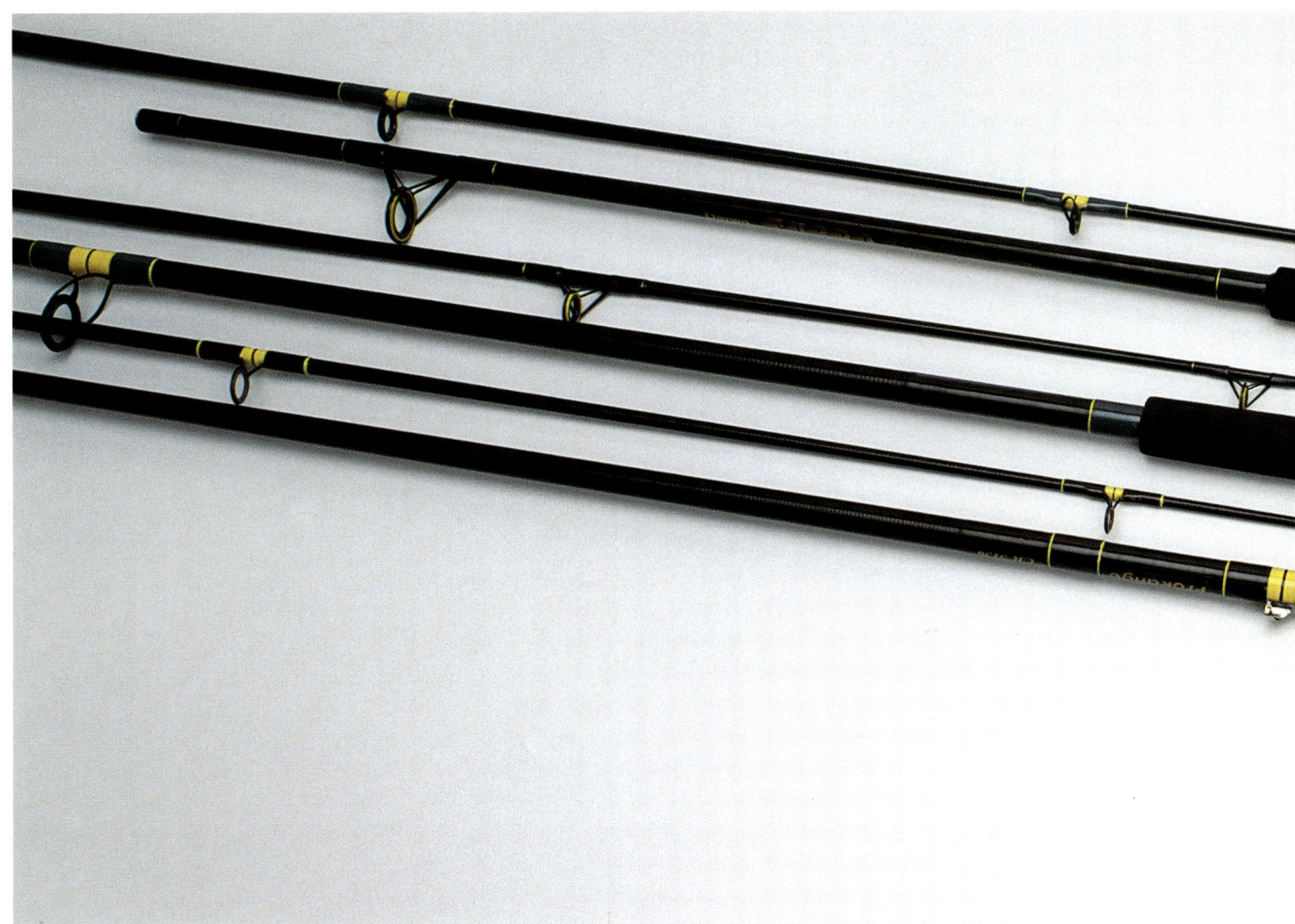

As their name implies, these rods are intended to be cast using both hands, in contrast to the single-handed spinning rods described on the previous pages. In Australia, this class of rod is sometimes known as a 'barra stick', despite the fact that double-handed spinning rods are generally less popular than baitcaster or plug rods among dedicated barramundi specialists.

Double-handed spinning rods are designed for use with medium-size spinning (threadline) reels, which are used underneath the rod. The lighter models in this category are suited to lines with breaking strains in the four to eight kilo range, and casting weights of 15 to 40 grams. Heavier 'magnum' double-handed spinning rods will cope with lines as heavy as 10 or 12 kilograms, and casting weights from 20 to 60 grams.

Double-handed spinning rods are much favoured by boat anglers targeting offshore species such as snapper, trevally, mid-range kingfish, the smaller tunas, mackerel, dolphin fish and even light-weight billfish such as sailfish and juvenile marlin. They are also used in some shore-based scenarios — particularly from jetties and deep water rock ledges — to catch a similar range of fish.

As mentioned earlier, double-handed spinning rods are also applicable to tropical fresh and saltwater fishing for barramundi and various associated species, although more experienced northern anglers tend to opt for single or double-handed baitcaster (plug) rods in this application. Nonetheless, the generic title of 'barra rod' or 'barra stick' has tended to become associated with some of the lighter and shorter rods in the double-handed spinning category.

Longer, heavier rods in this group are variously known as 'magnum spin sticks', 'bluewater spinning rods' or even as 'Moreton Bay spin sticks', because of their immense usefulness and popularity in that area of southern Queensland.

Nowadays, double-handed spinning rods are made almost exclusively from hollow, high-modulus fibreglass, kevlar, graphite fibres, boron, or a combination of those substances. These 'high-tech' materials offer the optimum combination of strength-to-weight, sensitivity, casting performance and fish-fighting power.

Most rods in this category measure between 1.8 and 2.8 metres, with the standard 'barra-style' model typically ranging from 2.0 to 2.4 metres and the heavier 'magnum' or 'bluewater' versions ranging from 2.2 to 2.6 metres. Both styles should carry between five and seven line guides or runners, and the inside

TACKLE

ABOVE: From top to bottom — Daiwa Turbo TS 25 M, Ol' Mate Fishing Rod, Pro Range CR 5136.

diameter of the runner closest to the reel (the stripping guide) should be over 2.5 centimetres.

The reel seat on a double-handed spinning rod is usually located between 30 and 50 centimetres from the butt, and the handles or grips are made from rubberised hypalon, duralon, cork, leather or wraps of nylon cord.

As with their single-handed counterparts, double-handed spinning rods are available in reasonable quantities 'off the rack' in tackle stores, or may be custom built to suit the angler.

ROD ACTION AND TAPER

The way in which a fishing rod bends under load is called its 'action'. This action is dictated by the materials used in the blank's construction, its diameter, the thickness of the blank's walls and — most importantly — the rate of taper of the rod from butt to tip.

Some rods taper very gradually from butt to tip. These are called slow taper rods and tend to exhibit a relatively even, parabolic bend when loaded. Slow taper blanks are traditionally used in the construction of fly rods, blackfish rods and some older style beach, rock and game rods.

Rods with a dramatic taper from butt to tip are said to have a fast taper. Under load, the top third of the rod bends quite easily, but the lower two thirds resists bending. Fast taper blanks are much favoured in the construction of modern jig rods, 'stand-up' game rods and many other rod styles. Most rods used today, however, fall between these two extremes and may be classified as medium taper or multi-taper.

RIGHT: A traditional-style game rod with a relatively progressive or parabolic bend under load.

Baitcaster Rods

Baitcaster or plug rods are designed to be used with baitcasting reels, smaller casting overheads and closed-face reels; all of which are intended to be used on top of the rod. Many of these rods feature a butt or handle with a moulded pistol-grip and trigger, although there has been a recent trend towards straight butts — with or without a simple trigger under the reel seat — especially on heavier, double-handed plug rods.

Baitcaster or plug rods range from light and ultra-light single-handed models measuring anywhere from 1.6 to 2.2 metres in length, up to double-handed versions typically measuring between 1.8 and 2.5 metres.

Shorter plug rods should be fitted with five to seven line guides and a tip, while longer models may require as many as

ABOVE: A handsome Australian bass taken while casting a lure with a single-handed baitcaster or plug outfit. Although this style of tackle is very popular with freshwater anglers, it also has many marine applications.

TACKLE

LEFT: From top to bottom — Silstar Powertip PT-60STB, Compleat Angler Custom Composite Developments BC-2B, Daiwa Rod Harrison Collection RH 21H, Shimano Black Magnum BKM-1552.

ABOVE: A big black jewfish — the northern cousin of the mulloway — taken on single-handed baitcaster gear. The rod is an American-made Loomis graphite baitcaster with a straight butt and trigger grip.

eight or even nine guides. Such a large number of runners are needed to keep the line clear of the blank under load, and to remove potential friction 'hot spots'. These guides or runners do not require particularly large inside diameters.

Light, single-handed baitcaster rods are typically used with lines testing between two and eight kilos, and casting weights from three or four grams up to about 25 or 30 grams. They are very popular among more experienced anglers pursuing freshwater species such as bass, barramundi, golden perch, Murray cod, sooty grunter and saratoga, as well as saltwater fish like flathead, mangrove jacks, queenfish, snapper and smaller kingfish, tuna and mackerel.

Heavier, double-handed plug rods may be mated with lines ranging from four to 15 kilos in breaking strain, and casting weights from 15 to 60 grams. They are much favoured by experienced anglers targeting large barramundi in brackish tropical waters, as well as trevally, middle-weight tuna and kingfish, mackerel, big snapper, small sharks and even the smaller billfish such as sailfish and juvenile marlin.

Today, most baitcaster or plug rods are made from hollow, high-modulus fibreglass, kevlar, graphite, boron, or a combination of those substances, these materials offering very high strength-to-weight ratios and providing great sensitivity, casting and fish-fighting power.

Many fine single-handed baitcasting rods and an increasing number of double-handed plug rods are available 'off the rack' in better tackle stores, although some anglers prefer to purchase a blank and construct their own rod, or have one custom built by a professional rod builder.

BUILDING YOUR OWN ROD

Making your own fishing rod is a viable alternative to buying a factory-made product. Custom rod building appeals not only to the home handyman looking to save a few dollars, but also to specialist anglers seeking a rod style or configuration not available commercially. Rod blanks and the various components or fittings needed to assemble a rod can be purchased from larger, better-stocked tackle stores or specialist mail-order outlets.

The rod is built by gluing on the handles or grips, reel seat, butt cap and tip runner, and binding the line guides in place with rod binding thread. A large part of the skill involved in custom rod building lies in working out which components to use, how many guides to fit and where to locate them. Experienced tackle shop staff may be helpful in this regard. In addition, there are many good books and even a few instructional videos on the market which will prove extremely beneficial to the first-time rod builder.

For those requiring a special, one-off rod, but lacking the time, inclination or skill to make their own, there are professional custom rod builders in most large cities or country centres who will perform this service for a fee.

Rock, Beach and Breakwall Rods

Casting rods for shore-based fishing from beaches, ocean rocks, breakwalls and jetties vary enormously in their construction, dimensions and appearance. To begin with, they may be specifically intended for use with any one of three different reel styles: spinning (threadline), overhead (including larger baitcasters) or sidecast. The type of reel used will dictate the configuration of the rod; especially in the area of butt dimensions, placement of the reel seat, the number of runners and the spacing of those runners.

Furthermore, specific rods in this category may be suited to light-weight applications — such as the pursuit of small fish, including whiting, mullet and bream — or heavy-duty work targeting the likes of snapper, salmon (kahawai), tailor, drummer, groper, kingfish, sharks or mulloway.

Generally, all of these rods are intended for double-handed use and must be reasonably long to facilitate distance casting, as well as to help the angler lift his or her rigs and hooked fish clear of shoreline obstructions such as weed, rocks and pylons. Most double-handed casting rods used by shore-based anglers in Australia and New Zealand measure between 2.5 and 4.4 metres, with by far the majority falling into the 2.8 to 3.6 metre range.

Those intended to be used with sidecast reels are usually the longest, and should have their reel seat located close to the butt — no more than 10 to 20 centimetres from the lower end of the rod. They should carry between four and six runners or line guides, with the line guide closest to the reel (the 'stripper') having an inside diameter of at least five centimetres.

Shore-casting rods for use with medium to large spinning (threadline) reels may have the same butt and runner configuration as sidecast rods, although the majority of Australasian anglers prefer to mount their spinning reels at least 35 to 50 centimetres from the bottom end of the rod, and to fit five to seven guides, depending on the length and taper of the blank. Again, the stripping guide should have an internal diameter of at least five centimetres to facilitate the flow of line from the reel when casting.

Overhead casting rods for shore-based work typically have a reel seat located 45 to 60 centimetres above the bottom end of the rod and carry six to nine line guides. The internal diameter of these runners is less critical than those fitted to sidecast and spinning reel models, as the line does not leave an overhead reel in large coils when casting.

Beyond these basic rules of thumb, there is scope for variation in shore-casting rods, especially when considering that

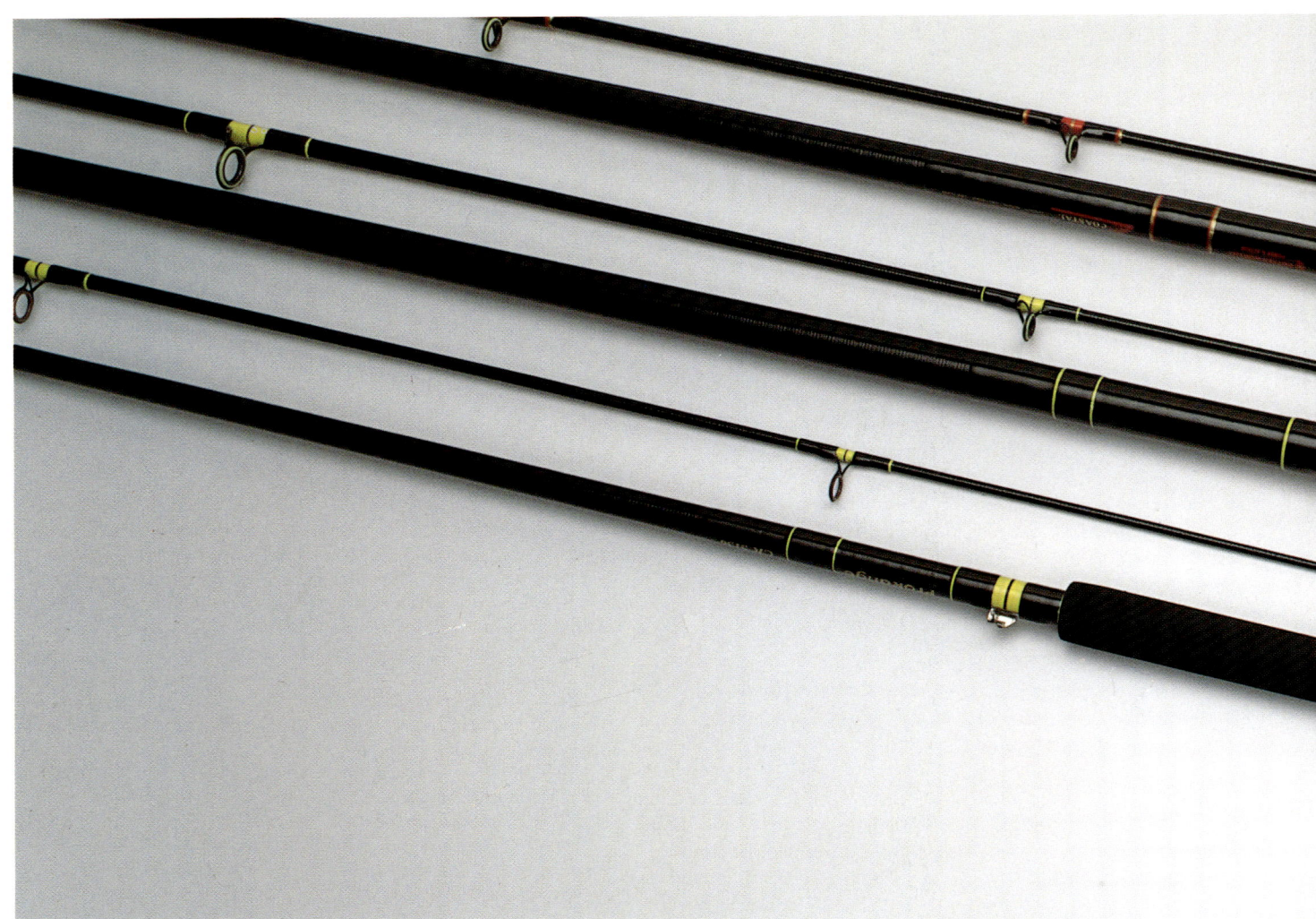

32

ONE-PIECE OR TWO?

Most rod styles discussed in this chapter are available in one- or two-piece configurations. A few rods designed specifically for the travelling angler break down into three, four or even five pieces, while yet another style of fishing rod is telescopic, with one section sliding inside the next for storage and transport.

The only real advantages of multi-piece rods are in the areas of storage and travel. If these factors are not major considerations when buying or building a rod, you are better off to opt for a single-piece model.

Ferrules or other connections add a potential weak spot to any rod and may also dampen or flatten the blank's action when casting or fighting a fish. These days, with modern glass-to-glass or graphite-to-graphite ferrules largely having replaced the older brass styles, such problems are minimised; nonetheless, they still exist to some extent.

some may be used with lines as light as four kilos breaking strain and sinkers or lures weighing less than 10 grams, while others are matched with 15 to 25 kilo line and casting weights as heavy as 120 grams!

RIGHT: A silver drummer taken on a one piece, four metre rock fishing rod.
BELOW: Three shore casting rods. From top to bottom — Butterworth Coastal 6144 2PM, Pro Range MT 7144, Pro Range CR 5136.

Sport and Game Rods

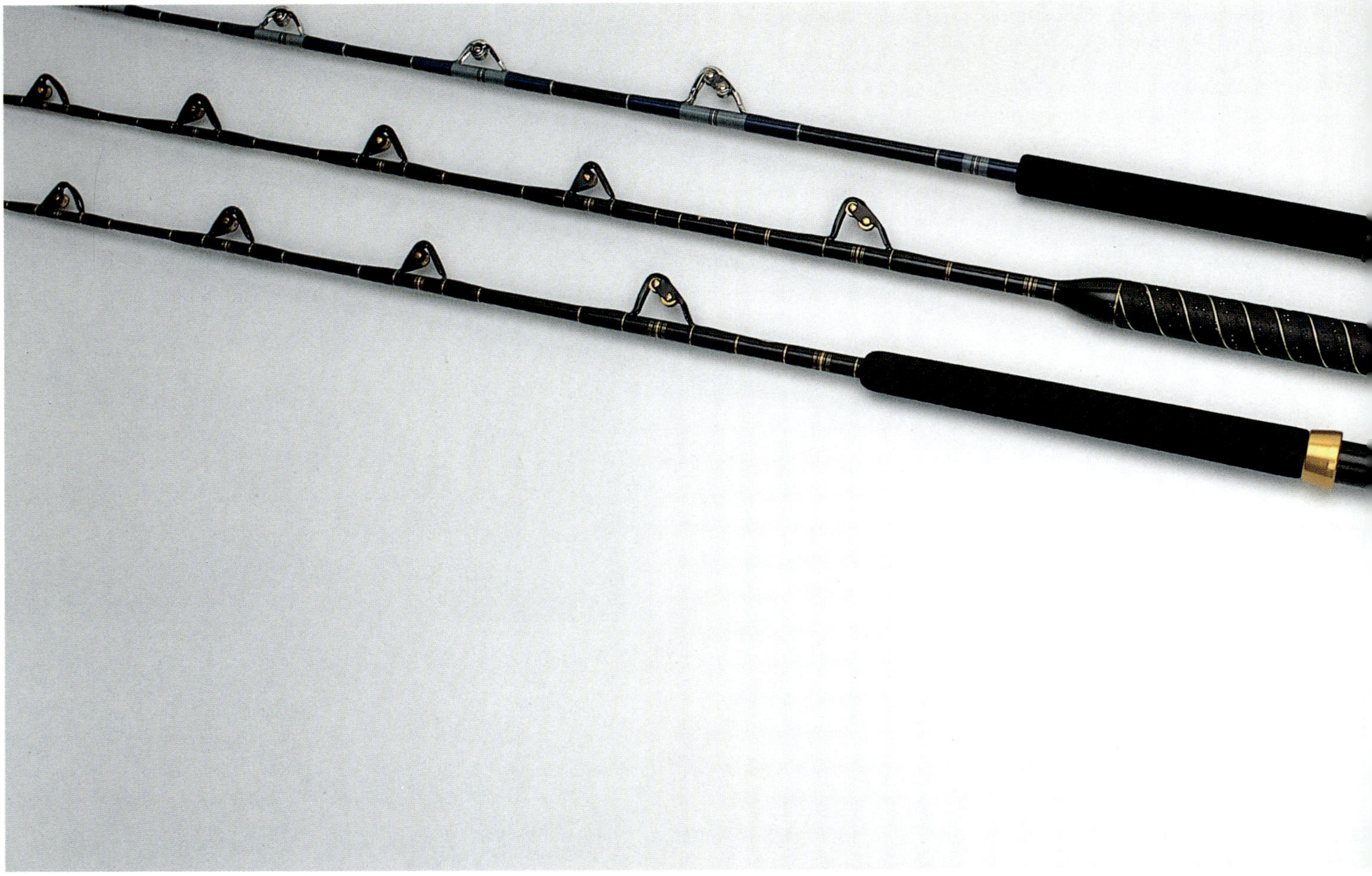

As with the shore-casting rods discussed on the previous pages, offshore or 'bluewater' rods for sport and game fishing cover a very broad range of angling options, from light-weight work on small species to big game fishing for giant sharks and marlin.

At least three major reels find favour with boat anglers trolling, drifting or bottom fishing for sport and game species in Australasian waters. These are spinning or threadline reels, baitcasters and overheads. The overhead reels may be further divided into casting models and those not intended for casting — including special-purpose, lever-drag game reels. Each of these reel styles calls for a different type of rod, and some of these rods fall into categories already discussed, such as double-handed spin sticks and plug rods.

The rod styles most specifically designed and engineered for offshore sport and game fishing are jig rods and game or trolling rods. Both categories are intended for use with overhead reels — either overhead casting models or true game and trolling reels.

One of the most significant aspects of these 'bluewater' rods is the fact that almost all of them are designed to be used

TACKLE

with just one or two specific line test 'classes', as set down by the rules and regulations of the International Game Fish Association (IGFA) and its world-wide affiliates. The line classes commonly used by offshore anglers in Australasian waters are the 4, 6, 8, 10, 15, 24, 37 and 60 kilo categories.

Jig rods are actually used for a great deal more than vertical jigging with lures. They are also popular for trolling, drifting, presenting live and dead baits,

LEFT: A sailfish taken on game tackle.
ABOVE: From top to bottom—Compleat Angler Custom Composite Developments 15kg, Custom Built 'Stand-Up' 15-24kg, Custom Built 'Stand-Up' 15-24kg (bent butt).
ABOVE RIGHT: A Cairns' deckie sets up a 60 kilo game outfit for giant black marlin.

bottom fishing and even casting lures. Most measure between 1.8 and 2.2 metres, and different models are suited to line classes with breaking strains from six to 15 kilos. The majority of jig rods will cope with at least two adjacent line classes; 10 and 15 kilo, for example.

These rods carry between five and eight conventional line guides or runners and may or may not be fitted with a special roller tip and a slotted gimbal butt cap. Jig rods typically have their reel seats located 30 to 50 centimetres above the butt cap, and have handles or grips made of rubberised hypalon, duralon, cork or leather.

True game or trolling rods are special-purpose tools intended for trolling, drifting or bottom fishing. Each rod is specifically designed to fill the requirements of one of the line classes nominated earlier, although most will handle a class above or below their designated category, especially in the lighter line tests below the 15 kilo mark.

Traditionally, game rods measured anywhere between 1.8 and 2.2 metres in the lighter line classes, and up to 2.5 metres and more in the heavier classes. A quarter or more of this length was made up by a detachable metal butt designed to be used in conjunction with a special game chair mounted in the cockpit of a large boat. This butt was usually straight in the classes up to and including 24 kilos, and bent or curved in the two heavy-weight classes: 37 and 60 kilos.

These traditional, two-piece (detachable butt) game rods were almost always fitted with five or six roller guides and a roller tip. They were built on relatively slow tapering blanks and had a progressive or parabolic bend under load.

In recent years, there has been a swing towards much shorter game rods, often featuring one-piece construction. The most radical of these are called 'short strokers' and are intended for non-chair, stand-up fishing with line classes from six to 24 or even 37 kilos. These rods may be as short as 1.4 metres, although most are in the 1.6 to 1.8 metre range. Their butts have also been dramatically shortened to facilitate stand-up fishing, with the reel being located anywhere from 20 to 30 centimetres above the gimbal-slotted butt cap. They may or may not carry roller guides.

Chair-fishing rods for the heaviest tackle classes (24, 37 and 60 kilos) have also undergone significant changes, with tip sections becoming much shorter in relation to the straight or curved detachable butts. These new chair rods are sometimes called 'high levers', and have proven much more effective on large fish, especially in experienced hands.

Due to the demanding conditions and the generally high level of commitment of those who participate in it, offshore sport and game fishing sees an almost constant evolution in tackle design. 'Bluewater' rods are at the leading edge of this evolution, and are sure to experience further refinements and modifications during coming years.

Fishing Lines

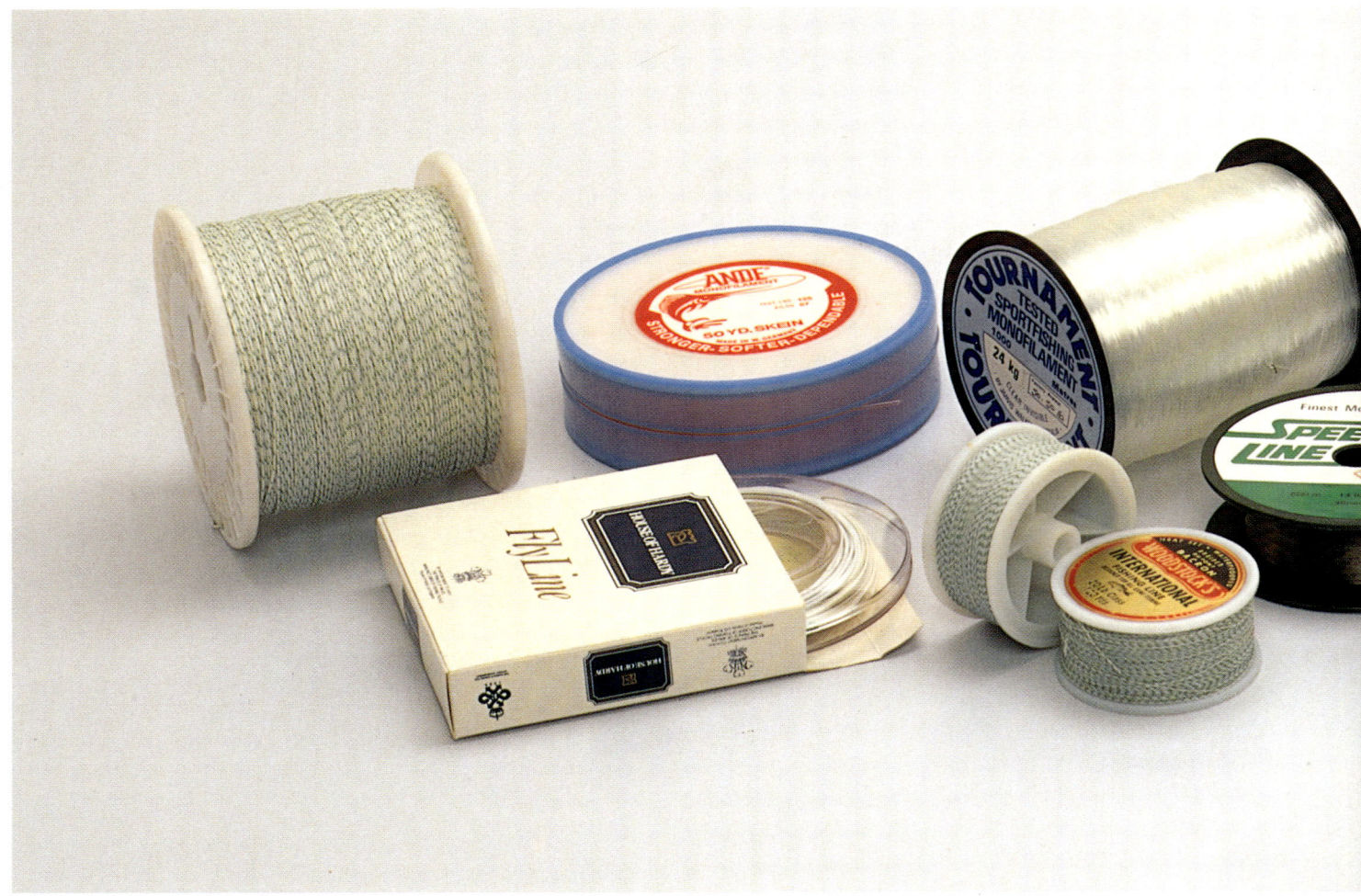

There are several types of fishing line available to the modern angler. These may be divided into two groups; multifilament lines and monofilament lines. As these names imply, multifilament lines are made from numerous fine strands of material woven or twisted together, whilst monofilament lines are a single strand.

Common multifilament line styles are braided nylon, dacron and micron. Older types of multifilament included braided 'cuttyhunk' cord and linen line, although neither of these see much use now. Today, the universally popular single strand line is made of nylon and is called nylon monofilament or sometimes just 'mono'. This grouping includes the newer co-polymer and tri-polymer nylons.

Multifilament and monofilament lines have quite different characteristics. Multi-strand lines have a low stretch factor, are not as smooth and are generally much more expensive than monofilament nylon. On the other hand, nylon is quite stretchy, very smooth and relatively inexpensive compared with dacron and micron.

Nylon monofilament line would nowadays account for approximately 98 per cent of the fishing line sold in Australia and New Zealand each year. This proportion may be a little lower in countries such as the United States and Canada, but even in those places — where dacron, micron and braided nylon are frequently used — nylon 'mono' is a popular choice among the ranks of recreational anglers.

Fly anglers are one major exception to this rule. They commonly use multifilaments as 'backing' on their reels, tied on behind their short length of thick fly line. Multi-strand suits this purpose because of its low stretch and its ability to be packed tightly around a narrow spool core without forming into tight 'memory coils' or spring-like loops. Most fly casters choose dacron or micron backing with a rated breaking strain of somewhere between eight and 15 kilos.

Some game anglers — particularly those using very heavy tackle for marlin and sharks — also like multifilament (mainly dacron) because its low stretch offers more control over big fish, and it can be spliced to give a smooth connection, with no knots and little reduction in breaking strain.

This ability to splice dacron allows the heavy tackle game angler to constantly fill up or 'top-shot' his or her reel, ensuring a full spool and fresh, strong line where it is most needed. However, the only two line classes or categories in gamefishing where dacron still enjoys reasonably widespread use are the 37 and 60 kilo breaking strain divisions. Apart from these two specific areas, multi-strand lines are not popular in Australia and New Zealand. As a result, supplies are small and prices high — in direct contrast to the situation with nylon monofilament lines.

Nylon was a product of the spurt of industrial development which accompanied World War

ABOVE: *A range of modern multi-filament, monofilament and fly lines. Specialist lines are available for every style of angling, although 90% of line sales in Australia and New Zealand are nylon monofilaments.*

2, although reasonable supplies of the material did not become available until well after 1945. Prior to that date, anglers got by as best they could with a variety of cantankerous and highly-strung lines such as linen, cuttyhunk, cat-gut and a Japanese forerunner of nylon commonly known by the trade name of 'Cherry Blossom'.

Probably no other single development did more for the widespread growth and popularisation of fishing as the advent of good, reasonably cheap nylon monofilament line during the latter part of the 1950s. Nylon line — and, to a lesser extent, fibreglass fishing rods — have transformed angling from a rather elitist and difficult undertaking into what it is today — our most popular outdoor activity.

Those early nylon monos were thick, springy and wire-like compared to the superb product available to us in the 1990s. Today, mono is incredibly thin for its strength, supple, resilient and — because of the variety of additives available — diverse in its colour, visibility and exact behavioural characteristics. Nowadays we can choose from an incredible array of brands and breaking strains, colours and gauges to ensure that we buy the nylon best suited to our particular style of angling.

Of course, as good as modern monofilament is, it is not indestructible. Being the vital link between the angler and the fish, line is constantly exposed to all manner of abrasive and damaging forces. It is pulled across rocks, sand and submerged timber, regularly soaked and dried, stretched and relaxed, coiled and uncoiled.

As well as these fairly obvious physical forces acting to degrade nylon fishing line, there is the long term damage caused by ultra-violet radiation from sunlight. Like many other plastics, nylon is gradually broken down and weakened by exposure to this form of radiation. You can fight this deterioration by storing your gear indoors or under cover when not in use, but eventually the unavoidable exposure to ultra-violet radiation experienced while fishing will begin to weaken any mono.

Because of all these adverse forces acting upon nylon fishing line, the product must be seen as having a limited life span. Nylon line may no longer be 'cheap', but it must still be regarded as an expendable item, and replaced regularly if unexpected breakages are to be avoided.

When you stop to consider the effort and money invested in your fishing through expenditure on tackle, bait, boats, fuel and trips away, it is obviously a false economy to scrimp on line.

Experienced anglers refill or top-up their reels with fresh line once a year or more. If you fish a clearly defined 'season', renew your line just prior to the season.

Hooks

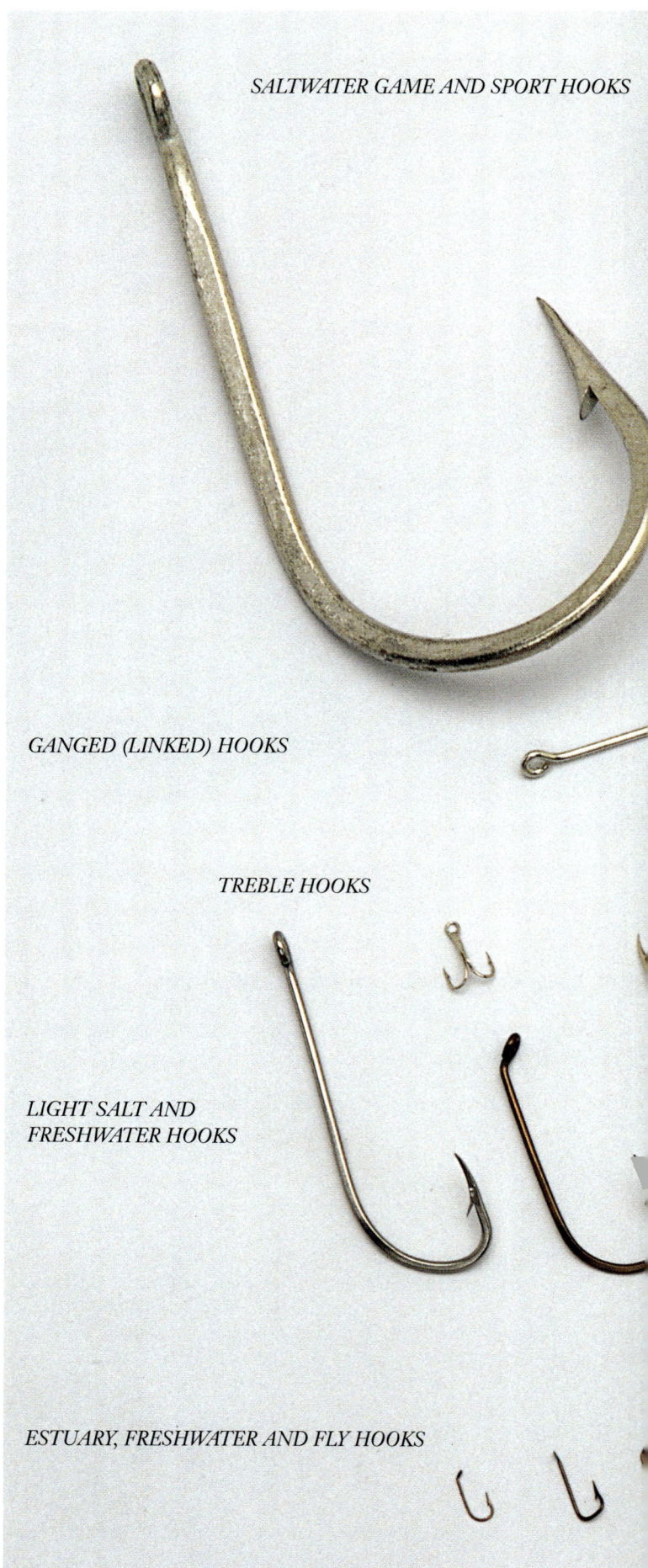

SALTWATER GAME AND SPORT HOOKS

GANGED (LINKED) HOOKS

TREBLE HOOKS

LIGHT SALT AND FRESHWATER HOOKS

ESTUARY, FRESHWATER AND FLY HOOKS

A hook is a curved piece of wire with a point; it usually also has a barb of some sort. Most hooks have eyes, but once they were simply flattened at the end so that a knot tied around the shank would not slide off. A few 'flatted', spade or eyeless hooks are still made, and these remain popular with certain specialists, such as traditional blackfish (luderick) anglers on Australia's east coast.

The bigger hook makers all offer catalogues listing thousands of hook patterns, each in dozens of different sizes. However, the average angler will get by using no more than a handful of these patterns in perhaps 10 different sizes. All hook patterns catch fish, but different shaped bends, shank lengths and wire gauges suit various types of bait and target species. This is why there are so many patterns on offer.

More important than a hook's exact pattern, and whether it has an upturned or down-turned eye, is its size. More bites are missed, or fish hooked and lost, because a hook was the wrong size rather than because it was the wrong pattern. Hook size should firstly be matched to the size and shape of the bait. A small hook in a large bait is unlikely to secure a solid hook-up, while a very large hook carrying a small bait looks unnatural and will 'spook' shy fish.

Secondly, hook size should be roughly matched to the weight or strength of the tackle being used, especially the line. It is simply too difficult to set or drive home a large hook with light line, while heavy line is likely to straighten a small hook or pull it from the fish's mouth before it can be landed.

The final consideration is the size of the fish. It is easier to catch a big fish on a small hook than a small fish on a big hook!

Hook size is expressed by a rather unusual numbering system. Very small hooks carry the largest numbers — a No.10 being a slightly bigger hook than a No.12. The size of the hook continues to increase as the numeral decreases, right on up to a No. 1. At that point the designation alters to an ascending number followed by a slash and a zero. Thus, the next size up from a No.1 is a 1/0, followed by a 2/0, 3/0, 4/0 and so on up to the enormous 16/0 and 18/0 shark and marlin hooks used by game fishermen.

The majority of fishing situations encountered by Australian and New Zealand anglers are more than adequately covered by the 24 sizes between No.12 and 12/0. Hooks smaller than 12s are mainly of interest to trout fly anglers tying imitations of tiny insects, while sizes larger than 12/0 are the province of heavy tackle game fishermen.

As the variation in size between each number hook is small, numbers can easily be skipped when putting together a collection of hooks. The following list of 10 different sizes covers 99 per cent of local angling situations; No.12, 10, 8, 6, 4, 1, 2/0, 4/0, 8/0, and 10/0.

Hooks may be bought by the box (there are usually 50 or 100 in a box) or in smaller lots of 10 or 12. If a few of an odd size or pattern are needed, lots of 10, 12 or 20 are more economical.

All hooks will rust after prolonged exposure to water and salt air. Keep your hooks in a watertight container and dispose of rusted hooks immediately. It pays to keep bulk boxes of hooks at home, away from corrosive elements.

Few hooks are sharp enough for use straight out of the box. With the exception of the chemically and laser sharpened models, hooks should be touched up on a fine-grained sharpening stone or file before being baited.

TACKLE

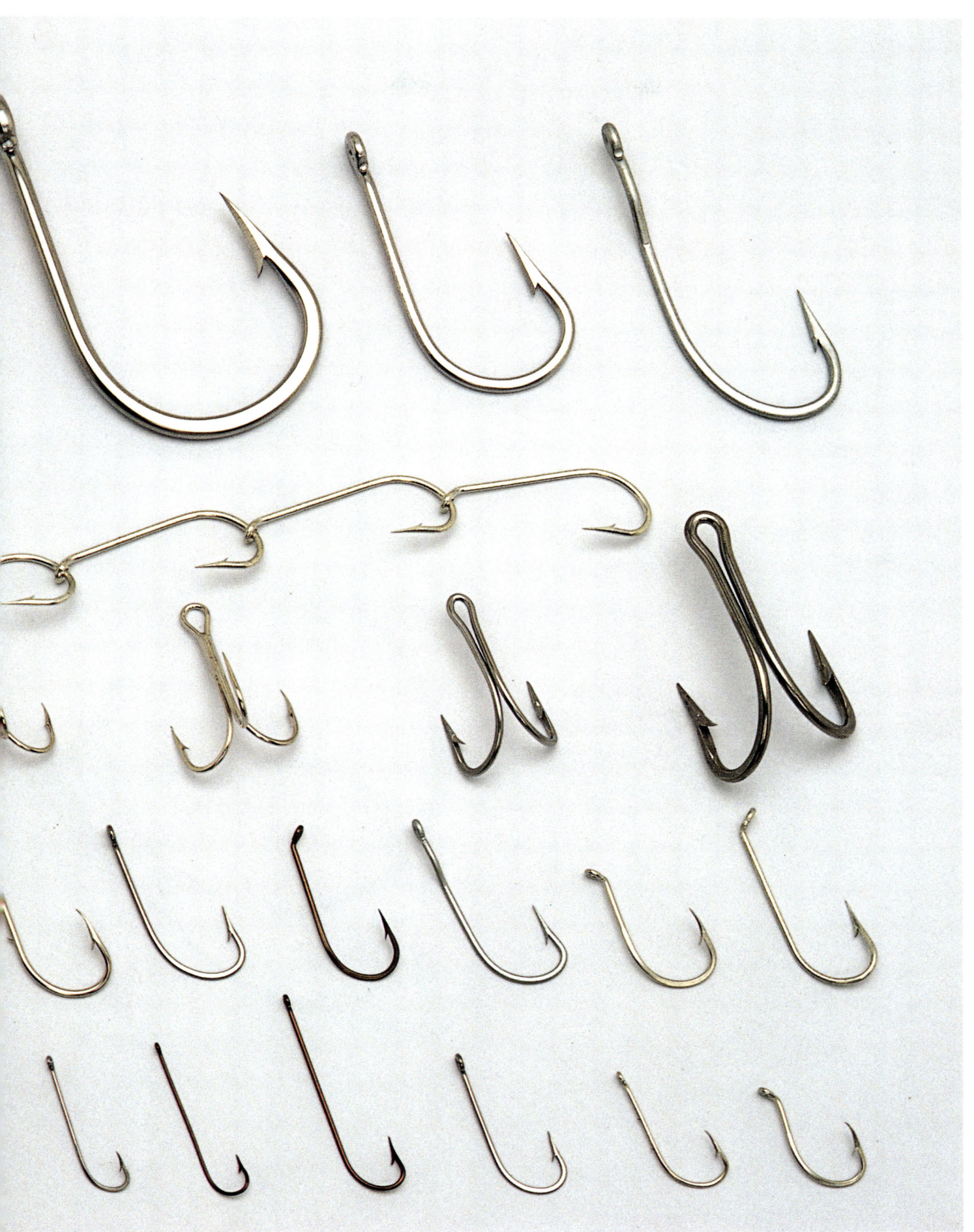

39

Leaders and Traces

Certain styles of fishing demand the use of a length of thick, strong nylon or wire at the business end of the line to prevent bite-offs and abrasion from the teeth, gills and tails of hooked fish, as well as to aid in the landing of those fish. These lengths of extra-strength line are called leaders or traces.

In contrast, some other kinds of angling require a lighter length of line above the hook or fly. These light, sometimes tapered, pieces of nylon line are also known as leaders.

Both types of leader are available commercially. The most common variety are 20 to 40 centimetre lengths of nylon-coated, multi-strand wire with a swivel at one end and a clip at the other. These wire traces are adequate for light to medium tackle and smaller fish with sharp teeth; however, they are prone to failure on big, strong fish. Most anglers who regularly use wire or heavy nylon leaders eventually make their own.

Commercially-made tapered leaders for fly fishing are a more trustworthy product, and many very experienced fly anglers continue to use the factory made product rather than tying up their own.

In recent years, several brands of special purpose nylon monofilament and co-polymer line have appeared on the market. These tough monos are intended especially for the construction of heavy-weight leaders. They are often 'annealed' during their manufacture or extrusion to give a hard outer skin that will cope with the abrasions caused by marlin and sailfish bills, or the teeth and gill cover cutters of other species.

Some of these heavy-duty leader lines form part of a complete leader-making system, which may include crimping sleeves, protector collars, crimping pliers and other accessories. Using these systems, it is possible to easily assemble very efficient leaders for game and sport fishing.

Similarly, wire of several types is also sold for those anglers who wish to make up their own shark traces or bite-proof leaders for other fish with sharp teeth. The most common types of wire are single strand (both stainless and galvanised) and multi-strand or cable wire. Multi-strand wires usually contain either seven or 49 individual strands woven together. For demanding applications such as heavy tackle gamefishing for white pointer and tiger sharks, some anglers favour tough aircraft control cable, or even chain traces!

In complete contrast, anglers employing light leaders or 'hook links' when pursuing trout, bream, luderick and other small fish will usually opt for the thinnest, most supple and neutrally-coloured leader material they can buy. The intention of these fine leaders is to mask the tackle from the fish. A secondary purpose is to allow a snagged hook or fly to be broken off without sacrificing floats, sinkers or other items of terminal tackle rigged on the heavier main line.

In some areas, anglers buy pre-rigged leaders or traces which already have a hook or hooks knotted to one end and a small loop or a swivel affixed to the other. These 'snells' or premade hook lengths enjoy regional popularity in places such as South Australia, but are practically unknown elsewhere. Most experienced fishermen agree that it is better — and cheaper — to tie up their own rigs.

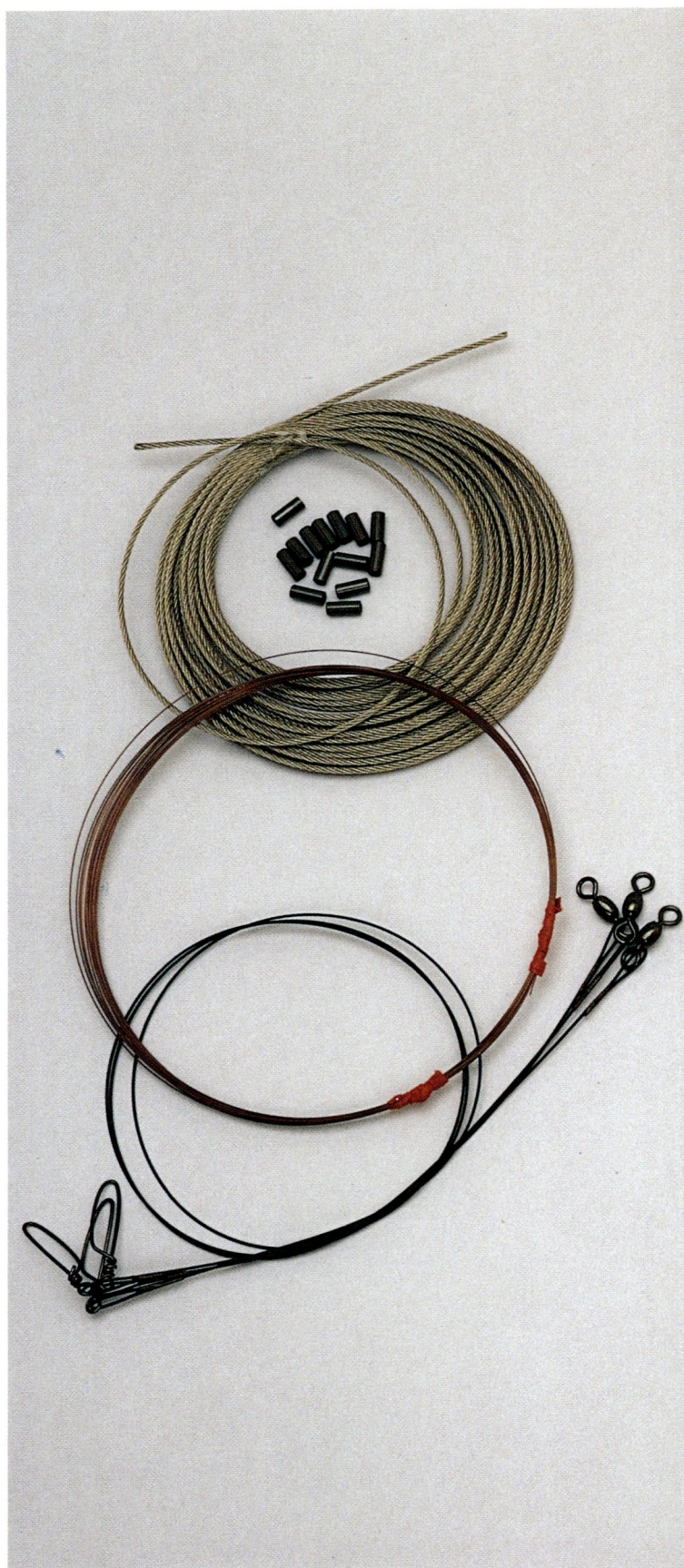

RIGHT: Different styles of leader or trace material including — from left to right — wire leaders, crimpable Jinkai leader material and two types of Sabre leader material (light and heavy).

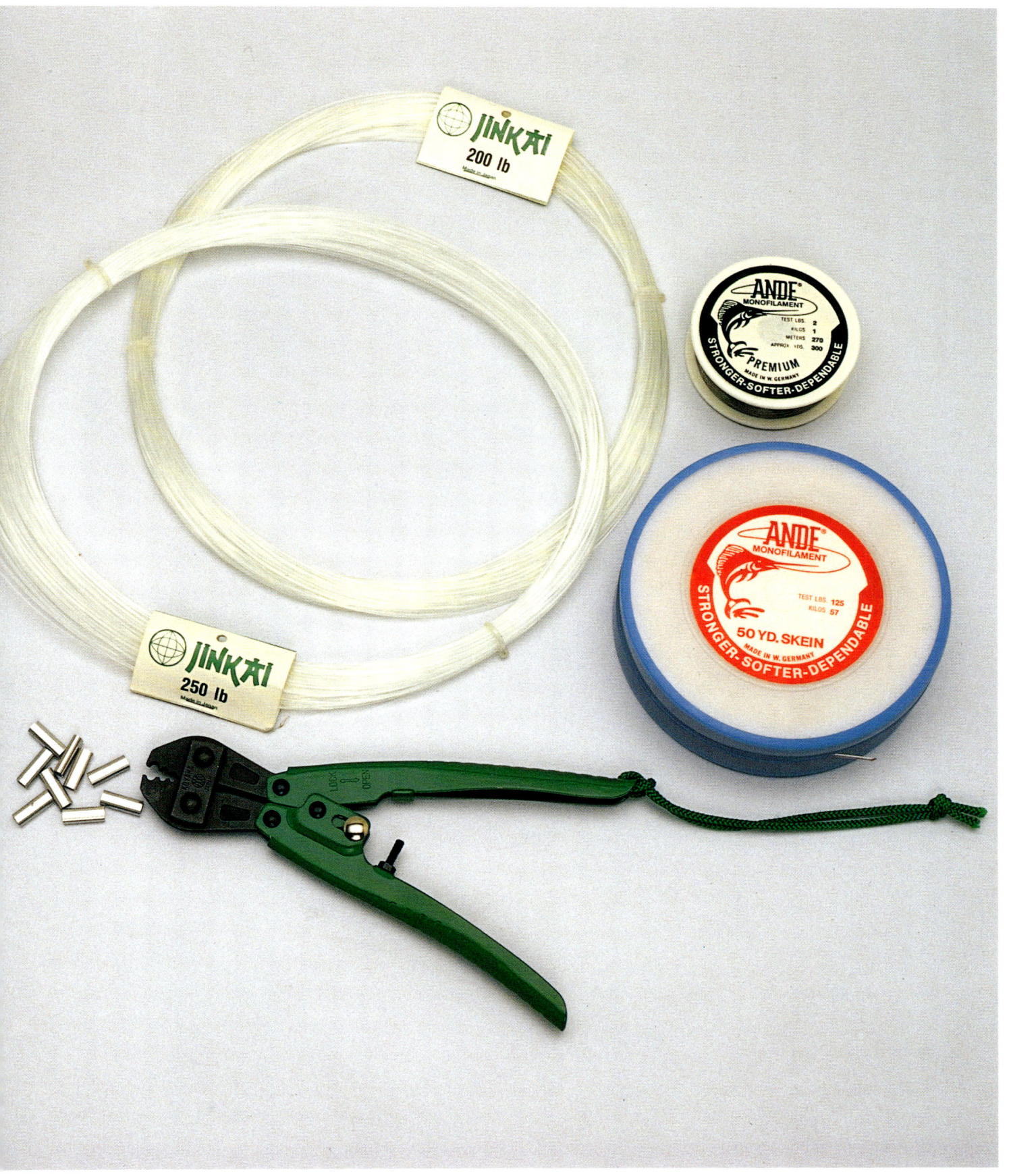

Sinkers and Shot

Sinkers are lead weights which can be added to your line to provide additional weight for casting, to hold a bait at a desired level in the water, keep the line down in a strong current, or balance a float so that it will register bites. Sinkers should not be used as anchors!

Too many anglers seem to think that a sinker should hold their bait firmly in one place and allow them to maintain an absolutely tight line at all times so that bites can be felt. The fact is, most bites will be easily registered through a slightly slack line, and far fewer fish will shy away from your bait or pluck at it timidly if it is allowed to move in a natural way.

In nearly every case, the smallest sinker you can manage with is the one to use. Picking the actual shape or design of the sinker is less important. Just as with hooks, choosing a suitable size is 90 per cent of the battle; shape merely allows for some fine tuning, and for the selection of certain special functions.

A couple of specific sinker shapes with useful applications are the snapper lead — which sinks fast, straight and without spinning, as well as travelling through the air with little resistance — and the star or helmet style of sinker — which offers a good hold in sandy bottom strata along ocean beaches when strong cross currents are evident.

A step beyond the star or helmet is the grapnel sinker, which is fitted with little wire prongs. This sinker goes completely against the adage that sinkers are not anchors, because that is precisely what it is — a small anchor! Grapnels have specific uses on storm-torn or current-ravaged beaches, and are particularly popular in eastern Victoria and parts of New Zealand.

Spoon sinkers have largely gone out of favour, despite the slight benefits they offer when used over very snaggy bottoms, and the channel sinker or 'picker's doom' also seems to be fading towards obscurity.

With those more offbeat sinkers out of the way, the choice really comes down to ball, bean, bug and barrel sinkers. The decision here is largely based on angler preference, although each has very slight variations in behaviour and usefulness. The needs of the vast majority of anglers will be covered by ball or bean sinkers, with a few of the specialist sinkers described above on hand to be used in specific situations.

The numbering or sizing system of sinkers is much less standardised than that used for hooks. Some shops number their smaller sinkers (especially ball sinkers) starting with the designation 00 for the smallest and moving up through 0 to 1, then 2, 3 and so on. However, it is common for this labelling to switch over to the weight in grams or ounces on sinkers larger than about 28 grams (one ounce), and most heavy sinkers are described in this way.

Sinkers may be bought in tens or dozens, or in packages according to weight. Moulds are also available for the angler who wishes to cast his or her own sinkers from lead or lead alloys. This is a viable and money-saving alternative for the fisherman who uses a great deal of sinkers, or where limited finances are a constraint.

Generally, it is better to have a large number of relatively small sinkers in your kit than fewer, heavier leads. That way, extra weight can be added by sliding two, three, four or more small sinkers onto the line.

Split shot, or shot, are small, ball-shaped sinkers with a slice halfway through rather than a central line channel. They are held in place by being crimped or squeezed closed into the line. Split shot are useful for fine-tuning the balance of a float, or providing a very small amount of weight at a set distance above a bait, fly or lure. They are also convenient in that they can be

Ball Sinkers

Bombs

Channel Sinker

TACKLE

Bean Sinkers

Spoon Sinker

Pyramid or Star Sinker

Large Snapper Lead

Helmet Sinker

Small Snapper Lead

Split Shot

added to the line without cutting and re-tying the rig.

Drawbacks of split shot include the damage they do to the line if applied too tightly, and their habit of rattling and banging about in tackle boxes so that the split closes up, rendering them almost useless. The best shot are made of very soft lead or lead alloy and come in a handy, circular dispenser with a sliding lid. Note that split shot should not be closed onto the line by biting them, as this can permanently damage your teeth.

ABOVE: A range of popular sinker and split shot styles in several sizes.

43

Swivels, Rings and Connections

The function of swivels is to prevent or reduce line twist. They also make convenient sinker stoppers, spacers and rig connectors.

The commonest type of swivel is made from brass or steel and is called a barrel swivel. Slightly stronger and more expensive is the box swivel, also made of brass or steel The torpedo swivel is stronger again, and suited to thick, heavy lines, while at the top of the range are various stainless steel ball bearing swivels, which are very pricey, but also extremely strong and effective. Ball bearing swivels are used mainly by game fishermen. For the majority of fishing with lines lighter than about 20 kilos breaking strain, quality brass barrel and box swivels are the best choice.

Swivels are sized in a manner similar to that used for hooks; with a No. 16 or the slightly larger No. 14 being the smallest swivel found in most ranges (box swivels are rarely available in sizes smaller than No. 10). The size range No. 14 up to No. 4 covers the majority of fishing situations. If larger swivels are needed, they should be torpedoes or ball bearing models. These may be sized differently, with ball bearing swivels, in particular, often rated on their tested breaking strength. The secret with swivels of any type is to use the smallest size suited to the line in use. Only then do they spin or 'swivel' as intended and remove line twist.

The novice may wonder, if that's the case, why No. 14 or No. 12 swivels cannot be used for all line strengths. The reason is that strong line may well tear a small swivel apart. Even if that doesn't happen, the very fine wire used in the eyelets of tiny swivels would soon cut into thick line and cause breakages at the knot. In most cases, you should choose a swivel on which the eyelet wire is one and a half to two times as thick as the line.

For lines with strengths up to about three kilos, use No. 14 or No. 12 swivels. With four to eight kilo line, use 10s and 8s. When using nine to 15 kilo line, try No. 6 and No. 4 swivels. Swivels are commonly sold in packets containing one dozen, 20 or 25 units. Torpedo and ball bearing swivels are sold in smaller packs, or singly.

Being made of brass or stainless steel, swivels require relatively little preventive maintenance, although barrel swivels will jam up with sand and grit if this is allowed to build up in the tackle box, and all swivels will eventually corrode if used around saltwater.

Snaps and snap swivels are safety-pin devices made of brass, steel and wire. They are commonly used to connect lures, leaders or even hooks to your line when frequent changes of terminal tackle are expected. Snaps may be either separate, or attached to a swivel. Some are rather weakly constructed and will not withstand the pressures exerted by large fish on heavy tackle. Price is a fair guide to quality and strength.

Keels, also called anti-twist or anti-kink keels, are flat plastic or lead semi-circles with eyelets. Sometimes they also have a swivel attached to one or both ends. They are used to prevent line twist with baits or lures that are especially prone to spinning in the water, particularly when trolling. Keels are mainly used by freshwater anglers.

Berley cages or 'swim feeders' are wire or plastic devices which may be attached to sinkers, floats or used on their own. These cages are designed to hold and disperse a small amount of berley such as soaked bread, bran or pollard. These are useful with species such as garfish, tommy ruff, mullet, carp, tench or roach, and are popular with anglers pursuing those fish.

There are two types of rings used by anglers: split rings and solid brass rings. Split rings are similar to those found on a key ring and are made of brass, chromed brass or stainless steel. They are mainly used for hanging hooks on lures. As a rule, nylon lines should not be

tied directly to a split ring, as the knot can easily slide into contact with the sharp ends of the coiled wire or, in rare cases, unwind completely out of the ring.

Solid brass rings make very useful connectors, spacers and sinker stops when a swivel is not required. They are cheaper, lighter and stronger than swivels, but do not prevent line twist as a swivel does.

Both types of ring are available in a range of sizes and are sold in packets of 12 or more.

A range of swivels, rings and connectors. Note the ball bearing swivels (centre and top right) used in sport and game fishing. The unusual models at lower left are three-way swivels, used to make dropper rigs.

Floats

Fishing floats are used to suspend a bait at a predetermined depth below the surface of the water, and also to give a visual indication of bites.

There are several styles of float. Perhaps the most common is the stemmed float, which has a shaped body of foam, cork or wood and a shaft of dowel, bamboo, plastic or metal. This shaft is fitted with either metal or plastic eyelets, or carries lengths of tight-fitting plastic tube to hold the float to the line.

Stem floats are very popular with blackfish (luderick) specialists on the east coast of Australia. They are also used by some anglers pursuing drummer, bream, mullet, sweep and similar species. Very light stem floats with no body at all are called 'quills' because they were once made from porcupine quills and the stems of large feathers. These are best used in still or slow-flowing waters to present baits to trout, garfish (piper), mullet and the like.

With the arrival in Australia and New Zealand of good supplies of British and European 'coarse' fishing floats, local anglers can now choose from a much better range of stemmed floats. These include such specialist designs as wagglers and antennas, which have specific applications in calm and slow-moving water. Most of these imported coarse fishing floats offer far greater sensitivity than locally-made products.

Floats without stems mainly take the form of bobby corks, 'bobbers' and bubble floats. Bobby corks are made of foam, cork, timber for hollow plastic. Most have a hole running right through the middle to carry the line. Corks range in size from as small as a thumb-nail through egg-size to giant floats as big as grapefruit or rock melons.

Bubble floats are mainly constructed of clear plastic or soft, transparent rubber and are fitted with plugs or slits so that they can be partially filled with water to provide casting weight. The line is attached by way of moulded eyelets or a central channel. Bubble floats remain popular with many Australasian trout anglers using baits such as live mudeyes (dragonfly larvae), shrimps and worms.

Game and sport fishermen — both shore- and boat-based — often use empty detergent or fruit juice bottles and inflated balloons as floats to suspend large baits intended for sharks, tuna or marlin. By the rules of gamefishing, these large floatation devices must be attached to the line in such a way that they break free after a fish is hooked. This is usually achieved through the use of rubber bands, light cord or adhesive tape.

Floats of most types may be used either fixed in position on the line, or allowed to run freely below a stopper of some sort; either a piece of knotted line, wool or rubber on the main line, or a swivel or ring tied into the rig. Little rubberised float stops are now sold in packets, each one on a small loop of fine wire. These may be easily slipped onto the line and adjusted to control the depth at which a bait is presented below a float.

In general, fixed floats are best when fishing at relatively shallow depths, while running-float rigs are preferred by anglers wishing to present a bait deep below a float. Most floats, especially the stemmed variety, work best if they are weighted or ballasted so that they are at least three-quarters submerged and take only a soft bite to sink. Insufficient weighting of a float will result in many missed bites and 'spooked' fish.

Three major styles of floats — top to bottom — quill and pencil floats, stemmed floats and bobby corks.

TACKLE

47

Landing Tackle

Anglers pursuing larger fish, using light lines, or operating from boats, piers, high rock ledges or steep banks must give careful consideration to the landing of their fish. Attempting to lift or winch a fish clear of the water in these situations will often result in a broken line or a pulled hook. The two major forms of landing gear employed by Australasian anglers are nets and gaffs. Both have their advantages and disadvantages.

A landing net can be very useful — even essential — in some fishing activities. The best application for nets is in boat fishing scenarios where the target species run from half a kilo to six or seven kilos. Bigger fish really do demand the use of gaffs. If you fish from a boat, buy the biggest, strongest net you can afford, even if it looks over-sized alongside the fish you regularly catch. One day you'll need all of that extra capacity.

Nets are also useful for bankside fishing, although they can sometimes be a problem for the mobile angler who hikes through scrub and bush. The various fold-away, collapsible nets now available do go some way towards alleviating these problems, but they too have their drawbacks. Finally, develop the habit of examining the mesh in your net regularly for holes and rips. At the same time check for rotted or weak mesh by punching your fist hard into the bottom of it.

Bigger and more active fish — especially those weighing in excess of five or six kilos — generally demand the use of gaffs. A gaff is a stout hook fixed to a pole and used to secure and lift a fish fought to the bank, shore or boat-side. Another style of gaff used for big, active game fish is slightly different in that it has a detachable head on a rope. This is called a flying gaff. When a big shark or marlin is gaffed with a flying gaff, the head detaches from the pole and the fish is secured by way of the rope, which is normally cleated off to a strong point in the boat.

Still another type of gaff can be clipped to a taut length of nylon fishing line and slid down to the water on a cord. This is called a cliff gaff, and is an invaluable tool when fishing from high rock ledges, cliffs or very tall piers and jetties.

When buying gaffs, check that the hook strength and gape are adequate for the fish you'll be catching. In addition, the handle must be long enough, and the metal used reasonably rust-resistant. Keep your gaffs sharp using a file, stone or grinding wheel. A smear of grease or vaseline over the hook point prevents corrosion and also aids in penetration. Finally, you should always protect your gaff heads with a cork, block of wood or length of plastic tube to prevent injury when transporting and storing these potentially dangerous devices.

Other items of landing gear include tail ropes, nooses and meat hooks, although these are mostly used by game fishermen pursuing sharks and other heavy-weight target species. Another device called a 'tailer' was originally designed for salmon angling in Europe, but has found a small following among Australasian offshore anglers, particularly those wishing to practice catch-and-release.

A sturdy glove such as the type worn while gardening or welding can also be a useful adjunct to landing fish. Gloved hands are much less likely to be cut or otherwise damaged when holding onto leaders, tailing fish or removing hooks from their mouths.

ABOVE: The author with a tropical dogtooth tuna, landed with the aid of a sturdy fixed-head gaff.
BELOW: Nets are best for landing smaller fish such as these fine trout, taken in a wooden, snow-shoe style landing net. These nets can be hung from the belt or back until needed.

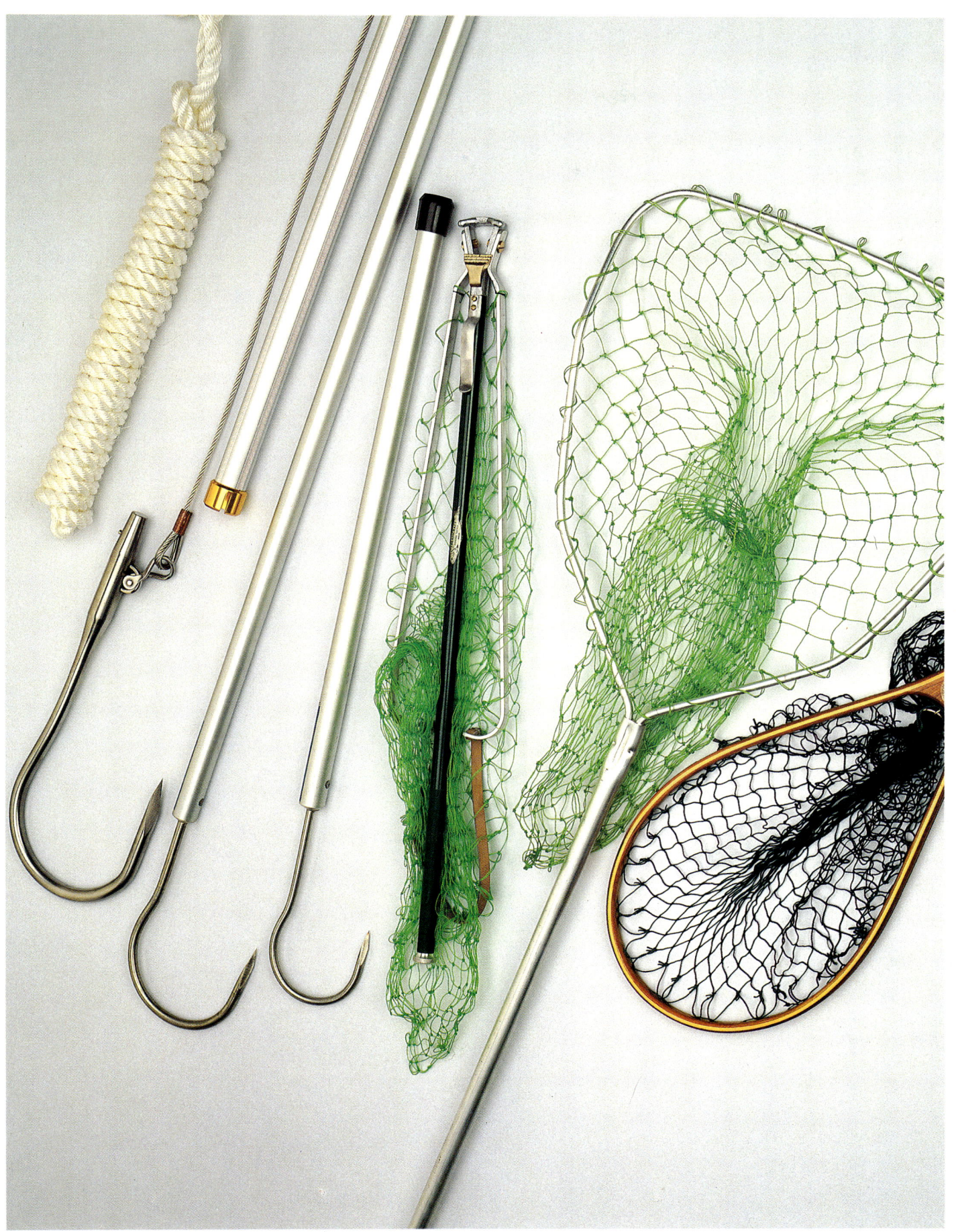
A range of modern landing tackle. From left to right — a flying gaff, two fixed-head gaffs, a collapsible net, standard landing net and trout angler's 'snow-shoe' net.

Fishing Electronics

There are several modern electronic devices which can help boat fishermen find and catch more fish. The most notable and widely accepted of these is the electronic depth sounder, also known in some literature as a 'fish finder', or by the wartime acronym of SONAR.

Depth sounders work by firing sound waves from a transducer mounted directly in the water, or against the inside of a fibreglass hull. These sound waves travel down through the water column and bounce back off various objects, including fish, air bubbles, weed, distinct temperature changes and — most importantly — the sea bed or lake floor itself. The returning echoes of sound are detected by a receiver within the transducer and relayed to the on-board sounder unit, which uses the time delay between the outgoing and incoming signals to plot a picture of what is currently beneath the vessel.

In the most basic types of sounders — called 'flashers' — this picture is conveyed by rapid bursts of light on a circular dial. These cheap, simple units can tell us little more than the depth of the water, but are still extremely useful in helping to locate the structural elements (reefs, weed beds, etc.) which are likely to hold fish.

Paper chart sounders represented a quantum leap beyond flashers, and revolutionised angling electronics through the 1970s and into the '80s. These units used a moving stylus to trace surprisingly accurate 'graphs' of the sea bed, large fish and bait schools onto a roll of specially sensitized paper which scrolled across a display area on the face of the sounder unit.

In early paper or graph sounders, the print-out was curved and rather distorted, but over time more and more sophisticated depth finders appeared on the market. Today's top-line paper sounders are regarded by many experts as the very best fish finders available. They create extremely accurate impressions of the sea bed and are sensitive enough to detect and 'draw' isolated strands of weed, sunken tree branches and individual fish down to a few centimetres in length.

The major disadvantage of paper sounders is the fact that they continually use up rolls of quite expensive sensitized paper. The best paper sounders are also very expensive.

During the latter part of the 1980s, liquid crystal displays (LCDs) began to replace the paper charts in many depth sounders. At first, the images created were inferior to those traced on moving paper by a stylus. In time, however, LCD sounders matched their graph print-out counterparts in most areas and actually surpassed them in others. The modern LCD sounder is a remarkable machine that is, in real dollar terms, much cheaper than the original paper units.

State-of-the art LCD sounders offer extremely life-like pictures and have a myriad of special functions which allow the operator to enhance the unit's sensitivity, screen out electronic 'noise' and even select and enlarge narrow bands within the water column for closer examination. Many are also equipped with built-in temperature gauges, speed indicators and distance logs! Best of all, they can be left running for hours with minimal battery drain, and without using expensive paper.

Yet another family of sounders employ video readouts displayed on cathode ray tubes not unlike small televisions. The best of these even use colours to differentiate between, for example, schools of bait fish and patches of kelp! Video sounders are more expensive than either paper or LCD units, and it might be argued that their advantages are marginal for the recreational angler. Nonetheless, increasing numbers of these sophisticated units are being used on sport fishing craft.

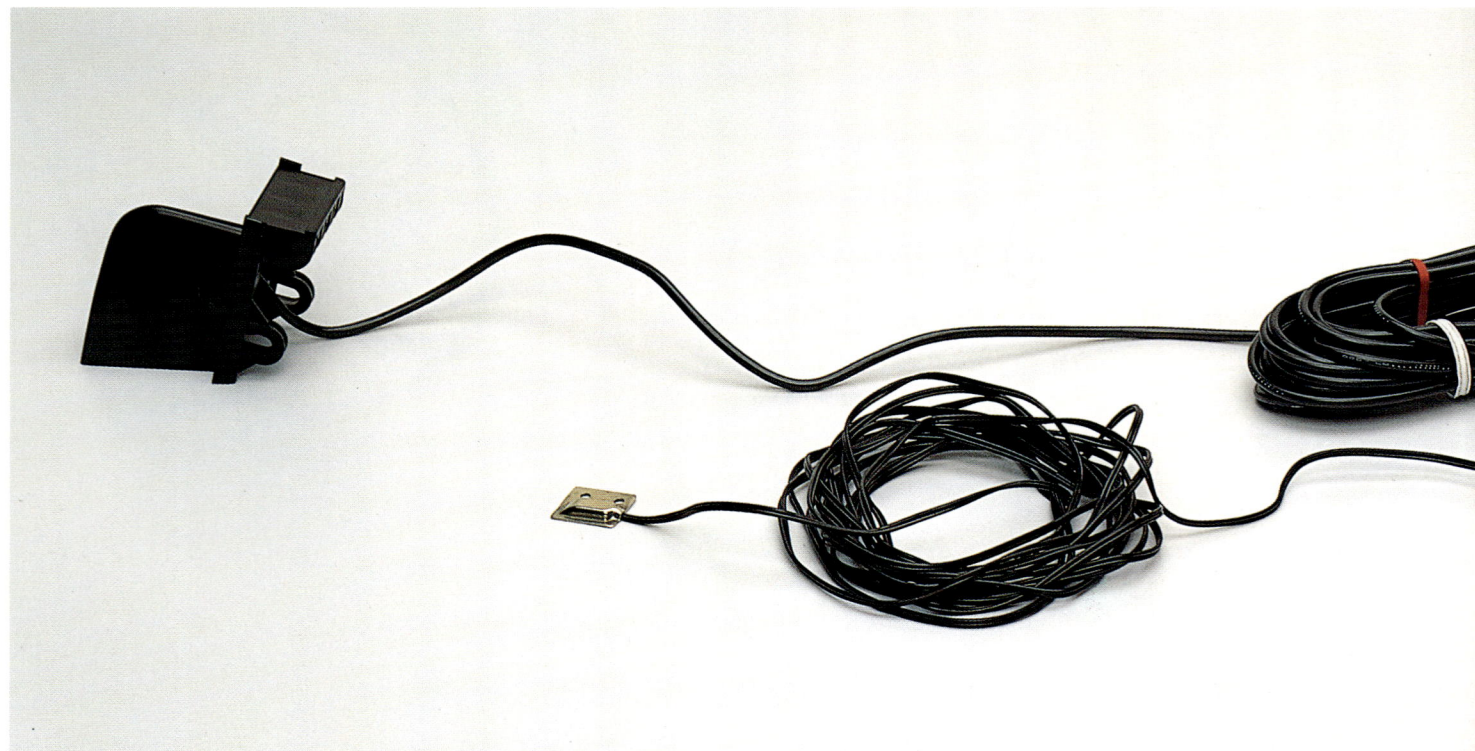

TACKLE

Depth sounder manufacture is one of the fastest changing areas of angling evolution, with new features appearing almost every week. It is difficult for the layman to keep up with these developments, and even harder for him to apply many of them to his day-to-day fishing needs. Thankfully, however, there is a strong swing towards automatic, 'user-friendly' units which will adjust themselves to present the optimum bottom picture and reveal significant objects between the hull and the sea bed. These functions fulfil at least 90 per cent of our requirements from a fishing depth sounder.

Radar is another electronic feature gradually finding its way onto smaller and smaller pleasure boats as the price, size and complexity of modern units comes down. While mostly a safety and navigational aid, radar can also be used to pin-point fishing 'marks' such as reefs or drop-offs in all weather and at any time of the day or night.

The next major leap forward for Australasian anglers will come with the spread and increased availability of satellite navigational systems such as GPS and Loran. This technology is still in its infancy in local waters, but in the past decade it has literally changed the way American and European offshore anglers go fishing. Satellite navigation allows an angler to return with absolute accuracy to a specific reef pinnacle or deep canyon, as well as to plot his or her true position to within a few metres at any time of the day or night.

As more navigation satellites are put in orbit over the Southern Hemisphere, and onboard equipment becomes cheaper, many Australian and New Zealand anglers will benefit.

ABOVE: This hefty coral trout was taken over a deep coral drop-off located with the aid of a depth sounder.
LEFT: From left to right— Templus Water Temperature Gauge, Eagle Fish I.D. Depth Sounder.

Baits and Lures

The purpose of any bait, lure or fly, is to trick a fish into taking a hook. Within that broad definition, there is an amazing range of possibilities — one that many newcomers and more than a few experienced anglers seem to find daunting and confusing.

Basically, baits, lures and flies fall into two broad categories. There are those which imitate — either closely or in a very general way — something edible that is familiar to the target species. Then there are those that bear little or no resemblance to anything living or dead which a fish ever ate. These rely on the curiosity, aggression, territorial behaviour, belligerence or just plain stupidity of a fish in order to illicit a strike! Neither category is totally rigid. Baits that are natural and ultra-realistic in one scenario may be outlandish in another, yet they might still catch fish.

When considering why fish so often respond to unlikely baits or artificials, we should remember that they have no arms and hands. If they wish to examine an intriguing object, they usually do so with their mouths. Therefore, some baits and lures may act in much the same way as a 'Wet Paint' sign does to humans. Just as we can't help confirming the sign's message by touching the tacky surface, so the fish is compelled to 'taste' the tantalising object... often with fatal results!

Having said that, it should be stressed that long term angling success — especially on difficult species in hard-fished waters — mainly comes to those who make something of a science of using the best, most natural and appealing baits, and offering them in a life-like manner. Many fish have an inbuilt suspicion about unfamiliar objects that largely over-rides the 'Wet Paint' syndrome. This suspicion is more pronounced in large fish and among populations which see a significant number of baited hooks, lures or flies each season. For these fish, we need to more closely imitate the real thing, and to keep to an absolute minimum the signs, scents and tastes that spell man.

Freshwater fly fishermen have a useful piece of terminology for closely imitating natural food items — they call it 'matching the hatch'. This refers to the insect hatches that are so important to trout anglers, but it is just as valid to a tropical lure caster pursuing barramundi, or a deep sea game fisherman trolling for marlin. In many instances, matching the hatch is a matter of common sense. If longtail tuna or skipjack are feeding voraciously on tiny whitebait, you will obviously stand a better chance of hooking one by casting a small, thin-profile silver lure into the school than a large, red surface-popper or a frozen prawn!

By the same token, it is certainly possible to too closely match the hatch. In the same scenario just described, where tuna are feeding on tens of thousands of tiny whitebait, it would be counter-productive if your lure or fly looked and behaved exactly like one of those little fry! It would then stand only a small chance of being eaten, unless there were a great many predators feeding for a long period of time.

Instead, we must slightly exaggerate the attractive features of the natural food and make our offering stand out from the pack. Our lure should be just a little more silvery, a shade larger, and perhaps a bit quicker and more erratic than the naturals. It should also be swimming away from the relative sanctuary of the school and out into open water.

These principles of matching the hatch, but of also identifying and exaggerating the 'attack response triggers', can be carried through to nearly every form of fishing. Our live bait for kingfish should be ever so slightly injured, and flashing or vibrating more strongly than the rest of the bait fish in the nearby school. Our prawn bait for bream should be plumper, slower and more vulnerable than the live prawns swimming in the same area. Our grasshopper-imitating fly for trout should have a slightly more yellowish body and kick just a little more energetically than the hundreds of natural 'hoppers blown onto the pool by a strong summer wind.

Most of the really good anglers — that often-quoted 10 per cent who catch at least 90 per cent of the fish — have an almost instinctive and unconscious 'feel' for matching the hatch and exaggerating the attack response triggers. The rest of us must work at it — at least during the early months and years of our fishing careers. Above all else, we must observe what is happening in and around the water we are fishing, and try to understand how these things affect our results, and what we must do to improve those results.

Despite the importance of what we attach to our hook — which is the subject of this chapter — the fact remains that the way we then present that baited hook to the fish is of paramount importance. A great angler can get by with a second or third rate bait, lure or fly — and still catch fish. Most of us, however, need all the help we can get!

Estuary, Harbour and Beach Baits

The humble frozen prawn is without doubt the most popular bait among Australia's vast army of estuary, harbour and beach anglers. Tens of thousands of packets of these crustaceans are sold every year from tackle shops, boat hire sheds, garages and even general stores right around our coastline, with sales reaching their highest levels during the school holiday periods. Because of their immense popularity and acceptability, there is also no doubt that more inshore and estuarine fish are caught each year on frozen prawns than on any other single bait type. This is not to say, however, that they are the best offering available for all forms of beach, bay and estuary angling.

Packet frozen prawns are chosen by most anglers because of their convenience and the fact that many of us grew up using this form of bait — occasionally taking some fine catches on it. This is hardly surprising, as prawns form a major part of the diet of many inshore species — especially during summer, when these crustaceans are prolific.

It is also true that properly handled and snap-frozen, prawns are only slightly inferior to the fresh or live item. You can assess the quality of frozen prawns by examining them through the clear plastic bag they are sold in. The individual prawns should be of a roughly similar size and their bodies should be a semi-transparent greenish brown. The heads must be firmly attached to the bodies and show no sign of dark discolouration in the gut region. Avoid buying packets of prawns containing lots of small or broken specimens, or those with a very dark colouration.

Frozen prawns are best thawed by placing them in a bucket of sea water half an hour before beginning to fish. They should all be used within four or five hours, and will keep much better if stored in a small styrofoam cooler out of the direct sunlight. Excess prawns may be re-frozen or brined in a solution of salt and sugar, but will be a significantly inferior bait when next used. It is much better to add the leftovers to your berley trail.

Apart from the frozen prawn, estuary and beach anglers have a wide range of possible baits to choose from. Some — such as squid, mullet gut, chicken gut, cockles, pilchards, whitebait and so on — can be bought in frozen packets at bait outlets. Others — like whole fresh mullet, garfish and octopus — are best purchased at fresh fish shops, or captured by the angler.

Two of the very best bait types available to the beach, estuary and harbour angler are marine worms (beach, blood, squirt and red wriggler) and pink nippers or bass yabbies. These are rarely available for purchase, although some of the better bait outlets along the coast stock live worms and nippers for at least a part of the year, and preserved, frozen beach worms are sold by many stores. The latter, however, are distinctly inferior to the live, fresh item. All worms and nippers are only really useful as baits when alive and kicking.

The best tool for bait gathering in our estuaries is a bait pump — also known as a worm or nipper pump. This is an Australian invention consisting of a metal or plastic tube with an internal piston that is drawn upwards to suck sand, mud, water and burrowing invertebrates from the tidal estuary flats. These pumps are ideal for extracting nippers (yabbies), squirt worms and certain types of blood worm from their holes in the sand flats. Anglers without such a pump must rely on shovels, spades and garden forks to gather their bait.

Beach worms are captured by washing a bag full of smelly fish scraps in the receding backwash of the surf on a falling or low tide. The worms poke their heads from the sand in an effort to locate the source of the smell, leaving a tiny V-shaped wake in the receding water. The bait gatherer then allows the worm to chew on a small, tough 'finger bait' of pipi (cockle) or fish flesh while he or she manoeuvres into a position to grab the worm by hand or with a special pair of pliers and pull it from the sand.

The bivalve shellfish called pipis (known as eugaries in Queensland and cockles in South Australia) are also very useful baits for beach and estuary angling. These bivalve molluscs are collected from the inter-tidal zone on beaches. They are located by digging with a fork, or twisting your feet and toes into the sand as a wave runs back and feeling for their hard, smooth shells. Pipis are best used fresh, but may be frozen or salted.

Squid, octopi and cuttlefish are three cephalopods which all make fine bait for many species of inshore and estuarine fish. Very small squid (sometimes called 'bottle squid') and baby octopi may be used whole, while larger specimens are best skinned and cut into strips.

BAITS AND LURES

A collection of popular estuary, harbour and beach baits including — from left to right — mullet, pilchards, whitebait, prawns, pipis (cockles), sand crabs, pink nippers (bass yabbies) and several types of marine worm, including beach worms.

These strips make tough, attractive baits and can be frozen for long periods with little loss of quality.

Bait fish and fish flesh are useful saltwater offerings in nearly all scenarios, including estuary and beach angling. Some of the most popular are whitebait, pilchards, anchovies and 'glassies'. All of these are available in frozen packs, and sometimes sold fresh at seafood outlets. They may be used whole or cut on single or linked (ganged) hooks to take a wide variety of predatory fish.

Larger fish such as mullet, garfish and tuna are usually cut into chunks or strips when used as estuary or beach baits, although anglers targeting large predators such as mulloway and barramundi may use whole dead or live fish as bait. Small live mullet (sometimes called 'poddies') are especially effective, and will also take large dusky flathead. Mullet can be captured on tiny hooks baited with bread, dough or worm pieces, or trapped and netted. Local fishing regulations should be consulted first.

Crabs of various kinds are popular estuary baits in some regions, especially among anglers targeting bream. The small black or dark brown estuary crab found under inter-tidal rocks is best, although blue soldier crabs will also take fish at times, including very large whiting.

The fine-stranded, filamentous algae known as green weed is a specialist bait used by estuary and harbour anglers seeking luderick (blackfish). It may be bought from many New South Wales tackle stores, or gathered from quiet backwaters in brackish lagoons, storm water drains and similar locations.

Finally, there are the various man-made offerings and so-called 'butcher's baits'. These include bread, dough, long-life packet baits, pudding mixtures, steak strips, chicken intestines, ox heart, liver, tripe and so on.

All of these baits catch fish at times — especially bream — although they seem to work best in areas near large population centres or holiday resorts, where the fish are more familiar with eating man's scraps and refuse. In most cases, natural baits will match or exceed the results obtained with these less natural offerings.

Rock, Jetty and Breakwall Baits

ABOVE: Popular rock and jetty baits, including: cunjevoi, sea lettuce, crabs and sea urchins (the latter are used as berley).
RIGHT: A thumping big blue groper of more than 10 kilos taken on a bait of live, red crab, which was caught right on the rock ledge from which the fish was eventually hooked and landed. Fresh, local baits are usually best.

Most of the productive estuary, harbour and beach baits described on the previous pages are also popular with experienced rock, breakwall and jetty anglers. In particular, various types of prawn — both frozen and fresh — produce excellent results when used around our rocky foreshores and wharves.

Small, whole bait fish species such as pilchards, whitebait, anchovies, garfish and mullet are also effective rock and jetty baits, especially when pursuing predatory species such as salmon (kahawai), tailor, trevally, snapper and kingfish. Several of these bait fish, as well as slightly larger yellowtail, slimy mackerel and herring, are also used alive or freshly killed by specialist land-based game and sport fishermen pursuing kingfish, tuna, mackerel, sharks, mulloway and the like.

Cut fish flesh is another productive offering around the rocks and off retaining walls and wharves. It may be cut into cubes, chunks slabs or strips, and is best taken from oily, blood-rich fish species such as tuna, bonito, mackerel and mullet. Fresh fish flesh is usually best, but some types (especially tuna) are just as effective or even better when salted. Salting preserves the flesh and toughens it, without significantly detracting from its taste, smell or appearance.

Squid, octopus and cuttlefish are favourite baits for anglers casting long distances in pursuit of snapper, kingfish, mulloway or similar species. The tough flesh of these cephalopods is also useful when large numbers of small fish ('pickers') become a nuisance. Squid, octopus and cuttlefish may be used whole or skinned and cut into strips. Small, fine strips are excellent for catching bait fish, leatherjackets and whiting.

Bread is a much overlooked bait in these shore-fishing scenarios The best type of bread for hook baits is a fresh, unsliced white loaf. Small balls of this can be squeezed to form a pliable dough that will stay on the hook reasonably well, while unpressed cubes or squares of bread and crust make an attractive — if fragile — floating bait for bream, drummer, sweep, luderick and the like. It should be used with a bread-based berley trail for best results.

Apart from these baits — which are also popular in many other saltwater angling scenarios — rockhoppers and jetty anglers have access to a range of specialist baits that grow or live in and around the inter-tidal zone on ocean rocks and wharf pylons. Perhaps the most popular and well known of these are the seasquirts or cunjevoi, which are commonly called cunje (sometimes spelt 'cunji').

Cunjevoi are filter-feeding animals that live in a hard, leathery case attached to rocks or jetty pylons near the low water mark. When pressed, they expel a strong jet of sea water from a small hole in the top of their case. Cutting this case open reveals a body of dark red meat and a gut of softer orange and green organs. This flesh may be used as bait, either fresh or after freezing, salting or drying.

Various other organisms found clinging to the inter-tidal rocks may also be pressed into service as baits. These include chitons, limpets and various shellfish such as turbans and periwinkles. Most of these are regarded by experienced anglers as emergency baits, but are actually quite attractive to many rock-dwelling fish, especially if a few are also crushed and thrown into the water as berley.

The abalone (called paua in New Zealand) is a large, roughly circular univalve shellfish much prized as a human delicacy. It sometimes ranges up to the low tide mark on our southern rocks, but is more common in ledges

BAITS AND LURES

and gutters a short distance offshore. The tough meat of the abalone is usually kept for the table, but the soft gut portion makes a superb offering for drummer, bream, leatherjackets and many other species.

The various crab species encountered along our ocean foreshores also make very good rock, breakwall and jetty baits. Some of the more common types are the black or green crab, the so-called 'Scotchy' crab and the red crab. These may all be captured with the aid of a single-pronged crab spear, or by hand. They can be used as whole baits or cut into portions and are especially attractive to species such as groper, drummer, bream, snapper, wrasse and parrot fish.

Another crab of great value as bait is the hermit crab, which is a soft-bodied crustacean that lives in the empty shells of molluscs such as turban and cone shells. It may be removed from its home by cracking the shell with a hammer or rock, but this often damages the soft, succulent body. It is much better to place live hermit crabs in the refrigerator or freezer for a short period of time, causing them to relax so that they may be easily withdrawn from the shell by hand.

A marine weed growth colloquially known as 'cabbage' or 'lettuce' weed is also common on the inter-tidal rocks around the southern half of Australia. This weed — which is usually presented on a relatively small hook suspended beneath a float — is an especially attractive offering for luderick or blackfish. It will also take black and silver drummer, sweep and even bream at times, as well as less desirable species such as the black spinefoot (also known as rabbitfish or 'happy moments') and the rock cocky or sea carp.

The filamentous green weed described in the previous section on Estuary, Harbour and Beach Baits may also be used from the ocean rocks and jetties, as may the man-made baits discussed in that section.

Offshore and Deepsea Baits

Nearly all of the natural and man-made bait types discussed earlier in this chapter under the headings of Estuary, Harbour and Beach Baits and Rock, Jetty and Breakwall Baits may be used with varying degrees of success by offshore boat fishermen.

Particularly popular and productive baits among those anglers fishing on or near the sea bed for reef dwelling species are: prawns, squid, cuttlefish, octopi, cut fish flesh and small, whole fish such as herrings, pilchards, garfish and 'poddy' mullet.

Very tough baits are often best when fishing in very deep water or where bait stealing 'pickers' are abundant. Under these conditions, many experienced offshore anglers choose squid flesh or salted tuna as their main hook bait, sometimes adding a small segment of prawn or marine worm to the hook point to increase the bait's attractiveness.

Anglers fishing lightly weighted or unweighted floater baits in a berley trail for snapper, trevally and similar fish are not so concerned with the durability of their offerings. Rather, these baits should be highly attractive to the target fish and at least similar to some of the chunks and scraps in the berley trail. The ubiquitous blue pilchard or 'mulie' is hard to beat in this application, and may be fished either whole or in halves, thirds or smaller segments. Tuna and bonito flesh — both fresh and salted — also makes superb floater baits, as do garfish, fillets or strips of mullet, large prawns, and fresh, whole bottle squid or squid strips.

Offshore game and sport fishermen have somewhat different needs when it comes to bait selection. They use all of the baits just described when pursuing fish such as snapper, tuna, mackerel and so on, but need larger offerings when targeting the likes of marlin and sharks.

Game and sport fishing baits could range from a whole pilchard or garfish drifted back down a berley trail for yellowfin tuna or Spanish mackerel, right up to a whole, or even live, yellowfin tuna or Spanish mackerel rigged as a trolling bait for marlin or a float-suspended offering for big sharks.

Trolling places special restrictions on the selection and presentation of baits. They need to be tough enough to withstand the wear and tear of being pulled through the water for several hours, and they should be rigged in such a way as to look natural and alive. It is also important to minimise the bait's tendency to spin in the water. Rigging trolling baits can be turned into something of an art form, and the better game-fishing deck-hands around the country take great pride in their specialist rigs, many of which have taken years to develop and perfect.

Favourite species for rigging 'swimming' troll baits include: garfish, mullet, mackerel, scad and small tuna. The keys to success in rigging an effective bait lie in the use of a symmetrical arrangement of terminal tackle, and of carefully centring the towing point in the bait's head. The bait rigger needs to be especially careful that the finished bait can lie straight, flat and loose in the water, pulled only from one point in the centre of the head.

Live baits are another popular option with offshore sport and game anglers. Again, the range of possibilities is immense, from a live yellowtail or mullet aimed at kingfish and small tuna, to live small tuna such as skipjack and frigate mackerel intended to lure really

BAITS AND LURES

big tuna, sharks and marlin.

These live fish may be drifted on an unweighted line, plumbed deep with the aid of a heavy sinker, float suspended, or slow trolled. Regardless of the presentation technique, they should always be hooked in a manner that minimises damage to the bait fish and allows it to swim and kick in a way that will appeal to predators. In particular, the angler must be careful not to damage the bait fish's lateral line, backbone or internal organs. To this end,

LEFT: *Popular offshore and deepsea baits, including skipjack (striped tuna), pilchards, octopus and squid.*
ABOVE LEFT: *A fine haul of fingermark and Venus tusk fish taken on fresh strips of tuna and trevally on an offshore reef mark in the Northern Territory.*
ABOVE: *A handsome 18 kilo mulloway taken by an experienced deepsea angler.*

hooks are typically inserted through the bait's back above the lateral line, or in the mouth or nose region. The latter option is especially useful when slow trolling a bait, or fishing it in a strong-flowing current.

Nose or mouth hooking may be taken a step further by bridal-rigging a live bait. This involves using of a large bait sewing needle to take a length of fine but strong cord through the bait's eye sockets (above the eyes) or nose area, then tying this cord to the bend of a big hook. This option is especially popular when slow trolling live skipjack or similar large baits.

The final point to remember in offshore fishing is that the angler is often operating far from the convenience of a tackle shop or bait outlet. Self-reliance is important, and skilled deep sea anglers are constantly on the lookout for additional bait and berley among the fish they catch.

Berley

Berley (sometimes spelt burley) is the name given by Australian anglers to bait scraps and other edible matter introduced into the water in order to attract and excite fish. Berley is known as 'chum' in North America and 'ground bait' in Britain.

In Australasia, berley is mostly used in saltwater fishing, although it does have applications on inland lakes and streams. As local freshwater anglers begin to make greater use of British coarse fishing techniques, we are likely to see an increased use of berley or ground bait in Australian and New Zealand freshwater fishing.

The simplest and most basic form of berleying involves throwing or dropping any mutilated baits, bait offcuts and similar scraps into the area where you are casting your lines. All anglers should get into the habit of doing this.

This process can be taken a step further by saving and freezing left-over bait, fish offal and other food scraps for use as berley during future outings. A couple of large plastic containers, such as empty ice cream buckets, make fine receptacles for this frozen berley, and their tight-fitting lids prevent odours from contaminating foodstuffs kept in the same freezer.

A basic berley of bait and fish scraps can be greatly enhanced by the addition of cereals such as bread, boiled wheat, pollard or chicken feed pellets etc. These substances should be thoroughly soaked in a bucket of water, mixed with the bait scraps and distributed as evenly as possible into the area being fished. Adding sand will increase the sink rate of the berley mixture.

Stale bread forms the basis of many proven berley mixes. Again, this can be accumulated in the freezer by saving household scraps in plastic containers or bags, although this does tend to take up rather a lot of freezer space. Anglers who make heavy use of bread-based berley usually attempt to establish a direct source of stale bread. Some bakeries and other retail outlets will sell one-, two- or three- day-old-bread at reduced rates, although in many areas, primary producers such as pig farmers buy up nearly all of the baker's stale bread supplies to use as stock feed.

A further worthwhile addition to most berley mixes is fish oil of some type. The most common varieties are tuna oil and pilchard oil, both of which are available commercially. If unavoidable, vegetable cooking oil can be substituted with reasonable results. These oils form a plainly visible surface slick and help to carry the smell of the berley further afield. Such a slick is often called a 'berley trail' and under ideal circumstances, it may stretch for several kilometres. Long, oily slicks or berley trails are particularly favoured by game and sport fishermen pursuing sharks, although oily surface slicks are also useful in attracting and exciting surface feeding table fish such as mullet, garfish, Tommy ruff (herring), tailor and salmon (kahawai).

The rules of berleying are that it should not feed the fish to such a degree that they become satiated and stop feeding, that the berley stream or trail be kept as unbroken as possible, and that there should be at least some similarity between substances in the berley and the hook baits being used.

Think of a berley trail as a stream of attractive smells wafting from the kitchen while a meal is being prepared. These smells grab our attention and get us thinking about food. If the smells are attractive enough, or we are sufficiently hungry, we may move towards the kitchen.

So long as we don't encounter enough solid food along the way to satisfy our hunger, we will most likely track the smell trail right to its source. In effect, we have been aroused and excited by the promise of food, at least partially conditioned into expecting a certain type of food, and attracted towards the location of that food. In fishing terms, we have been 'berleyed'!

There are a number of ways of dispensing berley into the water. It can be mixed in a bucket and ladled or tipped into the water, placed in a porous bag such as an onion sack and hung in the water, or dispersed from a specially constructed berley bucket. Berley buckets are usually attached to the stern of a boat. They consist of a plastic or metal tub perforated with holes. Older style spin dryer units from early model twin tub washing machines make excellent berley buckets. Berley is placed in this

Boat anglers berleying for snapper near Whyalla, in South Australia. Berleying works almost anywhere!

tub or bucket and allowed to permeate out through the holes. Tougher berley items such as whole fish or fish frames may be mashed up in the bucket using a pole or stick.

Smaller amounts of berley may even be released from specially constructed floats, such as the 'blobs' favoured by West Australian herring fishermen, or from cage sinkers known as 'swim feeders'. These berley-dispensing floats and sinkers are almost always used in conjunction with a larger berley trail dispensed by hand.

Another innovative method of dispensing berley involves packing soaked bread, bait scraps, cut pilchards and other items into a heavy paper bag, along with a stone or half-house brick. A cord is then tied to the top of this bag and it is lowered to the desired fishing depth, or the sea bed. After waiting a minute or two to allow the bag to become sodden and soft, the cord is jerked several times. This causes the stone to rip through the bag, dispensing the berley at the desired depth.

The use of berley results in increased catches in almost all saltwater and at least some freshwater scenarios. However, if done incorrectly, it can actually decrease your results by carrying fish away, or overfeeding them before they reach your baits. For this reason, berleying is best done in a relatively closed environment rather than one where current and wave action quickly carry the berley away. If berleying in an open fast flowing area, it is absolutely vital to maintain a steady, unbroken trail.

Try berley wherever you fish.

Freshwater Bait

Some of the saltwater baits described in the previous pages are also applicable to freshwater use. In particular, fresh and frozen prawns are useful when pursuing species such as bass, perch and sooty grunter. Saltwater mussels will take trout, particularly in discoloured streams after flooding, and small marine bait fish such as whitebait appeal to large trout and land-locked chinook (quinnat) salmon.

For the most part, however, freshwater anglers prefer to use specific freshwater baits. The most popular of these are: earth worms, scrub worms, bardi and witchetty grubs, shrimps, crayfish (yabbies), small live fish (gudgeons and minnows) and insects or their larvae. Man-made baits such as packet, long-life 'putty-style' mixtures and so-called bait eggs of flavoured gelatin are also useful, although usually less productive than natural items.

Generally, freshwater baits are much less easy to obtain through commercial outlets than their saltwater counterparts. An increasing number of worm farms are now supplying anglers with quality earth, tiger and scrub worms. These are usually sold in plastic tubs containing anywhere from 50 to 500 individual worms. It is also possible to buy live crayfish (yabbies) and dragonfly larvae (mudeyes) at some specialist outlets close to popular fishing waters. However, supplies are often limited and relatively expensive. For these reasons, freshwater anglers tend to be much more self-reliant concerning bait supplies than their marine counterparts. Keen inland anglers tend to catch, gather, dig or breed the bulk of their bait needs.

Earth worms are available in most gardens, especially in the damp, rich soil under compost heaps. Larger scrub worms live in leaf litter, bark and other detritus along creek gullies and storm water drains. Still other types of worms, such as active little red wrigglers, are best located in muddy soils around stockyards or under pats of cow manure.

Shrimps and crayfish (yabbies) may be captured in several ways. One of the most productive is to build a fine mesh cage with several funnel-shaped entrances, or perforate a large drum or tin with many small holes. These traps are then baited with a fish head or scrap of meat, weighted with rocks and placed on the stream or lake bed near submerged timber and weed beds. Within a few hours at most, reasonable quantities of shrimps and/or yabbies should have moved into the trap, which can be emptied, re-baited and moved if necessary. Small fish will also be caught in these traps from time to time and, where legal, these can be used as live or fresh baits.

Shrimps and small yabbies may also be captured with a scoop net or a rake run through the weed and mud in inland dams and quiet river backwaters. Larger yabbies will respond to pieces of slightly smelly meat tied to light cord or string. The crayfish will grasp these baits firmly enough to be drawn slowly towards shore and netted with a scoop.

Shrimps and small yabbies are best fished alive — hooked lightly through one or two segments of their tail shell and allowed to swim and kick. Very large yabbies may be killed and their tails peeled and placed on the hook whole or in segments.

Dragonfly larvae (mudeyes) and other aquatic insects or their larvae are also best captured with a fine-meshed scoop net run through submerged weed beds. In addition, mudeyes can be caught by pulling pieces of waterlogged timber ashore and peeling back the loose bark. Such logs should always be returned to the water later to provide a future habitat for these and other creatures. Mudeyes and other insect larvae are best fished alive, hooked lightly through the wing case with a small, fine gauge hook.

Terrestrial insects such as grasshoppers, crickets, beetles and cicadas may be caught by hand or with the aid of a butterfly net. Most of these insects are more easily captured during the cool of dawn, when they are relatively slow moving. Wherever possible, they should be presented alive, hooked lightly through the body or attached to the hook with a small rubber band.

Bardi, witchetty and wattle grubs are the fat, creamy white larval grubs of various moths and other insects. They make productive baits, especially for Murray cod, golden perch and trout. Most are found in burrows at the bases of large, riverside trees. These holes are revealed by scraping the leaf litter away. The grub may then be removed by digging, or by twisting a length of flexible wire (such as a car's speedometer cable) with a corkscrew coil at the end down the hole until it grips the grub, allowing it to be withdrawn. Other types of grubs will be found boring into wattle trunks and the timber of certain bank-side trees. These may be removed by chopping the softened, honey-combed wood with an axe or chainsaw.

The keen freshwater angler needs to be constantly on the lookout for natural bait sources. In particular, they should develop the habit of examining the stomach contents of captured fish and matching their bait choices to the favoured food types of their quarry.

ABOVE: A range of popular freshwater baits including — artificial 'bait eggs', crayfish (yabbies), minnows, shrimp and earthworms.
RIGHT: This angler is preparing to trot a bunch of float-suspended worms through a productive looking rapid on a healthy trout stream during spring. Mudeyes (dragonfly larva), mayfly nymphs or even maggots could all be used as effective hook baits in the same scenario.
FAR RIGHT: Choosing the right bait for freshwater fishing can lead to a handsome dividend — such as this beautiful 4.5 kilo brown trout taken by the author.

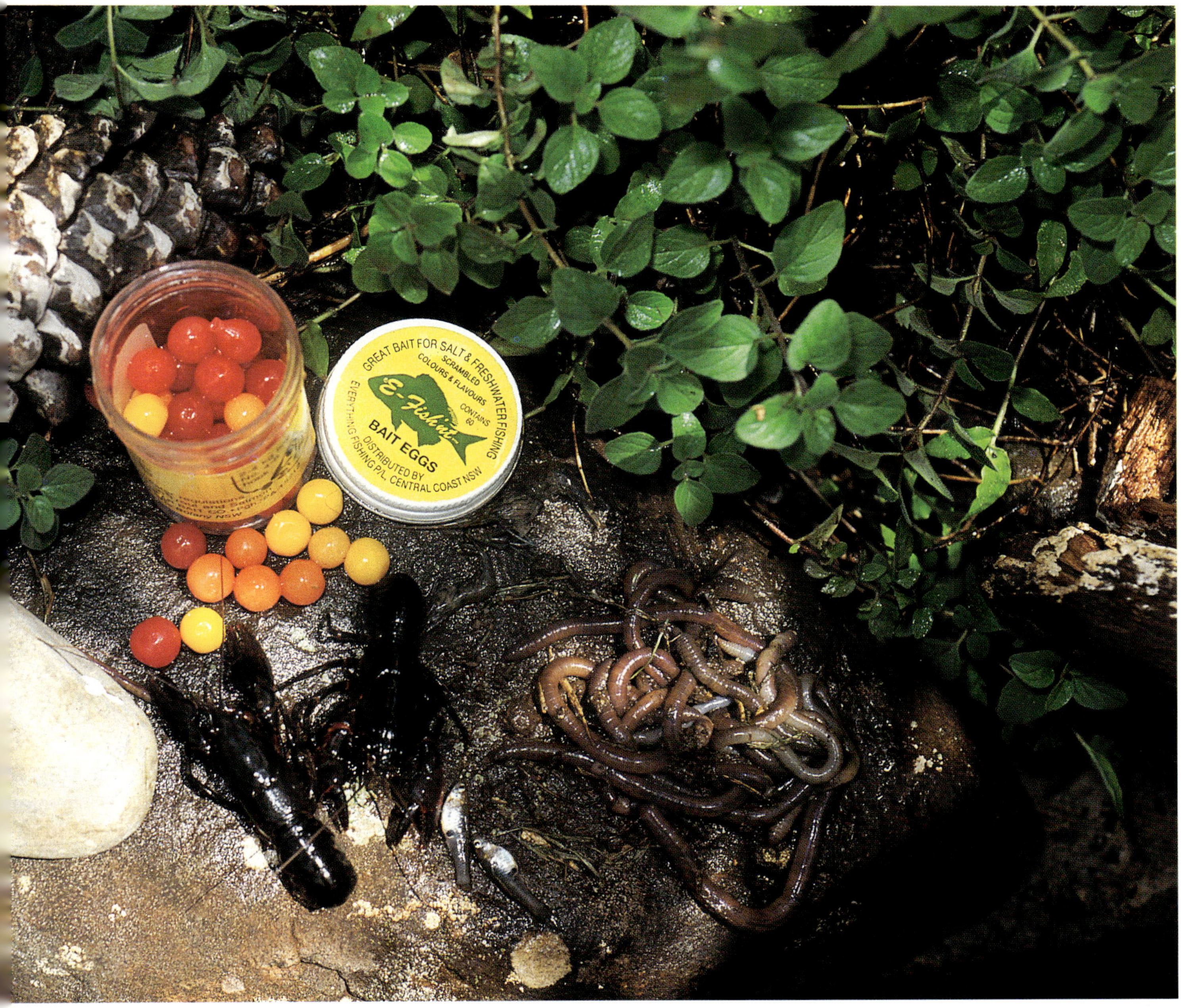
GREAT BAIT FOR SALT & FRESHWATER FISHING
SCRAMBLED
COLOURS & FLAVOURS
CONTAINS 60
BAIT EGGS
DISTRIBUTED BY
EVERYTHING FISHING P/L, CENTRAL COAST NSW

TSN

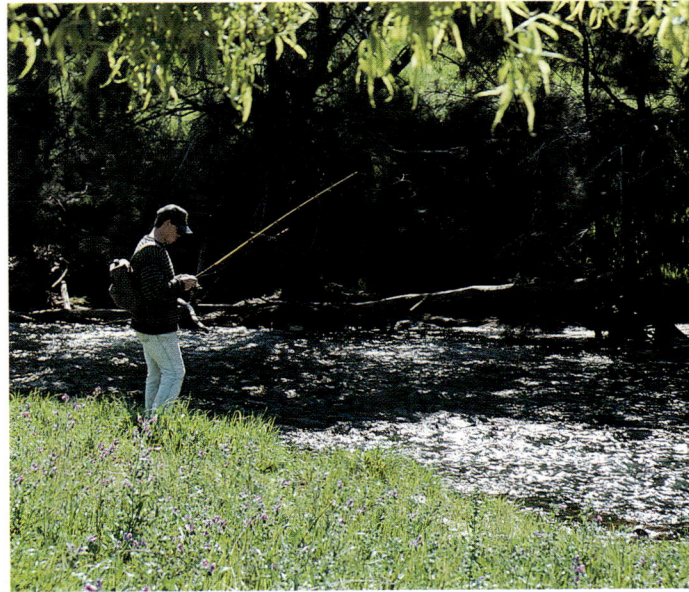

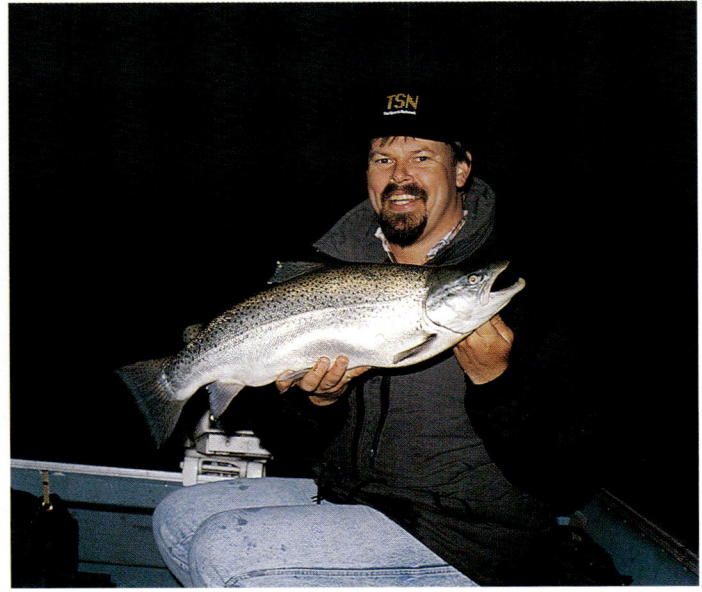

Saltwater Casting Lures

Saltwater casting lures are those artificial baits intended to be cast and retrieved by the angler, either from the shore or a drifting or anchored boat. Many of these lures may also be trolled (pulled along behind a moving boat), although as you will see on the following pages, there are several specific lure types better suited to trolling, especially at relatively high speeds (above about six knots).

Freshwater lures are often used in brackish and saline waters with good results, although care should be taken, as many freshwater models are not fitted with the tough, corrosion-resistant hooks and split rings required for marine use.

Of the saltwater casting lures, the most popular and versatile group are the spoons. These dished, metal lures come in a huge range of shapes, sizes, weights and colours. They vary from almost circular, oval or egg-shaped, through to long, thin models with a distinct longitudinal kink or S-bend. The designations and varying actions of these shapes are covered more thoroughly under the heading of 'Freshwater Lures', later in this chapter. Suffice to say that longer, thinner and heavy gauge spoons with a reasonably quick, tight action are better suited to saltwater use than wide-bodied models with a strong, slow beat. Spoons are particularly effective on flathead, tailor, salmon (kahawai), barracouta and mackerel.

Another very productive group of metal casting lures much favoured by anglers in Australia and New Zealand, are called 'slugs', sildas or — more commonly — bait fish profiles. These are long, thin lures cast from lead or lead alloy and meant to represent pelagic bait species such as whitebait, pilchards, anchovies and sprats. These lures are easy to cast long distances and work best with a reasonably rapid retrieve, occasionally interspersed with brief pauses. They may also be jigged on or near the sea bed, or allowed to sink and then retrieved rapidly towards the surface with rod sweeps and sudden stops. Bait fish profiles are particularly effective when targeting small to medium tuna, bonito, kingfish, mackerel, dolphin fish and even snapper.

Iron-style lures, pencils, hexagonals and 'flat bars' fall mid-way between spoons and bait fish profiles in their design and use. Most are made from metal alloys or solid brass bar stock. They may be boat-shaped, flat sides, hexagonal or sliced from a circular section of brass rod; most are chromed or painted. They cast well and should be retrieved quickly with occasional rod sweeps or pauses. This family of lures are at their best when used to pursue tailor, salmon (kahawai), barracouta, pike, mackerel, smaller tunas and bonito.

Lead-head jigs are another versatile and productive group of saltwater casting lures. Most have a ball, egg or boot shaped lead or alloy head cast around a strong, single hook designed to ride point uppermost in the water. The head is typically painted and adorned with eyes, and the tail dressed in deer hair, synthetic fibres, feathers or soft

ABOVE: *A broad selection of modern, saltwater casting lures. Those on the left are minnows, topwater poppers and rattle baits, while those on the right include metal spoons, jigs, irons and bait fish profiles or slugs.*

plastic fish and grub replicas.

Lead-heads cast well and sink rapidly. They may be cranked rapidly through the water, fished with a stop-start, lift-drop retrieve, bounced on the sea bed or jigged vertically. In slower presentation modes — especially vertical jigging — their effectiveness is greatly increased by the addition of a fish flesh or squid strip to the hook.

Lead-head jigs will catch every lure-eating fish that swims, but are especially deadly on mackerel, tailor, tuna, cod, coral trout and snapper.

Another group of saltwater casting lures are the plugs and minnows. These are fish-shaped baits made of timber, plastic, epoxy, high-density styrofoam or — more rarely — metal. They may or may not be fitted with a small paravane device called a diving lip or 'bib'. Some are designed to float and others to sink at various rates. Many are fitted with internal rattles to enhance their appeal.

This grouping — called 'body baits' by American anglers — is the largest and most diverse of all. Interestingly, these lures all owe their ancestry to freshwater fishing, although some of the saltwater plugs and minnows made today are larger than most trout or bass!

As well as an extensive range of imported plugs and minnows, some superb products are now made here in Australia and New Zealand. These have evolved specifically for local angling styles and offer the best combination of features available. Plugs and minnows are proven producers on barramundi, mangrove jacks, queenfish, trevally, kingfish, cobia, tailor, salmon (kahawai), barracouta and a host of other tropical, sub-tropical and temperate species. They are also effective on many reef fish, such as cod and coral trout. Smaller plugs and minnows score well on flathead, bream and snapper at times.

The final family of saltwater casting lures are the poppers or topwater plugs. These are also made of timber or various plastics, but are designed to run across the surface like an injured bait fish when retrieved, causing a great deal of fuss and commotion. Most float at rest, although a few sink, requiring a constant retrieve to keep them on the surface. The floating models are more versatile, as they may be fished with a stop-start action. Topwater plugs are especially effective on kingfish, cobia, queenfish, tropical trevally and even shallower reef species such as coral trout and red bass.

The saltwater lure caster should assemble a collection of lures in several styles, carefully matching the weight and optimum retrieve speed of each model to his or her intended fishing styles and target species. Generally speaking, factors such as colour are less important in saltwater lure fishing than size, shape and action.

Saltwater Trolling Lures

ABOVE: *A range of modern, skirted trolling lures, ranging from small models used to catch skipjack, bonito and other bait, right up to magnum marlin and tuna lures.*

All of the saltwater casting lures described on the previous pages may be trolled behind a moving boat, although many will not work well at speeds in excess of five or six knots. This is not a problem when targeting tailor, salmon (kahawai), bonito, barracouta, snook and the like, as these fish typically respond best to lures moving at three to six knots.

Especially productive at these slower trolling speeds are certain spoons, minnows and so-called 'Smith's Jigs'. The Smith's Jig is a boat-shaped plastic lure with a screw-mounted double hook. It was once favoured by professional trollers for catching tuna and similar fish, but is significantly inferior to modern designs, particularly at speeds in excess of five or six knots.

Some of the modern saltwater minnows will cope with much higher speeds than spoons or Smith's Jigs, and are great producers of tuna, wahoo, mackerel, dolphin fish and reef species. However, they are generally unsuited to very large, active game and sport fish in excess of 25 or 30 kilos. The leverage imposed by such heavyweights often results in pulled or straightened hooks when trolling with minnow lures. Many highly prized saltwater game and sport fish — notably tuna, wahoo, Spanish mackerel, sailfish and marlin — prefer lures travelling at five to 15 knots, and it is in this area that specific trolling lure styles have evolved.

Among the most popular of all the families of trolling lures are the squids, Evil Eyes, Christmas Trees and lead-head feathers. These all have bullet-shaped heads made of lead, alloy, plastic or some other material and tails of feather, hair, shredded plastic, vinyl or rubber. A hole running through the centre of the lure carries the line or leader and one or more hooks are attached behind. Some — called jets or shower-heads — have several additional holes running through the body to create a bubble trail.

Feather jigs, Evil Eyes, jets and squids are available in a multitude of sizes, weights, shapes and colour combinations. The smaller models — up to 10 or 12 centimetres in overall length — are much favoured when pursuing small tuna and mackerel. Very large feathers and squids have largely been superseded by the more modern

BAITS AND LURES

ABOVE: A beautiful bull dolphin fish or mahi-mahi taken on a troll lure.
RIGHT: Magnum minnows make useful trolling tools for kingfish.

Konahead-style lures and pushers.

Konahead is the generic name now given to a family of lures which originally evolved along the Kona coast of Hawaii's Big Island. They feature a resin or plastic head fitted with one or more layered skirts of shredded plastic, vinyl or similar material. They are further characterised by having an angled or scooped face to create splash and action when pulled through the water at speeds of six to nine knots. As with feather jigs and squids, a central channel carries the leader, and the hooks are attached behind. Konaheads were once the basic lure of the marlin and tuna troller, but are not so widely used today.

'Pushers' have nowadays largely replaced Konaheads as the last word in big fish lures. These specialist lures are constructed in much the same manner as the older Konaheads — with resin bodies and shredded plastic skirts — but have a flat, square-cut head, a very slight nose angle, or a scooped-out (concave) nose. As a result, they travel through the water in a relatively straight line, creating a strong bubble trail. They work best at speeds between seven and 12 or 14 knots and have accounted for the capture of many exceptional marlin, tuna, wahoo and mackerel in Australasian waters. The very best pushers are made in Hawaii, the United States and Australia.

When trolling more than one line, it is important to establish a pattern of lines with the lures staggered at different lengths to avoid cross-overs and tangles. It is also vital to select lures with similar operating speeds. For this reason for example, it is not generally possible to mix, spoons, minnows, Smith's Jigs and pushers. The best results will be obtained if the spread or pattern of lures are fine-tuned and balanced to swim together at an optimum speed.

Freshwater Lures

While many lures on the market today may be used in both salt and fresh water, specialist lake and stream anglers tend to select the bulk of their artificial baits from ranges made specifically for freshwater use.

Among the most traditional of the freshwater lure groupings are the spoons. These dished, metal lures bear at least some resemblance to the bowl of a teaspoon or tablespoon, and the earliest models were probably made by sawing up kitchen cutlery. Fresh-water spoons come in an array of shapes, sizes, weights, metal thickness and colour combinations.

The overall shape of spoon lures can be divided into three classes.

The almost circular, oval or egg-shaped designs are called Colorado spoons. They have a strong, wide-swinging action when retrieved or trolled, and work best at relatively slow speeds. Somewhat longer and narrower kidney- or teardrop-shaped models are called Indiana spoons. These are the most versatile of all freshwater spoons, and this grouping accounts for the majority of spoons sold in Australia and New Zealand. They have variable actions, but most work well at slow and medium speeds.

The longest, narrowest models are called needle spoons. Although they are more popular among saltwater anglers, they also enjoy a following in certain areas of freshwater fishing, particularly lake trolling for trout and salmon. These spoons have a tighter, faster action and work better at higher speeds than either Colorado or Indiana designs. A fourth classification, called flutter spoons, come in all of the shapes described above. They are characterised by the extremely thin metal used in their construction. Their light weight makes it almost impossible to cast flutter spoons, but they are extremely effective when trolled.

A separate lure grouping related in some ways to the spoon family are the so-called 'Tassie lures'. Originating in the Australian island state of Tasmania, these lures are now also popular on the mainland and in New Zealand. They consist of a cylindrical lead insert coated in plastic and featuring wings or fins that produce their distinctive action. Although originally developed for trout trolling, they are also favoured by some shore-based lure casters working the banks of lakes and large rivers.

Spinners are another traditional and time-proven family of freshwater lures. The most popular type are called in-line spinners and consist of a small, spoon-like blade revolving freely on a metal shaft ahead of a plastic or metal body. Two other spinner styles, known as weight-forward spinners and spinner-baits, are popular in North

America, but do not yet enjoy a large following here in Australia and New Zealand.

In-line spinners come in many sizes, weights and colours, although the smaller models are favoured by local anglers. They can be cast and retrieved or trolled behind a slow moving boat, although it should be noted that some models may cause severe line twist at times. To prevent this, always use a small, quality swivel tied into the line 25 to 50 centimetres ahead of the lure or, better still, a small anti-kink keel.

Lead-head jigs of the type described in the earlier section on 'Saltwater Casting Lures' are also useful in freshwater, although much smaller sizes are usually favoured by inland anglers. In fact, very small lead-heads — called 'micro jigs' — are great producers when fishing streams and lake margins for trout, perch and other freshwater species.

The largest grouping of freshwater lures are the plugs, minnows, rattle baits and topwater lures. These are all body baits, with bodies constructed of timber, plastic, injection-moulded foam, rubber or some other material. Some float, others sink, and many are fitted with diving lips or bibs to give them action and cause them to dive down through the water column when retrieved or trolled. Today, the majority of hollow body baits also feature an internal rattle of some type.

These body baits range from tiny, thin-profile minnows ideal for catching stream-dwelling trout, through fat-bodied plugs and 'crankbaits' favoured by bass and perch anglers, right on up to giant, deep-diving models aimed at big Murray cod. Mid-range, thin-profile minnows also form the basis of any lure collection used to catch barramundi, saratoga, sooty grunter and other tropical sport fish.

Some excellent plugs and minnows are constructed locally, especially in the deep diving category favoured by outback anglers targeting Murray cod and golden perch, and among the ranks of tough, tight-actioned minnows used by

Modern freshwater lures come in a huge array of shapes, sizes, colours and patterns. The cross-section displayed here includes floating/diving models, rattle baits, topwater plugs, spoons, spinners and wigglers.

barramundi specialists. The topwater members of this enormous family include poppers, chuggers, sliders and fizzers — floating lures with cupped or slanted faces, metal arms or little propellers that create splash and fuss on the surface as the lure is retrieved. These are good choices for bass, barramundi and saratoga.

It is true, however, that half a dozen well-chosen lures will often catch just as many fish as a collection of several hundred!

Freshwater Flies

Freshwater fly fishing has a long and rich record. The early Macedonians were probably the first to recognise fact that wisps of bird feather and animal fur tied to a hook and dangled on the surface from a long pole and length of plaited horsehair line would trick fish.

The fish those Macedonians captured were wild brown trout, and it is the pursuit of the trout and salmon clan (the salmonids) that dominated so much of the recorded development of freshwater fly fishing. Today, the vast majority of freshwater fly fishermen still target salmonids, although an ever-growing minority are expanding the sport pursuing 'warm water' sport fish such as carp, bass, barramundi, saratoga, sooty grunter and jungle perch. Fly patterns for cool water (salmonid) and warm water (non-salmonid) fly fishing have tended to evolve separately, although there are many areas of overlap, and a host of patterns that are applicable to both branches of the sport.

Basically, cool water fly patterns can be divided into three classes: dry flies, nymphs and wets. Warm water flies fall into the same groupings, with one additional class — the 'action' topwater flies such as poppers, chuggers and darters .

As the name implies, dry flies are intended to float on or in the surface film of the water. They achieve this through the use of light gauge hooks, buoyant or semi-buoyant materials and devices such as stiff hackles (feather fibres) which support the fly on the layer of surface tension known as the meniscus. Dry flies are meant to imitate hatching or emerging insects such as mayflies and caddis, egg-laying adults of the same species, dead or spent insects, and hapless terrestrial creatures such as beetles and grasshoppers which fall or are blown onto the water. Larger dries and the topwater patterns of the warm water angler may also imitate frogs, lizards or cicadas.

Famous dry fly patterns for trout include traditional British ties such as Tup's Indispensable, Wickham's Fancy, Greenwell's Glory and the Iron Blue. Two British patterns that have proven especially productive locally are the Coch-y-Bondhu and the Red Tag. The latter, in particular, is regarded as an essential fly by many Tasmanian anglers.

Innovative North American patterns — especially those evolved for use in the more boisterous streams of the Rockies — are becoming increasingly important to Australasian anglers. Famous examples include the various Wulffs, the Humpy or Goofus Bug, Irresistible, Elk Hair and Deer Hair Caddis, Compara Dun and Adams. In addition, there are many fine grasshopper patterns, including some — like the Nobby Hopper and Glenn Innes Hopper — developed specifically to match insect types found in Australia.

Most of the dries intended for trout are fished 'dead drift' or with very subtle jiggles and twitches. They are tied on small hooks — right down to size 22 or even 24 in extreme cases! The majority, however, are between No. 18 and No. 12, with some of the grasshoppers tied on No. 10 to No. 6 hooks.

The dry or topwater patterns of the warm water angler are generally larger and designed to be fished with some action — jiggled, popped or actively stripped by the fisherman. The most famous is the Dahlberg Diver and its derivations; a spun deer hair 'slider' which produces a loud plop when stripped and wiggles its way several centimetres beneath the surface. Other topwater patterns include deer hair bugs, poppers and mice, as well as cork and styrofoam creations in sizes ranging from about No. 10 or No. 8 right up to 3/0 and 4/0. Special wide-gape 'stinger' hooks are favoured by many specialist tyers of warm water bugs.

Nymphs may be regarded as an intermediate stage between dry flies and the lure-style wets. They have a tradition almost as long as that of the classic dries, and fishing them properly requires just as much finesse.

Nymph patterns imitate insects such as mayflies, caddis, dragonflies, damselflies and stoneflies. They may also represent shrimps, scud, daphnia and other copepods, or even small fish, water beetles and tadpoles. Famous patterns include the Hare's Ear, Pheasant Tail, Sawyer's Nymph, Seal's Fur and stonefly and mayfly imitations. Most are tied on hooks in the No. 18 to No. 10 size range. Nymphs are cast upstream and fished dead drift, twitched and retrieved slowly, or cast across

and swung down-stream.

Wet flies are also known as fly rod lures. They range from traditional winged wets and soft-hackled flies or 'spiders' — meant to imitate drowned insects, emerging adults or egg-laying caddis — through to streamers and Atlantic salmon flies. The latter types represent small fish, crayfish, shrimps, tadpoles, leeches or nothing in particular — relying on an instinctive response or outright aggression to trigger a strike.

Some of the better known winged wets and spiders include the wet version of Wickham's Fancy, the Invicta, Mallard and Claret, Dunkeld, Olive Quill, Black and Peacock and wet Red Tag. Australian and New Zealand patterns like Mrs Simpson and the Taihape Tickler are also productive. Established streamers include the Matuka, Zonker, Mickey Finn, Sweeny Todd and wet Muddler Minnows. Others, like the very effective Woolly Bugger and Sloane's Rabbit Fur Fly, defy accurate classification, being mid-way between soft-hackle wets and streamers, but able to be fished like a nymph!

Most of these wets are tied on hooks in the size range between No. 12 and No. 4, while traditional salmon and sea trout patterns like the Thunder and Lightning, Jock Scott and Silver Blue may be dressed on hooks as large as a No. 1 or 1/0. They are all fished with a steady series of strips, slow twitches, dead drift,

The study and hand-crafting of freshwater flies can become an all-consuming passion! Patterns shown here range from relatively large bugs and divers (top left), through streamers (top right), nymphs (centre left) to delicate dry patterns.

or an across-and-down swing.

Slightly larger versions of all these flies, or scaled-down saltwater patterns, are the preferred choice of many warm water fly casters targeting bass, perch and barramundi.

Saltwater Flies

Saltwater fly fishing began as an extension of the freshwater branch of the art. Atlantic salmon anglers in Europe and North America often plied their sport in the tidal reaches of coastal rivers, and occasionally they captured other species in addition to the noble salmon. Later, trout fishers began taking their fly outfits to the ocean and fishing the sand flats, mangrove creeks and reefs with increasing success.

The evolution of saltwater fly fishing followed a similar path here in Australia and New Zealand, although it was not until the late 1960s and early 1970s that reasonable numbers of local anglers began to cast flies into saltwater.

Today, saltwater fly fishing (sometimes colloquially known as 'swoffing') is one of the major growth sectors of the recreational sport fishing world, both here and overseas. As a result, tackle, techniques and fly patterns have rapidly evolved to accommodate the increased interests and aspirations of swoffing's devotees.

The first saltwater flies were freshwater patterns upgraded with larger, corrosion-resistant hooks. Nowadays, however, there are entire families of specific marine patterns intended to imitate such ocean-going fodder as garfish, mullet, pilchards, prawns and crabs.

Perhaps the most popular and successful of the saltwater patterns are the streamers. These are tied in a multitude of styles, sizes and colour combinations, although most are intended to represent a fleeing bait fish when stripped briskly through the water.

Some of the more famous and well established streamers include the Blonde series, often referred to as Brooks' Blondes in recognition of Joe Brooks, their American originator. These are very basic and easy-to-tie flies, with a tail and wing of bucktail or some synthetic equivalent and a body of mylar tubing or tinsel. They are extremely effective on a wide range of fish, and have the added advantage of being quite durable — an important consideration when dealing with sharp-toothed adversaries such as tailor, barracuda and mackerel. Blondes can be tied in a myriad of colour combinations on hooks as small as a No. 4 or as large as a 4/0 or 5/0. The most popular options, however, are all-white or white and red in sizes 1/0 to 4/0.

Slightly more involved, but a great deal more effective in many scenarios, are the Deceivers. These were developed by American fly fishing guru, Bernard 'Lefty' Kreh, and feature a tail constructed of soft, flowing saddle hackles (from the back of a chicken) with a collar-style wing of bucktail, polar bear or synthetic material. Few other fly patterns — salt or fresh — can match a well-tied Deceiver for action and 'life' in the water.

Deceivers are usually tied on hook sizes between about No. 2 and No. 6/0. They are not so effective in smaller sizes, as it is difficult to achieve the flowing, pulsating action that is this fly's key attribute when using very short saddle hackles. Colour combinations are almost unlimited, although all-white,

BAITS AND LURES

FLY TYING

Although many fly fisher-men start out buying their flies or having them custom tied, almost all of those who continue on with the sport end up tying at least a percent-age of the patterns they use. Fly tying is not especially difficult. With a small amount of practice, anyone can pro-duce workable, basic flies that will catch fish in many situations.

The essential requirements for fly tying include the following:
- A vice to hold the hook firmly.
- A pair of small, sharp scissors.
- One or two bobbin holders to help control the thread.
- A pair of hackle pliers.
- A half-hitch tool and/or whip finish tool.
- A stout needle or bodkin.
- A jar or bottle of clear lacquer or head cement.
- Spools of tying thread in white, black and brown.

Don't buy additional fly tying materials such as furs, feathers and tinsels until you know exactly which patterns you will be making. Start out with easy recipes that have the minimum number of steps, such as single-winged streamers or soft-hackled wets like the Black and Peacock. Many materials are available around the house or at haberdashery outlets, while others will need to be purch-ased from special-ist outlets.

With the necessities listed above, and a good book on beginner's fly tying, you will soon be well on the way towards catching fish on your own flies — a truly rewarding experience!

LEFT: Many saltwater flies are adaptations of freshwater patterns, especially streamers. Interesting variations here include the hair bug and popper fly (far left) and the Aussie-made Pink Thing (far right).

white and green, white and blue or white and brown are very popular. All-black or black and red Deceivers are especially potent when pursuing barra-mundi, threadfin salmon and other tropical targets in discoloured northern estuaries. Most tiers also add some flash to their Deceivers and other salt-water streamers in the form of thin mylar strands or fibres of synthetic material such as Flashabou, Lure Flash or Krystal Flash.

Some of the American tarpon patterns are used locally with considerable success. The best known of these is the Seaducer, which consists of several flared (back-to-back) saddle hackles tied in at the hook bend, with another hackle or two wound or 'palmered' ahead of the tail, and the remainder of the hook shank left bare, or lightly dressed in mylar or tinsel. Eyes may be added to the head if so desired. This fly is usually tied on relatively large hooks (2/0 to 6/0) and has an attractive, pulsating action when stripped.

Several local streamer variants have been developed for Australasian fish. These include Graeme White's Pink Thing, a heavily dressed Deceiver-style fly with bead-chain eyes that has earned a strong following among barramundi specialists in Australia's north. Similarly, Rod Harrison's Zedabou — originally developed for catching sea-run chinook salmon in New Zealand — has developed a reputation on many saltwater species, while the author's own Crooked Creek Special — a derivation of the long-established Bendback pattern — has a proven track record on flathead and bream.

Beyond the streamers — which cover the majority of saltwater fly fishing scenarios — there are many specialist patterns. These include the Mother of Epoxy (MOE) flies, which have bodies crafted from two-part epoxy or glue and are shaped to represent crabs, shrimps or prawns. There are also fur and feather prawn patterns, bonefish flies such as the Crazy Charlie and Chico's Special, rabbit-strip Zonkers, squid imitations, fluffy berley flies (tied to imitate a chunk or cube of cut fish flesh) and a host of topwater patterns including poppers, chuggers and sliders.

Topwater flies are especially effective on fish such as barramundi, trevally, kingfish, queenfish and cobia. The best known is the Dahlberg Diver — a spun deer hair freshwater bass pattern readily adapted to marine use. Other topwater flies are constructed with buoyant bodies of cork or styrofoam and are tied in a wide range of sizes, from No. 4 or No. 2 versions intended to catch 'chopper' tailor or small salmon (kahawai), right on up to giant bluewater poppers on single or tandem 7/0 hooks that can be cast at sailfish and small marlin.

Saltwater fly fishing is an exciting and fast changing facet of angling, with new patterns and methods of fishing emerging every month. One of the nicest things about the sport is that every participant can play a part in its evolution, and that an innovative new fly design is only as far away as the workbench and vice!

Fish Species

Almost 3 000 species of fish have been recorded in Australian and New Zealand waters during our two centuries of European settlement. No doubt there are still many others out there awaiting discovery and classification. The vast majority of these fish are of little more than academic interest to recreational anglers. They live in very deep water far from shore, or never grow large enough to be deliberately targeted. Only about 200 species of salt and freshwater fish are taken by Australasian anglers on a regular basis.

In this chapter, I have chosen to look at approximately 100 different types of fish. These represent our favourite angling species — those which account for at least 90 per cent of the recreational fishing effort taking place in our waters. I will have certainly left out some fish which enjoy a specialist or regional following. Just as surely, I have included a few which appeal to a relatively small handful of devotees. These facts simply reflect the incredible diversity of angling opportunities in Australasian waters.

When considered, 100 species is quite a substantial list of angling targets! Few of us will ever account for more than half of that list in a full lifetime of angling. Only a skilful handful of fishermen could hope to approach a 'full house' of 100 species, although it would certainly be a lot of fun trying!

The aim of this chapter is to give a thumb-nail sketch of each of the species chosen. As well as providing an invaluable aid in identifying your catch, it will give you vital information on the distribution, typical size range, habitat preferences, availability and eating qualities of the various fish discussed. Tackle and bait choices will also be summarised, although these subjects are dealt with in far greater detail elsewhere in the book.

As far as the names of the fish are concerned, I have tried wherever possible to give the more popular and widely-used common names, as well as the most up-to-date scientific descriptions. This is not always easy, as there are wide geographical variations in common names, and one species may have several different titles. For example, the name skipjack or 'skippy' could be applied to a tailor in Victoria, a silver trevally in Western Australia and a striped tuna in New Zealand!

Similarly, scientific titles are by no means set in stone. Just recently, an international conference of fisheries biologists agreed on a broad-sweeping re-classification of the trout and salmon families. As a result, the rainbow trout is no longer *Salmo gairnerii*. Today, it carries the even more tongue-twisting scientific title of *Oncorhyncus mykiss*.

Laymen typically avoid these long-winded and seemingly unpronounceable scientific names, but they do provide a valuable aid in identifying fish and are especially useful when comparing publications from different countries. For example, the immensely popular North American bluefish carries the scientific handle *Pomatomus saltatrix*. This tells us that the bluefish is exactly the same species which we call tailor here in Australia, and which South African anglers know as the elf; this knowledge is only available through use of the scientific name.

I trust that this chapter will make it much easier to identify your catch. I also hope that the information contained in these pages helps you add a few new species to your personal tally. There are few things more exciting in angling that catching a brand new fish you have never before seen! We are fortunate indeed to live in a part of the world which offers such a diversity of fishing opportunities. We owe it to ourselves to learn as much as we can about the fascinating creatures which provide us with so much challenging sport and excitement.

Anatomy

Although there are almost 25 000 species of fish throughout the world and 3 000 in local waters, they may be broadly divided into just two groups. The vast majority belong to the class known as bony fish (Teleostomi). These so-called 'true fishes' have internal skeletons composed mostly of bone. In contrast, the cartilaginous fishes have skeletons made entirely of a softer material called cartilage. Most of the cartilaginous fish are sharks or rays. Within these two broad groupings, there are wide variations in the physiology and life cycles of fish. Some lay eggs, others bear their young alive. Some live totally in saltwater, others in fresh, while still others are able to move between the two mediums.

The respiratory systems of both bony and cartilaginous fishes are similar in function — despite the fact that the bony fish have gill filaments covered by a pair of gill plates or opercula, whilst sharks have between four and seven gill slits, and rays have additional breathing apertures called spiracles. Despite these variations in the physical construction of their respiratory apparatus, fish, sharks and rays all breath by taking in water through their mouths (or spiracles, in the case of rays), extracting oxygen from that water as it passes over a series of blood-rich gill filaments, then expelling the water through their gill slits or openings. Waste carbon dioxide in the blood is released back into the exhaled water at the same time.

Being surrounded by water, fish also need to cope with the effects of a phenomena known as osmosis. This is the process whereby concentrated solutions of salts or sugars are separated from plain water by means of a thin, permeable membrane (such as the skin or mouth-lining of a fish). The two liquids attempt to equalise. Water from the weaker solution will begin to pass through the membrane in order to dilute the stronger solution, while salts or sugars pass in reverse direction, from the strong solution towards the weak one.

This means that freshwater fish — whose bodies represent a stronger solution than the surrounding water — fight a constant battle to avoid the loss of salts and the absorption of water. Saltwater fish have exactly the opposite problem, with the sea water attempting to leach fresh water from their bodies and replace it with a saltier solution.

Despite these apparent problems, many species move easily from highly saline to almost completely fresh water. Such fish are said to be euryhaline, and include Australasian species like the Australian bass, barramundi and some mullet.

Other fish need access to waters of varying salinities in order to reproduce. Two common types are those fish which are said to be anadromous, and those called catadromous. Anadromous fish spend most of their lives in the sea, but migrate into freshwater to spawn. Migratory or sea-run chinook salmon from New Zealand's South Island are a good example. In contrast, catadromous fish live their lives in fresh or brackish water and move down towards, or into, the sea to spawn. Our freshwater eels and the barramundi are typical representatives of this group.

The sensory systems of fish are highly evolved and complex. Their senses of sight, hearing, touch, smell and taste are generally well developed. In addition, they possess an extra sense best described as vibration detection. This is achieved through receptors in the fish's lateral line or similar organs in the skin. It allows a predator to detect the unnatural tail beats of an injured bait fish in murky water, or the individual members of a school of tuna to stay close together, even at night. It seems likely that there are other, even more subtle, senses at work in many fish species. One we know of exists in some sharks, and allows them to detect electrical fields as weak as a millionth of a volt! That is about equivalent to the electrical output of a flounder's breathing.

Most fish and sharks move through the water by flexing their bodies from side to side or sending a long S-shaped wave from nose to tail. Low speed manoeuvering may be performed by the beating of pectoral (side) fins and perhaps the rippling of dorsal and anal fins. For the most part, however, these fins are only used for adjusting trim, steering and braking. Exceptions include species such as the leatherjackets, wrasse and toad fish, which do the bulk of their swimming with rhythmic fin movements.

Muscle tissue within a fish's body is divided into two types: white meat and red meat. Red meat is highly blood saturated and is used for sustained power output. It gives the tunas their migratory stamina and makes the blue and mako sharks the open ocean wanderers that they are. In contrast, white muscle is used mostly for short burst activity, such as the lunge of a flathead or flounder from the sea bed as it grabs at a passing prawn.

The bodies of many bony fish are covered in scales. These show regular growth rings, like a tree, and are replaced if lost. Whether they have scales or not, most fish also have a mucous or slime coating, which is vital in resisting infections and overcoming the osmosis effects discussed earlier. Serious damage to this slime coat may easily cause the eventual death of a fish, and this should be borne in mind when handling fish intended for live release or retention in an aquarium.

NAPE

PRE-OPERCULUM

BARBELS

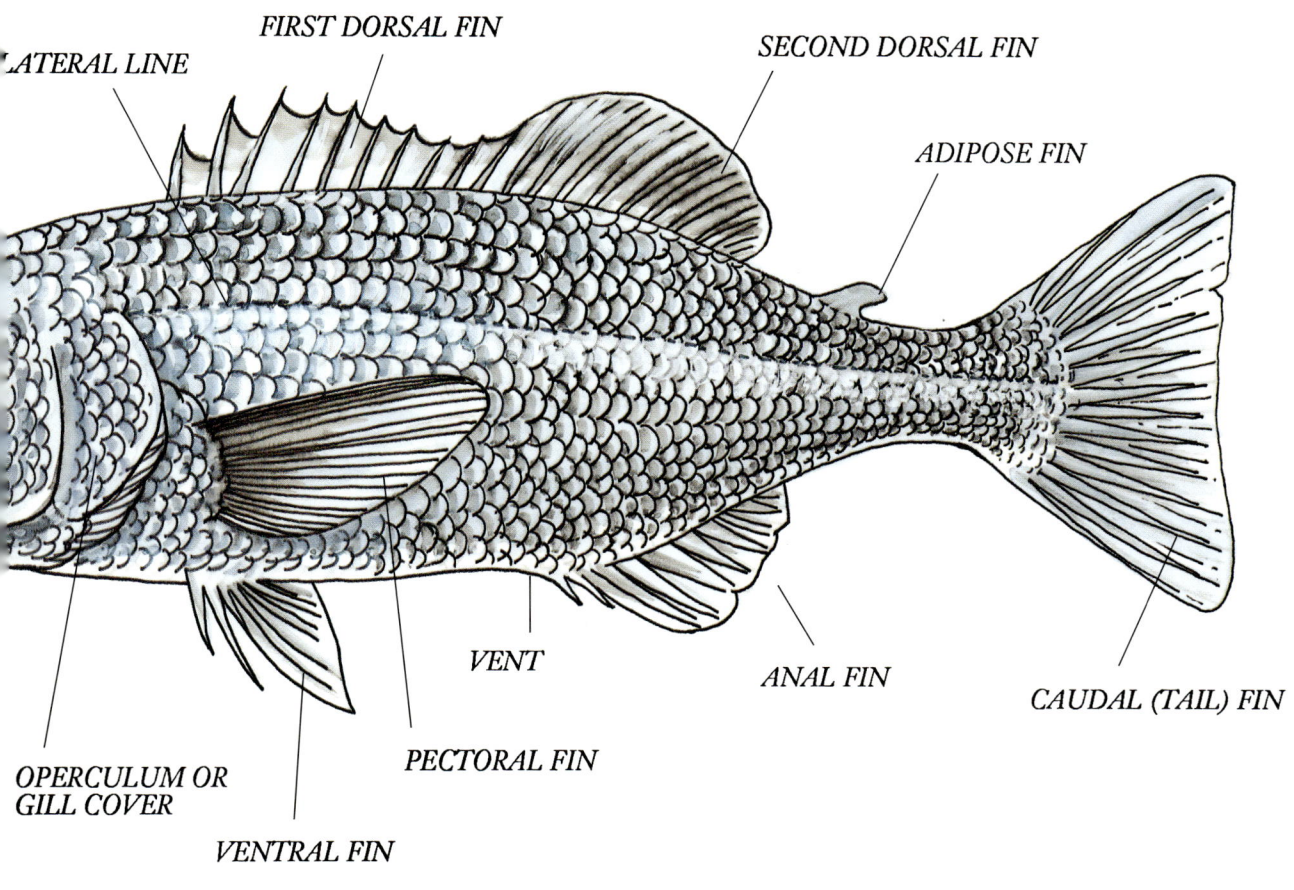

Finally, it should be noted that many fish species have defensive mechanisms that may make them potentially dangerous to handle. The most common are stout, sharp spines in the first dorsal, anal and pectoral fins. In many cases these are coated with a venomous mucous which may vary in its intensity from mildly irritating to outright life-threatening. There may also be spines and cutting edges on the gill covers or sharp teeth. Learn which species are potentially dangerous, and how to handle them.

Study the labelled illustrations of fish on these pages and try to remember the common names of the various fins and other body parts, as these are often mentioned in identification texts or warnings concerning dangerous species.

Albacore *Thunnus alalunga*

The albacore is a middleweight member of the tuna family found mainly in sub-tropical, temperate and cooler seas around Australia and New Zealand. They are mostly encountered in deeper, oceanic waters, near the edges of the Continental Shelf and beyond. However, favourable currents occasionally carry them inshore.

Albacore are characterised by their extremely long, strap-like pectoral or side fins. These reach back well beyond the base of the second dorsal fin, and are significantly longer than those found on any other tuna, with the possible exception of juvenile bigeye tuna (*T. obesus*), which are rare in our waters.

Albacore in Australasian waters commonly attain weights of two to 12 kilos, with exceptional specimens reaching 20 kilos. Elsewhere in the world, they have been taken to twice that size.

This species occurs in large schools, although individual fish rarely break the surface or jump in the manner of many other tunas. Albacore schools tend to make rapid vertical movements within the water column, and spend much of their time at depths outside the range of conventional fishing techniques.

Albacore respond to a wide range of angling techniques, including bait fishing, lure casting, trolling and fly fishing. They are often taken by game and sport fishermen targeting yellowfin tuna, sharks and marlin, especially in the cooler currents encountered at the beginning and end of the season.

They are a delicious table fish, with pinkish flesh that turns white when cooked. Most culinary experts rate them as the tastiest of all the tunas.

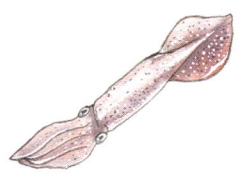

Natural Food

Barracouta *Thyristes atun*

Barracouta are found in sub-tropical, temperate and cooler seas around Australia and New Zealand. They occur mostly in the lower reaches of larger tidal rivers, bays, inlets and harbours, and over reefs and gravel beds extending offshore towards the edge of the Continental Shelf. Extensive schools are often encountered in cold, offshore waters around the southern half of mainland Australia, Tasmania, and New Zealand's South Island.

This species is characterised by its long, thin, silvery body and large jaws armed with sharp teeth. Despite some superficial similarities, barracouta should not be confused with the unrelated barracudas (*Sphyraena spp.*) of northern, tropical waters.

Barracouta are caught primarily by boat anglers using a variety of offshore fishing techniques. In particular, they respond aggressively to trolled or cast lures, such as metal spoons, jigs, feathers and minnows. They are also taken by shore-based anglers in some locations.

Although dark fleshed, oily and prone to infestations of parasitic worms, barracouta are a popular table fish in southern areas, and support a valuable commercial fishery. In more northerly waters, they are commonly regarded as a pest by anglers pursuing more desirable table fish.

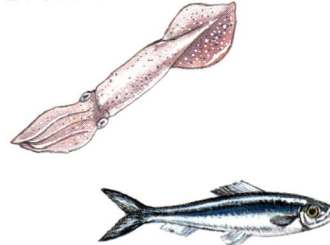

Natural Food

Natural Food

TECHNIQUE	ROD	REEL	LINE	TERMINAL TACKLE	HOOK	WEIGHT	BAIT
Trolling, lure casting or drifting.	Light to medium boat rod.	Small to medium overhead or game reel.	4-15 kg	Wire leader.	4/0-8/0	None, or small barrel.	Skirted trolling lures, minnows, live and dead fish.

FISH SPECIES

TECHNIQUE	ROD	REEL	LINE	TERMINAL TACKLE	HOOK	WEIGHT	BAIT
Trolling, drifting with live and dead baits.	4-15 kg class sport or game rod.	Lever or star-drag trolling reel or large threadline.	4-15 kg nylon.	4-15 kg nylon leader.	3/0-7/0	none	Skirted trolling lures, minnows, pilchards, small live fish.

TECHNIQUE	ROD	REEL	LINE	TERMINAL TACKLE	HOOK	WEIGHT	BAIT
Trolling, lure casting, live and dead baiting.	Beach or rock casting rod, light boat rod.	Small overhead, medium threadline or sidecast.	4-12 kg	Ganged hooks and/or light wire leader.	3/0-7/0	Small ball or barrel.	Casting lures, spoons, pilchards, small live or dead fish.

Barracuda *Sphyraena barracuda*

Known in some literature as the 'sea wolf', and carrying a largely undeserved reputation for ferocity towards humans, the great barracuda is found in tropical and sub-tropical waters around the northern half of Australia.

It is much thicker and heavier in build than the unrelated southern barracouta (*Thyrsites atun*). The barracuda also has two small, relatively widely separated dorsal fins, in contrast to the barracouta's long, high and connected dorsal fin structure.

Barracuda are a fish of estuarine and inshore waters, occurring mostly in the lower reaches of larger tidal rivers, bays, inlets and harbours, and over reefs and gravel beds extending offshore towards the edge of the Continental Shelf. Larger specimens are most commonly encountered over offshore coral reefs, around islands, bomboras and undersea pinnacles. They are a potentially large fish, reaching a metre or two in length and weighing as much as 20 or 30 kilos, although most of those encountered by anglers are considerably smaller.

Barracuda are usually an incidental catch taken by anglers fishing for more desirable target species such as Spanish mackerel, wahoo and tuna. They provide quite exciting sport on light tackle, with fast runs and occasional jumps, but lack the stamina of many other gamefish.

Barracuda have greyish flesh and are not considered highly as table fish. They have also been linked with serious incidences of ciguatera poisoning, and should not be eaten in areas where this toxin is known to occur.

Barramundi *Lates calcarifer*

The barramundi or 'barra' is one of Australia's most famous and highly regarded fish, renowned for both its sporting prowess and its edible qualities.

Barramundi are a species of the tropical north, ranging from the Mary River in Queensland to the Ashburton River in Western Australia, but occurring in greatest numbers north of the Tropic of Capricorn.

Barra live in fresh, brackish, estuarine and inshore waters, rarely straying far beyond the mouths of tidal rivers, harbours and inlets. They require access to saline, tidal waters in order to reproduce, but will live for many years in land-locked lagoons and billabongs without breeding.

They are a large, handsome and alert fish, commonly encountered at weights of one to six kilos. Fish over 10 kilos are far from abundant these days, although the occasional 20 kilo-plus monster is still a possibility in more isolated areas.

One of the most fascinating characteristics of this species is its ability to change sex as it matures! All barramundi are born male, but at a certain size (which appears to vary from place to place), they develop ovaries and become females.

Sadly, barramundi populations have been greatly reduced by over-harvesting and habitat destruction in many regions, particularly along the eastern seaboard of Queensland. Today, southern anglers must travel to the Northern Territory or the Kimberley region of Western Australia in order to find consistently good barra fishing.

Barramundi respond to a wide range of angling techniques, including bait fishing, lure casting, trolling and fly fishing.

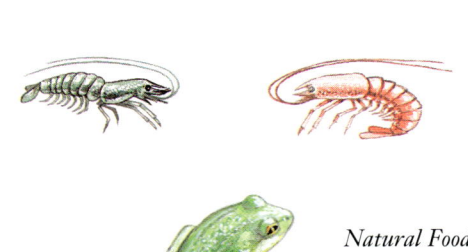

Natural Food

TECHNIQUE	ROD	REEL	LINE	TERMINAL TACKLE	HOOK	WEIGHT	BAIT
Casting or trolling lures, drifting live baits, fly fishing.	Light, single-handed spinning or baitcaster rod, No. 5-9 fly rod.	Light threadline or baitcaster. Fly reel.	2-6 kg WF5-9 fly line.	Line tied directly to hook or lure.	1/0-3/0	None	Casting lures, plugs, minnows, live insects or large fresh water flies.

TECHNIQUE	ROD	REEL	LINE	TERMINAL TACKLE	HOOK	WEIGHT	BAIT
Casting or trolling lures, drifting and float suspending live baits. Fly fishing.	Single or double-handed spinning or baitcaster rod. No. 8-11 fly rod.	Medium baitcaster or threadline. Fly reel.	4-12 kg WF8-11 fly line	30-60 kg nylon leader or light wire.	2/0-6/0	None, or small ball.	Casting lures, minnows, plugs, live bait, fish, prawns.

Bass, Australian *Macquaria novemaculeata*

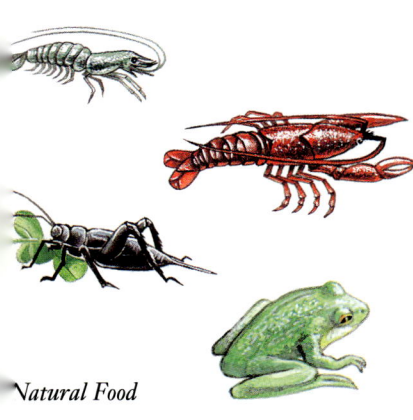

Natural Food

For all intents and purposes, the Australian bass and its cousin, the estuary perch (*M. colonorum*) can be treated as a single species. So similar are they in appearance and habit that most fishermen have trouble in telling them apart.

Bass and estuary perch occur in coastal rivers, creeks and lakes from the Mary River in southern central Queensland to the mouth of the Murray River, in South Australia. They range upstream only as far as the first impassable waterfall, dam or weir, and require winter-time access to brackish, tidal waters in order to reproduce.

These attractive, alert species are relatively small fish, not often exceeding a kilo in weight, although occasionally reaching twice that size. Exceptional specimens — mostly estuary perch — may very rarely approach weights of five or six kilos.

During the summer months, when they are more available to anglers, bass prefer clean, running fresh water with a reasonably high oxygen content and a diversity of food types. They prey mostly on shrimps, crayfish, frogs, insect larvae and terrestrial creatures such as beetles, cicadas and even mice.

In most areas, bass and perch are a relatively specialised angling target, requiring the use of specific tackle and techniques. Although they respond avidly to natural baits such as live crickets or earthworms, most sport fishermen prefer to catch them with lures such as plugs, minnows and poppers. They are also a superb fly rod target.

Although they are fine to eat, these days responsible anglers tend to release all or most of the bass and estuary perch they catch.

Bonito

There are two closely-related and almost identical species of bonito in Australian waters. These are the Australian bonito *(Sarda australis)* of the eastern seaboard, and the generally smaller Oriental bonito *(S. orientalis)* of Western Australia. A third, smaller fish — the leaping bonito or Watson's leaping bonito *(Cybiosarda elegans)* — is less closely allied.

Despite some superficial similarities in appearance, the bonitos should not be confused with the skipjack or striped tuna *(Katsuwonis pelamis)*. Bonito are striped on the back and sides rather than the belly, and have much more prominent teeth than skipjack.

The Australian and Oriental bonitos are pelagic, migratory Indo-Pacific species with reasonably extensive ranges. Mostly, however, they occur in sub-tropical and temperate waters off New South Wales and southern Western Australia.

Both fish are commonly encountered at weights of one to three kilos, although the Australian bonito may occasionally exceed six or seven kilos.

Bonito form moderate-sized schools and prey on small forage fish such as pilchards, anchovies and whitebait. Their sharp teeth and powerful jaws also allow them to take larger prey such as yellowtail, slimy mackerel, mullet and squid.

Bonito are caught by both shore-based and boat anglers using a variety of lures and live or dead fish baits. They are strong fighters.

Many anglers overlook the fine eating qualities of bonito, expecting them to have dark, strongly-flavoured meat like that found in skipjack tuna. In reality, bonito are pink-fleshed and tasty, if a little dry.

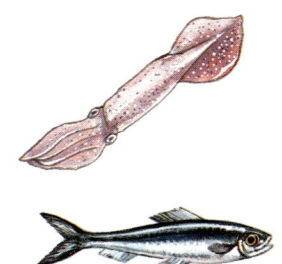

Natural food

Black Bream

Southern Bream

TECHNIQUE	ROD	REEL	LINE	TERMINAL TACKLE	HOOK	WEIGHT	BAIT
Casting or drifting with lightly weighted baits.	Ultra-light or light weight spinning rod, light rock or jetty casting rod.	Small threadline or light sidecast.	2-8 kg	Running sinker, line tied directly to hook.	2-2/0	Smallest suitable ball or bean.	Live worms, yabbies, prawns, cut fish flesh, crabs.

FISH SPECIES

TECHNIQUE	ROD	REEL	LINE	TERMINAL TACKLE	HOOK	WEIGHT	BAIT
Trolling, casting or drifting.	Rock or jetty casting rod, light boat rod.	Medium threadline, large baitcaster, small overhead or sidecast.	4-12 kg	Ganged hooks and/or 20-40 kg nylon leader.	3/0-6/0	None	Trolling and casting lures, pilchards, small live or dead fish.

Bream

Pikey Bream

Natural Food

There are three common bream species in Australian waters, each one of them prized by anglers.

The eastern black bream or yellowfin bream (*Acanthopagrus australis*) occurs along the eastern seaboard of Australia, from the southern or central coast of Queensland in the north, to Green Cape or Wilsons Promontory in the south.

Eastern black bream are a fish of estuarine and inshore waters, occurring mostly in the lower reaches of larger tidal rivers, bays, inlets and harbours, and over reefs and gravel beds extending well offshore. They will also range up coastal rivers beyond the upper limits of tides at times, and even enter fresh water for short periods.

In contrast, the southern or southern black bream (*A. butcheri*) lives almost exclusively in estuarine and inshore waters, rarely straying far beyond the mouths of tidal rivers, harbours and inlets unless pushed out of these enclosed waters by heavy flooding. It ranges from the far south coast of New South Wales in the east, around the southern coast (including Tasmania) to about Shark Bay in Western Australia. The tropical representative of this popular family is the pikey bream (*A. berda*). Pikey bream are found in tropical waters around the northern half of Australia, preferring mangrove-lined estuaries, bays and inlets.

All three bream are very similar in appearance. Indeed, a layman would find it hard to separate them. Adding to this difficulty is the fact that each species can display considerable colour variation between individuals, depending on their habitat.

These are all relatively small fish, rarely exceeding a kilo in weight, although occasionally reaching twice that size. The eastern and southern black bream have both been recorded at weights in excess of three kilos, although such giants are exceedingly uncommon.

All three bream species are very popular angling targets, pursued by large numbers of fishermen representing all levels of experience and commitment. Most are caught by anglers using relatively light tackle, fine lines and small hooks baited with prawns, crabs, saltwater yabbies, various marine worms, fish pieces, meat, cheese or dough-based 'pudding' mixes.

The three bream species are all highly rated table fare, with succulent, white flesh that remains sweet and moist when cooked.

83

Carp *Cyprinus carpio*

The European carp actually originated in Asia, but has been transplanted to every continent on earth except Antarctica. The carp found in Australian waters were introduced from Europe late in the nineteenth century, but only spread extensively through the continent's inland river systems with the arrival of a new strain during the 1960s.

Carp are sometimes confused with the smaller goldfish *(C. auratus)*, but may be separated by virtue of the fact that carp possess a pair of small barbels or 'feelers' on either side of their mouths, while goldfish have no such protrusions. Hybrid carp/goldfish are also encountered, and are best identified by a single barbel either side of the mouth.

In some parts of the world, European carp reach 30 kilos and more in weight. Here in Australasia, they are more common at weights of one to nine kilos.

Carp are regarded as noxious pests in Australia and New Zealand. This is due to their propensity for over-population, their competition with more desirable native and introduced species, the way in which their feeding stirs up mud and sediment, and their potential for transmitting fish diseases.

In Australia, carp are caught mostly in warmer, turbid outback rivers, lakes and man-made impoundments. They also occur in some clearer, cooler waterways near the headwaters of inland river systems. In New Zealand, they are found in coastal streams and some lower altitude trout waters.

Once hooked, they provide a spirited tussle. Unfortunately, they are not rated highly in the culinary department by most who have tried them.

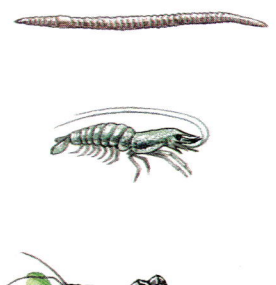

Natural Food

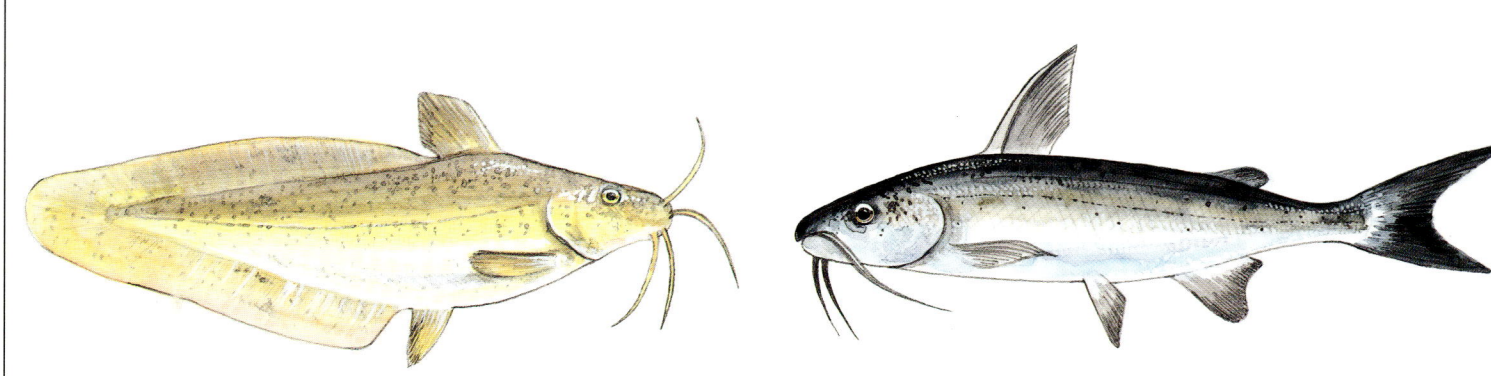

TECHNIQUE	ROD	REEL	LINE	TERMINAL TACKLE	HOOK	WEIGHT	BAIT
Eel-tailed: casting or drifting lightly weighed baits. Fork tailed: Casting or trolling lures, drifting and float suspending live baits.	Light spinning or baitcaster rod.	Small to medium threadline, baitcaster or closed-face.	3-8 kg	Running sinker, line tied directly to hook.	2-2/0	Smallest suitable ball or bean.	Worms, yabbies, shrimps, grubs.

TECHNIQUE	ROD	REEL	LINE	TERMINAL TACKLE	HOOK	WEIGHT	BAIT
Trolling, lure casting, jigging, drifting with live and dead baits.	6-24 kg class sport or game rod, sturdy shore-casting rod.	Game reel, casting overhead, large sidecast.	6-24 kg	30-80 kg nylon leader.	4/0-8/0	None	Trolling and casting lures, live and dead whole fish, sand crabs.

TECHNIQUE	ROD	REEL	LINE	TERMINAL TACKLE	HOOK	WEIGHT	BAIT
Casting or drifting with lightly weighted baits.	Light spinning rod, single-handed baitcaster.	Small threadline, baitcaster or closed-face.	2-6 kg	Running sinker or quill float, hook tied directly to line.	10-1	Smallest suitable ball or shot.	Worms, dough, bread, corn kernels.

Catfish

Natural Food

Two families of catfish are of interest to Australian anglers. They are the eel-tailed catfish or tandans (*Plotosidae*), and the fork-tailed catfish (*Ariidae*).

There are many species of tandans, sometimes called freshwater jewfish, dewfish or even 'dhufish', in our outback waters. However, one variety (*Tandanus tandanus*), is by far the most important. This species of eel-tail catfish is found in the freshwater rivers, lakes and dams of inland Australia, particularly those of the Murray/Darling system, as well as in the upper reaches of some eastern coastal streams. It is at its most abundant in central and northern New South Wales and the south western areas of Queensland.

Tandans are caught mostly in warmer, turbid outback rivers, lakes and impound-ments. They also occur in some cooler waterways near the headwaters of inland river systems.

Tandans or eel-tail catfish are small fish, rarely exceeding a kilo, although occasionally reaching twice that size.

Although rather unattractive and possessing three powerful, venomous spines in their dorsal and pectoral fins, eel-tail catfish are good to eat, especially when taken from clearer waters. Most of the common fork-tailed catfish occur in the tropical rivers, swamps and billabongs of northern Australia, occasionally ranging downstream into brackish areas. The blue and salmon catfish (*Arius graeffei* and *A. leptaspis*) commonly reach weights of a kilo or two, and may occasionally grow up to 10 or even 15 kilos.

Fork-tailed catfish are mostly an incidental catch taken by anglers fishing for more desirable target species.

Cobia *Rachycentrum canadum*

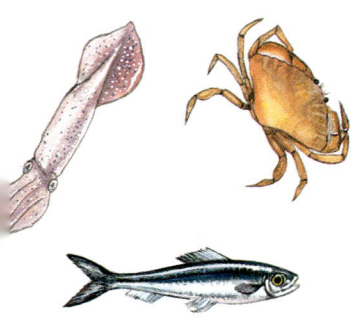

Natural Food

The cobia or black kingfish is an enigmatic fish found in discontinuous pockets throughout the tropical and subtropical oceans of the world.

In Australia, cobia are mostly encountered over offshore reefs and gravel beds, around islands, bomboras and undersea pinnacles, and near navigation buoys, drilling platforms and similar structures. However, they will also show up in large estuaries, bays and harbours.

While mostly encountered in Queensland, the Northern Territory and northern Western Australia, they will occasionally stray as far south as Jervis Bay on the east coast and Fremantle on the west.

Cobia are large fish, commonly reaching a metre or more in length and weighing as much as 20 or 30 kilos. Exceptional specimens may reach twice that size. Their flattened, almost shark-like head, dark longitudinal bands and eight to 10 stout, stubby dorsal spines separate them from most other fish, although small cobia do bear a passing resemblance to the suckerfish or remora (*Echeneis naucrates*).

Cobia respond best to live or fresh-dead baits of whole or cut fish, squid and octopus. They will also strike at a range of lures and large flies, either cast and retrieved, or trolled behind a moving boat. Because of their highly variable abundance, cobia are mostly an incidental catch taken by anglers fishing for more common target species such as Spanish mackerel, yellowtail kingfish and tuna. However, in light of their striking appearance, powerful struggle when hooked, and delicious, white flesh, they are always a welcome addition to the catch.

Cod

The name 'cod' is used to describe many salt and freshwater fish species in Australasian waters, despite the fact that the true cod family of the Northern Hemisphere does not occur in these waters.

In particular, the title is used to describe a number of members of the *Serranidae* or sea perch family, which are called groupers in North America. Two of these — the estuary cod and the black cod — are of particular interest to Australian anglers.

The estuary cod *(Epinephelus suillus)* is also known as the greasy cod, spotted cod and brown spotted rock cod. It is found in tropical and sub-tropical waters around the northern half of Australia, occurring mostly in estuaries, bays, harbours and over inshore reefs. Juveniles tend mainly to inhabit estuarine waters, while large adults move to offshore reefs.

Like its close relative, the Queensland groper *(Promicrops lanceolatus)*, the estuary cod is a very large fish, growing to weights in excess of 150 kilos and lengths of two metres and more. Most of those encountered in rivers and bays are much smaller.

The black cod or saddled rock cod *(E. damelii)* is a similar fish found in more temperate waters along the eastern seaboard of Australia, from the southern or central coast of Queensland in the north, to Green Cape or Wilsons Promontory in the south.

Sadly, the black cod's numbers have been dramatically reduced by both line and spear fishermen, to the point where it is now totally protected in New South Wales' waters. It is no longer common on the mainland, but is still taken in good numbers around Lord Howe Island and its nearby reef systems.

Larger specimens of both these cod are caught primarily by boat anglers using a variety of offshore fishing techniques. Juvenile estuary cod are frequently encountered by sport fishermen casting baits or lures around snags while pursuing barramundi and mangrove jacks.

These cod are fine table fish in their smaller sizes, though large specimens tend to be coarse and dry.

Natural Food

TECHNIQUE	ROD	REEL	LINE	TERMINAL TACKLE	HOOK	WEIGHT	BAIT
Bottom fished baits, jigs and casting lures.	Double-handed baitcaster or spinning rod, medium boat rod.	Large baitcaster, large spinning reel, sidecast or handline.	8-20 kg	Dropper rig above sinker, heavy nylon or light wire leader.	4/0-8/0	Snapper lead on large barrel.	Small whole fish, cut fish, squid, jigs and casting lures.

FISH SPECIES

TECHNIQUE	ROD	REEL	LINE	TERMINAL TACKLE	HOOK	WEIGHT	BAIT
Estuary: casting or trolling lures, drifting baits.	Single or double handed spinning or baitcaster.	Medium spinning or baitcaster.	6-15 kg	30-60 kg nylon or light wire leader.	3/0-7/0	None	Small live or dead whole fish.
Reef: bottom fishing with bait or jigs.	Sturdy boat rod or handline.	Sidecast, centrepin or handline.	15-40 kg	Hooks on droppers above sinker.	5/0-9/0	Snapper lead	

Coral Trout

Natural Food

The coral trout family (*Plectropoma*) contains several very important tropical reef species much sought after by northern anglers.

Coral trout are found in tropical and sub-tropical waters around the northern half of Australia. They are mostly encountered over offshore reefs and gravel beds, as well as around islands, bomboras and undersea pinnacles. They also occur in wave-washed, inshore waters adjacent to rocky shorelines, headlands and the edges of fringing coral reefs.

The most abundant species of coral trout (*P. maculatum*) commonly reaches weights of a kilo or two, and may occasionally grow much larger. On more isolated reef complexes far from shore, specimens in the 10 to 20 kilo range are still occasionally encountered.

This species shows wide colour variations, with specimens from deeper water tending to be reddish, while those living in the shallows have a green or rusty brown base colouration. Most have an overlay of blue spots.

Coral trout are voracious predators, preying mainly on smaller reef fish and various crustaceans. They are caught primarily by boat anglers using a variety of offshore fishing techniques. In particular, they respond to bottom-fished baits and jigs, but will also rise towards the surface in shallower areas to strike at floating baits, minnow-style lures and surface plugs.

Coral trout are one of our most highly rated tropical table fish, although larger specimens have been linked to incidences of ciguatera poisoning in regions where this toxin occurs.

Dart

The dart family *(Trachinotus)* contains several fish of interest to Australian anglers. The most widespread and commonly encountered is the swallowtail dart *(T. coppingeri)*. These are relatively small fish, rarely exceeding a kilo in weight, although very occasionally reaching almost twice that size. They occur along the eastern seaboard of Australia, from the central coast of Queensland to Jervis Bay in the south.

An almost identical fish, called the common dart *(T. botla)*, is found on the west coast between similar latitudes. It grows a little larger than its eastern counterpart.

Dart are a fish of our estuarine and inshore waters, occurring in the lower reaches of larger tidal rivers, bays, inlets and harbours. They are especially common along ocean surf beaches. They are mostly an incidental catch taken by anglers fishing for more desirable target species.

Despite their small average size, dart provide a spirited struggle when hooked and have reasonably tasty flesh.

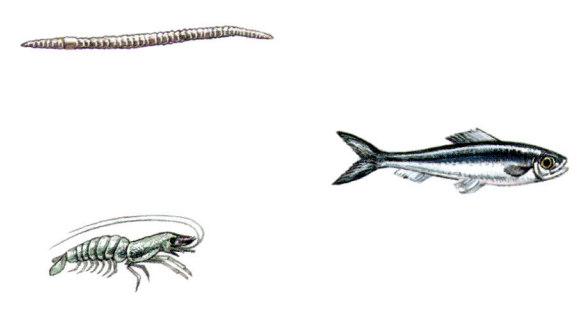
Natural Food

Dolphin Fish *Coryphaena hippurus*

Known in many parts of the world as dorado or mahi-mahi, the dolphin fish is in no way connected to the marine mammal called dolphin or porpoise.

This beautiful, fast-swimming pelagic game fish is found in tropical and sub-tropical waters around the northern half of Australia. It also makes occasional visits to the North Island of New Zealand during the summer and early autumn months.

Dolphin fish are mostly encountered in deeper, oceanic waters, near the edges of the Continental Shelf and beyond. However, favourable currents and water conditions will occasionally carry them much closer to shore. In particular, they favour warm, blue ocean currents flowing over offshore reefs and gravel beds, around islands, bomboras and undersea pinnacles, and near navigation buoys, drilling platforms and similar structures.

Dolphin fish are caught primarily by boat anglers using a variety of offshore fishing techniques. They respond to live or fresh-dead baits of whole or cut fish, squid and octopus. They will also strike at a range of lures and flies, either cast and retrieved, or trolled behind a moving boat.

In tropical waters, mahi-mahi are often large fish, commonly reaching a metre or more in length and weighing as much as 20 or 30 kilos. Further south, small juveniles in the one to four kilo range are more common.

Regardless of their size, dolphin fish are one of the most delicious of all the gamefish, with succulent, pinkish-red flesh.

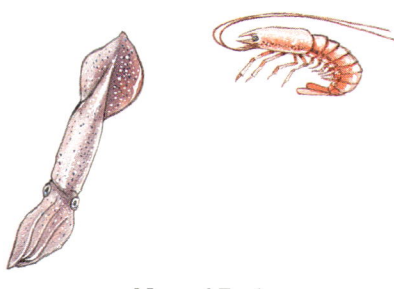
Natural Food

TECHNIQUE	ROD	REEL	LINE	TERMINAL TACKLE	HOOK	WEIGHT	BAIT
Casting lightly weighted or float-suspended baits from the shore.	Medium to heavy 3-4 metre double-handed rock casting rod.	Large threadline or sidecast.	4-12 kg	Running sinker, fixed or running stem float or bobby cork.	1-3/0	Smallest suitable ball, bug or bean.	Cunjevoi, bread, prawn tail, abalone gut.

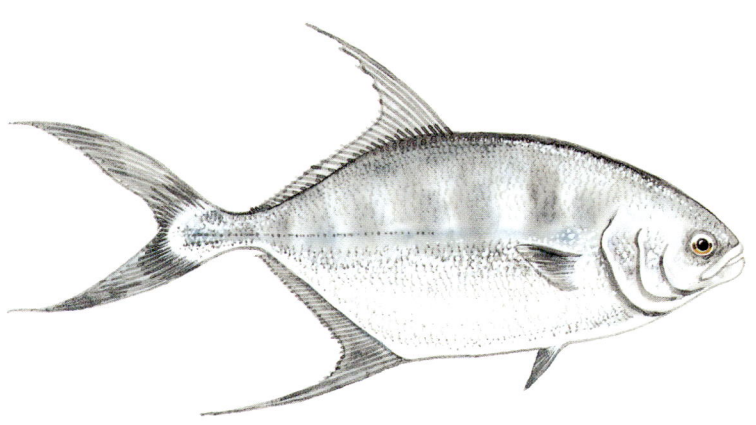

TECHNIQUE	ROD	REEL	LINE	TERMINAL TACKLE	HOOK	WEIGHT	BAIT
Shore casting.	Light double-handed beach or rock rod.	Medium threadline, light overhead or sidecast.	3-7 kg	Running sinker, hook tied directly to line.	4-1/0	Smallest suitable ball or bean.	Worms, prawns, pipis, small fish, catfish.

TECHNIQUE	ROD	REEL	LINE	TERMINAL TACKLE	HOOK	WEIGHT	BAIT
Trolling, lure casting or drifting with live and dead baits	4-15 kg class sport or game rod, light boat rod, medium spin or bait caster.	Light game reel, overhead, large spinning or baitcaster.	4-15 kg	30-60 kg nylon leader.	3/0-6/0	None	Trolling and casting lures, small live or dead fish.

Drummer

Natural Food

Two fish commonly known as drummer are important to Australian anglers. The first is the silver drummer or buffalo bream (*Kyphosus sydneyanus*). These robust, largely herbivorous fish occur along the eastern seaboard of Australia, from the southern coast of Queensland in the north, to Green Cape or Wilsons Promontory in the south. They also occur at times in north eastern Tasmania, are common in South Australia, and range up the West Australian coast to about Shark Bay.

The second species commonly known as drummer is the eastern rock blackfish, black drummer or 'pig' (*Girella elevata*). This darker, more omnivorous fish is confined to the east coast, although an almost identical fish (*G. tephraeops*) occurs in smaller numbers along the west coast.

Both silver and black drummer occur in wave-washed, inshore waters adjacent to rocky shorelines, headlands and stone breakwalls. They are taken mostly by shore-based anglers casting baits such as cunjevoi, prawns, cut crab, bread and marine weed.

Both species commonly reach weights of a kilo or two, and may occasionally grow much larger. Silver drummer have been recorded to 14 or 15 kilos on rare occasions, while black drummer are known to reach nine kilos.

Both fish are exceptionally hard fighters when hooked, and will attempt to sever the angler's line on submerged ledges and reef outcrops. The black drummer is a delicious table fish which should be filleted and skinned for best results. In contrast, the silver drummer is rather unpalatable, with coarse, tough flesh.

Emperor, Red *Lutjanus sebae*

This large, attractive fish is one of the most sought-after angling targets in the waters of northern Australia.

Red emperor are mostly confined to the seas off Queensland, the Northern Territory and northern West Australia. They favour areas of offshore reef and gravel beds, particularly those around islands, coral cays, bomboras and undersea pinnacles. They are most active at night, but will also be taken during daylight hours in deeper water.

Red emperor commonly reach weights of a kilo or two, and may occasionally grow much larger. Exceptional examples in excess of 18 or 20 kilos have been recorded.

Red emperor are caught primarily by boat anglers using a variety of offshore fishing techniques. In particular, they favour bottom-fished or lightly weighted live or fresh-dead baits of whole or cut fish, squid and octopus. They will also occasionally strike at lures.

When hooked, red emperor are strong fighters. They are also arguably the tastiest fish found in our tropical seas.

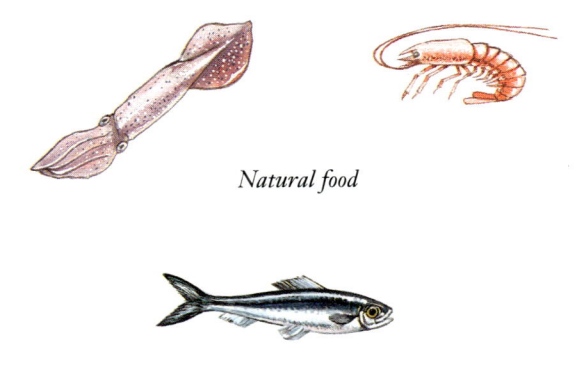

Natural food

Emperor, Spangled *Lethrinus nebulosus*

The spangled emperor or north west snapper is an attractive, medium-sized fish found in tropical and sub-tropical waters around the northern half of Australia, from about Sydney Harbour in the east to Rottnest Island in the west.

Spangled emperor commonly reach weights of a kilo or two, and may occasionally grow much larger. They have been taken at sizes in excess of seven kilos.

Spangled emperor favour sand, gravel and coral 'marl' seabeds in tropical reef lagoons and behind protective reefs. They respond to a wide range of angling techniques, including bait fishing, lure casting, trolling and fly fishing. Most, however, are taken by boat anglers using a variety of offshore bait fishing techniques. In particular, spangled emperor are a common incidental catch boated while fishing for target species such as red emperor, coral trout and snapper.

Spangled emperor are fine table fish, although not held in the same high regard as red emperor.

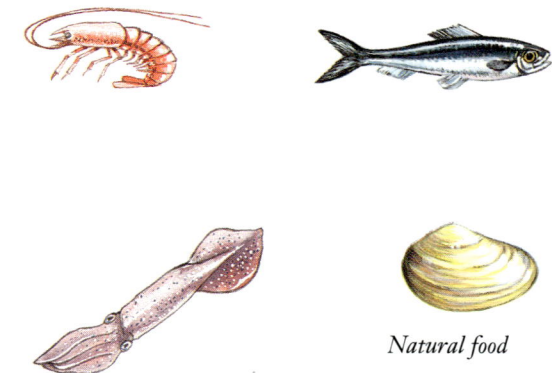

Natural food

Fingermark *Lutjanus johnii*

The fingermark or fingermark bream is also known as the red chopper, spotted scale sea perch and golden snapper. It is a strikingly handsome fish much sought after by northern anglers.

Fingermark are found in tropical and sub-tropical waters right around the northern half of Australia. They live mainly in estuarine and inshore areas, rarely straying far beyond the mouths of tidal rivers, harbours and inlets, although larger adults will sometimes be encountered on deeper offshore reefs.

Fingermark commonly reach weights of a kilo or two, and may occasionally grow much larger. Exceptional specimens to 10 kilos have been recorded.

These fish are caught mostly by estuary and inshore anglers pursuing barramundi, mangrove jacks and other tropical sport fish. In more recent years, specific techniques have evolved for targeting fingermark. These include the pin-point presentation of live baits or diving lures in deeper holes or gutters within northern estuary systems.

The fingermark is an exceptionally fine table fish, and is rated more highly than either barramundi or mangrove jack.

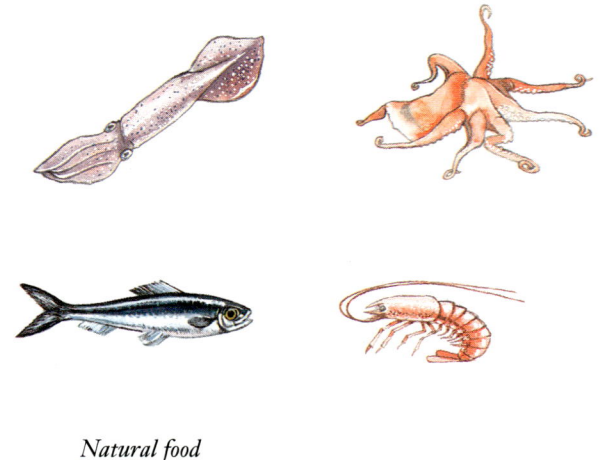

Natural food

FISH SPECIES

TECHNIQUE	ROD	REEL	LINE	TERMINAL TACKLE	HOOK	WEIGHT	BAIT
Bottom fishing from an anchored or drifting boat, or 'floater' bait in berley trail.	Medium to heavy boat rod, jig rod or double-handed spinning or baitcaster rod. Also handlines.	Casting overhead, large baitcaster, spinning reel or centrepin.	6-30 kg	Dropper rig above heavy sinker or running sinker rig. Heavy nylon leader if using light line.	3/0-8/0	Snapper lead, bomb, large running barrel, small ball.	Squid, octopus, small live or dead fish.

TECHNIQUE	ROD	REEL	LINE	TERMINAL TACKLE	HOOK	WEIGHT	BAIT
Bottom fishing from a boat, shore casting, lure casting or jigging.	Medium boat or jig rod, double handed spinning or baitcaster rod.	Overhead casting reel, medium to large baitcaster or threadline, sidecast.	6-15 kg	Dropper rig above large sinker, light running sinker, jig or casting lure. Heavier nylon leader if using light line.	3/0-6/0	Snapper lead, bomb, running ball.	Squid, cut fish, crab, prawns, casting lure, jig.

TECHNIQUE	ROD	REEL	LINE	TERMINAL TACKLE	HOOK	WEIGHT	BAIT
Bottom fishing, drifting, trolling and lure casting.	Medium boat or jig rod, double-handed spinning or baitcaster rod.	Casting overhead, medium threadline or baitcaster, sidecast.	6-15 kg	Running sinker rig, running bobby cork or lure. Heavy nylon leader if using light line.	3/0-7/0	Smallest suitasble ball, bean or barrel.	Small live fish, live prawn, squid, cut fish flesh.

Flathead

There are over 30 species of flathead (*Platycephalidae*) in Australian waters, although only a handful are of particular interest to anglers. The rest live in very deep water, do not grow to an edible size, or are rarely encountered.

The largest and most important angling species is the dusky or estuary flathead (*Platycephalus fuscus*). This flathead occurs along the eastern seaboard of Australia, from the southern or central coast of Queensland to Green Cape or Wilsons Promontory.

Dusky flathead live mainly in estuarine and inshore waters, rarely straying far beyond the mouths of tidal rivers, harbours and inlets. They will also penetrate beyond the upper limits of tidal movement, into almost completely fresh water.

The dusky averages a kilo or less in weight, although specimens two and three times larger are relatively common in some areas. This species has been recorded at weights in excess of nine kilos, although examples over seven kilos are uncommon. It is replaced in northern and western estuary waters by the smaller bar-tailed flathead (*P. endrachtensis*).

The eastern sand or blue-spotted flathead (*P. caeruleopunctatus*), southern sand flathead (*P. bassensis*), southern blue-spotted flathead (*P. speculator*) and northern sand flathead (*P. arenarius*) are all very important species to offshore anglers operating around the southern half of the Australian continent, including Tasmania. They are found mostly between the shoreline and sand or gravel areas with depths of up to 100 metres.

Further offshore again, in waters deeper than 100 metres, the tiger or king flathead (*Neoplatycephalus richardsoni*) becomes the dominant species, although this reddish, thick-bodied flathead also moves into shallower areas in southern latitudes, particularly around Tasmania.

All of these flathead species are known by a wide variety of colloquial names, including 'lizard', 'frog' and 'yank'. They are popular angling targets, pursued by large numbers of fishermen.

Flathead respond best to live or fresh-dead baits of whole or cut fish, squid and octopus. They will also strike at a range of lures and flies, either cast and retrieved, or deep-trolled behind a moving boat. The emphasis should always be on the use of moving baits presented close to the sea bed.

All the flathead mentioned are fine table fish, although larger duskies tend to be dry.

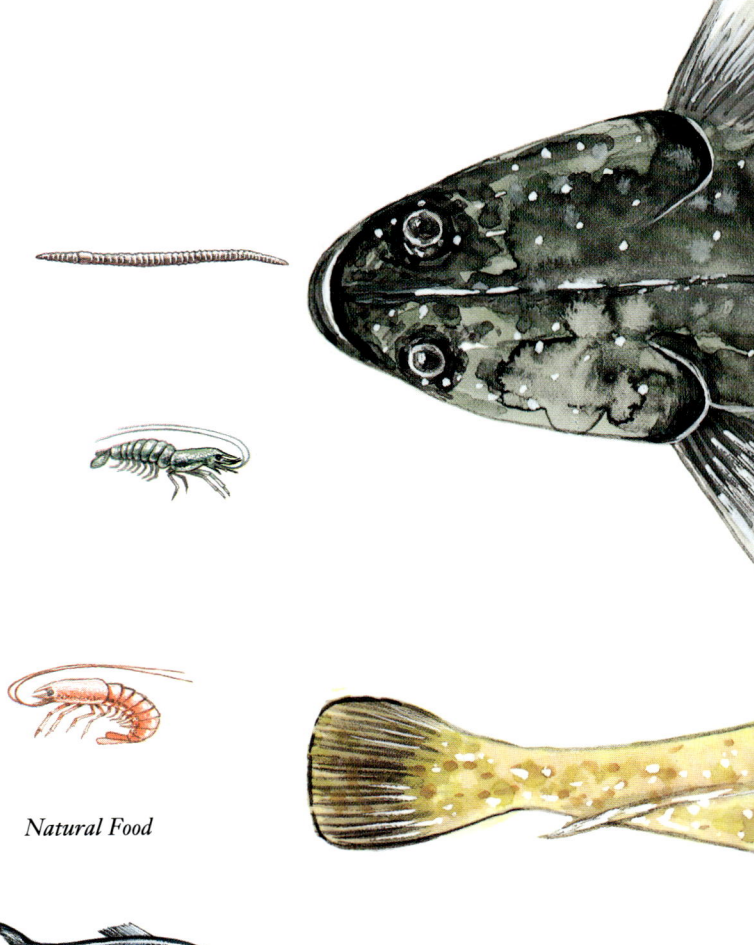

Natural Food

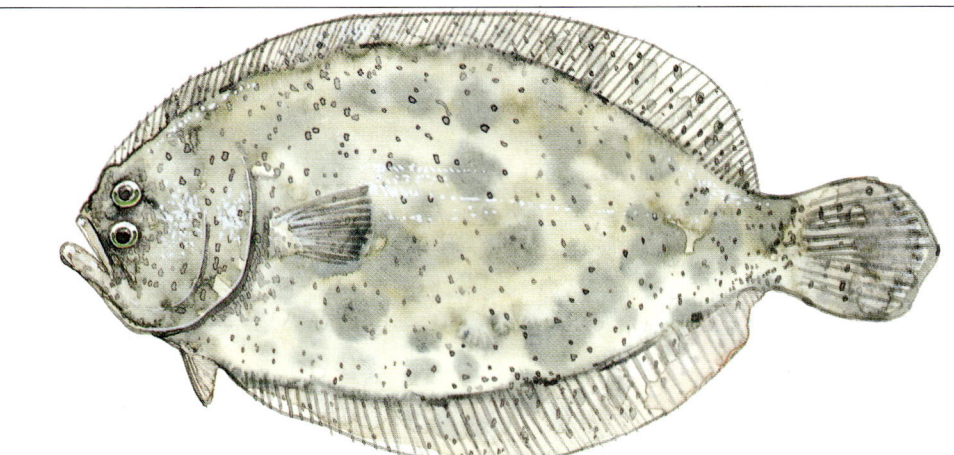

TECHNIQUE	ROD	REEL	LINE	TERMINAL TACKLE	HOOK	WEIGHT	BAIT
Drifting or shore casting with small baits or lures.	Light spinning, baitcaster or sidecast rod.	Light to medium threadline, baitcaster, closed-face or sidecast.	2-6 kg	Running sinker rig. Small lure or plastic tail jig tied directly to line.	4-1/0 (long shank)	Smallest practical ball or bean.	Estuary worms, prawns, nippers (yabbies), small fish and lures.

FISH SPECIES

Dusky Flathead

Sand Flathead

TECHNIQUE	ROD	REEL	LINE	TERMINAL TACKLE	HOOK	WEIGHT	BAIT
Estuary: Drifting or shore-casting with lightly weighted baits or lures.	Light to medium spinning, baitcaster or sidecast rod.	Light to medium threadline, baitcaster or sidecast.	2-8 kg	Running sinker rig or lure. Heavy nylon or wire leader.	1-5/0 (long shank)	Small ball or bean.	Live or dead fish, prawns, flesh strips, lures.
Offshore: Drifting with heavily weighted bottom baits.	Short boat rod, jig rod or handline.	Centrepin.	10-20 kg	Dropper rig above heavy sinker.	2/0-5/0	Snapper lead.	

Flounder

Natural Food

Several species of flounder are found in Australasian waters. The most important are the large-toothed flounder (*Psuedorhombus arsius*) and the small-toothed flounder (*P. jenynsii*).

Flounder are occasionally confused with the other major Australasian flatfish group; the soles (*Soleidaei* and *Cynoglossidae*), however, flounder are distinguished by their separate tail; in contrast, sole have a continuous fin running right around their tongue-shaped bodies.

As with other flatfish, juvenile flounder swim upright in the manner of normal fish. However, as they mature, one eye migrates around their head and they begin to swim on their side. Eventually, they spend most of their time on or very near the seabed, with their eyes facing upwards.

The two major flounder species mentioned are found in sub-tropical, temperate and cool waters around the southern half of Australia. They are a fish of our estuarine and inshore waters, occurring mostly in the lower reaches of larger tidal rivers, bays, inlets and harbours, and less commonly over sand and gravel beds extending offshore towards the edge of the Continental Shelf.

These two flounder are relatively small fish, rarely exceeding half a kilo in weight, although occasionally reaching twice that size.

Flounder are mostly an incidental catch taken by anglers fishing for more common target species such as flathead, bream and whiting. However, because of their delicious, moist, white flesh, they are always a welcome addition to the bag.

Garfish

The garfish family *(Hemiramphidae)* has many representatives in Australasian waters. In New Zealand, the same fish are known as piper.

The most important and commonly encountered garfish species are the near-identical eastern and southern garfish *(Hyporhamphus australis* and *H. melanochir)*, the river garfish *(H. regularis)*, the robust garfish or 'three-by-two' *(Hemiramphus robustus)*, and the snub-nosed gar *(Arrhampus sclerolepis)*.

These fish occur right around the coastlines of Australia and New Zealand, but are more important as angling species in the southern half of both countries.

Garfish are small, slender creatures. They rarely exceed 35 centimetres, and even very large specimens usually weigh less than 300 grams. Despite these diminutive sizes, gar are a popular angling and table fish.

Garfish are a relatively specialised target. They are caught mostly by anglers using light tackle, fine lines and small hooks. They respond best to lightly weighted or float-suspended baits.

Natural Food

TECHNIQUE	ROD	REEL	LINE	TERMINAL TACKLE	HOOK	WEIGHT	BAIT
Shore casting with baits using sturdy tackle	Double-handed sidecast, centrepin or overhead rod, 2.5 to 3.5 metres long.	Sidecast, large centrepin or heavy overhead casting reel.	12-40 kg	Dropper rig above heavy sinker, running sinker rig or running bobby cork.	3/0-6/0 (extra strength)	Spoon, snapper lead, bomb or ball sinker.	Rock-dwelling crabs, cunjevoi, abalone, chitons.

TECHNIQUE	ROD	REEL	LINE	TERMINAL TACKLE	HOOK	WEIGHT	BAIT
Drifting, anchoring or shore casting with baits and, occcasionally, lures.	Light to medium boat, jig, spinning or baitcaster rod. Also handlines.	Small overhead, medium threadline, baitcaster, sidecast or centrepin.	4-12 kg	Ganged (linked) hooks and/or wire leader. Large split ring for lifting fish. Running sinker.	3/0-6/0 (ganged or single)	Smallest practical ball, bean or barrel.	Small live or dead whole fish, pilchards.

FISH SPECIES

TECHNIQUE	ROD	REEL	LINE	TERMINAL TACKLE	HOOK	WEIGHT	BAIT
Casting lightly weighted or float-suspended baits in a berley trail.	Ultra-light to light spinning or sidecast rod.	Ultra-light to light threadline, closed-face, sidecast or centrepin.	1-5 kg	Running sinker or fixed quill, pencil or bubble float.	12-6 (long shank)	Tiny ball sinkers or split shot.	Dough, bread, maggots, worm, prawn or flesh pieces.

Groper, Blue

Natural Food

The eastern blue groper (*Achoerodus viridis*) and western blue groper (*A. gouldii*) are actually members of the wrasse family (*Labridae*), and are in no way related to the much larger Queensland groper.

There are several colour variations of blue groper, usually known as brown groper, red groper and blue groper. These differences are related to the sex of the fish, and do not indicate separate species.

All groper are born as females. The juvenile females are green or greenish brown. As they mature, they take on either a brown or a red hue, largely dependent upon the surrounding terrain and water depth (the red variation is more common in deeper water). Later, some of the larger females transform into males, becoming bright blue or deep navy.

Adult eastern blue groper are large fish, commonly reaching a metre or more in length and weighing as much as 15 kilos. The western variety grow even larger, and have been recorded at weights in excess of 35 kilos.

Groper are found in temperate and cool waters around the southern half of Australia in wave-washed, inshore waters adjacent to rocky headlands and breakwalls.

Groper are a specialised angling target, requiring the use of specific tackle and techniques. In particular, they are taken by shore-based anglers casting crab baits on very sturdy tackle, with thick lines and double or triple strength hooks. Once hooked, they provide a powerful fight, often severing the line on a rock ledge.

Larger groper are delicious eating fish, although juveniles under three or four kilos tend to be a little mushy and flavourless.

Hairtail *Trichiurus lepturus*

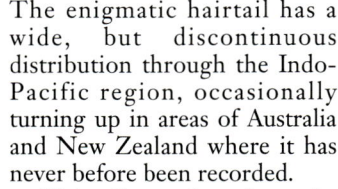

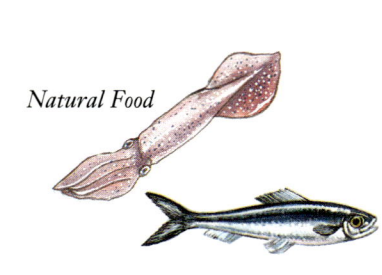

Natural Food

The enigmatic hairtail has a wide, but discontinuous distribution through the Indo-Pacific region, occasionally turning up in areas of Australia and New Zealand where it has never before been recorded.

Hairtail are thought to be deep ocean fish which make occasional forays into certain estuaries and harbours along the coast. Juveniles are seasonally abundant in tropical ports such as Townsville, while adults are fished for on a regular basis in just a handful of locations on the eastern seaboard of Australia, between Newcastle and Wollongong. In particular, they are targeted during the winter months in the Hawkesbury River estuary, Sydney Harbour and the deeper portions of Botany Bay.

These are striking fish, with their long, chrome-like bodies and sharp fangs. They should be handled with care, especially as they approach their maximum size of two metres and three to four kilos.

Hairtail are a relatively specialised angling target, requiring the use of specific tackle and techniques. Most are caught at night on baits of small, live fish or whole pilchards and garfish. A wire leader or ganged (linked) hooks should be used to prevent bite-offs.

Despite their unusual appearance and mysterious nature, hairtail are prized table fish with delicate white flesh that should not be over-cooked.

Javelin Fish *Pomadasys hasta*

The javelin fish or spotted grunter is a popular angling target found in tropical and sub-tropical waters around the northern half of Australia. They live mainly in estuarine and inshore waters, rarely straying far beyond the mouths of tidal rivers, harbours and inlets.

Javelin or grunter are relatively small fish, rarely exceeding a kilo in weight, although occasionally reaching three or four times that size. Many are taken incidentally by anglers fishing for bream, flathead and whiting, although they are targeted directly by some specialist bait fishermen. Javelin fish will also occasionally take a lure intended for barramundi or mangrove jack.

Javelin fish are a prized species for the table, with moist, white flesh that freezes without significant loss of quality.

Natural Food

Jewfish, Westralian *Glaucosoma hebraicum*

The Westralian jewfish or 'dhufish' is one of Western Australia's most highly-prized angling targets. It is a close relative of the eastern pearl perch *(G. scapulare)*.

Adult Westralian jewfish once commonly reached a metre or more in length and weighed as much as 20 or 25 kilos. Specimens of those dimensions are uncommon today.

Jewfish are mostly encountered over offshore reefs and gravel beds, around islands, bomboras and undersea pinnacles. They extend offshore all the way to the edge of the Continental Shelf. Their geographic range is confined to the south west coast, between about Recherche Archipelago and Shark Bay.

Westralian jewfish are caught primarily by boat anglers. In particular, they respond to live or fresh-dead baits of whole or cut fish, squid and octopus. They will also strike at a range of lures and jigs jigged near the sea bed.

The Westralian jewfish is one of Australia's most acclaimed seafood dishes, and has few peers among the other temperate water species.

Natural Food

TECHNIQUE	ROD	REEL	LINE	TERMINAL TACKLE	HOOK	WEIGHT	BAIT
Drifting and shore casting with live or dead baits and, occasionally, lures.	Medium spinning, baitcaster, sidecast or boat rod. Also handlines.	Medium spinning, baitcaster, sidecast or closed face.	4-12 kg	Unweighted rig, light running sinker, bobby cork or bottom dropper.	3/0-7/0	Smallest practical ball or bean.	Small live or dead fish, squid, lures.

FISH SPECIES

TECHNIQUE	ROD	REEL	LINE	TERMINAL TACKLE	HOOK	WEIGHT	BAIT
Drifting, anchoring or shore casting with baits and, occasionally, small lures.	Light to medium soinning, sidecast or baitcaster rod.	Medium threadline, baitcaster or sidecast.	3-8 kg	Running sinker rig or small lure on nylon leader.	2-3/0	Smallest practical ball or bean.	Worms, prawns, nipppers (yabbies) and small lures.

TECHNIQUE	ROD	REEL	LINE	TERMINAL TACKLE	HOOK	WEIGHT	BAIT
Deep water bottom fishing, drifting and long distance shore casting in specific locations.	Medium to heavy boat and jig rods or double-handed overhead and sidecast casting rods. Also handlines.	Casting overheads, sidecasts, centrepins.	8-30 kg	Dropper rig above a heavy sinker, running sinker or heavy jig.	3/0-9/0	Snapper lead, bomb, spoon, bean or barrel.	Squid, octopus, small fish, cut fish flesh.

John Dory *Zeus faber*

Natural Food

The unusual looking, but well known, John dory is found throughout the world, and occurs in good numbers around the southern half of Australia and most of New Zealand.

John dory inhabit a wide range of marine environments, from estuaries and bays to deep, offshore waters and trawling grounds.

They are relatively small fish, rarely exceeding a kilo in weight, although occasionally reaching twice that size and more. They are characterised by their laterally compressed bodies, large, protractile mouths and the distinct 'thumb print' marking in the middle of each flank.

John dory are mostly an incidental catch taken by anglers fishing for more common target species such as flathead, mulloway and kingfish. However, because of their delicious white flesh, they are an extremely welcome addition to any bag.

Dory respond best to live or fresh-dead baits of whole or cut fish, squid and octopus. They will also occasionally strike at lures and flies, although this aggressive behaviour appears to be more common in New Zealand than Australia.

This species is always mentioned in any short list of the top eating fish in Australasian waters. Because of this, it demands a consistently high market price, and is keenly sought by commercial fishermen.

97

Kingfish *Seriola lalandi*

The yellowtail kingfish, king or kingy is a big, powerful member of the same group of fishes as the trevallies, amberjack and samson fish.

Kingfish are found in sub-tropical, temperate and cool waters around the southern half of Australia and the northern part of New Zealand. Almost identical fish are found off the west coast of America and around southern Japan.

Kings are mostly encountered over offshore reefs and gravel beds, around islands, bomboras and undersea pinnacles, and near navigation buoys, drilling platforms and similar structures. Specimens will occasion-ally enter larger estuaries and harbours, especially in New Zealand.

Yellowtail kings are big fish, commonly reaching a metre or more in length and weighing as much as 20 kilos. Record-class specimens approaching two metres and weighing in the 40 to 60 kilo range are mostly encountered around offshore island groups such as Australia's Lord Howe and New Zealand's Three Kings and Poor Knights.

Kings are taken with a wide range of angling techniques, including bait fishing, lure casting, trolling and fly fishing.

When hooked, yellowtail kings provide one of the hardest battles of any marine species. As a result, they are greatly respected by most sport and game fishermen.

The eating qualities of yellowtail kingfish are variable. In certain areas, particularly southern Queensland, they are prone to a milkiness of the flesh which makes them unpalatable. In other locations they are highly rated table fare. Generally, the smaller specimens have tastier and more moist flesh.

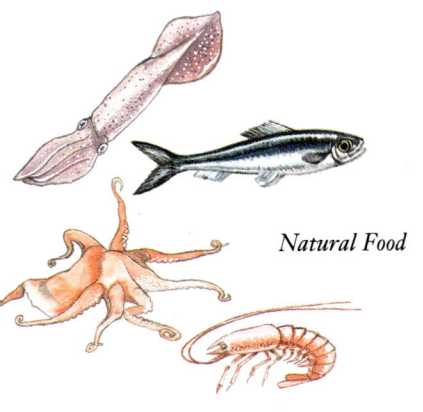
Natural Food

TECHNIQUE	ROD	REEL	LINE	TERMINAL TACKLE	HOOK	WEIGHT	BAIT
Shore fishing or offshore drifting with various small baits.	Light boat, spinning, baitcaster or sidecast rod. Also handlines.	Small to medium threadline, closed face, baitcaster or sidecast.	4-9 kg	Long shanked hook, runnning sinker or dropper rig.	6-1 (long shank)	Smalllest practical ball, bean, spoon or bomb.	Squid, cunjevoi, prawns, fish flesh.

Luderick *Girella tricuspidata*

The luderick is widely known as the blackfish, 'nigger' or 'darkie'. In New Zealand, the same fish is called parore.

Luderick or blackfish occur along the eastern seaboard of Australia, from the southern or central coast of Queensland in the north, to Port Phillip Bay in the south. They may also be encountered at times near Adelaide, and around the north eastern corner of Tasmania. In New Zealand, they are confined mostly to the waters of the North Island.

Luderick are a fish of our estuarine and inshore waters, occurring in the lower reaches of larger tidal rivers, bays, inlets and harbours. Outside of these enclosed areas, they are also found in wave-washed, inshore waters adjacent to rocky shorelines, headlands and stone breakwalls.

Blackfish are relatively small fish, rarely exceeding a kilo in weight, although occasionally reaching twice that size. They are omnivorous, consuming large quantities of weed and algae, as well as small invertebrates such as marine worms, shrimp and prawns.

Luderick are a relatively specialised angling target, requiring the use of specific tackle and techniques. They are caught mostly by anglers using light tackle, fine lines and small hooks, responding best to lightly weighted, unweighted or float-suspended baits of marine weed, algae, worm pieces, peeled prawn tails, bread or dough.

Although sometimes tainted by a slightly 'weedy' iodine taste, the flesh of the luderick or blackfish is quite popular. For best results, the fish should be cleaned promptly and the fillets skinned prior to cooking.

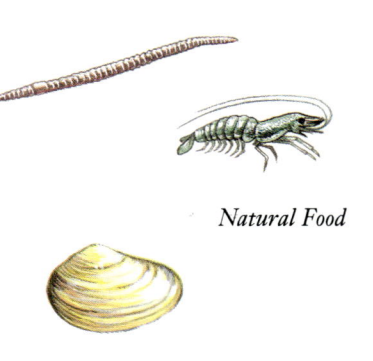
Natural Food

FISH SPECIES

TECHNIQUE	ROD	REEL	LINE	TERMINAL TACKLE	HOOK	WEIGHT	BAIT
Drifting, trolling or shore casting with live and dead baits or lures on sturdy tackle.	6-24 kg class game rods, jig rods and double-handed overhead, spinning and sidecast casting rods.	Game or trolling reel, large overhead, threadline or sidecast.	6-24 kg	Unweighted or float suspended live bait, weighted bait or lure. Heavy nylon leaders and doubles.	4/0-10/0	None or large, running bean or barrel in current.	Live or dead whole fish, squid, fish flesh and lures.

Leatherjackets

Natural Food

This is another extensive family of fish (*Monacanthidae*), containing several important angling species. They are characterised by their small mouths, sharp, beak-like tooth structure, sandpapery skin and the single, stout spine on their back, above the eyes.

Most of the better-known leatherjackets are found in sub-tropical, temperate and cool waters around the southern half of Australia. Among the most popular and commonly caught are the six-spined leatherjacket (*Meuschenia freycineti*), the horseshoe leatherjacket (*M. hippocrepis*), the Chinaman leatherjacket (*Nelusetta ayraudi*) and the fan-bellied leatherjacket (*Monocanthus chinensis*).

Most of these leatherjackets are fish of our estuarine and inshore waters, occurring primarily in the lower reaches of larger tidal rivers, bays, inlets and harbours, and over reefs and gravel beds extending offshore towards the edge of the Continental Shelf.

Leatherjackets are relatively small fish, rarely exceeding a kilo in weight, although occasionally reaching twice that size. The yellowish Chinaman leatherjacket is the largest species, occasionally reaching weights in excess of three kilos. On the other hand, the estuary-dwelling fan-bellied leatherjacket rarely tops half a kilo.

In many regions, leatherjackets are an incidental catch taken by anglers fishing for other target species. However, they have moist, sweet, white flesh and are a welcome addition to the catch of most anglers. They are also popular with younger fishermen, who regularly encounter these fish around wharves, jetties and breakwalls.

TECHNIQUE	ROD	REEL	LINE	TERMINAL TACKLE	HOOK	WEIGHT	BAIT
Casting or drifting float-suspended or lightly weighted baits in current.	Long (3-4.2 metre) soft-actioned float rods.	Lightweight sidecast, centrepin or threadline.	2-5 kg	Fixed or running float, light running sinker rig. Light leaders.	12-4	Tiny ball sinker or split shot.	Marine weeds and algae, bread, worms, cunjevoi and prawns.

Mackerel

Several species of large, tropical mackerel *(Scomberomorus)* are of great importance to anglers in the northern half of Australia. The biggest and best known is the narrow-barred Spanish mackerel or tanguigue *(S. commerson)*. The closely related broad-barrred Spanish mackerel or grey mackerel *(S. semifasciatum)* does not grow as large, but is seasonally abundant in some areas.

Smaller, but nonetheless important as angling species, are the Australian spotted mackerel *(S. munroi)* and the Queensland school mackerel *(S. queenslandicus)*. Another widespread species, the shark mackerel, scaly mackerel or large-scaled tuna *(Grammatorcynus bicarinatus)*, is less closely related, but belongs to the same general family.

All of these mackerel — which are erroneously called 'snook' in some regions — are found in tropical and sub-tropical waters around the northern half of Australia, although the narrow-barred Spanish mackerel occasionally strays as far south as Jervis Bay on the east coast, and Bunbury in Western Australia.

Narrow-barred Spanish mackerel are large fish, commonly reaching a metre or more in length and weighing as much as 20 kilos. Exceptional examples may be twice that size. The other mackerel species are smaller, with the broad-barred or grey mackerel and the shark mackerel rarely exceeding 10 kilos, while the spotted and school mackerels are most common at sizes of one to four kilos, rarely topping eight kilos.

All of these tropical mackerel range from the lower reaches of estuaries, through inshore waters, and out towards the islands and reefs of the Continental Shelf.

They are all very popular angling targets, pursued by large numbers of fishermen. Most are caught by boat anglers using a variety of offshore fishing techniques. In particular, they respond to live or fresh-dead baits of whole or cut fish and squid. They will also strike at a range of lures and large flies, either cast and retrieved, or trolled behind a moving boat. These tropical mackerel have powerful jaws and very sharp teeth, so wire leaders or linked (ganged) hooks should be used.

The flesh of the tropical mackerels is white, firm and delicious, although the shark mackerel is not as highly rated as the other species mentioned. It should also be noted that larger specimens of Spanish mackerel have been linked with outbreaks of ciguatera poisoning.

Natural Food

TECHNIQUE	ROD	REEL	LINE	TERMINAL TACKLE	HOOK	WEIGHT	BAIT
Casting unweighted, lightly weighted or float suspended baits in a berley trail. Also small lures and flies.	Ultra light to light spinning, baitcaster or sidecast rod. Also handlines.	Light threadline, closed-face, baitcaster or sidecast.	2-6 kg	Hook tied straight to line, minimal weight or fixed float.	10-2 (long shank)	Smallest practical ball, bean or split shot.	Fish flesh, squid, prawn or worm pieces.

FISH SPECIES

Shark Mackerel

School Mackerel

Narrow-barred Spanish Mackerel

TECHNIQUE	ROD	REEL	LINE	TERMINAL TACKLE	HOOK	WEIGHT	BAIT
Offshore trolling and drifting and shore casting in specific locations.	4-24 kg class game rods, jig, boat and double-handed spinning and baitcaster rods.	Game, overhead and troll reels, medium to large threadlines, baitcasters and sidecasts.	4-24 kg	Ganged (linked) hooks and/or wire leaders with all lures and baits.	3/0-8/0	None, or smallest practical bean or barrel.	Live and dead fish, trolling and casting lures.

Mackerel, Slimy *Scomber australasicus*

Natural Food

Also known as the blue mackerel, Pacific mackerel or common mackerel, the slimy mackerel is a small fish found right around the southern half of Australia and in northern areas of New Zealand. They are usually encountered near the surface or in mid-water over offshore reefs and gravel beds, around islands, bomboras and undersea pinnacles, and near navigation buoys, drilling platforms and similar structures. Schools also venture into bays, harbours and estuaries, being seasonally abundant around many wharves.

Occurring in large schools, this dark-fleshed, blood-rich species is a vital part of the marine food chain. It is eaten by most large game fish, from yellowtail kingfish and tuna to sharks and marlin.

Slimy mackerel are relatively small fish, rarely exceeding a kilo in weight, although occasionally reaching twice that size. They are more commonly encountered at lengths of 25 to 35 centimetres and weights between 200 and 800 grams.

Most slimy mackerel are caught by anglers using relatively light tackle, fine lines and small hooks baited with fish flesh strips, prawn pieces or squid strips. They also respond aggressively to small lures, flies and multi-hook baitfish jig rigs.

Slimy mackerel are especially popular with junior anglers and fishermen seeking bait for larger, offshore species. They are not a highly rated table fish, although their dark, oily flesh is well suited to smoking, drying, pickling and similar forms of preparation.

Mangrove Jack *Lutjanus argentimaculatus*

The mangrove jack or jack is also known in some areas as red bream, dog bream or red perch. It is closely related to both the fingermark bream *(L. johnii)* and the red bass *(L. bohar)*.

Mangrove jacks are found in tropical and sub-tropical waters around the northern half of Australia, south to about Sydney on the east coast and Shark Bay in Western Australia. They live mainly in estuarine and inshore waters, rarely straying far beyond the mouths of tidal rivers, harbours and inlets, although very large specimens are sometimes taken in reef waters well off the coast. Mangrove jacks are also capable of moving upstream into flowing fresh water at times.

Jacks commonly reach weights of a kilo or two, and may occasionally grow much larger. Exceptional examples from offshore reefs may weigh between eight and 10 kilos.

These handsome, aggressive fish respond to a wide range of fishing styles. Many are taken by sport fishermen casting lures or small live baits around snags, rock bars and other structural elements within tropical estuary systems.

When hooked, jacks are powerful fighters who immediately dive towards the line-cutting protection offered by submerged mangrove roots or oyster-encrusted rock ledges. Sturdy tackle and leaders of heavy nylon or light wire are recommended.

Mangrove jacks have delicious white flesh. However, it should be noted that the very similar red bass is often toxic. If there is any doubt at all about the identification and separation of these fish, the flesh should not be consumed.

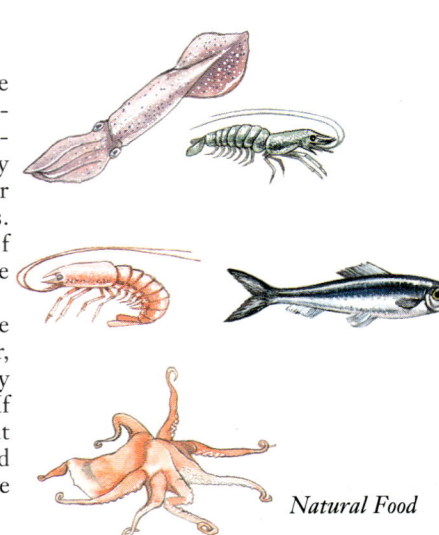

Natural Food

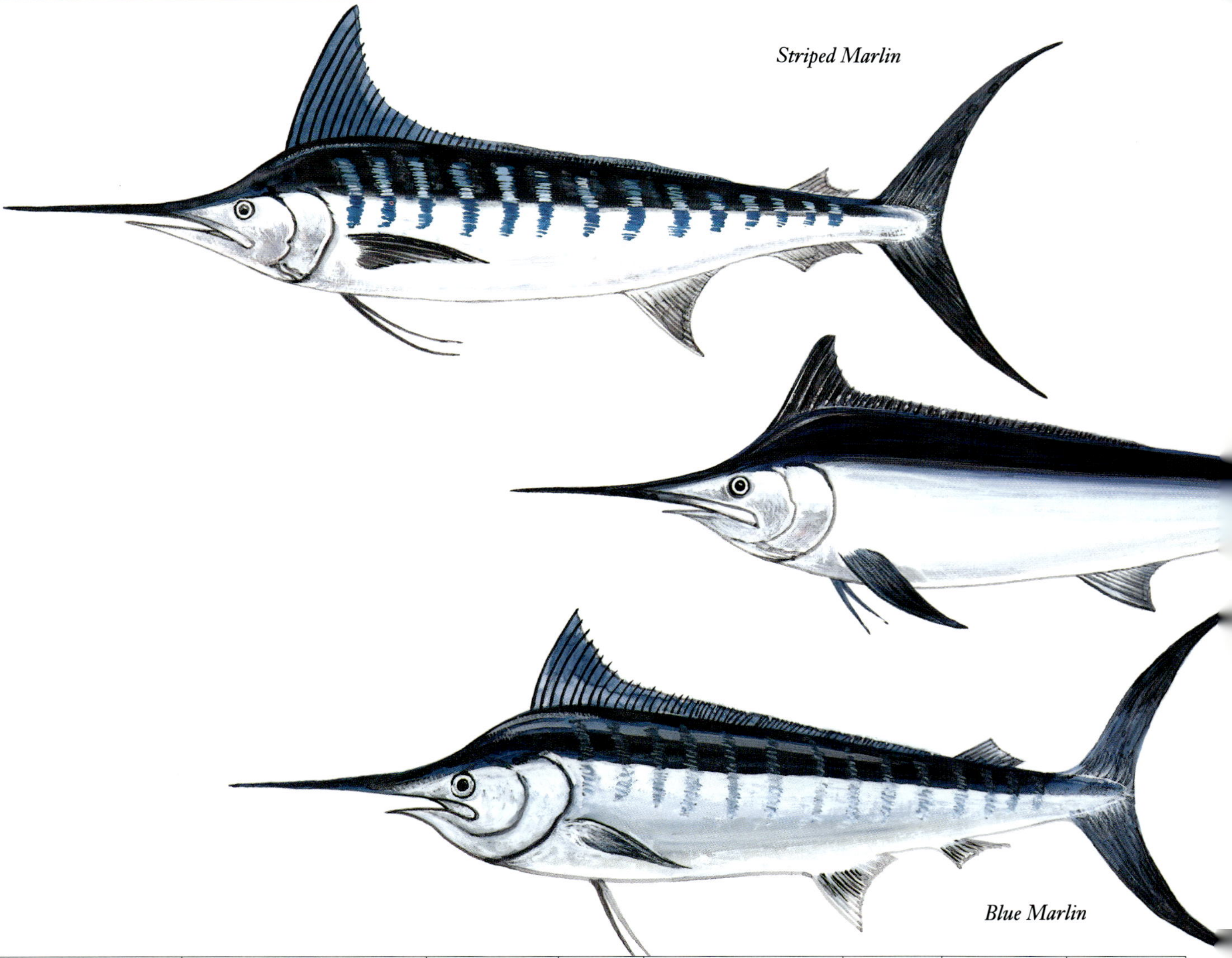

Striped Marlin

Blue Marlin

TECHNIQUE	ROD	REEL	LINE	TERMINAL TACKLE	HOOK	WEIGHT	BAIT
Trolling or drifting baits and lures in offshore waters with heavy tackle.	8-60 kg class game rods.	Lever drag game reels.	8-60 kg	Long, heavy leaders of very heavy nylon or wire, backed up by doubles.	5/0-14/0	None, or a small sinker to balance troll baits.	Live and dead fish or squid, trolling lures.

FISH SPECIES

TECHNIQUE	ROD	REEL	LINE	TERMINAL TACKLE	HOOK	WEIGHT	BAIT
Trolling, casting or drifting with baits and lures.	Medium spinning, baitcaster or sidecast rods.	Medium threadline, baitcaster or sidecast.	4-12 kg	Heavy nylon or light wire leaders, minimal weight or float.	2/0-5/0	Smallest practical ball or bean.	Small live or dead fish, squid or prawns.

Marlin

Marlin belong to the same family *(Istiophoridae)* as sailfish and spearfish. They are large, active marine predators, represented in Australasian waters by three species: the black marlin *(Makaira indica)*, blue marlin *(M. mazara)* and striped marlin *(Tetrapturus audax)*.

The black and blue marlin are the true heavyweights of this family, and among the largest fish in the sea. Both have been recorded at lengths of four to five metres and weights in excess of 600 kilos. They may rarely approach 1 000 kilos in weight.

Striped marlin do not attain such massive dimensions, although they have been recorded to 200 kilos and more, especially in New Zealand.

Marlin are mostly encountered in deeper, oceanic waters, near the edges of the Continental Shelf and beyond. However, favourable currents and water conditions will occasionally carry them much closer to shore.

Black marlin are more common in tropical and sub-tropical waters. In Australia, they are encountered at all sizes, from one metre juveniles weighing 10 kilos or less, right up to mature female spawners of 400 to 600 kilos.

Striped marlin take over from blacks as the most common inshore species in sub-tropical and temperate waters. They are particularly abundant off southern New South Wales, Tasmania and the North Island of New Zealand. Most examples caught in these areas weigh between 60 and 150 kilos.

Blue marlin are the true nomads of the family, ranging throughout the oceans of the world and preferring the deep, oceanic currents. Most of those encountered in Australia and New Zealand are mature female specimens, weighing anywhere from 90 to 500 kilos.

Marlin are caught primarily by boat anglers using a variety of offshore fishing techniques. In particular, they respond to live or fresh-dead baits of whole fish and squid. They will also strike at a range of lures and very large flies trolled behind a moving boat. Sturdy gamefishing tackle and leaders of heavy nylon or wire are needed to withstand the powerful struggle and repeated jumps of a hooked marlin.

Marlin flesh is white or pinkish white and has a pleasant flavour, although larger specimens tend to be a little coarse and dry. Big marlin may also carry relatively heavy accumulations of mercury and other heavy metals. The striped marlin has darker pink or orange flesh and is more highly rated by many seafood fanciers than either the black or blue.

Black Marlin

Natural Food

TECHNIQUE	ROD	REEL	LINE	TERMINAL TACKLE	HOOK	WEIGHT	BAIT
Offshore bottom fishing, drifting and shore casting with various baits.	Medium boat or jig rods. Double handed spinning, overhead or sidecast casting rods. Also handlines.	Overheads, boat reels, centrepins, sidecasts and medium threadlines.	8-15 kg	Hooks tied directly to line. Droppers above bottom weights or running sinker rigs.	1/0-5/0	Snapper leads, bombs, spoons, balls and beans.	Cut fish, prawns, squid, crabs and worms.

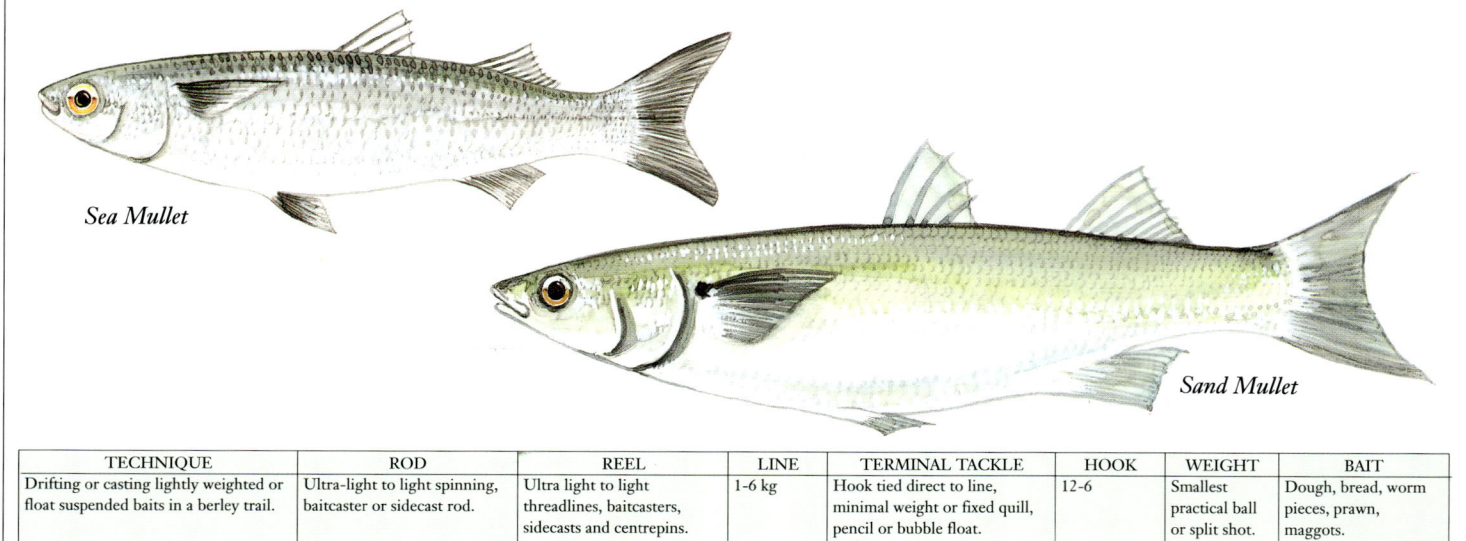

Sea Mullet

Sand Mullet

TECHNIQUE	ROD	REEL	LINE	TERMINAL TACKLE	HOOK	WEIGHT	BAIT
Drifting or casting lightly weighted or float suspended baits in a berley trail.	Ultra-light to light spinning, baitcaster or sidecast rod.	Ultra light to light threadlines, baitcasters, sidecasts and centrepins.	1-6 kg	Hook tied direct to line, minimal weight or fixed quill, pencil or bubble float.	12-6	Smallest practical ball or split shot.	Dough, bread, worm pieces, prawn, maggots.

Mulloway *Argyrosomus hololepidotus*

The mulloway is better known in the eastern states as the jewfish, jew or 'jewie'. In South Australia it is sometimes called butterfish or 'buttery', while in Western Australia, some anglers refer to them as king-fish, river king or silver king.

The mulloway's closest Australian relatives are its tropical cousin, the spotted or black jewfish (*Prontonibea diacanthus*), and the much smaller teraglin or 'trag' (*Atractoscion aequidens*).

Mulloway are are found in sub-tropical, temperate and cool waters around the southern half of Australia. They do not occur in Tasmania or New Zealand.

They are a fish of our estuarine and inshore waters, living mostly in the lower reaches of larger tidal rivers, bays, inlets and harbours, and over reefs and gravel beds extending well offshore. Mulloway also occur in wave-washed, inshore waters and in holes and gutters along beaches.

These are large, attractive fish, commonly reaching a metre and a half in length and weighing as much as 30 kilos. Isolated specimens to 45 kilos have been recorded. Small specimens in the half to three kilo range are sometimes called 'soapies', while slightly larger fish are known as 'schoolies'.

Mulloway are a very popular angling target, pursued by large numbers of fishermen casting from beaches, breakwalls and rock platforms, and by boat fishermen using a variety of offshore fishing techniques. In particular, they respond to live or fresh-dead baits of whole or cut fish, beach worms, squid and octopus. They will also occasionally strike at lures.

Mulloway are a highly rated table fish.

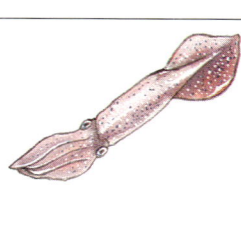

Natural Food

Morwong

Natural Food

The morwong family (*Cheilodactylidae*) contains several species important to anglers in Australia and New Zealand. The best known of these are the blue or silver morwong (*Nemadactylus douglasii*) — which is sometimes called the rubberlip — and the jackass fish (*N. macropterus*). In New Zealand, both are known as tarakihi.

Other morwong of some importance to anglers are the queen snapper or southern blue morwong (*N. valenciennesi*), the dusky morwong or butterfish (*Dactylophora nigricans*) and the red morwong (*Cheilodactylus fuscus*).

Morwong are found in sub-tropical, temperate and cooler seas around Australia and New Zealand. They are mostly encountered over offshore reefs and gravel beds, although they occasionally enter harbours and large estuary mouths. Red and dusky morwong occur mostly in wave-washed, inshore waters adjacent to rocky shorelines, headlands and stone breakwalls.

Morwong commonly reach weights of a kilo or two, and may occasionally grow much larger. The biggest are the dusky morwong and the queen snapper or southern blue morwong, both of which are capable of growing to a metre in length and 10 kilos in weight. Silver or blue morwong may reach five or six kilos, while the other species rarely top two kilos.

In many areas, morwong are an incidental catch taken by anglers fishing for more desirable target species. The big blue morwong or queen snapper is a top quality eating fish, and is actively sought by many southern anglers.

Mullet

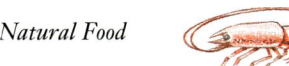

Natural Food

The mullet family (*Muglidae*) is a widespread one, found throughout the salt, brackish and fresh waters of the world. It is well represented in Australian and New Zealand waters, with at least three species being of importance to anglers. These are the sea or bully mullet (*Mugil cephalus*), the sand or lano mullet (*Myxus elongatus*) and the yellow-eye mullet or pilch (*Aldrichetta fosteri*).

All of these mullet are relatively small fish, rarely exceeding half a kilo in weight, although sometimes reaching twice that size. The exception is the sea mullet, which occasionally approaches five kilos.

The most easily captured of the mullet species is the yellow-eye, which is common around the southern half of Australia and much of New Zealand. It is a small fish, but one which bites well on baits of prawn pieces, marine worms, shellfish and even fish strips. Sand mullet are also taken in reasonable quantities, especially on the east coast of Australia. Sea mullet, on the other hand, are notoriously difficult to catch on a baited line, surviving for the most part on a diet of microscopic plants and animals.

Most mullet are caught in estuaries and bays or along ocean beaches. They rarely range far from shore, even when undertaking migrations along the coast.

Mullet are fair to very good table fish, and are also important to anglers as a bait source, used either alive, dead or cut into chunks and strips.

TECHNIQUE	ROD	REEL	LINE	TERMINAL TACKLE	HOOK	WEIGHT	BAIT
Casting or drifting baits from the shore or boats. Lure casting in specific scenarios.	Medium to heavy double-handed spinning, overhead and sidecast rods.	Large threadlines, overhead casting reels, sidecasts, large centrepins.	6-30 kg	Heavy nylon leaders if using lighter main lines. Minimal weight.	4/0-9/0	Smallest practical bean, ball or barrel.	Live or dead fish, squid, octopus, beach worms, cut fish flesh, casting lures.

Murray Cod *Macullochella peeli*

The Murray cod is Australia's largest freshwater fish, and among the three or four biggest freshwater species in the world. It may once have grown to lengths of two metres and weights in excess of 100 kilos, although these days, any cod over 30 or 40 kilos is an exceptional fish. Most of the Murray cod encountered by anglers today weigh between one and 15 kilos.

Murray cod are native to the Murray/Darling system and its many tributaries in western Queensland, New South Wales, northern Victoria and south eastern South Australia. They have also been introduced into rivers, lakes and dams outside this natural range, with varying degrees of success.

The smaller, but closely related, trout cod or blue nose *(M. macquariensis)* was once reasonably abundant in the cooler headwaters of some outback rivers, but is today present in just a handful of isolated localities. Similarly, the various east coast cod (which are yet to be accurately described in scientific terms) are now rare — possibly endangered — in their native waters along the upper Clarence, Richmond and Mary River systems.

Murray cod are caught mostly in warmer, turbid outback rivers, lakes and man-made impoundments. They also occur in some clearer, cooler waterways near the headwaters of inland river systems.

Murray cod are a highly esteemed table fish, although larger specimens from slow moving waterways may have a high fat content. The tastiest cod of all are two to six kilo fish from clean, moving water.

Natural Food

Nannygai *Trachichthodes affinis*

The nannygai, 'gai or redfish is a common reef species around the south eastern corner of Australia. Very similar fish, including the swallow-tail nannygai *(Centroberyx lineatus)* and the red snapper or Bight redfish *(C. gerrardi)* take over from the common nannygai in Tasmanian, South Australian and Western Australian waters.

Nannygai are mostly encountered over offshore reefs and gravel beds, around islands and near undersea pinnacles. They occasionally enter deeper harbours and bays in cooler, southern waters, but are more common on offshore grounds.

Nannygai are relatively small fish, rarely exceeding half a kilo in weight, although occasionally reaching twice that size. The swallow-tail and red snapper both grow considerably larger than the eastern nannygai.

Although they are an important commercial species, most nannygai or redfish taken by recreational anglers are an incidental catch, boated while fishing for larger and more desirable target species such as snapper, flathead and morwong.

Nannygai are caught primarily by boat anglers using a variety of offshore fishing techniques. In particular, they succumb to bottom-fished baits of fish flesh, pilchards, cut squid or prawns. They will also strike small lures and multi-hook bait jig rigs.

Nannygai are a tasty table fish with sweet, pinkish white flesh. Their small overall size and large heads result in a high degree of wastage, but this is offset by the fact that they are commonly caught in large numbers. Live nannygai are also a superb bait for large yellowfin tuna, yellowtail kingfish and even marlin.

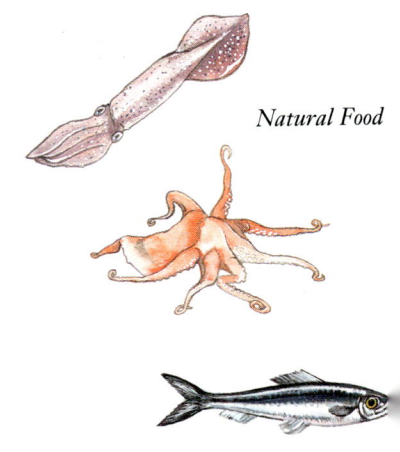

Natural Food

TECHNIQUE	ROD	REEL	LINE	TERMINAL TACKLE	HOOK	WEIGHT	BAIT
Offshore bottom fishing, drifting and 'floater' baits in a berley trail.	Boat or jig rod. Also handlines.	Boat or overhead reel, baitcaster or large threadline.	6-15 kg	Droppers above a sinker, running weight or unweighted in calm conditions.	3/0-6/0	Snapper lead, spoon, bean or ball.	Cut fish flesh, prawns, squid.

FISH SPECIES

TECHNIQUE	ROD	REEL	LINE	TERMINAL TACKLE	HOOK	WEIGHT	BAIT
Bait fishing, lure casting and trolling.	Medium spinning or baitcaster rods.	Medium threadline or baitcaster.	5-12 kg	Line or lure tied directly to line, minimal weight.	2/0-6/0	Smallest practical ball or bean.	Small, whole fish, yabbies, grubs, worms and various lures.

TECHNIQUE	ROD	REEL	LINE	TERMINAL TACKLE	HOOK	WEIGHT	BAIT
Offshore bottom fishing, drifting and distance casting in certain shore-based locations.	Boat or jig rod. Double-handed casting rod. Also handlines.	Boat reel or casting reel.	6-15 kg	Typically droppers above a heavy sinker.	2/0-6/0	Snapper lead, bomb, spoon.	Cut fish flesh, squid, octopus.

Pearl Perch *Glaucosoma*

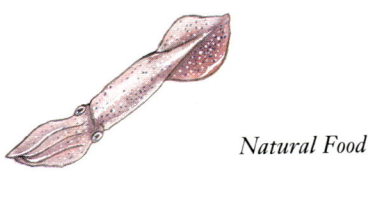

Natural Food

The pearl perch or 'pearly' is a bottom-dwelling fish confined to a relatively small stretch of coastline between about Fraser Island, in southern Queensland, and Port Macquarie, in northern New South Wales. It is closely related to the much larger Westralian jewfish (*G. hebraicum*).

Pearl perch are deep sea fish rarely encountered in water shallower than about 50 metres. They are mostly caught over rock, reef or rubble sea beds, particularly near pinnacles and undersea peaks.

Pearl perch commonly reach weights of a kilo or two, and may occasionally grow to twice that size. They are mostly taken while bottom fishing for snapper, teraglin and other reef species.

As one of our most delicious table fish, Pearl perch, like the Westralian jewfish, usually appear in any short list or 'top ten' of Australia's best eating species.

Perch, English *Perca fluviatilis*

The English or European perch is more commonly known to many Australasian anglers as the redfin perch, redfin or 'reddie'. It was introduced to Australia and New Zealand from its native waters in Britain and western Europe, and is regarded by many fisheries managers as a scourge because of its propensity for preying on juvenile trout and native freshwater species.

Redfin are caught mostly in warmer, turbid outback rivers, irrigation canals, lakes and man-made impoundments. They also occur in some clearer, cooler waterways near the headwaters of inland river systems. They do not generally move into the very warmest of our outback rivers and, as a result, are not found in the upper Darling or Coopers Creek drainage.

Redfin are most prolific in sections of the Murray, western Victoria and certain waters in south eastern South Australia and the south western corner of Western Australia. They are also regionally abundant in Tasmania and New Zealand's North Island.

Redfin perch are relatively small fish, rarely exceeding a kilo in weight, although occasionally reaching twice that size. Exceptional Australian specimens to four and five kilos have been recorded. This is considerably larger than the species grows in its European homeland. In many local waters, however, redfin perch are small and stunted, due to over-population.

The redfin is a fine table fish with firm, white flesh. It should be skinned, as the scales are very hard to remove.

Natural Fo[od]

Golden Perch

Macquarie Perch

TECHNIQUE	ROD	REEL	LINE	TERMINAL TACKLE	HOOK	WEIGHT	BAIT
Golden: Casting and trolling with baits and lures.	Light to medium spinning or baitcaster rods.	Medium threadline or baitcaster.	4-9 kg	Hook or lure tied directly to line. Minimal weight.	1-4/0	Ball or bean.	Worms, yabbies, grubs, shrimp and various lures.
Others: Casting or drifting with baits or small lures.	Ultra-light to light spinning and baitcaster or fly rods.	Light threadline, closed-face or baitcaster.	2-6 kg	Hook or lure tied directly to line, minimal weight or float.	6-1/0	Small ball or split shot.	

FISH SPECIES

TECHNIQUE	ROD	REEL	LINE	TERMINAL TACKLE	HOOK	WEIGHT	BAIT
Casting, trolling, drifting or jigging ('bobbing') with baits and various lures.	Ultra-light to light spinning or baitcaster rod.	Ultra-light to light threadline, closed-face or baitcaster.	2-6 kg	Hook or lure tied directly to line, sufficient weight to fish near bottom or cover.	4-1	Ball, bean or barrel.	Worms, minnows, yabbies and various lures or jigs.

Perch

Silver Perch

Natural Food

Three species of native freshwater perch are especially important to Australia's inland anglers. They are the golden perch or yellowbelly (*Macquaria ambigua*), the Macquarie perch (*M. australasica*), and the silver perch or bidyan (*Bidyanus bidyanus*).

Golden perch are our second biggest outback native species, growing to as much as 23 kilos under truly exceptional conditions. Generally, however, they run between half a kilo and four or five kilos, with specimens over eight kilos occasionally turning up in some food-rich dams.

Golden perch are variously known as yellowbelly, callop and even Murray perch. They have the greatest geographical range of any outback species, extending from the south eastern corner of the Northern Territory, right through inland Queensland and New South Wales to northern and western Victoria and the Murray in South Australia.

Macquarie perch are much smaller fish, rarely exceeding two kilos in weight. They are also known as mountain perch or white-eyed perch, and they live in cooler areas along the Great Divide in New South Wales, through the Australian Capital Territory and into Victoria. Small populations also exist in some eastern flowing streams, such as the Shoalhaven and Nepean Rivers.

Silver perch are known in many areas as grunter, bream or black bream, and belong to a large family of Australian freshwater fish, many of which are too small to be of great interest to anglers. Silver perch have a similar, though somewhat less extensive, range to that of the golden perch. They are typically small fish, averaging 200 grams to a kilo in weight, although occasional specimens will top three kilos.

All of these perch are a very popular angling targets, pursued by large numbers of inland fishermen, representing all levels of experience and commitment. They respond to a wide range of angling techniques, including bait fishing, lure casting, trolling and fly fishing. Silver and Macquarie perch are caught mostly by anglers using relat-ively light tackle, fine lines and small hooks, while goldens are often taken on much larger baits and lures by fishermen targeting Murray cod.

Golden and Macquarie perch are excellent table fish, especially when taken from relatively clear water. Silver perch are less highly rated and sometimes exhibit a 'weedy' or 'earthy' flavour.

Pike

Two saltwater species commonly known as pike are reasonably important to Australian anglers. They are the long-finned or yellowfin pike (*Dinolestes lewini*), and the striped sea pike (*Sphyraena obtusata*). A third species, the short-finned pike or snook (*S. novaehollandiae*), is important enough to be dealt with separately, under the heading of 'Snook'.

Long-finned or yellowfin pike are found in temperate and cool waters around the southern half of Australia, including Tasmania. They are relatively small fish, rarely exceeding a kilo in weight, although occasionally reaching almost twice that size.

Although specifically fished for in western Victoria and Tasmania, in most other localities, long-finned pike are an incidental catch taken by anglers fishing for more desirable target species such as tailor, snapper, flathead and bream.

Long-finned or yellowfin pike enjoy some regional popularity as an eating fish, although they are not held in high regard in New South Wales. Their flesh is quite tasty, but rather soft and prone to bruising. They make an excellent bait — alive or dead — for large predators such as kingfish and mulloway.

Striped sea pike are found in tropical and sub-tropical waters around the northern half of Australia. They are even smaller than the southern long-finned pike, rarely exceeding 250 or 300 grams in weight. They are mostly sought as bait for larger fish, although they are a fair table fish in larger sizes.

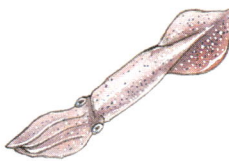

Natural Food

Queenfish *Chorinemus lysan*

Although there are several very similar species of queenfish, leatherskin or 'skinny' in Australia's tropical seas, one is the largest and most important.

The queenfish is a big, active saltwater sport fish, much prized by anglers for its fighting ability and acrobatics when hooked. It is found in tropical waters around the northern half of Australia, living mainly in estuarine and inshore areas, but occasionally straying well beyond the mouths of tidal rivers and inlets to frequent reef passes, bomboras and the tidal rips around off-shore islands.

Although growing to well over a metre, queenfish have laterally compressed bodies and are therefore quite light for their length. Most of those encountered by anglers weigh between two and seven kilos, although exceptional examples in excess of 12 kilos are occasionally reported.

Queenfish respond to a wide range of angling techniques, including bait fishing, lure casting, trolling and fly fishing. They are taken by both shore-based and boat anglers, and provide exceptional sport when hooked on light tackle.

Although queenfish are often denigrated as a table fish by tropical anglers, they actually have firm, white and slightly dry flesh which is well suited to many recipes and methods of preparation. They should be bled and iced promptly after capture.

Natural Food

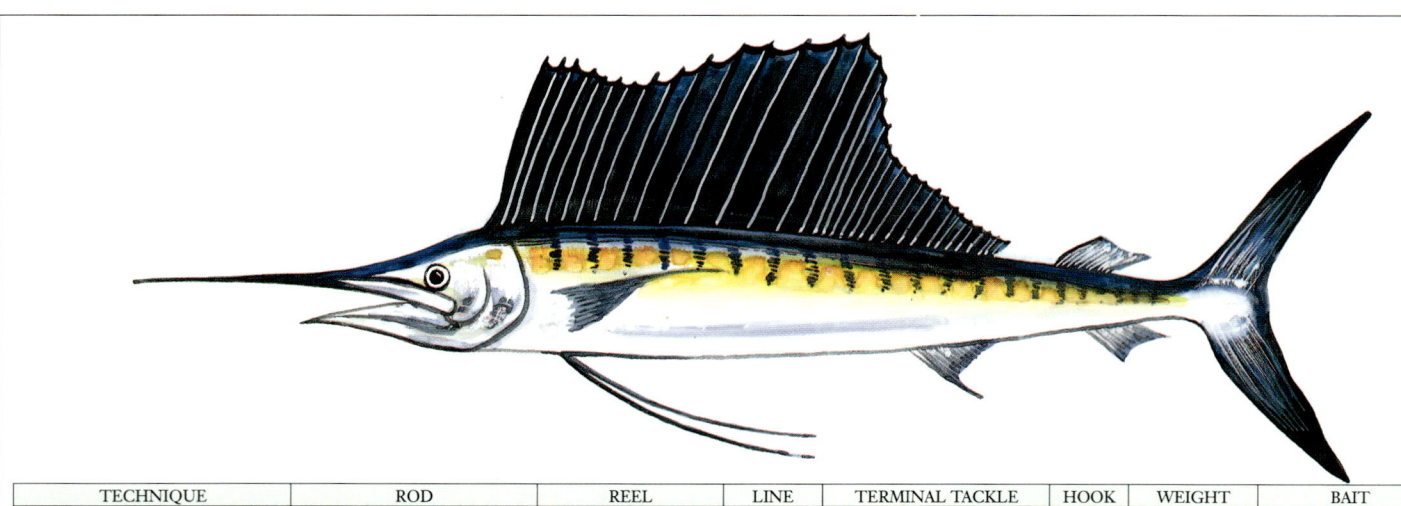

TECHNIQUE	ROD	REEL	LINE	TERMINAL TACKLE	HOOK	WEIGHT	BAIT
Offshore trolling and drifting with lures, as well as land-based live baiting in specific locations.	4-15 kg class game and sport rods.	Light game reels, star drag overheads, large capacity threadlines.	4-15 kg	Heavy nylon or wire leaders backed up with doubles.	3/0-7/0	None, or a small sinker to balance a troll bait.	Live and dead fish, especially gar and mullet, plus troll lures.

FISH SPECIES

TECHNIQUE	ROD	REEL	LINE	TERMINAL TACKLE	HOOK	WEIGHT	BAIT
Casting, trolling and drifting with baits and lures.	Light casting rods.	Light to medium threadline, baitcaster and sidecast.	4-9 kg	Ganged (linked) hooks, long shank hooks or short wire leaders.	2-3/0	Smallest practical barrel or bean.	Small fish, fish strips, squid and lures.

TECHNIQUE	ROD	REEL	LINE	TERMINAL TACKLE	HOOK	WEIGHT	BAIT
Casting, trolling or drifting with baits, lures and flies.	Medium baitcaster or spinning rods, 4-15 kg class game and sport rods, light boat rods. No. 8-10 fly rod.	Medium baitcaster or threadline, light game, overhead, sidecast or fly.	4-15 kg WF8-10F fly line	Heavy nylon or light wire leader and/or ganged (linked) hooks.	3/0-6/0	None or lightest practical bean or barrel.	Live or dead small fish, fish strips and lures, especially surface poppers.

Sailfish *Istiophorus platypterus*

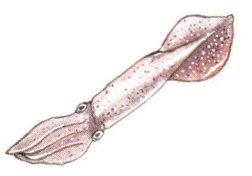

Natural Food

The Indo-Pacific sailfish is a billfish, belonging to the same group as the various marlin species and the much rarer shortbill spearfish.

Sailfish are found in tropical and sub-tropical waters around the northern half of Australia, rarely straying as far south as Sydney in the east and Perth in the west. They may very occasionally visit the islands to the north of New Zealand.

Sailfish swim mostly in deeper, oceanic waters, near the edges of the Continental Shelf and beyond. However, favourable currents and feeding conditions bring them much closer to shore. Some of the most famous sailfish grounds off Queensland and northern West Australia lie in depths of 40 to 60 metres, adjacent to major river mouths and around island groups or reef complexes.

Sailfish are large fish, commonly reaching two or three metres in length and weighing as much as 60 or 70 kilos, although specimens of half that weight are much more common. Record-size sailfish occasionally approach 100 kilos.

The sailfish is a highly prized sport and game species actively pursued by offshore anglers. Sails responds best to live or fresh-dead baits of whole fish and squid. They will also strike at a range of lures and large flies, either cast and retrieved, or trolled behind a moving boat. When hooked, they leap repeatedly from the water and make lightning fast runs, especially if relatively light tackle is used.

Although sailfish have palatable pinkish-red flesh that is well suited to smoking and other methods of preparation, most of those caught in Australian waters are released.

Salmon, Australian *Arripis trutta*

The Australian salmon or kahawai is a popular angling species throughout the southern half of Australia and around much of the New Zealand coastline.

Australian salmon are in no way related to the true salmon of the Northern Hemisphere. The only close relative of the Australian salmon is the much smaller Tommy ruff (*A. georgianus*).

Salmon or kahawai are a schooling species which occur mostly in wave-washed, inshore waters adjacent to rocky shorelines, headlands, break-walls, jetties and beaches. Juveniles, which are called salmon trout or bay trout in Victoria, are common in bays, harbours and larger estuaries.

Australian salmon commonly reach weights of a kilo or two, and may occasionally grow much larger. They have been recorded to weights of nine and 10 kilos in exceptional cases. The largest specimens tend to occur in the Great Australian Bight, Western Australia and New Zealand's North Island.

Salmon are a very popular angling target, pursued by large numbers of fishermen. They are taken by both shore-based and boat anglers using a variety of techniques. In particular, they respond to baits of whole pilchards or garfish, cut fish flesh, prawns and marine worms. They will also strike at a wide range of lures and flies.

Salmon have dark, reddish-grey flesh with a prominent blood line and a reasonably strong flavour. They are best suited to casseroles, fish cakes and similar dishes. They are also popular for canning and smoking.

Natural Food

TECHNIQUE	ROD	REEL	LINE	TERMINAL TACKLE	HOOK	WEIGHT	BAIT
Trolling, casting and bait fishing.	Light to medium spinning and baitcaster rods.	Medium threadlines, baitcasters and sidecasts.	3-10 kg	Hook or lure tied directly to line. Sufficient weight to reach fish.	4-1	Ball, barrel or bean.	Spoons, spinners, worms and minnows.

TECHNIQUE	ROD	REEL	LINE	TERMINAL TACKLE	HOOK	WEIGHT	BAIT
Casting, trolling and drifting with baits and lures. Fly fishing.	Medium spinning and baitcaster rods. No. 8-10 fly rods.	Medium spinning and baitcaster reels. Fly reels.	4-12 kg WF8-10 fly lines	Nylon leaders if using light main line. Minimal weight.	1-4/0	Smallest ball or bean practical.	Prawns, small live or dead fish, lures and flies.

FISH SPECIES

TECHNIQUE	ROD	REEL	LINE	TERMINAL TACKLE	HOOK	WEIGHT	BAIT
Casting, trolling and drifting with baits and lures. Also fly fishing.	Light to medium casting and trolling rods, overhead, spinning and sidecast. Also No. 7-10 fly rods.	Medium threadlines, baitcasters, overheads, sidecasts and fly reels.	4-12 kg WF7-10 fly lines	Line tied directly to hook or lure, minimal weight, running sinker rig.	1/0-5/0	Smallest practical ball, bean or barrel.	Small whole fish, fish flesh, squid, worms and various lures or flies.

Salmon, Freshwater

Natural Food

Two species of introduced salmon from the Northern Hemisphere are important to Australasian anglers. They are the chinook or quinnat salmon (*Onchorhyncus tshawytscha*) from the Pacific seaboard of North America, and the Atlantic salmon (*Salmo salar*) from Europe and the north east of North America.

The only established populations of sea-run chinook salmon outside of the fish's native waters are found in the South Island of New Zealand. These chinooks move offshore into the cool currents of the Pacific after being spawned in rivers. They remain in the sea for an average of four years before returning to the place of their birth to spawn and die.

Sea-run chinooks in New Zealand occasionally exceed 20 kilos in weight, although the average spawn-run fish weighs between six and 10 kilos. They are avidly pursued by anglers as they ascend the rivers towards their spawning beds.

Land-locked, non-reproducing populations of chinook or quinnat salmon also exist in Australia and New Zealand. The most famous are in Lakes Purrumbete and Bullen Merri, in western Victoria. These fish rarely exceed nine kilos.

Atlantic salmon have a different life cycle, and do not necessarily die after spawning. At present, no viable sea-run populations exist in Australasi. The Atlantic salmon found in a few of our lakes are totally landlocked and non-reproducing. They rarely exceed two or three kilos in weight.

Both freshwater salmon species are highly rated delicacies, especially when smoked or cured.

Salmon, Threadfin

Natural Food

There are two major species of threadfin salmon in Australia's tropical estuaries and inshore waters. These are the blue or Sheridan's threadfin (*Polydactylus sheridani*), and the larger gold threadfin, Burnett salmon or king salmon (*Eleutheronema tetradactylum*). Both are characterised by overshot mouths, hard, bony heads and finger-like filamentous rays extending from their lower flanks ahead of the pectoral or side fins.

Both species of threadfin are found in inshore tropical waters around the northern half of Australia. The blue salmon often forms large schools and averages a kilo or two in weight, sometimes approaching twice that size. Golden or king salmon typically form smaller groups or hunt alone. They are commonly encountered at weights of five and six kilos, and have been known to reach 15 or 16 kilos on occasion.

Both threadfin species are often taken by anglers fishing for better known target species such as barramundi, mangrove jacks and queenfish. However, because of their great speed, fast jumps and delicious table qualities, they are highly rated by northern fishermen, and always a welcome catch.

Threadfin respond to a range of estuarine and inshore techniques, especially the use of live or dead prawns, small live fish and relatively small lures and flies.

Samson Fish *Seriola hippos*

The samson fish is closely related and rather similar to both the amberjack (*S. dumerilli*) and the yellowtail kingfish (*S. lalandi*). It can be differentiated from these two fish by its deeper body, blunter head and darker, blotchy or barred colouration — although fin ray counts are sometimes required to separate juveniles of the three species.

Although confined mostly to the sub-tropical and warmer temperate waters of Australia's east and west coasts, samson fish also range through south western waters into the Great Australian Bight. Generally, they are more common in Western Australia — where they are often called sea kingfish.

Samsons are large fish, frequently reaching a metre or more in length and weighing as much as 20 or 30 kilos. Exceptional examples may approach two metres and 50 kilos.

Samson fish are caught by both land-based and boat anglers using live and dead fish baits, squid or lures. They are strong, active fighters and demand sturdy tackle in their larger sizes.

These fish make fine table fare, although very large specimens tend to be somewhat dry and coarse.

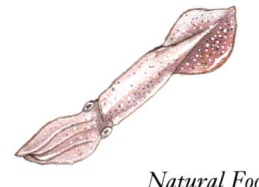

Natural Food

Saratoga

Saratoga are primitive, freshwater fish of the family *Osteoglossidae*, which also has isolated representatives in South East Asia and South America. Two similar but geographically separate, species occur in Australia. They are the northern saratoga (*Scleropages jardini*) and the Dawson River saratoga (*S. leichardti*).

The northern saratoga ranges from the Jardine River, on the north western tip of Cape York, to the Darwin area of the Northern Territory. It prefers billabongs and water holes, but is also found in some slower moving rivers.

The Dawson River saratoga was originally confined to the Dawson/Fitzroy system in central Queensland, but has now also been stocked in several man-made dams close to Brisbane. It prefers relatively clean, running fresh water with a reasonably high oxygen content and a diversity of food types, although it will also survive in still waters.

Both species are 'mouth brooders'. The female holds fertilised eggs in her mouth until they hatch, and also allows the fry to swim back into her mouth for protection after hatching.

Saratoga are mostly an incidental catch taken by anglers fishing for more desirable target species such as barramundi. However, in recent years, the saratoga has developed a well-earned reputation as a sport fish in its own right, and is now avidly pursued on a largely catch-and-release basis. Both species are particularly attractive targets for fly fishermen.

Saratoga are inferior table fish, with many bones and coarse, tasteless flesh. For this reason, most of those caught are returned to the water.

Natural Food

TECHNIQUE	ROD	REEL	LINE	TERMINAL TACKLE	HOOK	WEIGHT	BAIT
Shore casting and drifting or bottom fishing from boats with various baits.	Light to medium boat, jig or game rod, heavy spinning or baitcaster rod, double-handed casting rod.	Overhead, large threadline, baitcaster or sidecast.	7-18 kg	Heavy nylon or wire leader to prevent bite-offs and abrasion.	3/0-7/0	Ball, bean, barrel, helmet or star.	Fish flesh, pilchard, squid.

FISH SPECIES

TECHNIQUE	ROD	REEL	LINE	TERMINAL TACKLE	HOOK	WEIGHT	BAIT
Casting, trolling, drifting and jigging in offshore waters, as well as shore casting in certain locations.	6-24 kg class game and sport rods, double-handed casting rods.	Game and trolling reels, casting overheads, large threadlines and sidecasts.	6-24 kg	Heavy nylon leaders, backed up where necessary with doubles. Sufficient weight to reach fish.	3/0-9/0	Bean or barrel.	Live or dead fish, squid, lures and jigs.

TECHNIQUE	ROD	REEL	LINE	TERMINAL TACKLE	HOOK	WEIGHT	BAIT
Casting lures and flies close to overhanging bushes, weed beds and other structure. Occasionally taken while trolling.	Light to medium baitcaster and spinnning rods. No. 7-10 fly rods.	Light to medium threadline, closed-face and baitcaster. Fly reels.	3-8 kg WF7-10 fly lines	Nylon leader or shock tippet if using light line.	2/0-4/0	None.	Surface or diving lure, bushy fly, live frog or insect.

Shark, Gummy *Mustelus antarcticus*

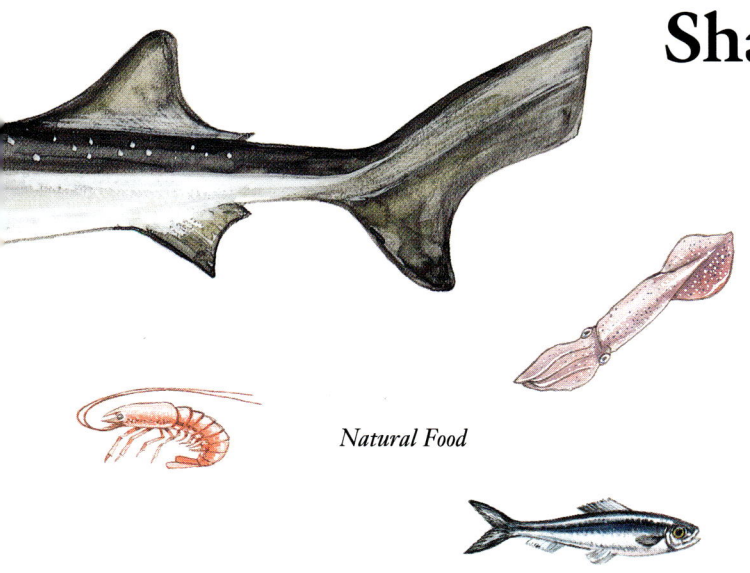

Natural Food

The gummy shark and the school shark, snapper shark or tope *(Galeorhinus galeus)* are both widespread throughout the temperate and cooler waters of Australia and New Zealand.

Both sharks are lightly built and rarely exceed 1.5 metres in length or weights of 20 kilos, although exceptional school sharks may approach 35 kilos.

These cool-water, slow growing sharks are relatively similar in appearance and habits, although the gummy is distinguished by its flat, grinding teeth, in contrast to the tope's small but sharp cutting teeth. The gummy is also peppered with light coloured spots on its upper flanks, while the tope rarely displays such markings.

Both of these lightweight sharks are taken by anglers on a regular basis, especially in large bays, harbours and along ocean surf beaches. They have firm white flesh and a sweet flavour much favoured by fish and chip shops, which traditionally market them as 'flake'. Larger specimens have been shown to contain high levels of mercury and other heavy metals, and should not be consumed on a regular basis.

Sharks

Hundreds of shark species occur in the seas surrounding Australia and New Zealand. Several also enter our tidal rivers, lakes and harbours, with a few even moving upstream into fresh water, particularly in tropical Australia.

The sharks of great interest to anglers are the smaller, edible species such as the previously described gummy and tope, and the large, active species classified as game fish.

Blue Shark

Blue sharks (*Prionace glauca*) are a migratory species with a world-wide distribution, including the southern, western and eastern coastlines of Australia and most of New Zealand. They are usually encountered in deeper, oceanic waters, near the edges of the Continental Shelf and beyond.

Although they reach lengths of at least four metres, blues are very lightly built and rarely exceed 100 kilos in weight. The biggest blue ever recorded weighed about 200 kilos.

Blue sharks are edible, though not highly rated in local waters.

Hammerhead Sharks

There are three species of large hammerhead sharks found in Australasian waters. The biggest and most potentially dange-rous to humans is the great hammerhead (*Sphyrna mokarran*) of tropical and sub-tropical waters. This large, aggressive shark with its characteristically high, curved dorsal fin may occasionally reach lengths of four metres and weights in excess of 400 kilos. It is largely confined to northern Australia, and mostly hooked accidentally whilst fishing for marlin and other big game fish.

The more common smooth hammerhead (*S. zygaena*) and scalloped hammerhead (*S. lewini*) are both found in sub-tropical, temperate and even cooler waters around the southern half of Australia and the North Island of New Zealand.

Smooth and scalloped hammerhead commonly reach two to three metres in length and weights of 40 to 150 kilos, with the occasional specimen topping 200 kilos. These temperate water hammerheads are actively pursued by game and sport fishermen, and provide a spirited fight when hooked. They prefer relatively small live or fresh fish baits.

Smaller hammerheads have quite tasty flesh and are often eaten.

Mako Shark

The mako or short-fin mako (*Isurus oxyrinchus*) is regarded by many anglers as the 'gamest' of all the sharks. When hooked, it often provides a fight equal to that of a billfish or tuna.

Makos have a world-wide distribution and are seasonally abundant in the sub-tropical, temperate and cooler seas around Australia and New Zealand. They also stray into tropical waters at times.

Occasionally reaching lengths in excess of four metres and weights of 450 kilos, makos are more commonly encountered at lengths between one and three metres and weights of 10 to 200 kilos.

Makos have very firm, tasty flesh which is pinkish-white prior to cooking.

Tiger Shark

The tiger shark (*Galeocerdo cuvieri*) is a big, dangerous species found throughout the tropical and sub-tropical oceans of the world, occasionally venturing into temperate waters during the summer months.

Tiger sharks grow to at least 4.5 metres and 800 kilos. In Australian waters, they are relatively common at sizes up to four metres and 500 kilos.

Tigers are not often targeted by tropical anglers, but are quite popular with east coast game fishermen working out of New South Wales' ports such as Sydney, Lake Macquarie and Port Macquarie. .

Tiger shark flesh is not often eaten, although small specimens are quite palatable.

Whaler Sharks

There are many species of whaler sharks in Australian and New Zealand waters. Some of the more common varieties include the bronze whaler (*Carcharhinus brachyurus*), the black whaler (*C. obscurus*), the sandbar shark or northern whaler (*C. plumbeus*) and the bull shark or river whaler (*C. leucas*).

All of these sharks are potentially large and dangerous predators. Most are capable of growing to at least three metres and 200 kilos, with exceptional examples of the black whaler having been recorded to 350 kilos.

Whalers are more abundant in tropical areas, but also occur in sub-tropical, temperate and even cool seas, especially during the summer months.

Small whaler sharks have tasty, white flesh much favoured as 'flake'. Very large specimens tend to be coarse and rank, with a strong ammonia taint.

White Shark

The white shark, white pointer or great white shark (*Carcharadon carcharias*) is the largest carnivorous shark on earth, having been reliably recorded at lengths in excess of six metres and weights of 2 500 kilos! Specimens of four to five metres and 1 000 kilos are far from rare in certain localities. It is a proven man-eater.

White sharks are most abundant in South and West Australia, from about Adelaide westwards to Albany. They also occur in smaller numbers in Tasmania, Victoria, New South Wales, southern Queensland and right around New Zealand. White shark populations are almost always associated with the presence of substantial seal or sea lion colonies, as these marine mammals — along with whales, dolphins, other sharks and rays — make up an important part of the white shark's diet.

Large white sharks are highly prized by big game fishermen, who pursue them with heavy tackle and large baits.

The few people who have eaten white shark report that the flesh is tasty and not unlike mako shark. It does, however, carry very high levels of mercury and other heavy metals.

Whaler Shark

Tiger Shark

Mako Shark

Natural Food

FISH SPECIES

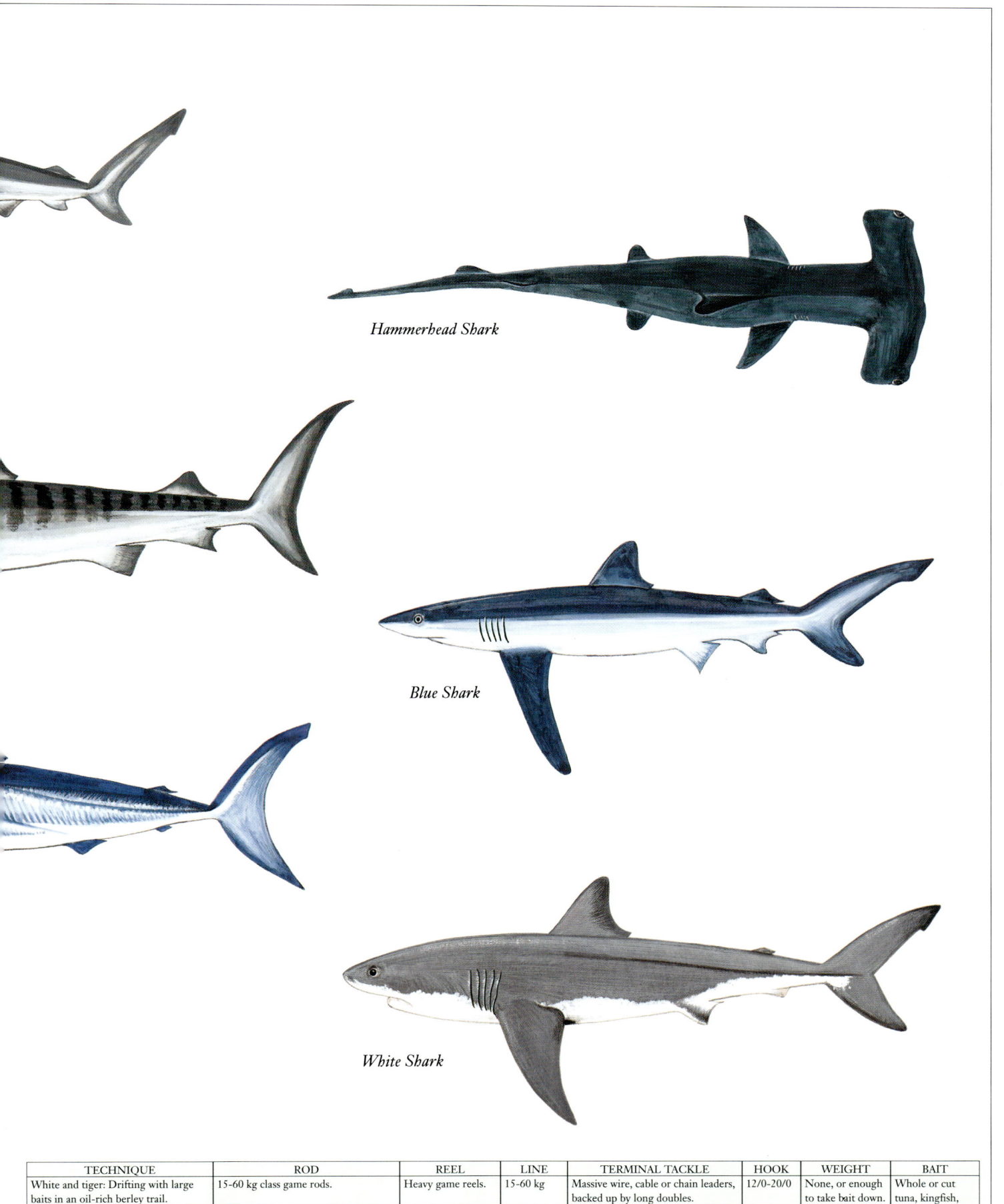

Hammerhead Shark

Blue Shark

White Shark

TECHNIQUE	ROD	REEL	LINE	TERMINAL TACKLE	HOOK	WEIGHT	BAIT
White and tiger: Drifting with large baits in an oil-rich berley trail.	15-60 kg class game rods.	Heavy game reels.	15-60 kg	Massive wire, cable or chain leaders, backed up by long doubles.	12/0-20/0	None, or enough to take bait down.	Whole or cut tuna, kingfish, salmon and mackerel.
Others: Drifting or slow trolling naits of live or dead fish.	6-24 kg class game and sport rods.	Medium game and trolling reels.	6-24 kg	Wire leaders and doubles.	6/0-14/0	None.	

Snapper *Chrysophrys auratus*

The snapper is also known as the pink snapper, red, reddie, red bream, squire and pinkie. It is, without a doubt, one of the most popular saltwater species in Australia and New Zealand.

In Australia, snapper are found around the southern half of the mainland, from about Rockhampton in Queensland to Carnarvon in Western Australia. They are rare in Tasmania. In New Zealand, the fish is found right around the North Island and as far down the east coast of the South Island as Christchurch. Snapper also occur at Lord Howe and Norfolk Islands.

The largest snapper are caught in South Australia, Norfolk Island and New Zealand. Exceptional examples to 20 kilos have been recorded, although any fish over 12 or 13 kilos is a real prize. On the east coast of Australia, the fish rarely tops 10 kilos these days.

Small snapper are called cockneys, red bream, squire, pinkies or ruggers in various locations. They are often encountered in bays and estuaries. Larger snapper move offshore, although they return to shallow bay waters period-ically to feed and spawn. Generally, snapper of all sizes prefer bottom strata of rocks and gravel, or transition areas between reef and softer sea beds.

Snapper are a very popular angling target, pursued by large numbers of fishermen representing all levels of experience and commitment. They are caught by both boat and shore-based anglers using a variety of fishing techniques. In particular, they respond to baits of cut fish flesh, whole, small bait species such as pilchards, gar (piper) and herring, squid, octopus and prawns. They will also take lures and flies on occasion, especially jigs fished on or near the sea bed.

Snapper are highly-rated table fish and command premium prices at fish markets in both Australia and New Zealand. Generally, smaller specimens in the half to two kilo range are regarded as having the best flavour, while very large individuals may tend to be a little dry.

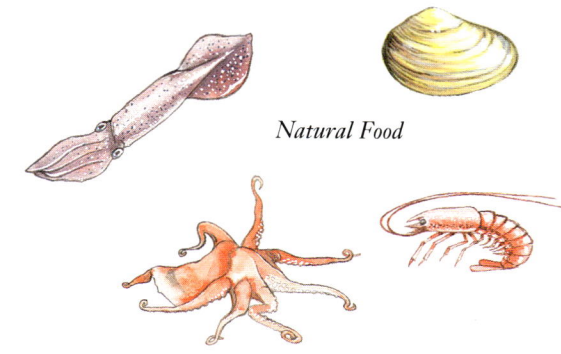

Natural Food

TECHNIQUE	ROD	REEL	LINE	TERMINAL TACKLE	HOOK	WEIGHT	BAIT
Casting, drifting and trolling with baits or lures.	Light boat, jig, spinning, baitcaster and sidecast rods.	Light to medium threadlines, baitcasters, sidecasts and centrepins.	4-10 kg	Light wire leader and/or ganged (linked) hooks. Paravanes effective when trolling.	2-4/0	Barrel, bean or paravane.	Small whole fish, cut fish, squid and lures.

FISH SPECIES

TECHNIQUE	ROD	REEL	LINE	TERMINAL TACKLE	HOOK	WEIGHT	BAIT
Offshore bottom fishing, drifting and fishing of 'floater' baits in berley. Distance casting from certain shore locations.	Medium to heavy boat, jig and sport rods. Double handed spinning rods, distance casting rods.	Boat and overhead reels, large threadlines, baitcasters and sidecasts.	6-18 kg	Use heavier nylon leaders if main line lighter than 8 kg. Shock leaders may be needed for distance casting.	1/0-7/0	Snapper leads, spoons, balls, beans, barrels.	Squid, octopus, cut and whole fish, prawns, some lures.

Snook *Sphyraena novaehollandiae*

The snook or short-finned sea pike is a cool water species distantly related to the tropical barracuda family. Surprisingly, it is not closely allied to the long-finned pike *(Dinolestes lewini)*, which is found in many of the same southern waters.

This fish should not be confused with members of the tropical mackerel clan, which are erroneously known as 'snook' in some regions.

Snook occur in temperate and cool waters around the southern half of Australia, including Tasmania. They are at their most prolific in parts of Victoria, South Australia and southern West Australia, preferring areas of relatively shallow inshore water over sea grass beds, sand or gravel.

Commonly reach weights of a kilo or more, snook may occasionally attain lengths in excess of a metre and weigh as much as three or four kilos.

Snook respond to a range of angling techniques. Most are taken on small, whole fish baits, fish flesh strips and lures.

This species is a popular table fish in southern areas, with moist, tasty white flesh that tends towards softness.

Natural Food

119

Sooty Grunter *Hephaestus fuliginosus*

The common sooty grunter is one member of a relatively large group of tropical fresh and brackish water species of the family *Theraponidae*, some of which are still to be fully described by scientists.

Sooty grunter are also known as black bream, khaki bream and 'blubberlips'. They occur in the tropical rivers, swamps and billabongs of northern Australia, occasionally ranging downstream into brackish areas. They generally prefer clean, running water with a reasonably high oxygen content and a diversity of food types, but will also be found in turbid lagoons, dams and water holes in some areas.

Sooty grunter are relatively small fish, rarely exceeding a kilo in weight, although occasionally reaching twice that size. They are often taken as an incidental catch by anglers fishing for more desirable target species such as barramundi, but are highly regarded as a sporting species in their own right, being one of our hardest-fighting freshwater fish on a kilo-for-kilo basis.

Sooty grunter respond to a wide range of natural baits, lures and flies. They provide reasonable to good table fare when taken from clean, flowing water, but may be a little 'weedy' or mud-tainted if caught in discoloured dams, lagoons and rivers.

Natural Food

Sweep

Three species of sweep are important to Australian anglers. They are the sea sweep or snapjack *(Scorpis aequipinnis)*, the banded sweep *(S. georgianus)* and the common sweep, silver sweep or 'Newcastle bream'*(S. lineolatus)*.

Sea sweep are the biggest and most important member of this group. They are largely confined to cool, southern waters; being most abundant along our southern coastline, from about Wilsons promontory in the east to Albany in the west, and around Tasmania. Banded sweep occur along with sea sweep in the western portion of this range, beyond Kangaroo Island, and up the coast of Western Australia at least as far as Shark Bay.

The common or silver sweep is a smaller, less prized fish found in large numbers along the New South Wales coast, in eastern Victoria and, less commonly, in north eastern Tasmania.

Sweep are quite small fish, rarely exceeding a kilo in weight, although occasionally reaching twice that size. They are caught mostly by anglers using relatively light tackle, fine lines and small hooks.

The larger sea sweep is a fine table fish. The other two species are not so highly regarded, and the common or silver sweep is often denigrated by New South Wales anglers. However, if cleaned promptly and eaten fresh, it has tasty, white flesh.

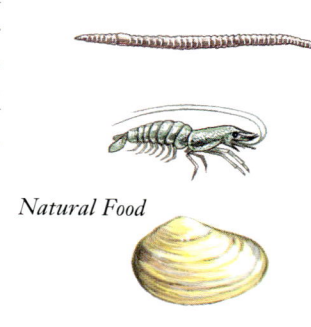

Natural Food

TECHNIQUE	ROD	REEL	LINE	TERMINAL TACKLE	HOOK	WEIGHT	BAIT
Offshore bottom fishing and drifting. Limited shore casting possibilities in specific locations.	Boat or jig rod. Medium to heavy spinning or baitcasting rod. Also handlines.	Boat or centrepin reel. Overhead, large threadline, baitcaster or sidecast.	8-20 kg	Dropper rigs above a heavy bottom sinker, running sinker rig or, more rarely, 'floater' bait.	3/0-7/0	Snapperlead, bomb, bean or barrel.	Cut fish, prawns, squid, small whole fish.

FISH SPECIES

TECHNIQUE	ROD	REEL	LINE	TERMINAL TACKLE	HOOK	WEIGHT	BAIT
Casting, fly fishing and, more rarely, trolling.	Ultra-light to light spinning or baitcaster rod. No. 6-8 fly rod.	Light threadline, closed-face or baitcaster. Light fly reel.	2-8 kg WF6-8 fly line	Lure, fly or hook tied directly to line. Minimal weight.	4-1/0	Smallest practical ball, bean or split shot.	Worms, shrimp, meat, lures and flies.

TECHNIQUE	ROD	REEL	LINE	TERMINAL TACKLE	HOOK	WEIGHT	BAIT
Shore and boat casting into aerated white water, bottom fishing and drifting.	Light to medium casting rods.	Medium threadline, baitcaster, sidecast or centrepin.	4-9 kg	Hook tied directly to line. Smallest possible sinker, or float. Running sinker rig.	6-1	Smallest practical ball, bean or split shot.	Fish flesh, prawns, squid, bread, worms.

Sweetlip *Lethrinus chrystostomus*

Natural Food

The red-throated sweetlip, sweetlip emperor or 'lipper' is a very important tropical and sub-tropical reef species taken in large numbers by party-boat customers and other anglers fishing in northern waters.

Sweetlip stray as far south as the New South Wales border at times, but are more prolific in northern reef waters, from about Rockhampton in the east to Carnarvon in the west. They are also taken in massive numbers at Norfolk Island.

Red-throated sweetlip commonly reach weights of a kilo or two, and may occasionally grow to three or even four kilos. The scarlet colouration in their fins, throat area and mouth lining is characteristic, and helps prevent confusion with other tropical species, including closely-related members of the emperor clan.

Sweetlip are caught primarily by boat anglers using offshore reef fishing techniques. In particular, they respond to weighted lines baited with fish flesh, small whole fish, squid or prawns. They are a highly rated table fish, not quite in the league of red emperor and coral trout, but nonetheless very tasty.

Tailor *Pomatomus saltatrix*

The tailor is widespread throughout the temperate and sub-tropical seas of the world. An identical fish occurs on the eastern seaboard of the United States, where it is called bluefish, while in South Africa this species is known as elf. Here in Australia, tailor are sometimes called choppers, skipjack or 'skippies'.

Tailor are found in sub-tropical, temperate and cool waters around the southern half of Australia, although they are uncommon in Victoria and rare in Tasmania. Tailor do not occur in New Zealand.

Tailor commonly reach weights of a kilo or two, and may occasionally grow much larger. Exceptional specimens in excess of 10 kilos have been recorded, although any tailor over six kilos is a prize catch.

Smaller tailor are a fish of our estuarine and inshore waters, occurring mostly in the lower reaches of larger tidal rivers, bays, inlets and harbours. Larger specimens are usually found over reefs and gravel beds extending offshore towards the edge of the Continental Shelf. They are also prolific at times in inshore waters adjacent to surf beaches, rocky shorelines, headlands and breakwalls.

Tailor form schools of varying sizes. Juvenile to mid-size specimens often congregate in very large numbers, feeding voraciously on shoals of pilchards, whitebait and other small forage fish. This activity creates foamy patches on the surface and attracts seagulls, terns and other sea birds.

Tailor are a very popular angling target. Fresh tailor which have been bled and cleaned promptly after capture are very tasty. They are also well suited to smoking.

Natural Food

TECHNIQUE	ROD	REEL	LINE	TERMINAL TACKLE	HOOK	WEIGHT	BAIT
Lightly weighted or float-suspended baits in an oily berley trail.	Ultra-light to light spinning, baitcaster or sidecast rods.	Ultra-light to light threadlines, closed-face, baitcaster, sidecast and centrepin.	1-5 kg	Tiny sinkers and/or a float, small hookks and light leaders.	10-4	Minimum practical ball, bean or split shot.	Maggots, worm pieces, prawn, cut fish and small lures.

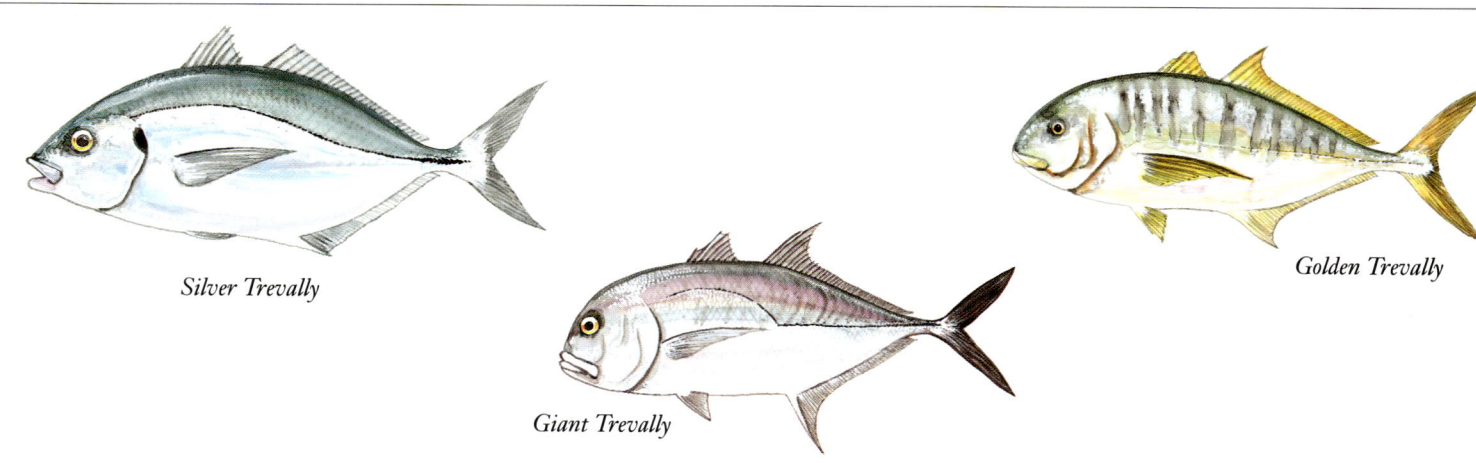

Silver Trevally

Giant Trevally

Golden Trevally

TECHNIQUE	ROD	REEL	LINE	TERMINAL TACKLE	HOOK	WEIGHT	BAIT
Silver: Casting and drifting various baits and sometimes lures.	Medium spinning, baitcaster or sidecast casting rod.	Medium threadline, baitcaster or sidecast.	3-10 kg	Hook tied directly to line. Minium weight on line.	4-3/0	Smallest practical ball or bean.	Various lures, cut and whole fish, prawns, squid, worms and octopus.
Tropical: Lure casting, trolling, jigging and bait fishing.	Medium to heavy spinning, baitcaster, sidecast or boat rod.	Medium to large threadline, baitcaster, sidecast or overhead.	4-18 kg	Heavy nylon or wire leader.	2/0-7/0	None, or bottom rig.	

TECHNIQUE	ROD	REEL	LINE	TERMINAL TACKLE	HOOK	WEIGHT	BAIT
Shore casting, spinning, trolling and drifting from boats with various baits and lures. Also fly fishing.	Light to medium spinning, baitcaster or sidecast rods, double-handed shore-casters, light boat and trolling rods. No. 8-10 fly rods.	Medium threadline, baitcaster and sidecast reels, light overheads. Fly reels.	4-10 kg WF8-10 fly lines	Ganged (linked) hooks and/or heavy nylon or wire leaders.	1/0-6/0	Sufficient ball, bean or barrel.	Whole or cut fish, squid, lures and flies.

Tommy Ruff *Arripis georgianus*

Natural Food

The Tommy ruff, rough or Australian herring is very closely related to the Australian salmon or kahawai (*A. trutta*). Indeed, many people mistake Tommy ruff for juvenile salmon.

Tommy ruff are found in temperate and cool waters around the southern half of Australia, rarely straying as far north as the New South Wales coast, or as far south as Tasmania. They are most prolific in South Australia and the south west corner of Western Australia.

Tommy ruff are small fish, rarely exceeding 300 grams in weight, although occasionally reaching twice that size. Rare examples may approach 800 grams or even a kilo in size.

What these little fish lack in size, they more than make up for in numbers. Massive schools are commonplace, and large catches are possible, especially in bays, harbours and relatively shallow inshore areas.

Ruff are caught mostly by anglers using relatively light tackle, fine lines and small hooks. They respond best to lightly weighted, unweighted or float-suspended baits of worm or prawn pieces, strips of fish flesh, pieces of squid or live maggots. A berley of soaked bread, pollard or boiled wheat mixed with a little tuna oil is very beneficial in attracting and holding a school. In certain areas, anglers use a berley-dispensing float called a 'blob'.

The Tommy ruff has somewhat dark, oily flesh, but is very tasty and enjoys great popularity as a table fish, especially in South and West Australia. They are best grilled, but are also ideal for smoking and pickling. Tommy ruff also make excellent bait for larger fish; alive, dead or cut up.

Trevally

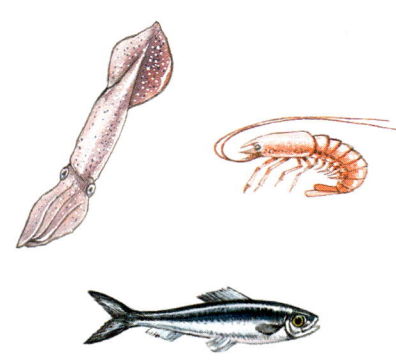

Natural Food

Several species of that branch of the *Carangidae* family known as trevally are important to Australasian anglers. These include the silver or white trevally (*Psuedocaranx dentex*) of southern waters, and tropical species such as the giant trevally (*Caranx ignobilis*) and the golden trevally (*Gnathanodon speciosus*).

Silver trevally, which are called skipjack or 'skippy' in parts of Western Australia, are found in large numbers in sub-tropical, temperate and cool waters around the southern half of Australia and much of New Zealand. They commonly reach weights of a kilo or two, and may occasionally grow much larger. The biggest specimens come from Lord Howe Island, some weighing over 11 kilos.

Silver trevally are a popular angling species, taken mostly in larger estuaries, harbours, inlets, bays and over inshore reefs. They are captured by both shore-based and boat fishermen.

Cleaned promptly after capture, silver trevally are a fair to good table fish.

The tropical trevallies are a large group, including the giant and golden trevallies already mentioned, plus less well-known varieties such as the big-eye trevally (*Caranx sexfasciatus*), bluefin trevally (*C. melampygus*) and the gold-spotted trevally or turrum (*C. fulvoguttatus*).

All of these tropical trevallies tend to grow larger than their southern counterpart. Giant trevally, in particular, are very big fish, commonly reaching a metre or more in length. Exceptional specimens may occasionally top 45 kilos.

Smaller tropical trevally — particularly goldens — are very good table fish. Larger specimens of giant trevally may be a little dry and coarse.

The Trout Family

Three species of introduced fish known as trout occur in Australasian waters. They are the brown trout *(Salmo trutta)*, the rainbow trout *(Oncorhyncus mykiss)* and the brook trout *(Salvelinus fontinalis)*. The last species named is actually a char rather than a true trout, although this distinction is largely academic from the fisherman's point of view.

All of these salmonids were originally introduced to Australia and New Zealand from the Northern Hemisphere during the second half of the nineteenth century. Brown trout are native to Europe, while rainbows and brook trout both come from North America.

Brown and rainbow trout have thrived in many Australasian waters, especially cooler alpine and sub-alpine streams and hydro-electric storage dams. Brook trout have fared less favourably, although isolated stocks do exist in some Australian and New Zealand waterways.

Trout in streams and smaller rivers are relatively small fish, rarely exceeding a kilo in weight, although occasionally reaching twice that size. Generally, they grow larger in lakes and dams, very occasionally approaching 10 kilos in some waters. However, any trout over four kilos is a real prize.

Trout prefer clean, running fresh water with a reasonably high oxygen content and a diversity of food types. They need such conditions in which to spawn and obtain their maximum growth potential, although they will also survive in some 'marginal' waters that were once considered to be too warm or turbid. Generally, the brown trout is the most resilient of the three species mentioned.

In Australia, trout are confined to the highlands and western slopes of New South Wales, Victoria, south eastern South Australia and the southern corner of Western Australia. They also thrive throughout Tasmania. Trout have found New Zealand waters even more to their liking, and this island nation now boasts some of the finest trout fishing in the world. Although most Australasian trout stocks are land-locked, small sea-run populations do occur, mainly in western Victoria, Tasmania and New Zealand.

Trout are a very popular angling target, pursued by large numbers of fishermen representing all levels of experience and commitment.

Trout of all species and sizes are highly regarded by gourmets, although some people prefer the taste of saltwater fish. The tastiest trout are generally those with orange or pink flesh — a result of dietary components. Trout flesh is well suited to smoking, salt or sugar curing and pickling.

Natural Food

Southern Bluefin Tuna

Skipjack Tuna

Longtail Tuna

Yellowfin Tuna

TECHNIQUE	ROD	REEL	LINE	TERMINAL TACKLE	HOOK	WEIGHT	BAIT
Skipjack: Trolling, casting and drifting with lures and small baits.	Light to medium boat, sport and game rods. Medium spinning rods.	Overheads, baitcasters and spinning reels.	4-15 kg	Heavier nylon leaders if using lighter main lines.	2/0-6/0	None	Trolling and casting lures, small live and dead fish, cut fish and pilchards.
Bluefin/yellowfin: Trolling, casting and drifting with baits and lures.	Medium to heavy sport and game rods, heavy spinning rods.	Overheads, game reels and large spinning or baitcaster reels.	8-37 kg	Heavy nylon leaders, backed by doubles.	5/0-10/0	Smallest necessary barrel.	

Brown Trout

Rainbow Trout

TECHNIQUE	ROD	REEL	LINE	TERMINAL TACKLE	HOOK	WEIGHT	BAIT
Stream: Casting lures, flies and baits.	Ultra-light spinning rod, or No. 2-7 fly rod.	Ultra-light threadline, closed face or fly reel.	1-4 kg DT2-7 fly line.	Lure, fly or hook tied directly to lightest practical line or leader.	18-8	None, or tiny ball or shot.	Worms, insects, minnows,
Lake: Casting, trolling and drifting with lures, flies and baits.	Light spinning or baitcasting rod, or No. 5-9 fly rod.	Light threadline, closed-face, baitcaster or fly reel.	2-6 kg DT or WF5-9 fly lines.	As above, plus occasional use of paravanes, attractors and similar devices.	12-4	Smallest practical ball or bean.	manufactured baits, lures and flies.

The Tuna Family

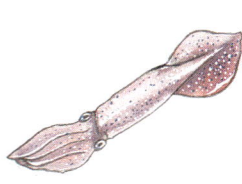

Natural Food

As well as the albacore, which was dealt with separately, there are six tuna species of interest to anglers in Australia and New Zealand. They are: the dogtooth tuna *(Gymnosarda unicolor)*, longtail or northern bluefin tuna *(Thunnus tonggol)*, mackerel tuna or kawa-kawa *(Euthynus affinis)*, southern bluefin tuna *(T. maccoyii)*, striped tuna or skipjack *(Katsuwonis pelamis)*, and the yellowfin tuna *(T. albacares)*.

The three most significant of these are the skipjack, southern bluefin and yellowfin.

Skipjack

The skipjack is widely known in Australia as the striped tuna or 'stripey'. In New Zealand it is sometimes called 'tunny', and in both countries it is erroneously referred to as bonito.

Skipjack are a small tuna which form large schools. They spawn in the tropics, but range deep into southern waters during summer and autumn.

Skipjack average one to four kilos, with occasional specimens exceeding seven kilos. In other parts of the world they have been recorded to 20 kilos!

Whilst they are an important canning, skipjack are not greatly favoured as table fare by most Australasian anglers.

Southern Bluefin Tuna

The southern bluefin tuna has a circum-polar distribution, being caught off South Africa and South America, as well as Australia and New Zealand.

Although southern bluefin once formed vast schools, they were fished to the brink of extinction during the 1960s and '70s. Only now are they beginning to make a slow comeback in certain areas.

Southern bluefin are large tuna, occasionally reaching two metres and at least 170 kilos. Highly rated by the canning and fish processing industries, southern bluefin are also one of the finest tuna for the preparation of sashimi (Japanese-style raw fish).

Yellowfin Tuna

Yellowfin tuna are a pelagic, migratory Indo-Pacific species with an extensive range. They are found in tropical and subtropical waters around the northern half of Australia, but make seasonal forays into cooler southern waters, ranging as far south as Tasmania and New Zealand's Bay of Plenty.

Yellowfin are mostly encountered in deeper, oceanic waters, near the edges of the Continental Shelf and beyond. However, favourable currents and water conditions will occasionally carry them inshore.

These are large tuna, regularly attaining weights of 50 to 100 kilos in our waters and occasionally approaching 120 kilos. .

Yellowfin have pinkish-red meat that cooks to near-white.

Wahoo *Acanthocybium solandri*

The wahoo is a fast, exciting game fish found in tropical and sub-tropical waters around the northern half of Australia, as well as elsewhere in the world. It also makes seasonal forays into temperate and cool waters, occasionally travelling as far south as Perth, Eden and the northern tip of New Zealand.

Although vaguely similar to the Spanish mackerel in body shape, wahoo are distinguished by their more cylindrical cross section, short, upright tail lobes and the even height of their first dorsal fin.

Wahoo regularly attain lengths approaching two metres and weights in excess of 20 kilos. They have been recorded to 50 or 60 kilos around Fiji and Tahiti. In Australia, most of those caught weigh between eight and 25 kilos.

Wahoo are encountered in deeper, oceanic waters, near the edges of the Continental Shelf. However, favourable currents and water conditions will occasionally carry them closer to shore.

These fish have wickedly sharp teeth set in scissor-like jaws and should be handled with extreme care at all times.

Wahoo respond to a wide range of angling techniques, including bait fishing, lure casting, trolling and fly fishing. They are caught primarily by boat anglers using a variety of offshore fishing techniques. In particular, they are taken as an incidental catch whilst trolling for marlin and tuna.

Wahoo have delicious white meat and are at least the equal of the tropical mackerels in the culinary department. The slug-like intestinal parasites often found in their gut have no detrimental effect on these fish.

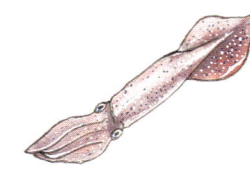

Natural Food

Whiting

Two species of whiting are especially important to Australian fishermen. They are the King George or spotted whiting (*Sillaginodes punctatus*) of cool, southern seas, and the sand, silver or yellowfin whiting (*Sillago ciliata*) of warmer temperate and sub-tropical waters. Other species such as Queensland's winter whiting (*S. maculata*) and Western Australia's yellow-finned whiting (*S. schomburgkii*) are of regional significance.

The King George whiting is by far our largest representative of this family, occasionally exceeding a kilo and even reaching two or three kilos in very rare instances. This is in contrast to the other whiting mentioned, which rarely top 400 grams.

King George whiting are found in temperate and cool waters around the southern half of Australia, being most prolific in Victoria, South Australia and Western Australia. They live mainly in estuarine and inshore waters, particularly favouring the relatively shallow sand and gravel flats or sea grass beds found in southern bays.

Sand or yellowfin whiting, on the other hand, are most prolific along the eastern seaboard of Australia, from the central coast of Queensland to Green Cape or Wilsons Promontory.

Yellow-finned whiting occur between similar latitudes on the west coast. As well as occurring in estuaries and bays, both these fish are found in the surf line along ocean beaches.

All of these whiting are a very popular angling targets and are highly rated table fish, none more so than the King George, which is rated by many experts as Australia's most delicious fish species!

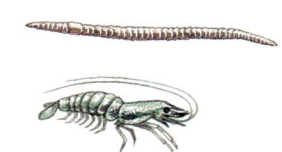
Natural Food

TECHNIQUE	ROD	REEL	LINE	TERMINAL TACKLE	HOOK	WEIGHT	BAIT
Casting or drifting small, soft baits on lightly-weighted or float-suspended lines. Also spinning and jigging with tiny lures. Usually with berley.	Ultra-light to light spinning or sidecast rod.	Ultra-light to light threadline, closed-face, sidecast or centrepin.	1-5 kg	Hook tied directly to line. Minimal weight or float.	14-8 (long shank)	None, or tiny ball or shot.	Mince meat, prawn, worm pieces, dough, bread, maggots, fish strips.

FISH SPECIES

TECHNIQUE	ROD	REEL	LINE	TERMINAL TACKLE	HOOK	WEIGHT	BAIT
Trolling, drifting and very occasionally casting in offshore waters with lures and baits.	6-24 kg class sport or game trolling rods. Double-handed overhead casting or jig rods.	Overhead casting, game and large capacity threadline reels.	6-24 kg	Stout wire leaders essential to prevent bite-offs.	4/0-9/0	None, or fixed bean or barrel on wire leader.	Trolling lures, whole small fish, squid.

TECHNIQUE	ROD	REEL	LINE	TERMINAL TACKLE	HOOK	WEIGHT	BAIT
Shore casting and boat fishing with various small, soft baits.	Ultra-light to light spinning, baitcaster or sidecast rod. Also handlines.	Ultra-light to light threadline, closed face and sidecast.	2-6 kg	Line tied directly to hook. Minimum weight on line.	6-2 (long shank)	Minimum practical ball, bean or barrel.	Worms, prawns, cockles (pipis), nippers (yabbies), squid.

Yellowtail *Trachurus novaezelandiae*

Natural Food

The yellowtail, yellowtail scad, yakka, chow or bung is prolific in the cooler waters around the southern half of Australia. A near identical fish — the koheru — is found in New Zealand.

The yellowtail belongs to a large group of fish including the very similar cowanyoung, horse mackerel or jack mackerel (*T. declivis*). This latter species is very common off Tasmania and New Zealand, forming huge schools which ripple the surface as they swim.

Yellowtail are small fish, rarely exceeding 300 grams in weight, although occasionally reaching twice that size. They are a fish of our estuarine and inshore waters, occurring mostly in the lower reaches of larger tidal rivers, bays, inlets and harbours, and over reefs and gravel beds extending offshore towards the edge of the Continental Shelf.

Yellowtail are caught mostly by anglers using relatively light tackle, fine lines and small hooks. Best baits include prawn and worm pieces, squid strips, mince, bread and dough. Yellowtail will also strike at small lures, flies and multi-hook bait jig rigs.

This species is very popular among junior anglers fishing from wharves and piers, and with sport and game fishermen seeking live or dead baits for larger predators. The flesh of yellowtail is edible and quite tasty — especially when smoked — but the species is rarely eaten due to its diminutive size.

Techniques

One of the most fascinating aspects of angling is the fact that its participants never stop learning, now matter how long they are involved with the sport. It is this feature, above all others, that best explains the captivating charm of fishing.

Ironically, the basic and essential techniques needed to catch fish — rigging up, knot tying, baiting and casting — are relatively simple to master. However, beyond those basics there are so many subtleties involved in angling that they will go on filling magazines, instructional videos and books like this one year after year, for as long as there are men and women to cast a line and fish to be caught.

Partly in response to the scope of these angling subtleties, more experienced fishermen tend to fall into two vaguely defined groups: the specialists and the jacks-of-all-trades.

Specialists devote the greatest part of their angling effort to mastering a fish species, a specific class of tackle, a type of environment, or even a single location. Some will combine several of these avenues of specialisation. Thus, we have fly casters who pursue trout in just one or two rivers with a small selection of flies, or blackfish devotees who drift their handmade floats along the same breakwall all their lives.

At the opposite end of the angling spectrum are those individuals who are forever seeking a new challenge; be it an exotic fish, a faraway destination, a revolutionary new style of tackle, or a different way of catching familiar species.

In our earlier years as anglers, most of us fall somewhere between those two extremes — concentrating primarily on one or two styles of fishing, but willing to give something else a try if it comes along. Later, as our expertise increases, we tend to gravitate in one direction or the other: towards greater specialisation, or increased versatility.

Whilst there is much to be said for specialisation, the angler who narrows his or her perspective too far tends to miss out on many things. There are a multitude of parallels and overlaps in angling technique, and smart, versatile anglers are constantly picking up ideas from one branch of the sport and applying them to others — often with spectacular results! Unless you occasionally practice different types of fishing, or at least read and talk about them, you will miss out on discovering many of these subtleties.

Recent examples of this flow-on from one branch of fishing to another include things like the growth of saltwater fly fishing — which initially developed as an offshoot of its freshwater counterpart — and the application of European-style 'coarse' fishing strategies to estuary bream angling or bait fishing for trout. These are just a couple of the more obvious instances where techniques, strategies and tackle from one branch of the sport have been taken, modified where necessary, and applied elsewhere.

The widespread availability of fishing magazines, books and videos from other countries has greatly accelerated this interchange of information. However, at the grass roots level, much of this adaptation of techniques to fit new scenarios springs from individual anglers talking to each other and trying something new.

All of these subtleties in technique, and the fact that new twists are coming along all the time, may seem a little daunting to the newcomer. Don't despair — the fundamental importance of tying a good knot, using a sharp hook and selecting the best bait remains as important as ever! Anglers who stick to those fundamentals will always catch fish, regardless of whether they embrace the latest 'fashion' in technique or tackle.

For that reason, this chapter begins with basic and not-so-basic knots and rigs before moving on to more specific analyses of modern angling styles such as jigging, bluewater trolling, saltwater fly fishing and land-based gamefishing.

As you read the chapter, remember that many of the strategies contained in it may be of little more than academic interest to you. On the other hand, be constantly on the look-out for gems of information from other branches of the sport that may be readily applicable to your favourite styles of fishing.

And remember, you never stop learning!

Basic Knots

There is a great deal of truth in the adage which states that the most important factors in fishing are a sharp hook and a good knot. Sophisticated tackle, fresh bait and the best of local knowledge all count for nothing if these basics are overlooked.

Lines which break mysteriously are a common symptom of failed knots. Too often, anglers blame their tackle for such failures, claiming that the line was of poor quality, or too light in breaking strain. In the vast majority of cases, these break-offs may actually be traced back to knot failure.

There are literally dozens of knots suitable for use in modern nylon monofilament line, but a handful of proven knots are both strong and relatively easy to tie, even in adverse conditions such as wind, rain, cold and darkness. These are the 'essential' knots which all anglers should know. Try the knots on these pages. Decide which ones you like best, and then practice them.

As important as it is to know a handful of essential knots, it is even more vital to adhere to a few basic rules that apply to all knots tied in nylon monofilament line.

The first rule is to check the working end of the line for nicks, chafes and flat spots before you begin to tie a knot or make up a rig. Do this by running it through your fingers or across your tongue. This is especially important if the previous rig was broken off on a snag or fish. Secondly, as you tie the knot, be sure to thoroughly lubricate it with water or saliva. This is best done by giving the half-tied knot a lick before tightening it.

Thirdly, draw the knot tight with slow, steady pressure, avoiding any sudden jerks. Snug the turns right down and test the knot by increasing the pressure smoothly until the force exerted is close to half the breaking strain of the line. This step is critical in drawing the knot really tight, and will prevent it from slipping later.

Finally, trim the tag end off the knot, leaving roughly half a centimetre for any slight slippage under load. This tag may be a fraction shorter in very light lines, and a shade longer in heavy lines.

TERMINAL KNOTS

The commonest knots used in fishing are those employed to tie on items of terminal tackle such as hooks, lures, flies, swivels, rings and sinkers. These are the connections all anglers should practise and perfect until they can be tied in total darkness, a feat which is not as difficult as it sounds!

HALF BLOOD KNOT

This popular connection is also called the Clinch Knot. It is a very widely used terminal knot. It is easy to tie and secure.

To commence the knot, pass the line through the eye of the hook, swivel, ring or lure and then wrap the tag end back around the main line five or six times as shown.

Pass the tag back through the loop, lubricate the entire knot with saliva and draw it tight by pulling evenly on both the tag end and the main line to begin with, then on the main line alone.

When the knot has been very firmly tightened and tested, trim the tag end off to half a centimetre or so.

IMPROVED HALF BLOOD KNOT

For more demanding situat-ons, the basic Half Blood or Clinch Knot may be improved to ensure greater retained line strength, and to reduce the chances of slippage. This improved version is a little more complicated, but well worth the effort when dealing with large fish or using very light lines.

To tie the Improved Half Blood Knot, the tag end is first passed through the eyelet twice, as illustrated, taken back around the main line five or six times, then back through the double loop, in much the same manner as a standard Half Blood Knot.

Next, the knot is 'locked' as shown, by passing the tag end through the larger loop. This greatly reduces the risk of slippage in the finished knot.

Once lubricated and thoroughly tightened, the tag end of this knot may be cut off very short without risk of slippage.

UNI KNOT

The Uni Knot, or Hang-man's Noose, is a viable alternative to the Half Blood Knot, and is preferred by many anglers, particularly as it is an easier hitch to tie in heavy, stiff lines. A well-tied Uni Knot pre-serves a very high percentage of the line's strength, and is less likely to slip than a basic Half Blood Knot.

To tie a Uni Knot, pass the end of the line through the eyelet and form a backhand loop alongside the main line, as indicated. Next, pass the tag end through the loop and around the two parallel strands four to six times (three turns are sufficient in very heavy lines over about 30 kilos breaking strain).

Lubricate the turns of line with saliva, then draw the knot tight slowly and steadily, pulling on both the tag end and the main line to begin with, then just the main line. When it is securely tightened, trim the tag off to about half a centimetre.

JOINING KNOTS

After terminal knots, the next most important hitches are

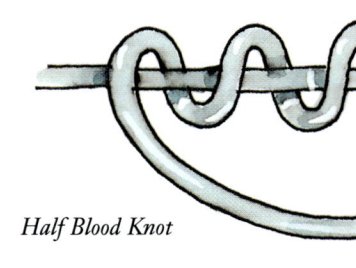

Half Blood Knot

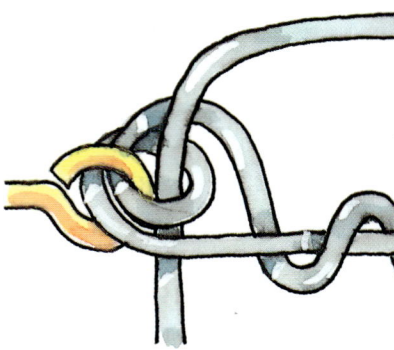

Improved Half Blood Knot

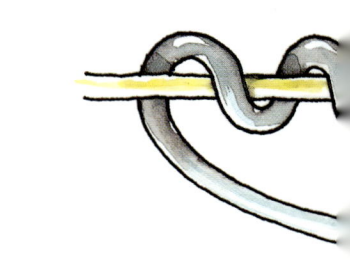

those used to join two lengths of line together. These are employed when a tangle or damaged section must be cut away, when 'top-shotting' with fresh line, or when connecting a heavier trace or lighter leader directly to the main line without a swivel or ring.

Just as with terminal knots, all joining knots should be lubricated, drawn tight smoothly, tested and trimmed before use.

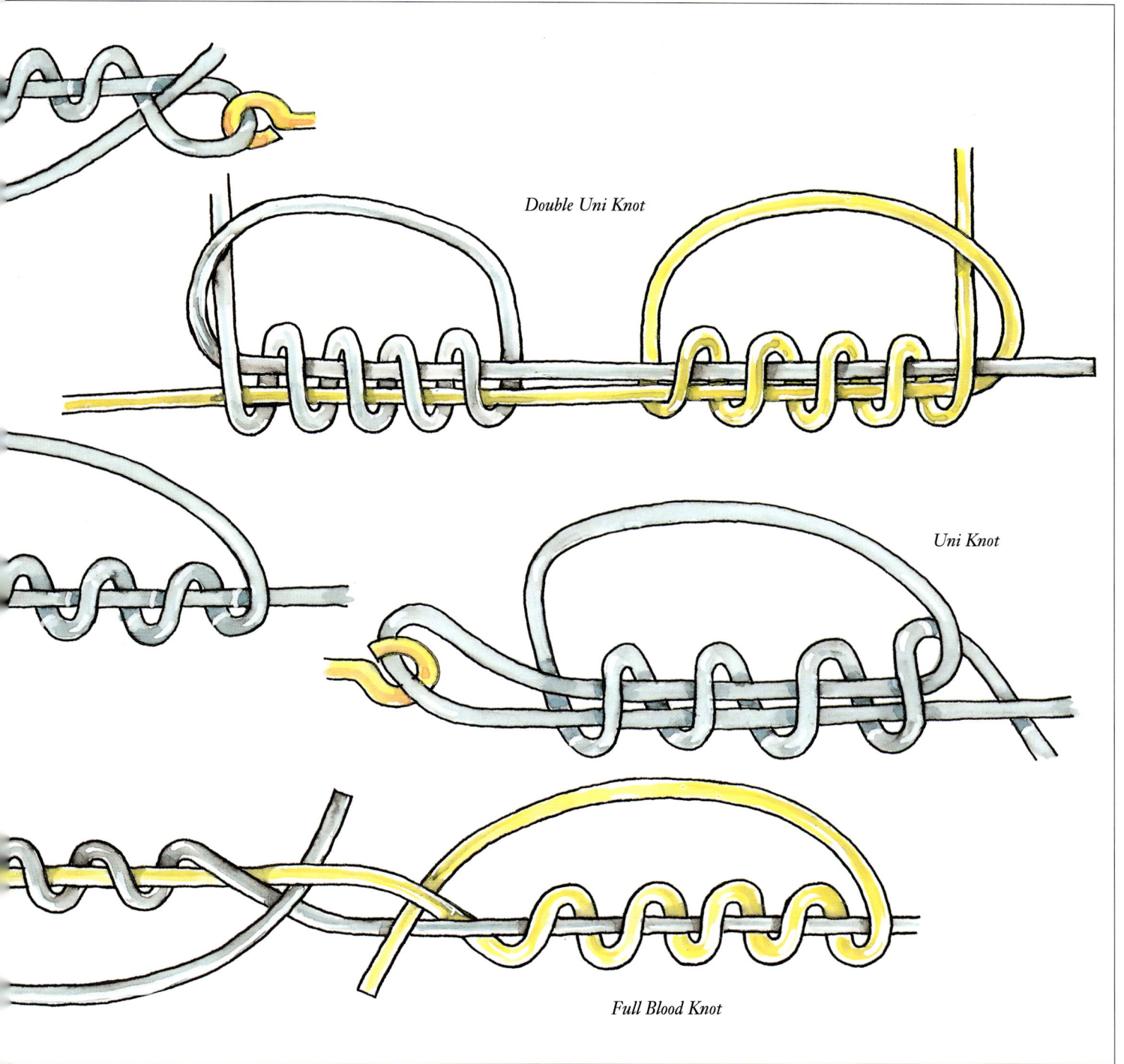

Double Uni Knot

Uni Knot

Full Blood Knot

FULL BLOOD KNOT
As the name implies, this connection utilises two Half Blood Knots to join two lengths of line. The Full Blood Knot is best suited for connecting lines of a similar or identical breaking strain, however it may also be used to join light line to heavy by first doubling over the thinner line before commencing the knot.

To tie a Full Blood Knot, cross the two strands of line 15 or 20 centimetres back from their tag ends. Next, wrap one strand around the other five times before passing is back between the two lines as shown.

Repeat this procedure on the other side, this time passing the tag through the middle from the opposite side.

Lubricate the knot with saliva and draw it tight steadily, test with firm, steady pressure, and then trim the tags off to less than half a centimetre.

DOUBLE UNI KNOT
Fans of the standard Uni Knot will find the Double Uni to be a superb connection for two lines of a similar strength. It is at least as strong as the Full Blood Knot and, as a bonus, the tags may be trimmed even closer without risk of slippage.

First, lay the two ends to be joined alongside each other with a 20 to 30 centimetre overlap. Tie one tag end around the other main line with a standard Uni Knot.

Repeat this operation with the other tag end. Now, as well as lubricating the two individual knots, lick the strands of line between them. Draw the two Uni Knots tight and slide the them together. Tighten, test and trim the tags to a couple of millimetres.

Advanced Knots

The basic knots described on the preceding pages will satisfy the vast majority of your angling needs, particularly in freshwater, estuary, beach, rock and inshore fishing. However, as your level of angling sophistication increases, additional knots and connections may be needed to obtain optimum results.

SPIDER HITCH
This knot is also known as the 'Cairns Quickie', and is very simple way to tie a doubled line once mastered, but not quite as strong as the Bimini Twist.

To tie a Spider Hitch, double the required length of line, then form a backhand look at the top as shown, holding the loop between thumb and forefinger.

Next, take the doubled length of line and wrap it five or six times around the end of your thumb, working from the back towards the front.

Now, take the end of the double, pass it through the loop, lubricate, and pull tight slowly, allowing the turns to slip off your thumb one at a time.

Draw the knot tight, test it, and trim the tag.

BIMINI TWIST
This is a very strong double knot, although somewhat cumbersome to tie single-handed when a double line longer than a metre is required.

Double the desired length of line and then twist it 20 to 25 times as indicated. Widen the loop between the double strands to force the twisted area down.

Now, as you continue to spread the two strands, pull the tag end out at 90 degrees to the twists until the tag begins to wrap back in tight spirals over the twisted line. Maintain pressure until the spiral reaches the end of the twists.

Grasp the knot here to stop it unravelling, then take a half hitch around one leg of the double, then around both strands together. Make several more half hitches around both strands, lubricating them as they are pulled tight. Trim the tag.

BLOOD BIGHT DROPPER
This strong, easy-to-tie loop is ideal for making up bottom fishing rigs which employ one or more hooks above a sinker.

To construct a Blood Bight, double the required length of line as shown, take the doubled end back around the doubled strands three to five times, then back through the loop at the end. Lubricate and pull tight with a strong, even pressure.

PERFECTION LOOP
Certain fishing applications demand the use of a small loop at the end of the line to allow the item of terminal tackle some mobility. This is particularly important when tying lures or flies to fairly stiff lines or leaders that might restrict their action.

One of the better loop knots for this purpose is the Perfection Loop which, although a little complicated at first glance, can be tied in most lines, even very thick mono.

It should be noted that the Perfection Loop does not offer quite as much retained line strength as a Uni or Half Blood Knot and should not be tied in very light lines. It is really at its best when formed in a leader

To tie a Perfection Loop, form a large, loose overhand or 'granny' knot in the line at least 20 centimetres from the end.

Next, pass the tag end through the eyelet of the lure or fly and back through the overhand knot, making sure to return from the same side of the overhand knot as the tag end originally emerged from.

Now, take the tag end behind the main line as shown and up from beneath. The next step is the most difficult to describe; as it involves pinching together the two strands of line emerging from the overhand knot and bringing the tag end through the loop from behind, over the two strands and out through the loop again.

To complete this knot, lubricate it with saliva, draw the turns tight, test it with strong, steady pressure and trim the tag.

MILLER'S SHOCK KNOT
A useful, easy knot for joining lighter line or doubles to a heavy trace of nylon or nylon-coated wire. The advantage of this connection over a swivel or ring is that it may be cranked through the rod runners and cast with minimal bumping.

To tie this Shock Knot, form an overhand or 'granny' knot in the heavy leader material. Pass the lighter line (single or doubled) through the overhand knot and then draw the overhand knot partially tight.

Tie a Uni Knot around the heavy leader with the lighter line. Lubricate the Uni Knot, tighten it, and slide it hard up against the overhand knot.

Next, pull the overhand knot up very tight (use pliers if necessary) and trim both ends.

WIRE TIES
Wire is often used at the working end of rigs intended for toothed or sharp-gilled species such as sharks, mackerel, wahoo, large flathead and barramundi. Commercially-made wire traces are available, but many anglers prefer to make up their own.
Three types of wire account for most traces used in this country. They are: non-coated multi-strand; nylon coated multi-strand, and single strand strand.
Multi-strand wires are most often crimped with metal sleeves or 'swages', which are squeezed onto the trace using a special tool. Multi-strand wire may also be knotted, and the nylon coated version lends itself to heat welding. Single strand wire is nearly always twisted.

CRIMPING
The most basic form of crimping involves running a sleeve onto the wire, passing the tag end of the wire through a swivel, hook eye, ring or whatever, pushing it back into the sleeve and crimping that sleeve firmly in place with a special tool available from your local tackle store.

Remember are that the sleeve size should be matched to the thickness of the wire (so that the two strands only just fit into it), and the sleeve must be firmly

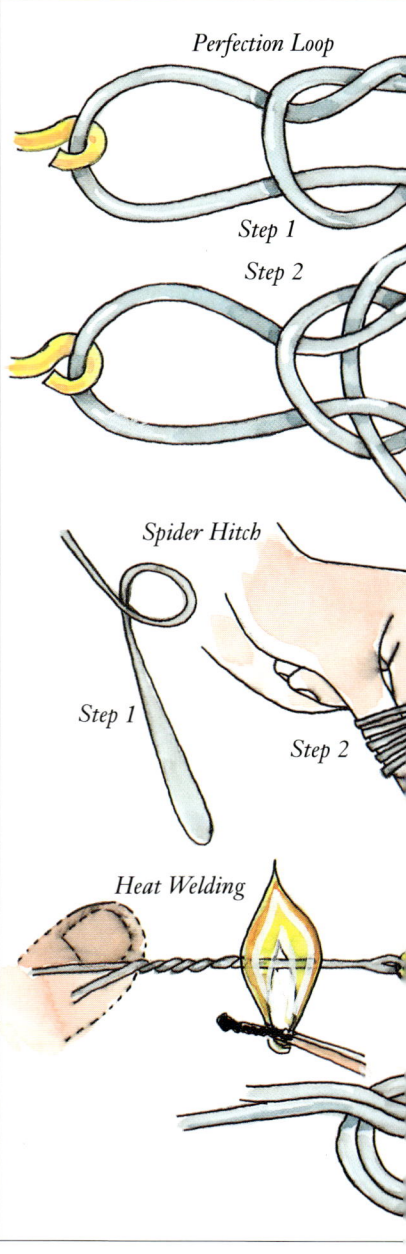

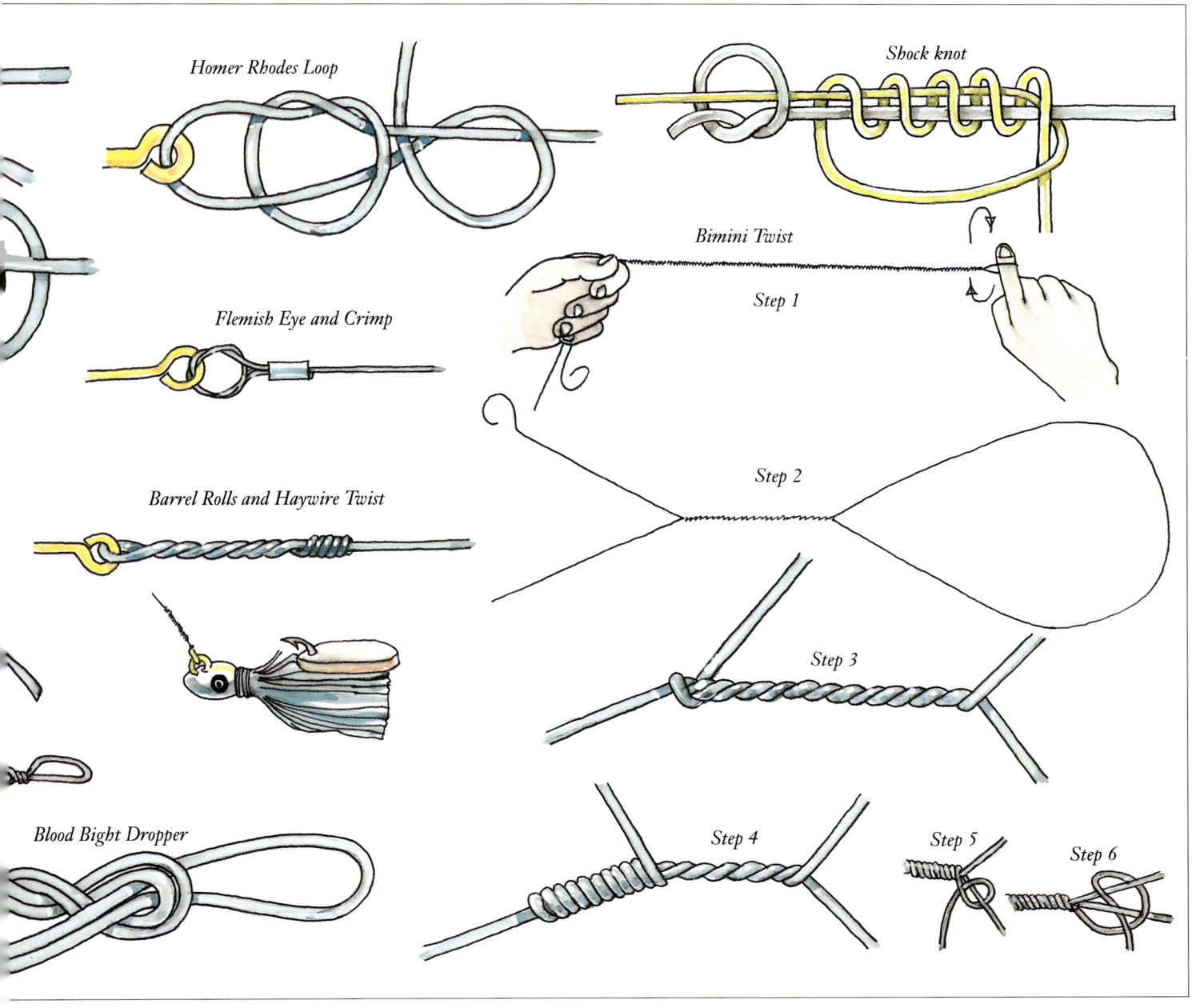

crimped in place using the correct recess in the tool.

FLEMISH EYE
For more demanding applications, such as heavy tackle angling for sharks and large gamefish, the wire passing through the eyelet of the hook or swivel should be formed into a Flemish Eye before the sleeve or sleeves are crimped in place.

The Flemish Eye will tighten under load, and even if the wire should slip through the sleeve, there is a good chance that the Flemish Eye itself will hold.

HOMER RHODE'S LOOP
This quick, easy loop knot can be used in nylon as well as multi-strand wire, but because it cuts the line's strength almost in half, it is best reserved for wire and very heavy nylon leaders.

To tie the Homer Rhode's Loop, form a loose overhand or 'granny' knot in the wire or heavy mono, pass the tag end through the hook, ring or swivel, back through the overhand knot, and then form another overhand knot with the tag end on the main line above the first. Lubricate, draw tight and trim.

HEAT WELDING
All nylon coated multi-strand wires may be heat welded to give a quick and surprisingly strong connection.

To heat weld coated wire, pass the end through the item of terminal tackle and twist the tag and main length of wire together for five centimetres or so.

Expose this twisted section of wire to the flame from a cigarette lighter, candle or match, turning the twists as the nylon coating melts and fuses. The longer the welded section, the stronger the bond.

HAYWIRE TWISTS AND BARREL ROLLS
The accepted method of forming connections in single strand wires — both stainless and galvanised — is to form Haywire Twists and Barrel Rolls after passing the tag end through the tem of tackle.

To form Haywire Twists, cross the two strands of wire at 45 degrees and wind them tightly around each other for two or three centimetres.

Next, straighten up the main strand and bend the tag end out at 90 degrees before wrapping it tightly and evenly around the main strand in six to eight neat, even Barrel Rolls.

To finish the tie the tag may be bent into a little crank handle which can be twisted to break off flush with the rolls.

Estuary and Harbour Rigs

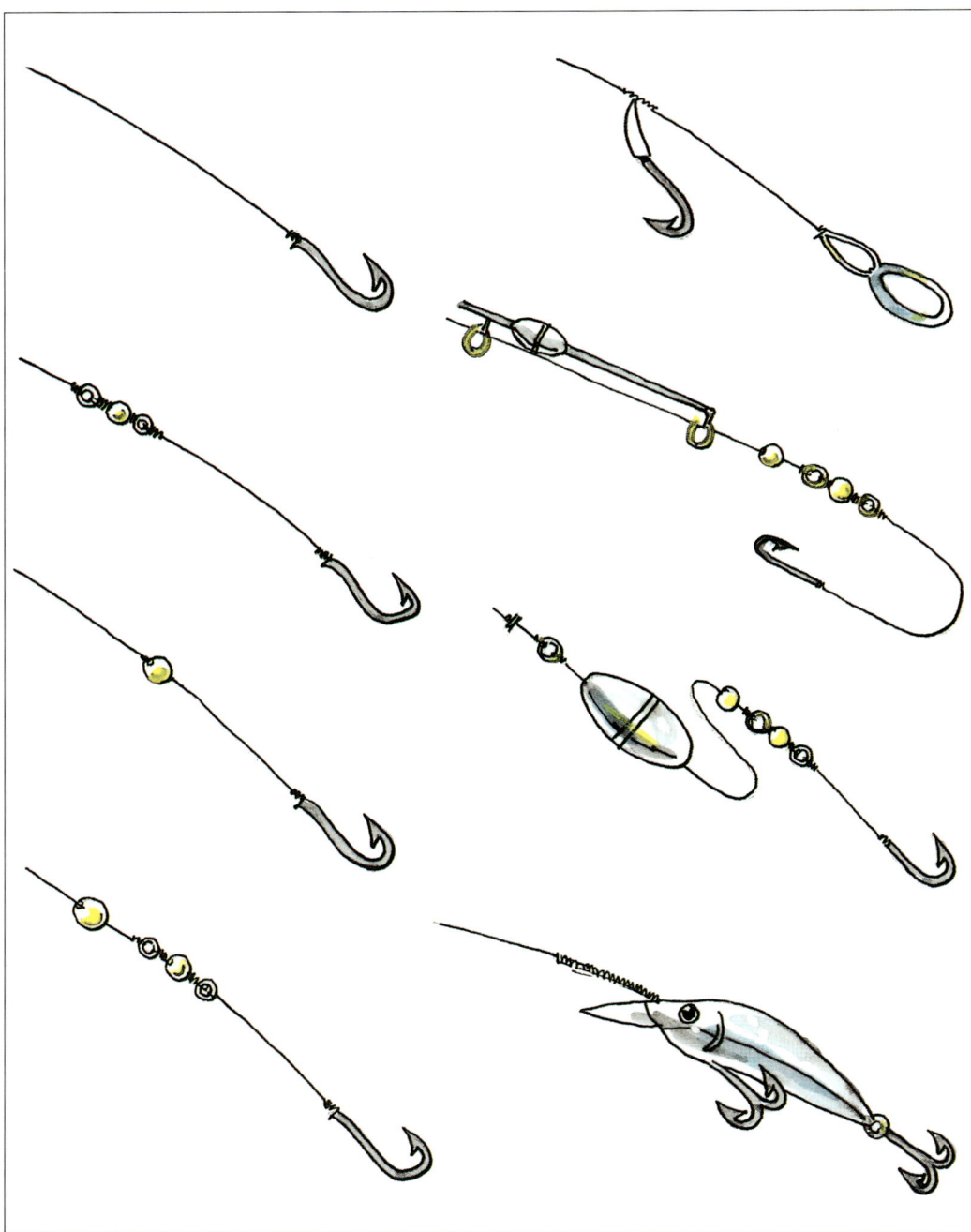

Being able to select and tie the best rig for the prevailing conditions and likely target species is a skill that develops with time on and around the water. It is one of the factors which separates experienced anglers from novices.

The best time and place to make decisions about rigging is at the fishing spot itself, just prior to commencing fishing.

Only then is it possible to accurately judge conditions of weather, water depth, tidal flow and so on, all of which ultimately dictate rig requirements.

For estuary, harbour and bay fishing in Australia and New Zealand, the simplest rigs are often the best. Those shown on these two pages will satisfy at least 90 per cent of your angling requirements for popular estuary species such as bream, flathead, whiting, smaller snapper, luderick and mulloway.

NO-SINKER RIG

This is the simplest of all fishing rigs: a sharp hook tied directly to the end of your main line!

Naturally, this rig is only applicable where short casts are sufficient to reach the fish, and where there is minimal current or tidal flow. However, those conditions often prevail in quiet estuary backwaters, around 'slack water' at the change of the tide, and on still nights.

This rig is often deadly on bream, snapper and school mulloway, and may be used with baits ranging from live blood worms or whole prawns to fish flesh strips or live 'poddy' mullet. Hook sizes should be adjusted to suit the bait and target species.

NO-SINKER RIG AND SWIVEL

If you are using a sidecast or spinning reel which may induce line twist, or your bait is likely to spin when retrieved through the water, add a small swivel to your rig. This may be tied in anywhere from 15 to 50 or 60 centimetres above the hook.

As well as reducing or eliminating line twist, a swivel adds a tiny amount of weight to this rig, helping to cast the bait further and holding it down in slight currents or tidal flows.

As a bonus, you can easily use a length of line that is thicker or thinner than your main line between the swivel and hook. A lighter hook link may be advantageous when pursuing small, finicky species such as whiting and bream, while a heavier length of line will reduce bite-offs from fish such as flathead and leatherjackets.

RUNNING SINKER RIG

When you need to add weight to a rig in order to cast it further, or carry it down through the water column in a tidal flow or current, it is often best to simply run one or more sinkers on the line above the hook.

Ball, bean, barrel or bug style sinkers are best for this purpose, and you should use the smallest sizes practical for the prevailing conditions. Often, it is better to use two small sinkers rather than a single, larger one.

When such a rig is retrieved and cast, the sinker will sit right on top of the knot or hook eye. However, as soon as the rig enters the water, the sinker will slide away up the line, descending through the water faster than the bait. This makes for a very natural presentation.

If using a sidecast reel, tie a swivel in above the sinker, at least 60 centimetres to one metre back from the hook.

RUNNING SINKER AND SWIVEL RIG

One of the most popular of all Australasian fishing rigs involves the use of a short (20 to 60 centimetre) hook link below a swivel, with one or more sinkers running on the main line above the swivel. Many anglers regard this as the most basic of all estuary and harbour rigs, although in reality, it can often be replaced by no-sinker or running sinker rigs of the type already described.

One of the best best features of the running sinker and swivel rig is that you can easily use a length of line between the swivel and hook that is either thicker or thinner than your main line. A lighter hook link may be an advantage when pursuing species such as whiting and bream, while a heavier length of line will reduce bite-offs from fish such as flathead.

FIXED PENCIL FLOAT

This very useful rig involves fixing a quill or pencil float to your line anywhere from a couple of centimetres to a rod length above your hook, and weighting the line between the float and hook with shot or sinkers to ballast the float.

Floats with metal or plastic eyelets may be fixed in place by passing the line through each eyelet twice. Other floats are fitted with plastic or rubber sleeves rather than eyelets. These are attached by passing the line through the tubing before pushing it firmly into place on the float stem.

Running floats should be used when presenting a bait deeper than a rod length below the float. Running float rigs are covered later in this chapter.

All pencil and quill floats should be weighted so that only the brightly coloured stem tip protrudes above the water. The exception is when fishing a very shallow bait. Here, the float may be left unweighted so that it will lie flat on the water, standing or tipping up to indicate a bite.

BELLOW: A mangrove jack taken on a lure rigged with a simple loop knot.

KEEP IT SIMPLE!

The simplest rigs are often the best, especially when fishing for smaller, inshore species or freshwater fish. Most of these do not demand the use of heavy, chafe-resistant leaders, wire traces or similar items of terminal tackle.

In many cases, a sharp hook tied directly to the end of your line will do the trick. If extra weight is required, it may be added in the form of one or two ball, bean, barrel or bug sinkers running freely on the line above the hook.

Add swivels only where line twist is a potential problem (such as when using a sidecast reel, or a lure or bait that spins in the water), or when you wish to separate the bait and sinker to avoid 'spooking' shy fish in clear water.

Simple rigs contain less knots, are quicker to tie and are often more effective than complicated set-ups. Whenever and wherever you fish, examine your rigging habits and see if you can simplify things by removing one or more steps. Your results may well improve as a result!

Fixed float rigs are especially useful for catching garfish (piper), mullet, luderick, small bait species and even bream in certain scenarios.

'PATERNOSTER' OR DROPPER RIG

'Paternoster' is a British name for a rig that has the sinker located at the end of the line, with the hook or hooks on short droppers above.

Although primarily used when casting from the ocean rocks or deep sea fishing, paternoster or dropper rigs have certain uses in estuaries, bays and harbours. They are useful when drifting these waters in a boat, or when fishing over soft, muddy bottom strata or beds of short sea grass and other weeds..

LURE CASTING RIG

A lure tied directly to the end of your main line can be used to pursue species such as flathead, bream, tailor, salmon (kahawai) and trevally in estuaries, harbours and bays.

Some of these species — notably flathead and tailor — are equipped with sharp teeth or other line-damaging devices. So, too, are many of the tropical lure-casting targets such as barramundi, mangrove jacks and queenfish. When pursuing these fish, it is best to add a swivel and short leader of heavy nylon or light wire to the rig.

Beach, Rock and Jetty Rigs

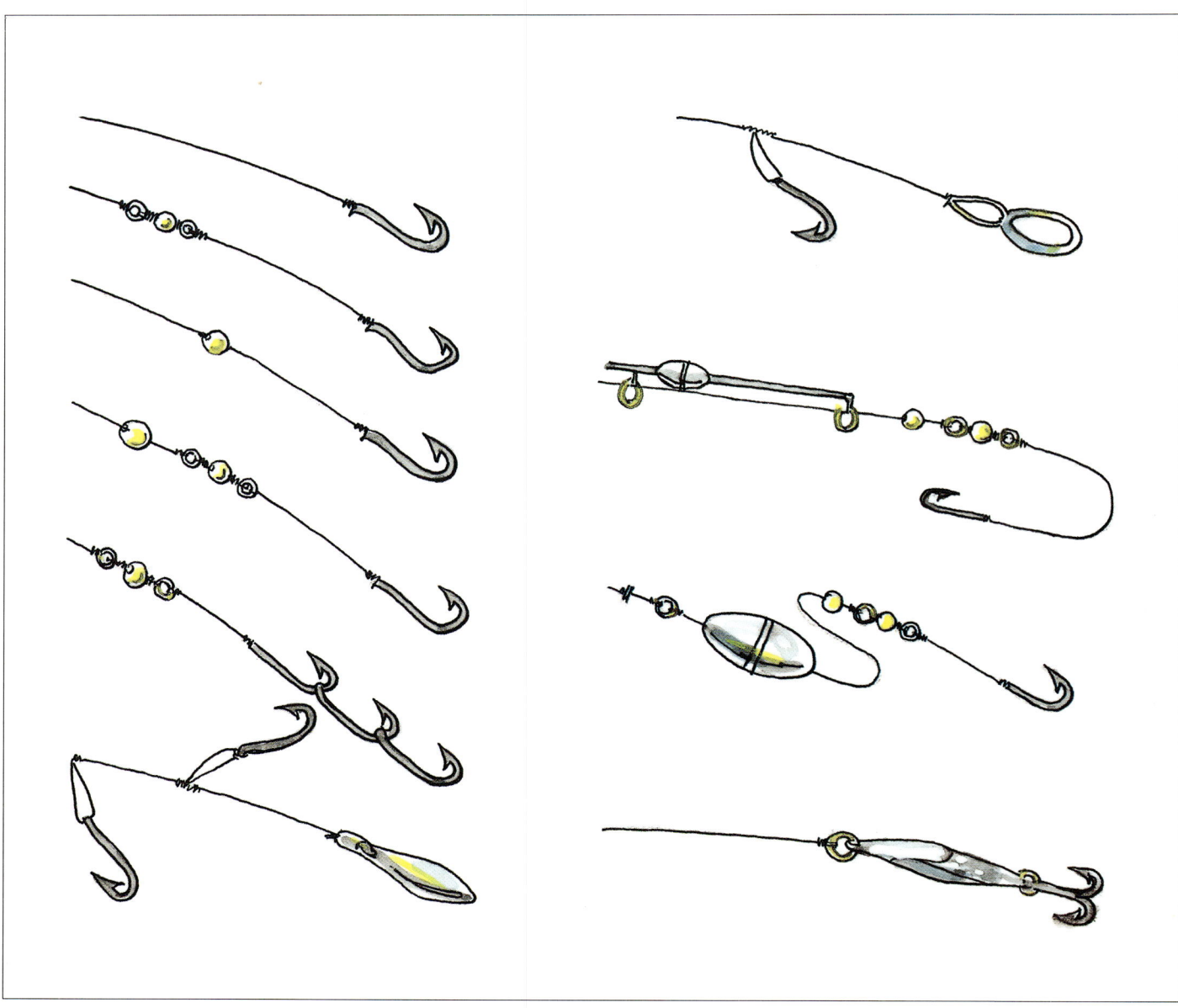

Most or all of the rigs already described for estuary, harbour and bay angling also have applications when casting from beaches, rocks or jetties. The rigs shown on these pages should be regarded as additional to those already examined.

RUNNING SINKER RIG

The simple, no-swivel running sinker rig described earlier for estuary and harbour fishing is also extremely useful for rock, beach, breakwall and jetty casters. It is made by running one or more sinkers on the line above the hook.

Ball, bean, barrel or bug style sinkers are best for this purpose, and you should use the smallest sizes practical for the prevailing conditions. Often, it is better to use two small sinkers rather than a single, larger one.

If using a sidecast reel, tie a swivel in above the sinker, well back from the hook.

RUNNING SINKER AND SWIVEL RIG

The most popular of all Australasian fishing rigs involves the use of a short (20 to 60 centimetre) hook link below a swivel, with one or more sinkers running on the main line above the swivel. Many anglers regard this as the most basic of casting rigs, although in reality, it can often be replaced by a no-swivel, running sinker rig of the type already described.

One of the best things about the running sinker and swivel rig is that you can easily use a length of line between the swivel and hook that is either thicker or thinner than your main line. A lighter hook link may be an advantage when pursuing species such as bream, while a heavier length of line will reduce bite-offs from fish.

GANGED HOOK RIG

Ganged or linked hooks are very popular in parts of Aus-tralia, especially among anglers targeting tailor and salmon (kahawai). They are also useful for catching snapper, kingfish, mackerel, mulloway and several other species.

A 'gang' consists of two to five hooks, linked together by passing the point of one through the eye of the next. Some angl-

TECHNIQUES

ABOVE: Dressed for the conditions, and with a bait bucket and shoulder bag to carry his gear, this rockhopper is fishing a productive 'wash' in southern New South Wales.

ers construct their own, although they are available ready-made from tackle stores.

The major advantage of ganged hooks lies in the way in which they present a bait such as a whole pilchard, whitebait, garfish or flesh strip. As a bonus, they effectively hook tail-biting fish, and help to prevent bite-offs from sharp-toothed species, even without a wire leader.

The most useful ganged hook rig involves tying the flight of hooks directly to the end of the line and relying on the bait itself to provide casting weight. However, gangs can also be used with any of the running sinker rigs already described in this chapter. When using a sidecast reel, a swivel should be incorporated in the rig.

'PATERNOSTER' OR DROPPER RIG

These rigs are extremely useful when casting from beaches, the ocean rocks or wharves and jetties, especially if the sea bed is rough and likely to snag conventional rigs.

Droppers may be formed used the Blood Bight Knot described earlier in this chapter, or by tying in place one or more special three-way swivels.

SPOON SINKER RIG

This is basically another form of paternoster or dropper rig, but employs a special spoon sinker instead of the convent-ional bomb or snapper lead.

Spoon sinkers have the advantage of rising fairly quickly through the water column when retrieved — planing or gliding up over rocky outcrops, kelp or other potential snags. They are also easily (and cheaply) manufactured at home, by pouring molten lead into an old dessert spoon bowl. For both these reasons, spoon sinkers are popular with anglers working reefs.

RUNNING BOBBY RIG

A bobby cork is an egg or oval-shaped float without a stem. It has a channel through the middle.

BALANCED RIGS

The concept of 'balanced tackle' extends beyond rods and reels to include the terminal items used in constructing a rig. Not only should the size of the hook or sinker suit the line strength, they should also match each other. Rarely does a large sinker go well with a very small hook, or vice versa. Similarly, thick, heavy leaders do little to enhance the appeal of small lures and flies.

If a rig is intended to delicately present a small bait or lure to a shy fish on light tackle, keep every part of the rig as small and inconspicuous as possible — even items such as floats, which may be well back up the line from the hook itself.

Balance in rigs is largely a matter of common sense. If the combination of terminals looks unwieldy, chances are it will not perform well.

Bobby corks are usually rigged to run freely on the line below a stopper of some sort, especially when used from the ocean rocks or wharves and jetties. The positioning of this stopper determines the depth at which the bait will be presented.

To construct this rig, the stopper is first attached to the line. This may be a short length of nylon or wool tied around the main line, a rubber band, a small split shot or, best of all, a specially made rubber stopper.

In some cases, a small bead may need to be run on the line between the float and stopper to prevent the stopper travelling through the float's line channel.

Beneath the float, all sorts of rigs may be constructed, ranging from a plain hook tied to the line through to any combination of swivels, sinkers, single hooks and ganged hooks. Whatever the case, the float should be ballasted with weight in the form of sinkers or shot until it is at least three quarters submerged.

Deepsea Rigs

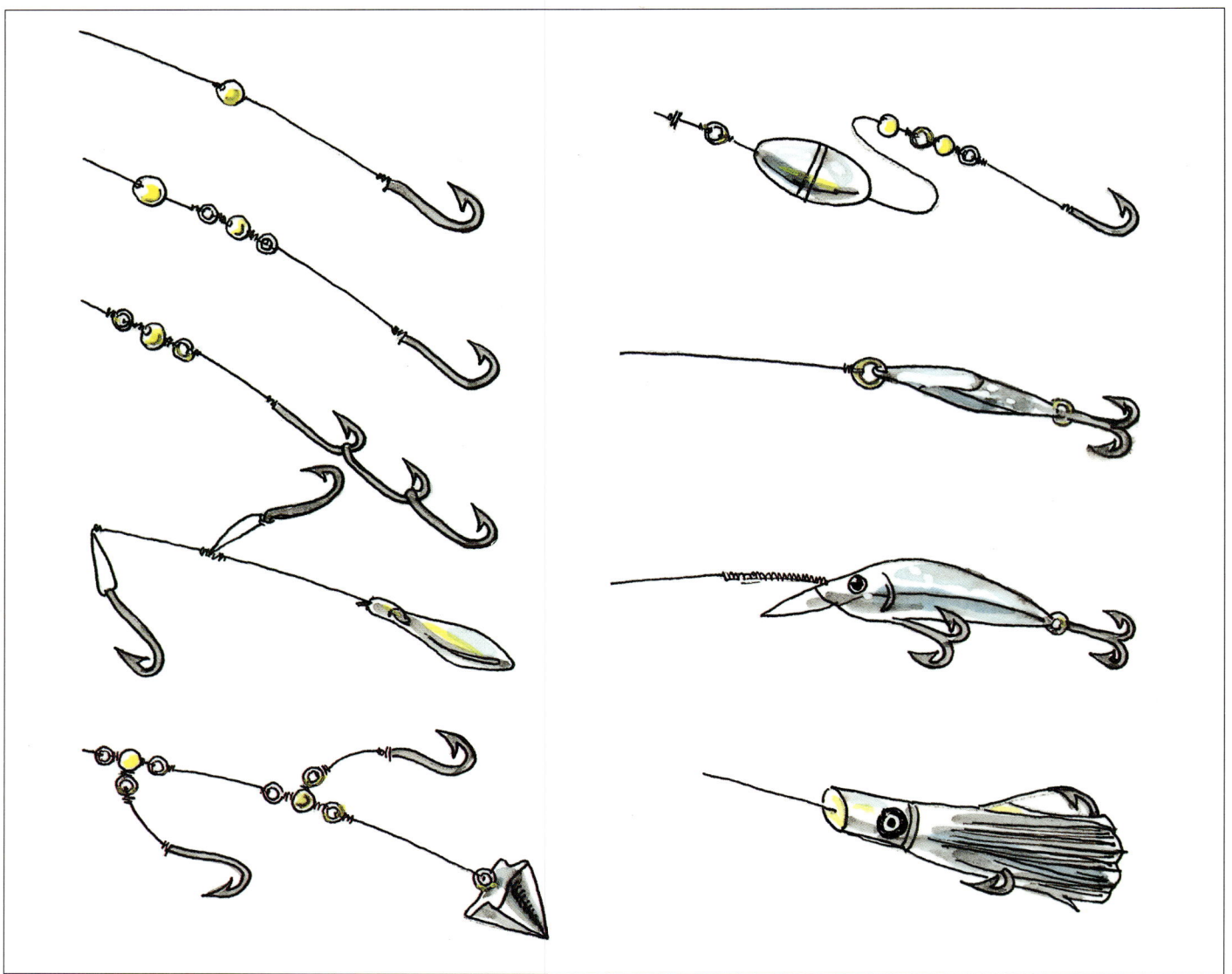

Offshore or deep sea fishermen use perhaps the widest variety of rigs of any group of saltwater anglers. This is because their fishing styles and target species range from shallow water, inshore angling for snapper, trevally and the like, through deep water 'bottom bouncing' for morwong, flathead and coral trout, right up to trolling, drifting, jigging and live baiting for all manner of game species.

Once again, many of the rigs already covered in this chapter are readily applicable to deep sea angling, and a few are repeated here with special notes on theirshore use.

RUNNING SINKER RIG

The simple, no-swivel running sinker rig described earlier for estuary and shore-based fishing is also extremely useful offshore.

Ball, bean, barrel or bug style sinkers are best, and you should use the smallest sizes practical for the conditions.

Running sinker rigs of this sort are especially popular with offshore anglers presenting floater baits in a berley trail. The size of the sinker should be altered to match current and drift conditions. In fact, the sinker may be dispensed with altogether in calm water.

If using a sidecastl, tie a swivel in at least 60 centimetres from the hook.

GANGED HOOK RIG

As explained earlier when discussing rock, beach and jetty rigs, ganged or linked hooks are very popular in parts of Australia, especially among anglers targeting tailor and salmon (kahawai). They are also useful for catching snapper, kingfish, mackerel, mulloway and several other species.

A 'gang' consists of two to five hooks, linked together by passing the point of one through the eye of the next. Some anglers construct their own gangs, although they are available ready-made from many tackle stores.

The major advantage of ganged hooks lies in the way in which they present a bait such as a whole pilchard, whitebait, garfish or flesh strip. As a bonus, they effectively hook tail-biting fish, and help to prevent bite-offs from sharp-toothed species, even if no wire leader is employed.

One of the most useful ganged hook rig involves tying the flight of hooks directly to the end of the line and relying on the bait itself to provide

TECHNIQUES

casting weight. However, gangs can also be used with any of the running sinker rigs already described in this chapter. When using a sidecast reel, or slow trolling a gang-hooked bait, a swivel should always be incorporated into the rig.

'PATERNOSTER' OR DROPPER RIG

'Paternoster' is the name for a rig that has the sinker located at the end of the line, with the hook or hooks on short droppers above. In offshore or deep sea fishing, the sinker is typically a snapper lead, pyramid or bomb-style lead.

These rigs are very useful when fishing the sea bed from a boat — either anchored or drifting. Droppers are especially effective if the bottom is likely to snag conventional rigs.

CASTING LURE OR JIG

In some offshore applicat-ions, a casting lure or metal jig may simply be tied to the end of your main line. However, many deep sea fish have teeth, sharp gill covers or other devices which can damage line. In addition, there is always the chance of the line brushing against the hull of the boat or the leg of the motor when a fish is brought close for netting, gaffing or tagging. To help resist this wear and tear to the working end of the line, many offshore anglers add a leader of some sort, often backed up with a length of doubled line.

By tying a one to five metre long double and using a swivel to connect a 40 or 50 centimetre leader of heavy nylon or light, multi-strand wire, the lure caster or jig fisherman greatly reduces his or her chances of being bitten off or having the main line damaged when the fish is close to the boat. This rig does not appreciably affect the casting of the lure, as the Spider Hitch, Bimini Twist or Plait used to form the double will travel smoothly through the guides and onto the reel.

BLUEWATER TROLLING LURES

Skirted gamefishing lures — often called 'bluewater' trolling lures — require special rigging. Because the fish taken on these lures are big and active, strong leaders of nylon or multi-strand wire are usually employed.

The lure itself runs freely on the leader, which may be anywhere from 1.5 to 4.5 metres in length. A hook or hooks are attached to the leader below the lure, and a sturdy ring, eyelet or swivel fixed to the top.

A pair of in-line hooks are favoured by many sport and game anglers targeting marlin, sailfish and tuna. Often, these are rigged on a short length of heavy cable wire. Nylon monofilament in the 80 to 200 kilo breaking strain range usually makes up the rest of the leader, although in tropical areas, some anglers use wire for the entire leader. A ball bearing swivel or swivel and snap is the most favoured connector between the leader and main line, or leader and double.

MAKE EVERY RIG COUNT!

Tie every rig you make — no matter what its intended use — as if the fish of a lifetime will be hooked on it.

All too often a really big fish will grab a rig intended for much smaller fare. This commonly happens when fishing for bait fish, with a large predator grabbing either one of the hooked and struggling baits, or the small hook or lure itself. If you've been at all haphazard in your preparations, such an encounter will not last very long. On the other hand, if each knot was carefully tied, and the working end of the line regularly checked for damage and weak spots, you have at least a fighting chance of success.

Some incredibly big fish have been landed on ultra-light line and tiny hooks by anglers with the right combination of cool-headed patience, skill, luck and attention to detail in their rigging.

BELOW: Anglers aboard a north Queensland charter boat prepare their rigs before a day at sea.

Sport and Game Rigs

Sport and game fishermen typically pursue relatively large and active fish, many of which are hooked on lines that are quite light when compared with the weight of the fish. For this reason, they tend to use more complex rigs than most other anglers. The rules of their various clubs and associations also place certain constraints on the style of rig used.

To tie these sophisticated rigs, sport and game fishermen are required to learn additional knots, especially those used to create doubled lengths of line, loop knots, heavy leaders and wire traces. Many of these special-purpose knots and connections were covered earlier in this chapter under the heading of 'Advanced Knots'. Anglers intending to become involved in sport and game fishing should carefully re-read those pages and practice the knots described there before attempting to construct the rigs discussed below.

It should also be stressed that almost all of the rigs described so far in this chapter are regularly used by sport and game anglers, although they are often strengthened with the addition of a doubled length of line above the rig and a heavy leader of some sort.

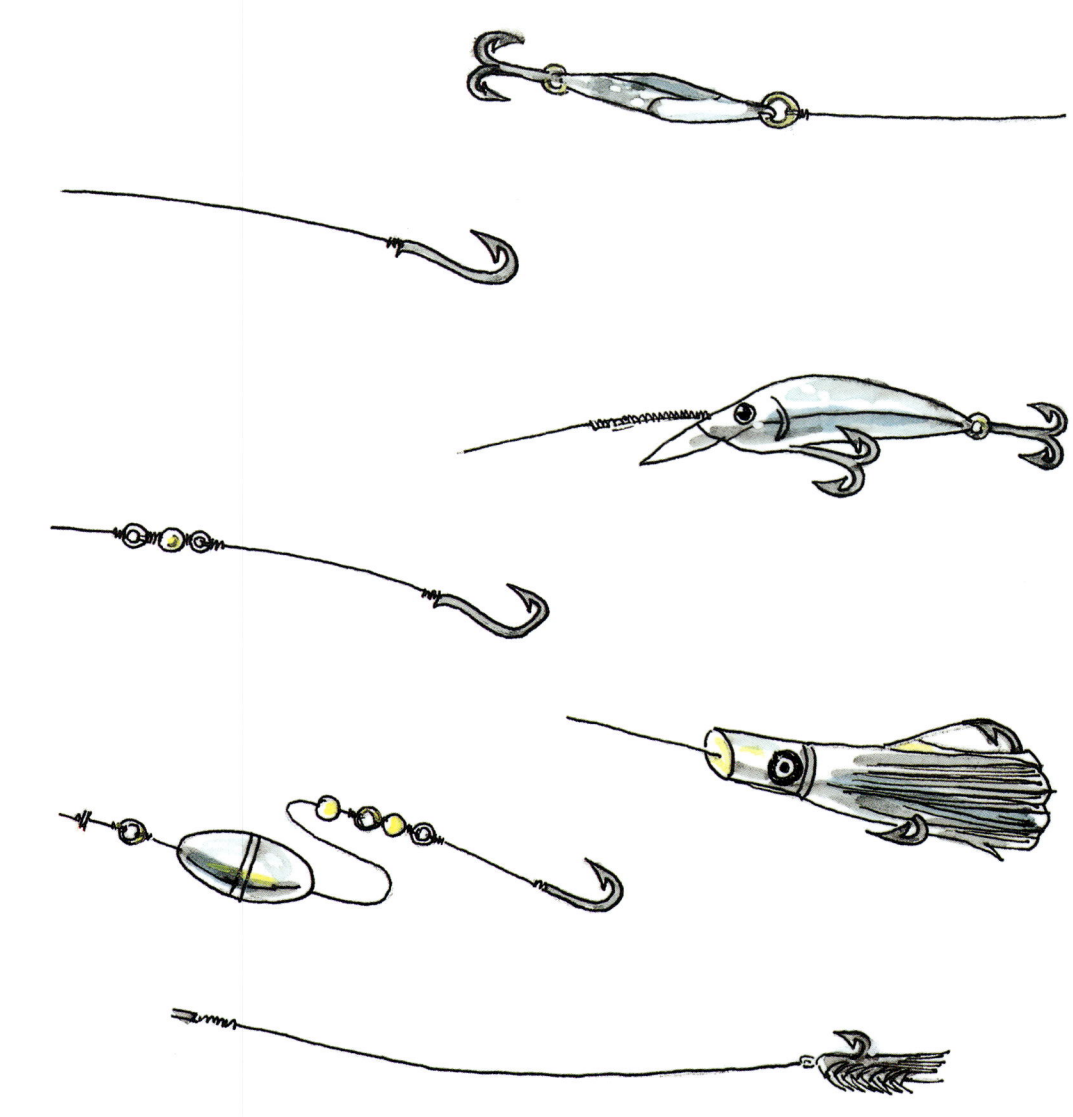

CASTING LURE RIG

In some lure casting scenarios — especially in freshwater — a minnow, plug, spoon, spinner or jig may simply be tied to the end of the main line. However, many tropical, estuarine and deep sea fish have teeth, sharp gill covers or other devices which can damage line. In addition, there is always the chance of the line brushing against submerged rocks, snags or the hull of a fishing boat or the leg of the motor when active, hard-fighting sport and game species are involved. To help resist this wear and tear at the working end of the line, sport and game anglers usually add a leader of some sort to their rig, often backing this up with a length of doubled line.

By tying a one to five metre long double and using a swivel to connect a 40 or 50 centimetre leader of heavy nylon or light, multi-strand wire, the lure caster or jig fisherman greatly reduces his or her chances of being bitten off or having the main line damaged by a hard-fighting fish. This rig does not appreciably affect the casting of the lure, as the Spider Hitch, Bimini Twist or Plait used to form the double will travel smoothly through the guides and onto the reel.

To prevent the stiffness of a heavy leader from inhibiting the action of a lure, a loop knot of some sort should be used for the final connection. The Perfection Loop and Homer Rhodes Loop are useful in this role, as is a Uni Knot tightened a short distance from the lure eyelet.

This rig may also be employed when trolling a plug, minnow or similar lure behind a moving boat.

GANGED HOOK RIG

As explained earlier in this chapter, ganged or linked hooks are very popular in parts of Australia, especially among anglers targeting tailor and salmon (kahawai). They are also useful for catching snapper, kingfish, mackerel, mulloway and several other species.

A 'gang' consists of two to five hooks, linked together by

TECHNIQUES

ABOVE: A big barracuda taken on a minnow lure trolled on a wire leader.

passing the point of one through the eye of the next. Some anglers construct their own gangs, although they are available ready-made from many tackle stores.

The major advantage of ganged hooks lies in the way in which they present a bait such as a whole pilchard, whitebait, garfish or flesh strip. As a bonus, they effectively hook tail-biting fish, and help to prevent bite-offs from sharp-toothed species, even if no wire leader is employed.

The most common ganged hook rig involves tying the flight of hooks directly to the end of the main line and relying on the bait itself to provide casting weight. However, sport and game fishermen tend to rig their gangs on short leaders of heavy nylon or light, multi-strand wire, often backed up by a one to five metre length of doubled line.

If additional weight is required for casting, or to hold the bait down in a strong current, sinkers may be run freely on the leader or the doubled line.

BOBBY CORK RIG

A bobby cork is an egg or oval-shaped float without a stem. It has a channel through the middle to carry the angler's line. These floats are much favoured by sport and game anglers presenting live and dead fish baits to large fish from the ocean rocks, jetties or boats.

When live or dead baiting, bobby corks are usually rigged to run freely on the line below a stopper of some sort — in this instance, the Bimini Twist, Plait or Spider Hitch forming the double makes an ideal stopper.

In some cases, a small bead may need to be run on the doubled line between the float and knot to prevent the knot travelling right through it, or becoming jammed in the bobby cork's line channel. Beneath the float, the double is tied to a sturdy swivel atop one to four metres of heavy leader material. Additional weight in the form of sinkers is not usually needed, as the weight and pull of the live or dead bait itself is usually sufficient to ballast the bobby cork so that only the brightly coloured upper portion is exposed.

This live and dead bait rig may be easily adapted for presenting a deep bait by dispensing with the bobby cork, or replacing it with a running bean sinker of an appropriate size.

SKIRTED TROLLING LURES

As explained earlier in this chapter, skirted gamefishing lures require special rigging. Because the fish taken on these lures are typically big and active, strong leaders of nylon or multi-strand wire are usually employed.

The lure itself runs freely on the leader, which may be anywhere from 1.5 to 4.5 metres in length. A hook or hooks are attached to the leader below the lure, and a sturdy ring, eyelet or swivel fixed to the top end of the leader.

A pair of in-line hooks are favoured by many sport and game anglers targeting marlin, sailfish and tuna. Often, these are rigged on a short length of heavy cable wire. Nylon monofilament in the 80 to 200 kilo breaking strain range usually makes up the rest of the leader, although in tropical areas, some anglers use wire for the entire leader. A ball bearing swivel or swivel and snap is the most favoured connector between the leader and main line or leader and double.

SPECIALISED RIGS

Don't specialise or complicate your rigging simply for the sake of the exercise. Wait until a clear need emerges, and only then add additional items of terminal tackle, or modify their arrangement within the rig.

Certain styles of fishing for specific target species require the use of specialised rigs right from the outset. For example, it would be pointless fishing for large sharks without a wire trace and a strong hook, or attempting catching garfish (piper) on a rig suited to snapper.

If you have some idea of what you are likely to catch, or wish to catch, gear up for it by all means, but remember that over-specialisation can limit your chances.

For the novice angler, chances of success — of catching something — are generally better if a more diverse approach is adopted. Many fine, big mulloway or snapper have been landed on general purpose or prospecting rigs more suited to bream, whiting or flathead. In contrast, very few whiting fall to the hefty baits and sturdy tackle of the specialist mulloway angler!

Freshwater Rigs

Freshwater anglers in Australia and New Zealand employ many of the rigs used by their saltwater colleagues. In particular, most of the terminal set-ups described earlier in this chapter under the heading of 'Estuary and Harbour Rigs' are readily applicable to stream, river and lake fishing scenarios. Refer to that section for details of the no-sinker, running sinker and sinker and swivel rigs.

The additional rigs described on these pages are specialised set-ups for freshwater fishing. Once again, however, versatility is the name of the game, and many of these so-called freshwater rigs have obvious saltwater applications.

FIXED QUILL FLOAT
This very useful rig involves fixing a quill or pencil float to your line anywhere from a couple of centimetres to a rod length above your hook, and weighting the line between the float and hook with shot or sinkers to ballast the float.

Floats with metal or plastic eyelets may be fixed in place by passing the line through each eyelet twice. Other floats are fitted with plastic or rubber sleeves rather than eyelets. These are attached by passing the line through the tubing before pushing it firmly into place on the float stem.

All pencil and quill floats used in freshwater should be weighted so that only the very tip of the brightly coloured stem protrudes above the water.

Fixed float rigs are especially useful for presenting mudeyes (dragonfly larva), shrimps and worms to trout and perch, live crickets or similar insects to bass, and bread, dough, maggots or worms to carp and tench.

BUBBLE FLOAT RIG
Bubble floats are much favoured by trout anglers cast-ing mudeyes (dragonfly larvae) and similar natural baits on lakes, dams and larger rivers. The greatest advantage of the bubble float is that it may be partially filled with water, thus providing casting weight without the need for sinkers.

One of the best and most popular rigs for delicately presenting natural baits with a bubble float involves passing the main line through one eyelet of the float and allowing the bubble to run freely on the line, without a stopper of any kind. The line below the float eyelet is then tied to a swivel, which is in turn attached to a short hook link. With this rig, the float acts solely as a casting tool, with the bait ultimately sinking through the water column towards the lake bottom or stream bed. Split shot can be added between the swivel and float to help take the bait down in wind or current.

A variation on this rig sees a small sliver or block of cork or styrofoam attached to the line between the swivel and the bubble. This acts as a tiny float, suspending the bait, but offering minimal resistance to a biting fish.

LURE TROLLING RIG
When trolling lures such as spoons and spinners in freshwater lakes and impoundments, it pays to tie an anti-twist keel or anti-kink swivel into the line anywhere from 20 to 80 centimetres ahead of the lure.

These semi-circular lead or plastic devices are a great help in preventing line twist, which can be a real problem with certain types of freshwater lure, particularly in-line spinners.

DEEP TROLLING RIG
The freshwater troller has several options for taking the bait or lure deeper in the water column. He or she may use a downrigger, paravane, sinking fly line, length of lead-core or wire line. An even simpler approach is to add weight to the line in the form of sinkers. These are best positioned at least 50 centimetres ahead of the lure.

ABOVE: This fisherman obviously knew the right rig to use, and ended up with a handsome brace of brown trout from a high country stream.

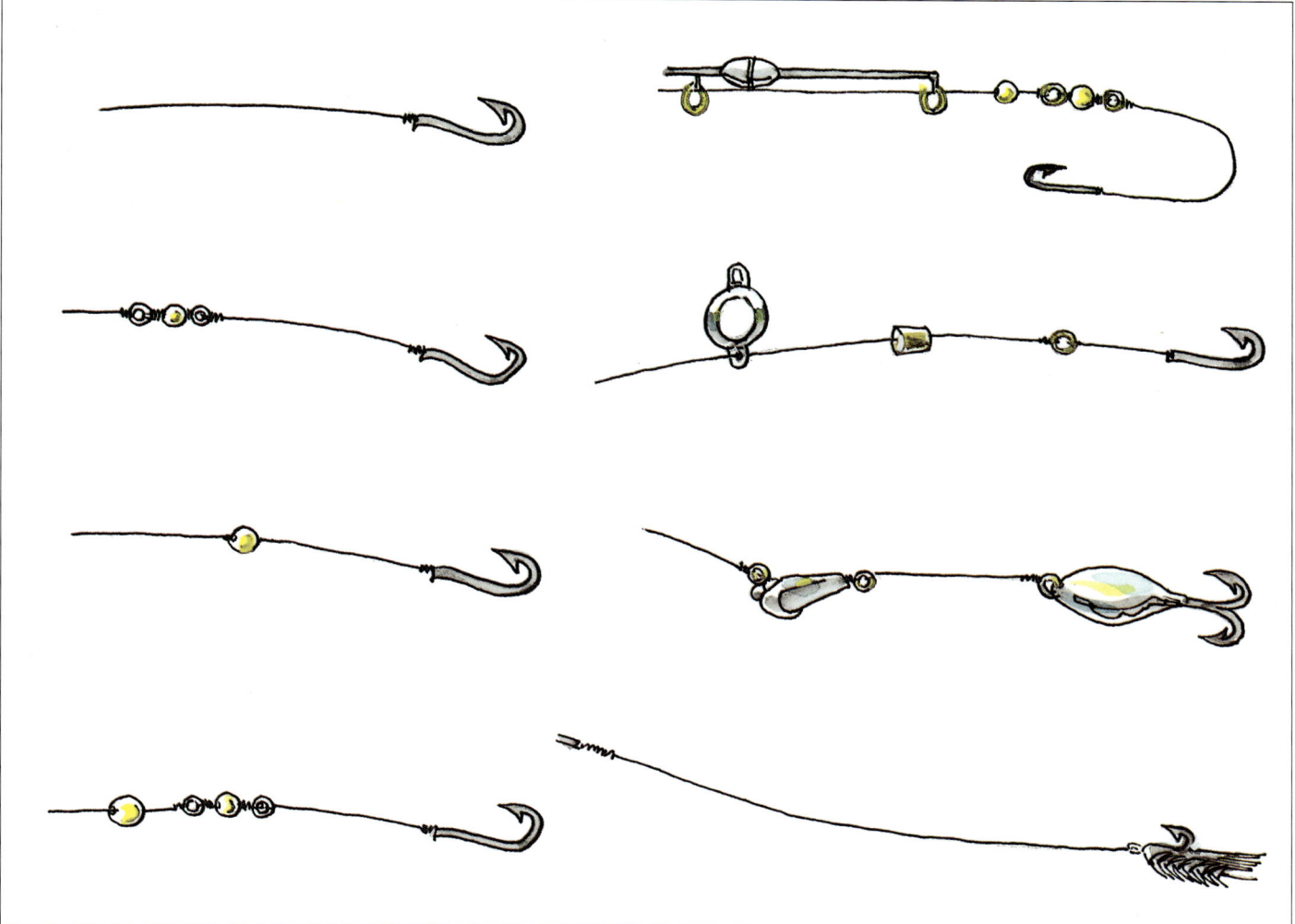

'SLIDING' ON A DOWNRIGGER

The use of downriggers (touched upon elsewhere in this chapter and throughout the book) has revolutionised freshwater trolling, especially among anglers targeting salmonids in lakes and dams.

The conventional way of using a downrigger involved running the lure or bait astern anywhere from 10 to 50 metres, then attaching the line to a special release clip on the downrigger weight or cable and lowering it to the fishing depth.

A second lure may easily be run off the same downrigger and rod and reel. This is done by sliding a second drop-back down the main line.

To 'slide' or 'stack' a second rig, deploy the first bait or lure as described above. Next, rig another bait or lure on a one to two metre length of nylon with a similar breaking strain to your main line. attach a snap swivel to the end of this dropper.

Clip the snap onto the line already deployed, feed the lure astern and let go of the dropper. It will run down the main line to approximately half the depth of the downrigger weight and hang astern on the belly of line.

FRESHWATER FLY CASTING RIG

Freshwater fly casters employ a special fly line to cast their very light flies out over the water, This fly line is usually about 30 metres in length, and is attached to anywhere between 20 and 100 metres of backing line, in case a large fish is hooked.

At the business end, the fly line is normally connected to a tapered leader between two and four metres in length. The leader is tapered to aid in the smooth transfer of casting energy from the fly line to the fly, and to assist in a delicate presentation.

High quality knotless tapered leaders are readily available, and are favoured by many freshwater anglers. Others prefer to make up their own leaders by carefully knotting together lengths of nylon line with different gauges and breaking strains.

The fine tippet or point of the leader is tied directly to the fly, although variations abound. Particularly popular is a rig which involves knotting an additional length (30 to 80 centimetres) of fine tippet material to the end of the leader, and leaving one long tag end on the connecting knot. A second fly may then be fixed to this short dropper so that the angler can fish two flies — thus experimenting with size, colour and pattern in order to determine the fish's preferences.

Some British anglers take the 'dropper fly' concept much further, adding as many as five flies to their leader! You should check the legality of such a rig in your area before trying it.

Light Tackle Spinning and Plug Casting

ABOVE: The author's son spins a pretty tidal system for flathead.
RIGHT: ...while offshore, similar tackle accounts for a 'rat' kingfish.

Casting and retrieving lures of various kinds with single-handed spinning (threadline) or plug (baitcaster) tackle is an enjoyable and productive technique. It is applicable to freshwater, estuary and inshore work on smaller fish up to five or six kilos in weight.

Most of the anglers who regularly practice light tackle spinning and plug casting adopt a highly mobile approach to their sport. If walking or wading, they carry their extra gear in a small haversack, shoulder bag or special fishing vest. Those who prefer to do their lure casting from a boat tend to choose canoes, punts and small dinghies which can be easily and quietly manouevred in shallow water. They rarely anchor, preferring instead to drift, or use oars and/or an electric motor to position the craft for short, accurate casts towards fish-holding structures.

Tackle choices for this style of angling vary considerably. Spinning (threadline) outfits are most often built around a 1.7 to 2.2 metre single-handed 'flick stick', small to medium spinning reel and one to five kilo breaking strain line.

Single-handed baitcaster rods are generally a little short-er, varying from 1.5 to 2 metres. They have a pistol grip or straight butt which carries a small to medium sized reel filled with two to eight kilo line.

Lure choices obviously vary with the target species likely to be encountered; from deep-diving plugs for Murray cod and golden perch to spoons and leadhead jigs for flathead. Freshwater anglers pursuing trout and redfin perch will carry a selection of light-weight spinners. spoons and minnows, while tropical fishermen seeking sooty grunter, jungle perch, saratoga and barramundi will pack some slightly larger plugs. jigs and a few surface poppers or 'chuggers'.

Other requirements are few. A spool of heavier nylon or light wire may be needed if leaders must be used on species with sharp teeth. Some small swivels and snaps are also convenient for preventing line twist and facilitating quick lure changes.

A broad-brimmed hat or peaked cap, polarised sunglasses, dull-coloured clothing and comfortable walking shoes complete the outfit of the light tackle spin-fisher— one of the most versatile members of the modern sport fishing clan.

GO BARBLESS

An increasing number of lure-casting sport fishermen are choosing to partially or completely crush down the barbs on their hooks. This is easily accomplished using a pair of long-nosed pliers. Barbless or semi-barbless hooks make it much easier and safer to release unwanted fish. They are also less painful to remove from human flesh. should an accident occur!

Contrary to popular opinion, the number of fish hooked and subsequently lost will not rise dramatically if barbless hooks are used. In fact. if the angler pays careful attention to keeping a tight line at all times while playing fish (especially aerialists such as barramundi and Australian salmon or kahawai), very few will 'throw' the hooks.

Barbless hooks are especially suitable when fishing isolated or wilderness locations. where most fish will be returned to the water alive. They are also useful when a really 'hot bite' is encountered and large numbers of fish must be handled in a short space of time.

TECHNIQUES

Distance Casting

Long distance casting is a technique frequently employed by shore-based anglers fishing from rock ledges, beaches. breakwalls and jetties. The ability to cast a rig anywhere from 90 to 120 metres is often critical to angling success in these land-based scenarios, as desirable target species are not always found close to shore.

Three types of tackle are favoured by long distance casters. The first and perhaps the simplest to master is the heavy, double-handed spin (threadline) outfit. This typically consists of a three to four metre rod, magnum threadline reel and six to 12 kilo breaking strain line.

While a heavy spinning rig is easy to cast. it does have its limitations. Threadline reels suffer dramatic reductions in casting efficiency as line diameter increases, making them largely ineffective for long range work with line heavier than about 12 kilos breaking strain. Even with lighter line, the spool must be kept well topped-up and the line-load smoothly and evenly packed. The newer 'long-spool' design threadlines greatly facilitate distance casting, although practical maximum ranges with the 80 to 100 gram weights commonly used are generally in the order of 80 or 90 metres.

Sidecast outfits offer substantial improvements in distance casting performance, especially if large diameter models are chosen. Once again, line gauge plays a significant part in the sidecast's long range efficiency. although lines to at least 15 kilos breaking strain can be used without major reductions in distance. A reasonably experienced shore-caster using a large diameter sidecast. 3.5 to 4.5 metre rod and casting weights in the 90 to 120 gram range can reasonably expect to throw the bait at least 100 metres under favourable conditions (still air or a slight tail wind).

For real long range casting. however, a powerful, double-handed overhead rod and well-tuned overhead casting reel gives the best performance. In expert hands, such an outfit can deliver baits at ranges between 90 and 110 metres using lines up to 15 kilos breaking strain, and at least 80 metres using very heavy lines in the 15 to 20 kilo range.

Optimum casting performance with all these tackle styles depends on balance, attention to

ABOVE: Rock fishermen, more than any other group of anglers, often need to be able to cast their rigs considerable distances in order to clear obstacles and reach fish-holding terrain.
TOP RIGHT: Casting can become a sport in its own right, as this father-and-son champion casting team prove with their many trophies and awards, won at specialist casting events held all over the country. In other parts of the world — particularly Japan and Europe — casting events attract huge audiences and television coverage.

detail and the correct matching of casting weights to rod actions and line strength. In general, there is no advantage in using sinkers much heavier than about 110 grams, as few rods (or anglers!) have the power to develop high rod tip speeds when pushing greater masses. Far more obvious benefits will be gained by reducing the line diameter, trimming the bait for aerodynamic efficiency and tuning the reel to bring out its best. Beyond those basics, distance casting comes down to practice and experience.

Careful thought should be given to all elements of the bait and terminal rig used in long-range fishing. Sinkers should be sleek, aerodynamic styles such as snapper leads or bombs. Knots should be well-tied and closely trimmed. And above all baits must be tough and reasonably compact. Soft offerings such as pilchards or mullet fillets can literally fly apart under the strains imposed by distance casting. For this reason, baits such as squid or cuttlefish tentacles. or tough strips of salted tuna (with the silvery skin attached) are preferred by most long range anglers.

Distance casting is not for everyone as, apart from other factors, it demands a reasonable level of strength and physical fitness. However, some anglers take to it with such fervor that they ultimately begin distance casting solely for the sake of the exercise, competing in various organised casting events that often take place in grassy fields, miles from the closest fish!

FAR LEFT AND RIGHT: These illustrations demonstrate the accepted distance casting styles when using overhead tackle (Far Left) and double-handed threadline or spinning tackle (Right). Individual anglers and competition casters may modify these casting styles to suit their specific requirements.

Fishing the 'Washes'

'Washes' are those areas of foaming, aerated white water that form when ocean swells. wind waves or currents strike headlands, reef outcrops or patches of shallow ground.

Such areas are natural magnets for predatory fish. The foamy water provides partial cover for bait and forage species, while the action of the moving water on weed, crustaceans and marine growth constantly dislodges small food items. This contributes a smorgasbord for larger hunters such as kingfish, snapper. salmon (kahawai), trevally, mackerel and many other species.

Anglers fish the washes from two directions: either casting into them from the shore itself. or standing off a short distance in a boat and throwing or drifting a line back into the 'strike zone'.

Both shore-based and boat fishermen employ a variety of techniques to explore the washes. Casting or drifting a lightly weighted or unweighted bait or pilchard, garfish (piper) or fish flesh strip is perhaps the most popular option. and is greatly enhanced by the introduction of a little berley into the immediate vicinity.

Casting and retrieving a lure such as a spoon. diving minnow, flat-bar, jig or popper can also be productive.and takes over from 'floater' bait fishing in tropical latitudes as the most popular option. Trolling the washes from a boat is yet another method of attack, although great care must be exercised not to travel so close to the rocks or reef that the hull strikes an outcrop. or a larger than average wave drives the boat onto the shore.

In fact, boat fishing the washes is potentially dangerous in almost all scenarios. and should only be practiced by more experienced crews. A sturdy anchor and length of rope should be ready at all times in case the motor stalls or the main anchor drag when lying close to the breaking water. In an emergency. this back-up anchor can be deployed to hold the boat off the rocks.

Washes attract fish most of the time. but some situations are better than others. To begin with, isolated and exposed reef edges or outcrops are almost always the most productive, especially if they are swept by strong currents.

Dawn and dusk are the prime times for working the washes, particularly in shallower waters,

TECHNIQUES

LEFT: A bruising giant trevally pulled from a tropical wash with the help of a big popper.
ABOVE: A haul of luderick or blackfish taken from a food-rich wash on the Australian east coast.
ABOVE RIGHT: This young angler has taken a beautiful big black drummer or 'pig' on a bait of abalone gut fished in a wave-washed area of white water beside an ocean headland in southern New South Wales.

although overcast conditions will prolong the bite in some instances, as will heavy mats of foam and scud which accumulate after prolonged bouts of rough weather. Even in bright, mid-day conditions, foaming wash areas will often harbour a few fish.

Learn to 'read' the washes, as described in Chapter Five, and always try a cast or two into these turbulent areas of food rich water.

'COUNTDOWN' LURE CASTING

When casting lures into washes and other areas, bear in mind the fact that predatory fish are not always confined to the surface layers. Often they will be hunting much deeeper in the water column, sometimes cruising just above the sea bed.

One of the best ways to thoroughly explore a wash is to use a series of 'countdown' retrieves. To do this, make your first cast and count slowly until the lure touches the bottom and the line begins to go slack. Commence your retrieve immediately in order to prevent the lure from hanging up on rocks or kelp, but remember the number you counted to as it sank.

On the next cast, commence the retrieve one number earlier in your count. This will cause the lure to travel just above the sea bed. Keep counting one number less on each retrieve until you have the lure skipping across the surface, then work back down through the water column by adding a number to each successive cast. If this proceedure fails to draw a strike or follow, move to another area and start again.

'Countdown' lure presentation is a very thorough and effective way of exploring a wash or similar area with a sinking lure, and will dramatically improve your overall results.

Land-Based Game Fishing

Land-based gamefishing, or 'LBG' as it is sometimes known, is a style of angling largely unique to sections of Australia, New Zealand, South Africa and a few of the Pacific island nations.

Land-based gamefishing involves the pursuit of true game fish species such as tuna, kingfish, sharks and even billfish (marlin and sailfish) from the shore. It is mostly performed from rock ledges fronting deep water, cliffs, breakwalls and jetties or wharves. Limited LBG opportunities also exist on certain beaches, particularly in tropical areas.

The best known land-based gamefishing venues in Australia and New Zealand include the following regions: the stretch of coast between Geraldton and Exmouth in Western Australia, certain headlands between Coffs Harbour and Sydney in northern New South Wales, the Jervis Bay and Green Cape areas of that state, and the north eastern and northern shores of New Zealand's Northland.

Secondary locations offering a more limited range of species also exist in other states and more southerly latitudes in New Zealand, while shore-based fishing for sharks is possible just about anywhere in both countries.

Land-based game fishermen typically use baits of live or dead fish. Favourites include yellowtail (koheru), slimy mackerel, garfish (piper), mullet, frigate mackerel, bonito, and small skipjack tuna. Juvenile kingfish, tailor and salmon (kahawai) are also useful baits. and even quite large specimens may be used by those targeting very big kingfish, tuna and sharks.

These baits are attached to sturdy hooks and leaders of heavy nylon or wire. Usually the rig is supported by a float of some description, ranging from

ABOVE: Some of the world's best LBG water, near Jervis Bay, New South Wales. However, it would be folly to fish these ledges on a day as rough as the one shown.

a large bobby cork to a balloon or empty plastic drink container or detergent bottle. In favourable conditions, large floats can actually be used as 'sails' to carry out the bait, in a similar manner to that employed in the unique Kon-Tiki style of shore-based fishing practiced in parts of New Zealand.

Some anglers in northern West Australia have taken this a step further, utilising helium-filled gas balloons to carry their baits far offshore in the prevailing easterly winds! The strike of a big Spanish mackerel

ROCK FISHING SAFETY

Rock fishing is a potentially dangerous sport, with several participants being killed or seriously injured each year. Most of the fatalities occur when rockhoppers are washed from ocean ledges by large waves, or fall from cliffs while attempting to reach their chosen fishing spot. Almost all of these deaths and injuries could be easily avoided.

Develop the habit of sitting a safe distance from the water and watching your fishing spot for at least 15 minutes before moving down to the water's edge and making that first cast.

During this period, observe the way in which the waves are striking the rock. Is water or spray reaching the ledge from which you plan to fish? Is the tide rising or falling? Are the waves increasing or decreasing in size? And, most important of all, can you identify ready escape routes in case a larger than normal wave appears?

Also consider what you would do if you or one of your companions were washed in. Do you have something buoyant to throw to the person in the water? Is there a more sheltered bay or beach nearby where he or she could come ashore without risk of injury? Where would you go for help?

If you ask yourself these questions each and every time you fish the ocean rocks, you'll circumvent most potential problems before they arise, and live to be an old and happy rockhopper.

or sailfish is made doubly exciting when the bait is skipping and bouncing wildly across the surface of the ocean behind a helium balloon!

Tackle used by land-based game fishermen varies considerably, depending upon the expectations of those involved and the fishing location. In most areas, overhead reels are favoured, and these are typically filled with at least 600 metres of line testing between six and 30 kilos' breaking strain. In some areas, sidecast or centrepin reels are preferred.

Rods range from two to three metres in length. Some are fitted with roller tips and a few carry roller guides throughout.

In some locations, live bait is readily available and may be caught as needed. Elsewhere, anglers carry their baits in buckets or large plastic drums, aerating the water with battery powered pumps to prolong the life of the captive bait fish. Once the fishing spot is reached, the baits are often transferred into a larger, storage container filled with clean seawater. Inflatable wading pools are much favoured for this purpose.

Because of the difficulty of reaching some of the better LBG locations around the country, this from of angling remains largely the sport of fit, active young men. However, piers and jetties stretching into deep water give anyone a chance to float a live or dead bait out to sea. And with the ever-present chance of connecting with kingfish in excess of 20 kilos, tuna to more than twice that weight, big sharks and even marlin, there is no denying the excitement of this uniquely 'Down Under' activity!

RIGHT: While kings, tuna and billfish hold the limelight, many newcomers to LBG are more than happy to start their careers with a shark such as this hammerhead, which fell to a live frigate mackerel.

Bluewater Trolling

Trolling skirted lures for offshore gamefish such as tuna, wahoo, mackerel, sailfish and marlin is a branch of the sport which has undergone significant changes during the past two decades. In Australasian waters today, 'bluewater' lure trolling is a finely-tuned art form which annually accounts for some of our most impressive game and sport fishing captures.

The traditional home of modern skirted lures is the Hawaiian island chain. It was from here, during the 1960s, that the so-called 'Konahead' style of trolling lure emerged — changing the face of offshore gamefishing forever.

The original Konaheads had contoured, scooped-out heads made of plastic, resin or even bone. They were fitted with shredded vinyl or plastic skirts, and exhibited an erratic action when dragged through the water at speeds between five and eight or nine knots.

Trolling lure design has gradually evolved over the intervening years to bring us today's highly sophisticated 'pushers', 'straight-runners' and 'jets'. Most of these, too, have resin heads, usually with reflective inserts, sometimes weighted, and always carrying one to three layered plastic skirts in a myriad of colour combinations. These lures are rigged with a heavy leader through the middle and one or two large, straight-patterned hooks behind. They are usually pulled on 15, 24, 37 or 60 kilo tackle, although smaller versions may be used on lighter lines.

Modern, skirted trolling lures are intended to run best at boat speeds between about six and 12 knots. Optimum trolling speed will vary with the sea conditions and — even more importantly — with the length and angle of the line between the lure and the towing point (rod tip, outrigger release, rubber band or roller troller).

At slower speeds, lures should be run closer to the transom, or from a higher towing points. At higher speeds, it is often necessary to drop the lure further astern, or to lower the height of the towing point. You should experiment for optimum results.

When running with the correct combination of speed, line length and towing angle, modern straight-runners and pusher-style trolling lures should spend approximately 25 per cent of their time on the surface and 75 per cent beneath the surface, creating a visible bubble path or 'smoke trail' through the water.

If the lure leaps clear of the water repeatedly and tumbles through the air, one should either reduce trolling speed, let out more line, or lower the towing point. On the other hand, if the lure fails to break the surface and does not create a smoke trail, it may be necessary to increase trolling speed, shorten the line, or raise the towing point.

By adjusting the line length and towing angle, it is possible to mix lures with slightly different actions and still obtain optimum performance and excellent results.

Nearly all of the modern bluewater trolling lures work best as part of a pattern of lures. It is advisable to troll no less than two lures, and ideally between three and seven, although outrigger poles are generally needed to run five or more lines. All of these lures should be run at staggered distances and, if possible, from towing points of different heights. This will help to prevent cross-overs and tangles while turning. The helmsman should still exercise great care whenever manoeuvring.

When trolling bluewater lures, the angler should set the strike drag on his or her reel at approximately one third the breaking strain of the line. In other words, if using 15 kilo line, set the drag tension at around five kilos. Use a spring balance or objects of a known weight to test this setting. The ratchet or strike alarm should also be engaged whenever trolling.

When a fish strikes the lure, the boat should be kept moving ahead until the rod loads fully and line is being pulled from the reel against the strike drag setting. In the case of marlin and sailfish, it can be an advantage to 'gun' the motor for a few seconds immediately following the strike, especially if the fish begins to jump or head shake. Gunning the boat assists in setting the hooks, maintains a tight line, and helps pull the rest of the lure spread clear of the hooked fish to avoid tangles.

Only when the fish is firmly hooked and running should the boat be slowed, stopped or manoeuvred to follow the fish.

At the end of a day's fishing, your bluewater trolling lures and rigs should be hosed down or washed with fresh water and thoroughly dried before being packed away. At the same time, the leaders should be checked for significant chafes and nicks, and the hooks re-sharpened with a file or stone if necessary. Sharp hooks are absolutely essential to successful lure trolling.

Do not store your trolling lures in direct sunlight or excessively warm or damp areas. If the skirts becomes matted, stained or dirty, wash the entire lure in warm, soapy water, rinse thoroughly and dry.

LEFT: Heading offshore in a well-equipped 'battle wagon'.
RIGHT: The pay-off! A massive marlin is hooked and takes to the air.

Offshore Shark Fishing

Fishing for sharks has always been an important part of the offshore sport and game fishing scene, especially here in Australasian waters, where so many of the world's biggest sharks are to be found.

The major shark species pursued by Australasian game fishermen include: makos, blue sharks, whalers of several species, hammerheads, threshers, tigers and whites. Incidental captures include seven gill, porbeagle and grey nurse (sand tiger) sharks, although the latter is protected in some areas, and not regarded as a particularly sporting adversary.

These sharks vary enormously in size. Some anglers pursue smaller specimens, up to 100 kilos or so, using the lighter gamefishing line classes, while others hunt the true giants with heavier tackle. Record-size sharks of all the species mentioned have been landed in Australian and New Zealand waters, and the dozen heaviest fish ever taken on rod and reel anywhere in the world are all South Australian great whites or white pointers, which occasionally run to 1 500 kilos and more in weight!

The standard techniques for catching sharks on game and sport tackle involve either anchoring or drifting and laying down a steady berley trail of fish oil, blood and chopped fish pieces. (It should be noted that berleying or 'chumming' with the meat, blood or fat of mammals is nowadays strictly prohibited by international gamefishing regulations.)

Baits may be deployed from the moment berleying commences, although some experienced shark anglers prefer to wait until they see the fish first, before deciding on the bait size and tackle strength to present it.

For general shark fishing, dead baits of various sizes are set at staggered depths in the water column. Some may be weighted and others suspended beneath balloons or similar large floats which are rigged to break away from the line when a fish is hooked. Favoured baits include whole or cut tuna, bonito, kingfish, Australian salmon (kahawai), mullet and trevally. Oily, blood-rich baits are preferred, and they should be as fresh as possible.

These dead baits are typically

rigged on heavy, multi-strand or cable wire leaders which test between 200 and 1 000 kilos, depending on the strength of the tackle and the anticipated size and species of the target sharks. Very big white pointers and tigers call for the use of the heaviest wire cable available, or even chain!

The leader should be as long as game and sport fishing rules permit (up to almost 10 metres in some cases), as many shark species will attempt to roll in the leader and sever the main line or double with their rough, sandpaper-like skin.

One or two hooks commensurate to the dimensions of the bait (usually 9/0 to 18/0) are sown in place and the bait paid out to the desired depth and distance from the boat.

Some sharks — notably makos and hammerheads — can exhibit great shyness and cunning in avoiding hooks and lines. They may, however, succumb to a live bait such as a slimy mackerel, small salmon (kahawai) or skipjack fished on smaller hooks and the lightest possible wire leader. In extreme cases, this leader might need to be constructed of fine, single-strand wire, although this will result in some lost fish due to kinking and wear during the course of a long fight.

When a shark seizes one of the baits, it is usually allowed to swim away with it against minimal drag for several seconds or longer. When the angler believes that the shark has the bait and hooks well back in its

LEFT: Golfing celebrity, Greg Norman, battles his namesake; a great white shark.
BELOW: Gloved hand poised tensely over the reel, an angler awaits the first run that heralds another big shark.

mouth, the strike drag is engaged and the fish struck — sometimes with the assistance of the helmsman, who starts the engines and moves the boat away to remove slack from the line and drive the hooks home.

BELOW: Shark fishing is often a waiting game, allowing time to catch smaller fry in the berley trail.
BOTTOM: No monster white or tiger this time, just a pesky little black tip whaler from the Barrier Reef.

The rest of the crew retrieve all other lines and ready the gaffs, tail rope or tagging pole.

The angler should have preset the strike drag on his or her reel at approximately one quarter the breaking strain of the line. In other words, if using 24 kilo line, the drag tension should be set at around six kilos. Use a spring balance or objects of a known weight to test this.

After the strike and first run of the shark, the drag may be eased up to about one third of the line's breaking strain, or slightly more. However, the angler should be ready to back off the pressure if the shark runs hard, sounds or jumps.

The fight of a shark is never predictable. It can range from dour and uninspiring to explosively violent. However, nearly all sharks keep something in reserve for the end play — when the gaffs or tag pole are struck home. Flying gaffs and a sturdy tail rope must be used to restrain heavy sharks, although an increasing number of anglers are choosing to tag and release these fascinating creatures.

Shark fishing is not for everyone, and it has its potential dangers, particularly if practiced from smaller trailer boats. In fact, it is not recommended for those operating vessels under about six metres in length. However, it provides most Australasian offshore anglers with their best chance of catching a fish over 100 kilos in weight, and offers undeniable thrills.

Jigging and Spinning From a Boat

While many offshore anglers confine their use of lures solely to trolling, there is some superb sport to be enjoyed while casting and retrieving or jigging lures from a drifting or anchored vessel.

Casting and retrieving or 'spinning' is at its best when there are obvious schools of predatory fish in the vicinity. The location of these is often given away by the presence of wheeling, diving seabirds, and by the fish themselves as they slash and chop at bait fish herded to the surface.

The species most often involved in such melees are small to medium-size tuna (especially skipjack, bonito, mackerel tuna, longtails and southern bluefin), tailor, salmon (kahawai), school kingfish, barracouta, queenfish and trevally. All of these fish respond avidly to cast and retrieved lures, as do dolphin fish (mahi mahi), cobia, Samson fish and amberjacks — although this latter group of species tend to be more frequently encountered around exposed reef pinnacles, items of flotsam, marker buoys and drilling rigs.

Standard practice involves cruising and watching for obvious activity, sometimes with a troll lure or two run astern. When feeding fish are sighted, the boat is quickly positioned upwind or upcurrent of the school and the engine cut. The anglers aboard then cast their lures beyond and ahead of the moving fish, let them sink for a second or two (unless using surface lures) and commence a brisk retrieve.

If there are no obvious signs of predatory activity, it is still possible to catch fish with cast and retrieved lures by concentrating on areas such as the foaming white water around headlands and reef breaks, shallow reef patches, channel markers, current lines, weed patches and flotsam.

A wide range of lures can be used for this style of fishing. Some of the best are the so-called 'flat bars' or 'half-by-quarters': very simple chromed or painted bars of metal with hooks and split rings attached. Also useful are the various pirks and Silda-style lures, bait fish profiles, 'slugs' and 'irons'. Poppers or other topwater patterns can also be effective at times, especially on kingfish, cobia, queenfish and the tropical trevallies.

Often, schools of fish are too deep in the water column to be located visually. Their presence may be indicated by marks on the depth sounder screen, or by the occasional specimen taken on a trolled lure or deep-fished bait. These are fish that may be better targeted by jigging or 'vertical spinning'.

Jigging involves spooling a lure to the sea bed or casting it a short distance and allowing it to sink well down in the water column before commencing the retrieve. This may be either a straight retrieve, or a more erratic, stop-start one accompanied by sweeps, lifts and stabs of the rod tip.

Taken to its ultimate, jigging can involve bouncing a lure up and down on the sea bed and only occasionally retrieving it, prior to another drop or a change of locations.

Although originally developed for the capture of yellowtail kingfish, jigging and vertical spinning have proven effective on a wide range of species, including Samson fish, cobia, amberjacks, Spanish mackerel, snapper and tropical reef fish such as coral trout and cod.

As well as the lures mentioned earlier when discussing spinning patterns, jig fishermen make use of various diamond jigs and heavy pirks or 'irons' as well as traditional lead-head jigs with tails of fur, synthetic fibres, feathers or soft plastic. Some of these jigs benefit greatly from the addition of a strip of fish flesh, belly strip or squid tentacle to the hook. Jigs 'sweetened' in this manner will often take fish when unadorned lures are drawing a blank. They also tend to be more effective on less likely lure takers such as snapper and some of the other reef-dwelling species.

Jigging is usually undertaken from a drifting boat, although if concentrations of fish are pinpointed, it is sometimes possible to anchor and jig with good results.

The same tackle may be used for both spinning and jigging, although many spin fishermen prefer longer rods than their jigging counterparts. Either way, fast-taper rods in the two to three metre range are best. These should be coupled with casting overheads or magnum spinning (threadline) reels with a relatively high retrieve ratio (at least 4.5:1) and a large line capacity. Lines from six to 15 kilos breaking strain are usually employed, although it is possible to use lighter tackle when spinning for small surface fish like tailor and frigate mackerel, and heavier gear when bottom jigging for big reef fish, kings and cobia.

Spinning and jigging add a whole new dimension to boat fishing, and are techniques that are sometimes capable of producing exciting action when trolling and bait fishing are in the doldrums.

ABOVE: A selection of modern lure casting gear.
ABOVE RIGHT: The author with a popper-caught king.
ABOVE FAR RIGHT: Dolphin fish are a regular lure casting target, especially around buoys and items of flotsam.
RIGHT: This monster Spanish mackerel almost demolished a timber-bodied minnow!
FAR RIGHT: Red bass are the reef-dwelling cousin of the mangrove jack. They love poppers, pull like blazes, but are, unfortunately, poisonous to eat.

TECHNIQUES

157

'Floaters' and Berley Trails

The presentation of so-called 'floater' baits in a berley trail has revolutionised snapper fishing in Australia and New Zealand, as well as having a profound effect on the way offshore anglers target several other significant species.

Actually, the term 'floater' is something of a misnomer, as these baits are not actually intended to float. Instead, they are meant to sink slowly, or waft down through the berley trail — just like an unencumbered chunk of fish flesh or a pilchard piece in the berley trail.

This is a far cry from the older-style, heavily weighted rig once used to catch snapper and other reef fish. Those rigs worked well in deeper water, or on shallow marks which had not been over-fished. However, as snapper numbers declined and it became increasingly difficult to catch these fish, more and more anglers shifted away from drifting the deep grounds with heavily weighted lines. Instead, they began anchoring on precise features such as pinnacles or drop-offs, berleying and casting or feeding astern 'floaters' on lightly weighted or unweighted lines.

The baits used in this style of angling are usually whole or cut pilchards, strips and chunks of fish flesh (especially tuna and bonito), large prawns, bottle squid or fresh squid pieces. However, the berley trail itself is a vital ingredient in successful floater fishing, and is worthy of closer attention.

Berley (sometimes spelt 'burley') is the name given by Australian anglers to bait scraps and other edible matter introduced into the water in order to attract and excite fish.

A basic berley of bait and fish scraps can be greatly enhanced by the addition of cereals such as bread, boiled wheat, pollard, chicken feed pellets and the like. Stale bread forms the basis of many proven berley mixes used by offshore 'floater' fishermen.

A further worthwhile addition to the berley mix is fish oil of some type. The most common varieties are tuna oil and pilchard oil, both of which are available commercially. At a push, vegetable cooking oil can be substituted with reasonable results. These oils form a plainly visible surface slick and help to carry the smell of the berley further afield.

The rules of berleying are that it should not feed the fish to such a degree that they become satiated and stop feeding, that the berley stream or trail be kept as unbroken as possible, and that their should be at least some similarity between substances in the berley and the hook baits being used.

There are a number of ways of dispensing berley into the water. It can be mixed in a bucket and ladled or tipped into the water, placed in a porous bag such as an onion sack and hung in the water, or dispersed from a special 'berley bucket'.

Berley buckets are usually attached to the stern of the boat. They consist of a plastic or metal tub perforated with holes. Older style spin dryer units from early model twin tub washing machines make excellent berley buckets. Berley is placed in this tub or bucket and allowed to permeate out through the holes. Tougher berley items such as whole fish or fish frames may be mashed up in the bucket using a pole or stick with cutters fixed to the end.

Another innovative method of dispensing berley involves packing soaked bread, bait scraps, cut pilchards and other items into a heavy paper bag, along with a stone or half house brick. A cord is then tied to the top of this bag and it is lowered to the desired fishing depth, or the sea bed itself. After waiting a minute or two to allow the bag to become sodden and soft, the cord is jerked several times. This causes the stone to rip through the bag, dispensing the berley at

the desired depth. This can often establish a 'hot bite' faster than conventional berleying.

The unweighted or lightly weighted baits are then dropped astern into the trail or cast a short distance and allowed to waft towards the sea bed. Tackle used may range from a simple handline to a medium-sized baitcaster (plug) outfit or spinning reel and 'barra rod' combination. Lines in the five to nine kilo range are preferred by most practitioners of the technique.

As well as producing good numbers of snapper, the floater technique is deadly for trevally, teraglin, mulloway, school kingfish, tailor and salmon (kahawai).

A derivation of this technique, known as strip baiting or cubing, has also changed the face of yellowfin tuna fishing over the past decade, producing more 80-kilo-plus tuna than all other methods combined. Naturally, much heavier tackle is used for these fish than for the snapper discussed earlier!

LEFT: Small boat anglers pioneered the art of fishing 'floaters' in a berley trail. Here, one shows off the spoils — a fine mulloway or jewfish.
RIGHT: The three species shown here — snapper, trevally and bream — are the mainstays of the 'floater' fishermen. Fine hauls like this one, which was taken by three anglers in a little over two hours, are still available on many shallow, inshore grounds when using the techniques described on these pages.

Deepwater Bottom Bouncing

Although the use of 'floater' baits in a berley trail (described on the previous pages) has led to great changes in the way offshore anglers target snapper and several other species, there will always be a place for 'bottom bouncing' with heavily weighted lines.

Bottom bouncing is typically practiced from a drifting boat, but may also be done at anchor in certain situations, particularly where fish are concentrated over known features such as reef pinnacles and drop-offs.

The scope for bottom bouncing extends from tropical reef waters, where the target species include coral trout, sweetlip, cod and emperor, through to cold, southern waters where flathead, morwong, leatherjackets and gurnard are on the menu.

Snapper were once the primary target of most temperate-water bottom bouncers, but such has been the depletion of this species that good catches are rarely taken today by those using this relatively unsophisticated technique. Happily, there are still enough flathead, morwong, nannygai, leatherjackets and similar fish around to keep the temperate-water bottom bouncer happy most of the time.

Traditionally, this style of angling was undertaken with relatively heavy handlines, while in deeper water, rail-mounted deck winches or stubby boat rods and centrepin reels took over. Lines testing anywhere between 40 and 80 kilos were the norm, and sinkers weighing half a kilo to a kilo or more were not uncommon.

These tactics may still produce bags of fish in lightly fished areas and around distant offshore reefs outside the reach of most small boats. However, increased sophistication is needed to take worthwhile hauls on the more popular fishing grounds today.

Most modern bottom bouncers have come down to 12 or 15 kilo line for anything other than big, tropical reef fish. These lighter, thinner lines suffer less from water drag, and have allowed anglers to reduce their sinker weights significantly. Snapper leads in the 100 to 250 gram range cover most conditions today.

Handlines are still popular, but so too are boat rods, including lighter, hollow glass or graphite composite models sporting geared, overhead reels with good drag systems.

Even more important than the refinements in tackle have been the increasing use of angling electronics such as fish finders, radars and satellite navigation systems. These high technology devices have all allowed the offshore bottom fisherman to pin-point his marks more precisely and return with great accuracy to proven grounds. These are invaluable benefits in this style of fishing.

Regardless of all these changes and refinements, the actual mechanics of bottom bouncing remain much the same today as they were 15 or 20 years ago. The most common rig is still a paternoster or dropper set-up, with the sinker fixed to the end of the line and anywhere from one to five or six hooks hung on short droppers above it. These hooks are baited with fish flesh strips, whole small fish, prawns, bottle squid or pieces of squid and dropped rapidly to the sea bed.

The angler then holds the taut line or rod and feels for bites, striking with an exaggerated action to help overcome the effects of line stretch and water drag. Hooked fish are hauled quickly to the surface.

When drifting, short lengths of line are occasionally paid out to keep the sinker and rig on or very near the bottom. Eventually, however, there will be so much line in the water that drag will lift the rig clear of the sea bed, necessitating its retrieval prior to another drop.

Bottom bouncing may not be as exciting and high profile as some other angling techniques, but it continues to put fresh fish on the tables of fishermen and their families in Australia and New Zealand, and will do so for many years to come.

BELOW: Tasmanian trumpeter are among the tastiest prizes available to the bottom bouncer, and they don't come much bigger than this pair!
RIGHT: Mulloway or jewfish are another highly rated catch much prized by offshore anglers.
BELOW RIGHT: What many deep water bottom bashers and drifters would call 'a bit of colour'! Hauls of fish such as these nannygai, gurnard perch and morwong account for the lion's share of catches taken by deepwater bottom bouncers. They also provide some fine meals.

Freshwater Trolling

In Australia, freshwater trolling can be divided into four different categories: trolling for trout and land-locked salmon in cooler, southern waters; trolling for Murray cod, golden perch and other inland species in outback rivers and dams; trolling the upper reaches of coastal streams for bass and estuary perch; and trolling in tropical freshwater for barramundi.

In New Zealand, freshwater trolling is exclusively aimed at the capture of trout and land-locked salmon.

Trolling for trout and land-locked salmon involves trailing lines behind a slowly moving boat or canoe. It is mainly practiced in lakes and dams, although success is also possible on larger rivers.

A wide range of tackle may be used for trout trolling, although most Australasian anglers prefer a light rod and reel spooled with two to four kilo breaking strain line. Troll lines for trout and salmon may carry lures similar to those used when casting and retrieving in similar waters. These include spinners, spoons and various plugs or minnow imitations. Troll lines for trout may also be rigged with streamer flies, or even natural baits such as scrub worms or mudeyes.

In addition to a lure, fly or bait, the line often carries some form of a metal and plastic flasher or attractor, such as a 'Cowbell' or a 'Ford Fender'. The water drag imposed by the spinning metal blades on these devices demands slightly heavier gear, and lines of four to six kilos breaking strain are suggested.

Specialist salmonid trolling methods such as downrigger fishing and the use of lead-core or wire lines are becoming increasingly popular. These tools allow the angler to troll the deeper thermoclines and temperature layers, where trout and salmon feed for much of the year. In fact trolling with a sinking fly line or length of lead-core is one of the most effective fish catching techniques on New Zealand's larger waterways, such as Lake Taupo. In New Zealand, this technique is called 'harling', and typically employs a streamer fly such as a Matuka in place of a hard-bodied lure.

The success of these deep trolling techniques reflects the fact that trout and salmon are not always found near the surface of our lakes and rivers. In fact, their location is highly variable, and tends to be dictated by factors such as the season, water temperature, availability of food and the specific species of trout or salmon present.

In lakes and other large bodies of water, trout spread out around the shoreline and relate to bottom strata and structures of various kinds. Brown trout tend to relate more strongly to the shoreline and to submerged features than rainbows and land-locked salmon, which sometimes hunt well away from shore, utilising the surface layers and mid-water areas of a lake or dam.

Seasons also play a significant part in locating and catching salmonid fishes in a lake or dam. For example, as the water in our impoundments warms up in middle and late summer, trout and salmon will tend to move deeper in the water column seeking thermoclines or zones of sudden temperature change. Later, as the water cools towards autumn, they will move back into the shallows and look for feeder streams in which to spawn. In spring and early summer, as they return from spawning, they will once again frequent the shallows.

Interestingly, those trout and salmon which remain in the main basin of the lake or dam through mid-winter tend to feed almost as deeply in the water column as they do in mid-summer. This is a response to the lack of life and shortage of food in the shallows, and also a reflection of the fact that the shallows and margins can become too cold, even for trout, during winter.

Trolling for Murray cod, golden perch, redfin and other freshwater species in mainland Australia's inland rivers and dams generally requires the use of heavier tackle and larger lures than those employed for trout and salmon.

Although the technique grew immensely in popularity through the 1980s, there is nothing particularly new about using trolled lures to catch inland native fish. The famous old Aeroplane Spinner was taking cod from our outback rivers before the Depression, while smarter anglers began catching large bags of golden perch on plugs and minnows in the early 1960s. However, it is only in the last 10 to 15 years that lure fishing — including trolling — for these fish has really gained in popularity and become a reasonably widespread practice.

There is absolutely no doubt that our native inland predators will fall for a well-presented lure. Murray cod, trout cod and golden perch are particularly aggressive lure takers, but so too are silver and Macquarie perch, especially if lures of the correct size are used. Eel-tailed catfish will also strike at trolled lures from time to time, especially near their nesting sites at spawning time. Introduced redfin perch are avid lure takers, and even carp can be induced to strike on artificials, so the outback lure troller is not necessarily limiting his or her options by sticking with 'hardware' as opposed to natural baits.

The one great limiting factor in outback lure fishing is the turbidity or muddiness of the water. All too often, our inland waterways are simply too discoloured for practical lure fishing. This problem has been compounded by the spread of carp and, more particularly, by poor farming and soil conservation practices among riverside land users. Today, throughout much of the Murray/Darling system and its tributaries, clear water is a rarity.

Just how clear the water must be in order to permit worthwhile lure fishing is a moot point. With certain lures, such as 'sonics' and rattling noise-makers, fish may be caught in extremely turbid conditions. However, as a rule, if you cannot see a pale coloured object, such as the palm of your hand, when it is held half a metre below the surface, success with artificials is likely to be limited.

In all inland lure fishing the emphasis is on strong-actioned spoons, spinners, plugs and minnows trolled as slowly as practical near fish-holding cover such as snag piles, rock bars, and the areas immediately below weirs and dams. In dams themselves, deep drop-offs associated with sunken river beds and stands of drowned timber are good places to start.

Trolling for Australian bass, estuary perch and barramundi is mostly confined to rivers, lagoons and a handful of stocked impoundments. Once again the emphasis is on keeping the trolled lure as close as possible to submerged structures such as fallen trees and the edges of weed beds. Bibbed, deep-diving plugs are preferred for catching bass and perch, while barramundi specialists typically employ medium-running minnow-style lures measuring between seven and 15 centimetres in length.

ABOVE LEFT: A big rainbow trout alongside a collection of flutter spoons which can be productive when trolling our lakes and dams.
ABOVE: This Victorian angler has taken a plump Macquarie perch on a live mudeye (dragonfly nymph) slow trolled around some sunken timber with the aid of a special 'Downunder' trolling sinker.

Light Tackle Breaming

ABOVE: A lady angler unhooks another keeper in Victoria's Tambo River. The Tambo is part of the vast Gippsland Lakes' system, and attracts thousands of bream anglers every spring, when wattle lines the banks and the fish are at their best.

Bream of one species or another are among the most popular angling targets around the southern half of Australia. They are pursued by thousands of fishermen, from Townsville and Cairns in the north, to Hobart in the south and Perth in the west.

As the objects of so much angling effort, it is hardly surprising that bream have inspired a range of specific techniques, tackle and rigs. These vary around the country, from the quiet lake backwaters of Victoria's Gippsland, to the tidal rivers of South Australia's Kangaroo Island and the pounding surf breaks of Yamba or Narooma in New South Wales.

However, despite the considerable geographic variations in bream habitat, certain common threads run through the philosophies of the country's best bream anglers. Foremost among these is the notion — supported by a great deal of practical evidence — that bream respond best to lightly weighted rigs and fresh baits presented in the most natural manner possible and on the finest line practical.

There are, of course, many exceptions to these 'rules', and large numbers of bream are occasionally taken on seemingly unsuitable heavy and unsophisticated rigs. However, for long term success in a range of environments, the budding bream angler will benefit from embracing the time-proven combination of light rigs, natural presentation, fresh baits and fine line.

In most areas, the threadline or spinning reel has emerged as a favourite tool among bream specialists. Small to medium sized spinning reels mated to soft-tipped 1.8 to 2.8 metre rods and spooled with two to four kilo line have become almost a standard in estuary, bay and lake fishing for bream, from Sydney Harbour to the Swan. The newer 'bait runner' or 'line feeder' style threadlines are particularly applicable to still water breaming.

Regional exceptions to this standard do exist. Handlines remain popular with some bream specialists, particularly the more senior members of this group, and those fishing from small boats and dinghies. Light sidecast outfits are also employed, especially in southern and central Queensland. Called 'Sloppy Joe' outfits in some circles, these combinations of shallow-spooled, 10 to 15 centimetre sidecast reels and very light, slow-tapered 3 to 3.5 metre rods continue to account for vast numbers of bream in areas such as Jumpinpin and the Southport Broadwater.

In New South Wales and southern Queensland, where anglers pursue bream from ocean headlands, rock ledges, breakwalls and beaches, slightly heavier gear is often used because of the more boisterous environment. Here, light to medium weight threadline and sidecast outfits carrying four to eight kilo line are preferred.

Regardless of their choice in rods, reels and line, almost all bream anglers agree on the merit of a running sinker rig. In most cases, the lightest sinker possible for the prevailing conditions is run freely on the main line above a small swivel. A further 20 to 60 centimetres of line or light leader separates this swivel from the hook.

Sometimes this rig is simplified even further by dispensing with the swivel and hook link altogether, allowing the sinker to run right down the line and sit atop the hook. This is an especially good rig in very snaggy or reefy areas.

One traditional rig that unfortunately seems to be dying out was once widely used by boat-based handliners. Called the 'Picker's Doom', it consisted of a very long hook link (two to 10 metres), with a relatively heavy channel sinker above the swivel, split shot or matchstick stopper. The heavy sinker kept the line on or near the bottom, but the extremely long trace allowed the bait to waft about in a very seductive manner, and also gave a timidly biting fish plenty of slack line on which to hook itself.

Naturally, the 'Picker's Doom' is not applicable to rod and reel fishing. However, the modern angler can make use of the same principles while using a standard running sinker and swivel rig. To do this, simply hold the sinker in one hand and drop the bait overboard into the current. Still holding the sinker, allow 10 or 15 metres of line to run out into the current, carrying the bait down-tide. Then drop the sinker overboard, let it sink to the bottom and engage the reel or close the bail arm. Just as with the 'Picker's Doom' the bait is now free to waft about down current on a very long tether.

The subject of baits for bream would fill a book by itself, and no two bream 'experts' would necessarily agree on a 'top ten' listing of the best baits for this species. For one thing, there are many regional favourites — from Goolwa cockles in South Australia to sand worms in Victoria; live nippers (yabbies) in New South Wales and blood worms in Queensland.

Less conventional offerings such as home-made 'pudding' concoctions, ox heart and chicken gut also have their followers, and more than a few fine bream have been taken on such simple household staples as cheese and fresh bread!

However, talk to enough serious bream specialists and several facts emerge concerning bait selection. First, it is nearly always best to offer the fish a food source with which they are familiar and which occurs naturally in the area being fished. Secondly, in clean, clear water, fresh, sweet-smelling baits are best. Finally, there is simply no substitute for gathering, making or catching your own bait in preference to buying it.

Bream angling is a wonderful pastime often pursued in aesthetically pleasing surrounds. However, as with any other fishing style examined in this book, returns depend heavily on the commitment and effort of the individual angler — you only get out what you put in!

ABOVE: Break out the frying pan! BELOW: The target of so much angling effort in Australia each year: the bream.

Freshwater Fly Fishing

Fly fishing in freshwater is one of the oldest and most traditional styles of angling in existence. It's history stretches back at least as far as the times of the ancient Macedonians, who caught wild brown trout on small fur and feather insect replicas dangled or 'dapped' on the surface of the water. Their tackle most likely consisted of braided horse hair lines tied directly to the ends of long, fine cane poles or reed stems.

Today's fly fishing tackle is very different from the horse hair lines and cane rods of the Macedonians; however, the philosophy of freshwater fly fishing remains largely unchanged. Modern fly fishermen still employ fur and feather insect imitations and in some instances, they still 'dap' them on the surface.

Other things have changed. To begin with, trout and salmon are no longer the only targets of the freshwater fly caster. Today, fly fishermen in Australia and New Zealand cast their flies in search of species as diverse as carp, bass, sooty grunter, saratoga and barramundi — as well as the introduced trout and salmon species.

The widening horizons of the fly caster have led to innovations in rods, reels, lines and — most especially — fly patterns. There are now tens of thousands of different fly patterns in use, and while some are 'traditional' styles that would be at least vaguely familiar to the ancient Macedonians or fly fishers from the Elizabethan age, many more are products of twentieth century materials and philosophies.

No longer do freshwater fly patterns represent only floating insects. Nowadays we also have drowned insects (soft-hackled wets), insect larvae and pupae (nymphs), small fish, tadpoles or leeches (streamers), frogs, lizards and even small birds (bugs, poppers and divers). For a more thorough description of these varying fly styles and the way they are fished, refer to the section entitled 'Freshwater Flies'.

New fly patterns and methods of fishing them have also spawned new tackle. Dangling a fly from the end of a long rod proved to be a very limited presentation technique. and by the Middle Ages, fly fishers were casting their imitations — albeit very short distances — to feeding trout and other fish.

In later times the thick, tapered lines of the modern fly caster were developed which allowed much longer casts to be made. When the plastics revolution of the mid-twentieth century arrived, 'plastic' fly lines brought fly fishing to the people in much the same way that nylon monofilament and fibreglass rods had taken angling in general away from the fortunate few and introduced it to the masses.

Today, fly lines are available in at least a dozen different weights, half a dozen taper configurations and several

TECHNIQUES

ABOVE TOP: The Comet is an old steelheaders' pattern from North America that works well in the salt. Perhaps it is taken as a shrimp.
ABOVE CENTRE: A surface 'slider' of the author's design with a track record on the elusive giant herring — so much so that it's been christened the GH Slider!
ABOVE BOTTOM: Another of the author's purpose-built patterns. This derivation of the old Bendback is called a Crooked Creek Special, and isdynamite on flathead and bream in estuarine waters.

169

Saltwater Fly Fishing

The sport of fly fishing in saltwater originally grew out of freshwater fly fishing, when trout and salmon anglers began taking their tackle to the seaside and pursuing all manner of marine adversaries.

Over the years, saltwater fly fishing has developed along parallel lines to the freshwater branch of the sport, with major advances in materials, tackle design and fly patterns. Today, experienced saltwater fly casters regularly take on strong, active saltwater game species such as trevally, salmon (kahawai), tailor, kingfish, bonito and the smaller tunas. A handful of experts have even taken big tuna, sailfish, small marlin and sharks on fly gear!

While saltwater fly casting for heavy-weight game fish requires extremely specialised (and expensive) tackle, there are many facets of this fast-growing sport open to the newcomer armed with nothing more sophisticated than a No. 6 or No. 7 trout outfit.

Estuarine and inshore fly rodding for species such as mullet, mackerel, juvenile salmon (kahawai), small trevally, bream, flathead and 'chopper' tailor requires little in the way of additional tackle. A standard freshwater fly outfit is perfectly adaptable to these species, and some of the nymphs and streamer-pattern flies will take the species mentioned. Mullet and garfish (piper) will rise to tiny dry flies, while salmon (kahawai), tailor and the tropical trevallies will avidly attack hair bugs and poppers of the type used for bass, barramundi and saratoga in freshwater.

Some of the species mentioed have sharp teeth or other line damaging devices, so a short shock tippet of heavy nylon or light wire may need to be attached to the working end of the leader before tying on the fly. Because this shock tippet need only be 10 or 15 centimetres long it will have little effect on casting or presentation.

Later, as the angler becomes more involved with saltwater fly rodding. he or she will begin to discover the wealth of 'new' fly patterns now available to followers of this activity. Most of these are streamer patterns intended to mimic marine bait fish species such as sardines, pilchards, herring and mullet, although some are meant to imitate crabs, prawns and other invertebrate food sources. For more details on specific saltwater fly patterns and how to fish them, read the section entitled 'Saltwater Flies' at the end of Chapter Two.

ABOVE: American saltwater fly fishing veteran, Jack Samson, fights a small black marlin on the fly near Townsville, north Queensland.
LEFT: A small mackerel tuna or kawa-kawa taken from the ocean rocks on fly gear.
RIGHT: The author proves that it doesn't take 'glamour' sport fish to bring a smile to the 'swoffers' face! These barracouta were a real handful on a trout outfit. They were taken by casting to the edge of a large school feeding close to the cliffs at Eagle Hawk Neck in south eastern Tasmania.

TECHNIQUES

FLY LINES

Fly casting is quite different to other styles of casting in that it relies on the weight of the line rather than a sinker, lure or bait to carry a nearly weightless artifical fly out over the water.

To this end, flyline is very thick and quite heavy. Because such a thick line would 'spook' the fish if it were tied directly to the fly, a leader of lighter nylon is tied to the working end.

There are several types of fly line available for different needs. To begin with, fly lines are available in a range of weights to suit different strength rods and fly sizes. Common fly lines used in this country range from ultra-light AFTMA (American Fishing Tackle Manufacturers Assoc-iation) No.4 weight, up to the very heavy AFTMA No.12 and No.13 lines used in saltwater fly fishing.

Secondly, the line may be either floating or sinking, depending on its density. This is indicated by the addition to the serial number of an 'F' for floating and an 'S' for sinking lines. In addition, some fly lines — called 'sink tips' — have a short sinking section at the working end. These typically carry the coding designation 'F/S'.

Finally, the actual taper of fly lines varies. This dictates the line's behaviour in the air during a cast, and also influences how far it can be cast. Common tapers include level (L), double taper (DT), weight forward (WF) and a special, short, heavy line called a shooting head or shooting taper (SH or ST).

All of this information about a flyline is incorporated into the serial number printed on its packaging, so that the buyer knows a DT6F line is a double taper, No.6 floating line — ideal for stream trouting. In contrast, a WF10S is a weight forward, No.10 sinking line — a popular choice for intermediate saltwater work, or barramundi fishing in the tropics.

densities, from high-floating dry lines to fast-sinking versions with descriptive titles such as 'Deepwater Express'! There are also short, heavy lines called shooting tapers for distance casting. and special sink-tip lines to present wet flies at controlled depths or over weed beds and other bankside obstructions.

The combined effect of all of these changes and innovations has been to greatly expand the horizons of the freshwater fly fisher. No longer is he or she limited solely to presenting dry flies at very short ranges to 'rising' or actively feeding trout. The same fish can now be targeted when they are lying deep in the water or further from shore. when they are feeding on bottom-hugging nymphs, darting minnows or emerging caddis larvae swimming upwards through the water column. Similarly, big streamers or popping bugs can be cast to bass or barramundi, life-like nymphs presented to cruising carp, or epoxy-bodied lure-flies dragged past snags and undercuts where golden perch or Murray cod lie in ambush.

Where once the 'standard' freshwater fly fishing outfit in Australia and New Zealand was a No. 6 or No. 7 rig carrying a full length floating line, anglers are now using feather-weight No. 4 outfits on stream-dwelling trout, No. 8 set-ups to throw hair bugs for bass and sooty grunter. No. 9s for casting heavily weighted nymphs and Glo Bugs at spawn run trout in big, fast rivers — or even No. 10 rigs for tackling big barramundi or high-flying saratoga in snag-studded tropical billabongs. And just as the weight and power of the outfit varies with its intended application, so do the taper and density of the line, length and design of the leader and size and pattern of the fly at the end of that leader. In short, freshwater fly fishing has broken free of tradition and become a dynamic branch of the sport of modern angling.

ABOVE: A pretty little brown trout from Sydney's Blue Mountains.

LEFT: This is the type of trout water that gladdens the heart of the fly fisher — small and intimate.
RIGHT: Cleaning the morning's catch.

Reading the Water

The ability to look at a stretch of water and make intelligent assumptions about the types of fish likely to be present, where they should be, and what they might be doing is one of the factors that identifies the successful angler. We call this ability 'reading the water'.

Being able to read water and make the most of any opportunity is more important than owning a rack of expensive rods or being a lucky angler. Those who consistently produce results — in a wide range of situations — do so as a result of their powers of observation. Being observant is a skill. Some people are naturally better at it than others, although we can all sharpen our powers of observation with practice and time on and around the water.

A talented angler is always observing the surroundings and making mental notes of the many small indicators that point the way to fishing success. In some cases, this kind of observation becomes an unconscious process — a kind of reflex action. Anglers who exhibit keen observation as a reflex action are usually uncannily successful. Their peers may call them lucky but the truth is that these people make their own luck!

You can begin to train yourself to be an observant angler by looking long and hard at every aspect of the environment each time you fish. Make mental notes or, better still, write down the key elements in a note book, diary or log. What sort of day is it? What direction is the wind blowing from, and how strongly? Is the water rough or calm? Clear or discoloured? Cool or warm? What state is the tide at? Are there obvious currents? Are any fish splashing or jumping? Are other anglers on the water enjoying any action?

Given time, you will begin to make many of these significant observations automatically. Then you can start to examine the less obvious ones. What is the current moon phase? Is the barometer high or low? Is it rising, falling or stable? What has the weather been like during previous days? What is the short term forecast? Has it been an unusually wet or dry season?

Tools exist to help you with these observations. Perhaps the most important are a pair of good quality, polarised sunglasses and a hat with a generous brim. The underside of this brim should be dark in order to reduce reflections and glare. With a pair of polarised sunglasses and hat, your powers of direct observation will be increased.

A barometer is also a useful tool for the angler, both in weather forecasting and helping to make guesses about the likely activity levels of many fish species. So, too, is a water temperature gauge or thermometer of some sort. This may be handheld if you are a freshwater or shore-based angler, or built right into your boat if you go offshore in search of marine species.

These days, few serious offshore anglers would leave port without a depth sounder or 'fish finder' aboard their vessel. These are also becoming increasingly important to freshwater fishermen working larger lakes and impoundments. Depth sounders are another tool to enhance your powers of observation.

In addition, you should begin to collect secondary aids to observation, such as tide charts, topographic maps, oceanographic charts, moon phase calendars and books or magazines dealing with your sport.

In the long run, however, all of these tools and your increasingly sharp observational skills are only as useful as your ability to apply what you see to a specific fishing scenario. You need to know what you are looking for!

Again and again you will come across the terms 'structure' and 'structural elements'. These are important concepts in angling, because almost all fish relate to structures.

This natural trait is known as thigmotropism or thigmotaxis. It is the reason that the greatest number of ants on a footpath will be found near the edges of the concrete, or along the cracks, rather than out in the middle of the squares. It is also why fish will gather around a floating marker buoy or submerged reef pinnacle.

Food and shelter play their parts, however, it goes beyond those basic necessities of life to include less tangible concepts such as 'living space' and 'points of reference'. These concepts help to explain why dozens of large tuna or dolphin fish will gather around a small floating log, which can offer them little in the way of additional food or shelter.

By recognising the importance of structure and the merits of different structural elements, and combining this with increased powers of observation and a growing understanding of fish behaviour, you will become a significantly better fisherman.

Reading an Estuary System

Estuaries are those sections of our coastal rivers, lakes, harbours and inlets between the open sea and the upper limits of tidal movement or significant saltwater intrusion. They are vitally important to our fishing, being the home, breeding ground, nursery and larder for so many species — including fish more typically associated with deep, offshore areas or inland, freshwater streams.

The dominant force acting upon the location and behaviour of fish in most estuaries is the tide. However, it should also be remembered that some estuary systems — particularly smaller coastal lagoons and lakes — may be closed off from the sea by sand bars for considerable periods of time. When closed, these systems become significantly more difficult to 'read'. Indeed, some of the guidelines used to understand non-tidal bodies of water such as freshwater lakes and impoundments may need to be applied to closed estuaries. Happily, the majority of our estuary systems are open and tidal, even if their tidal fluctuations are often considerably different to those experienced just outside the estuary mouth.

Most Australasian estuaries experience four reversals in tidal flow or direction during each 24 hour period. In other words, there are two high tides and two low tides each day. Extreme variations between high and low water range from six or eight metres in some tropical estuaries to less than a metre in other waterways. In addition, tidal variations change with the lunar calendar: the greatest variations (spring tides) occurring on the full and new moon cycles, and the smallest variations (neaps) during the first and last quarter of the moon.

A period of relatively little tidal flow — called 'slack water' — often occurs around each change of the tide. This may last from several minutes to an hour. For the rest of the time, the water flows in one direction or another: in from the sea on the rising or making tide, and back out towards the sea on the falling or ebbing tide. This tidal movement has a major influence on the positioning, behaviour and feeding of the estuarine fish species pursued by anglers.

To begin with, high water levels experienced during the last half of the incoming and first half of the outgoing tide give fish access to areas that might otherwise be very shallow or even completely dry. In tropical estuaries, these could be the flooded root systems of dense mangrove forests, while further south, such areas are typically composed of expansive mud or sand flats.

Such areas are rich with food life, particularly algae, marine worms, crabs, prawns, yabbies (nippers) and other invertebrates. Access to these feeding flats gives the major forage species such as mullet, garfish, bream, whiting, juvenile snapper, flounder and so on their best chances to feed. They are even more likely to take advantage of this access if it occurs at night, or in the half light of dawn or dusk. Rising and high tides at such times are typically prime periods during which to pursue these fish with a baited line, and efforts should be concentrated on the flats themselves, or over the drop-offs and gutters leading up into shallower areas.

Predators such as flathead, mulloway, barramundi, mangrove jacks and the like will also move up onto feeding flats during high water. They come to feed on both the invertebrate life forms and the smaller forage fish. However, the best time to

target predatory species in most estuary systems is during the run-out tide and around low water. At these times, forage fish are forced to spill back off the flats and shallows into deeper holes and gutters. Predators like flathead and barramundi will lie in ambush at gutter mouths and under the lips of drop-offs and shelves at these times, intercepting the smaller fish as they move with the falling water.

Low water levels around the bottom of the tide will also concentrate fish in smaller areas. There is literally less water between the fish, which often makes it easier to find and catch them! Remember, however, that forage fish and predators alike may become very nervous and easily spooked in very shallow, clear conditions, particularly during the day.

Tidal movements result in other changes, too. For example, a rising or making tide can bring clean, salty water in from the ocean. This may attract offshore species such as mackerel, kingfish and trevally into the estuary system. In contrast, run-out or ebb tides often carry very fresh, discoloured water down from the higher reaches of the system. This water is typically much less appealing to oceanic species, but may carry brackish or freshwater inhabitants such as barramundi, estuary perch, eels and even trout in some areas.

Prime structural elements within estuaries that will attract and hold fish include: current-

READING THE WATER

scoured holes and depressions, gutters running from shallow to deep water, the edges of weed beds, worm or yabby beds, mangrove roots, fallen trees, rock bars and man-made elements such as breakwalls, wharves, jetties, oyster leases, bridge pylons and boat moorings. Less tangible structures such as lines of demarcation between fast and slow moving currents, colour or temperature changes and back eddies are also important.

The basic points to remember when seeking fish in estuaries are that moving water will carry food — especially if it is moving in from the sea or across rich feeding flats — but that most fish do not choose to hold position within fast flowing water while awaiting their next meal. In other words, seek sheltered, slower moving bodies of water in very close proximity to faster running currents.

Work the tides, use natural baits or lures and be observant. Look for areas that will obviously concentrate food and feeders alike, and eliminate the vast, unproductive stretches common to so many estuaries.

LEFT: *A nice bream taken after a little 'code cracking' in a local estuary.*
ABOVE: *A fine haul of southern bream taken from a back eddy area beside the main current in a Victorian river.*
RIGHT: *A typical coastal creek at low tide. Low water and a high vantage point allow many key fish-holding features to be identified for later exploration. This one's at Hat Head, on the New South Wales north coast.*

Reading a Surf Beach

Surf or beach fishing is a popular pursuit around the southern half of Australia and in parts of New Zealand, especially on the North Island. It has a strong following among those who enjoy the solitude of the wave-washed shore, and the clean crunch of white or golden sand underfoot. Almost all of the species commonly taken from beaches are highly desirable table fish with a good average size. Very few unwanted species are encountered by the surf angler.

Many of our beaches are long, ranging from half a kilometre to two or three kilometres and in some instances spanning much more extensive stretches of coast.

Fish are often scattered in small numbers along these beaches, but densities can be very light. In this way, beaches are not unlike deserts — there is plenty of life, but it is thinly spread and often well hidden. As in a desert, we must locate the oases in order to find reasonable concentrations of activity. On an ocean beach, these oases usually take the form of holes, gutters or reef outcrops, especially if these structures are in close proximity to worm or pipi beds.

Unlike many other angling environments, ocean beaches change shape quite rapidly. Holes, gutters and sand banks can literally form and be destroyed in the course of a day, or even one tide cycle.

The major forces causing these physical changes are wave action, current or long-shore drift and tidal movement.

Waves may be either constructive or destructive in their effects on a beach. Constructive waves add sand to a beach and are associated with periods of stable weather. Destructive waves erode sand from the beach and carry it elsewhere. The commonest types of destructive wave are the shore-breaking 'dumpers' associated with storm seas and their aftermath.

Current and long-shore drift is a fact of life on nearly all ocean beaches. It picks up sand and moves it constantly, filling in gutters and forming others. The direction and force of this drift varies with the prevailing winds and fluctuating ocean currents. On a stable, crescent-shaped beach, experiencing calm weather conditions and an orderly surf break, there is often a current or long-shore drift running away from the centre of the beach, towards the headlands at either end.

Long-shore drift and currents along an ocean beach can result in a strong movement of water. Should such a flow encounter a gutter or depression in the sand leading seawards, it may race out along this to form a condition known as a rip. Rips are dangerous to swimmers and have caused many drownings. They also tend to scour even deeper gutters and holes; although further seawards, as they lose force and dissipate, they deposit their sediment load and begin to build a sand bank or bar.

The tides add a wild card to this water movement and wave action. Most Australasian beaches experience four tides during each 24 hour period. In other words, there are two high tides and two low tides a day, each approximately six hours apart. Variations between high and low water on most beaches

174

range from two or three metres to less than a metre. In addition, tidal variations change with the lunar calendar: the greatest variations (spring tides) occurring on the full and new moon cycles, and the smallest variations (neaps) during the first and last quarter of the moon.

A period of relatively little tidal flow — called 'slack water' — often occurs around each change of the tide. This may last from several minutes to an hour. For the rest of the time, the water is either increasing or decreasing in depth.

Flooding or incoming tides tend to 'fill-in' waves and alter their nature from destructive to constructive. At such times, holes and gutters may be partially filled with sand. Ebbing or falling tides cause the shore break to stand up more sharply, and may scour additional gutters or make existing holes deeper and more defined.

Despite the dynamic and fluctuating physical nature of ocean surf beaches, they remain one of the easiest of all angling scenarios to read. This is because the water is quite clear — readily showing deep and shallow areas — and because the actual shape and speed of waves over the sea bed give us a very good picture of what is going on below.

As an ocean swell moves into shallow water near a beach, the 'foot' of the swell begins to drag on the sea bed. This friction causes the swell to slow and grow in height and steepness. Eventually, the top of the swell will form a classic wave and begin to curl over. As the top of the wave attempts to travel faster than its base, the face of the wave steepens, curls over and breaks.

By watching how the waves travel towards a beach and where they break, we can paint a very clear picture of the sea bed. For example, waves breaking far off shore and rolling in as foamy white water — perhaps re-forming and breaking several times on their way — indicate a shallow, gently shelving bottom structure. In contrast, low swells coming almost to the beach before standing up abruptly and breaking right on the shore as 'dumpers' indicate a very deep and sudden drop-off.

Waves which slow down, stand up, almost break, then return to being low, fast moving swells have almost certainly passed across a sand bar or reef before reentering deep water. Similarly, low, unbroken 'saddles' in a line of waves indicate a gutter, outflowing rip, or both.

A few hours spent sitting high on a sand dune or headland watching a beach will prove illuminating and help greatly in sharpening your water reading skills. Such an exercise is especially useful if you can repeat it at high, low and mid-tide.

Dead low tide is a very good time during which to examine beach formations, as structures such as holes, gutters and bars are often plainly visible to the naked eye. These can be fished on the rising and high tide — traditionally productive times on many beaches.

A great many anglers place heavy emphasis on the importance of holes in beach fishing, and work these structures almost exclusively. Holes hold fish on many occasions, but there can also be great fishing in gutters, on sand banks and bars, and along drop-offs or ledges linking shallow and deep water.

Remember that the optimum combination of conditions occurs where relatively clear, deep and slow moving waters lie adjacent to current areas and wave-scoured feeding flats. In many cases, this means a deep gutter running alongside or through the middle of a sand bar. Recognise also that gutters leading out to sea provide 'highways' for fish — especially predators like mulloway, tailor, salmon, kingfish and sharks — to move into and away from the surf.

Perhaps the ideal set-up is a T-junction, where a gutter running in from deep water meets a gutter or hole that is parallel with the beach. Should this junction lie close to a pipi or worm bed in the process of inundation by a rising tide, so much the better! Put all of this together at dawn or dusk, and you are guaranteed of success.

FAR LEFT: Catching beach worms on a low tide beach. Low tide is also one of the best times to 'read' the surf and identify concentration zones for fish later on in the tide cycle.
ABOVE: High tide, rough seas and the fish are biting.

Reading the Rocks

Fishing from rocky shorelines is popular throughout the southern half of Australia and in many parts of New Zealand, particularly the east coast of the North Island. A staggering array of saltwater fish species is available to the Australasian 'rockhopper', from mullet to marlin. There are few other places on earth where fishermen can cast a line from the shore and hope to connect with such a diversity of fish.

Rock fishing locations cover a broad range of geographic forms, from sheltered sandstone platforms in large bays and estuary mouths, to rugged granite ridges and basalt razor-backs plunging into the deep, open ocean. However, the rock hopping structures of Australia and New Zealand can be divided into three broad types or classes: shallow reefs, mixed depth locations and deep-water ledges.

Shallow reef locations are common in bays and harbours, as well as along some open ocean shorelines. They feature low rock ledges or platforms which may be awash at high tide. Water within casting range of these rocks ranges from half a metre to three or four metres in depth, and the sea bed consists of broken reef, boulders, rocky outcrops, kelp beds and occasional patches of gravel or sand.

Life is prolific in these shallow, wave-washed areas. There is an abundance of crabs, shellfish, cunjevoi and other invertebrates, as well as algae and weed of several types. Fish are also abundant although many are small, or species not popularly targeted by anglers. However, highly desirable fish are also encountered in such locations, particularly on rising tides, at night or during and immediately after a stormy sea.

Fish commonly taken in shallow reef locations include bream, black and silver drummer, luderick, groper, trevally and sweep. Snapper will also enter these shallow areas, particularly after heavy seas.

The geographic category classed as mixed depth covers the vast majority of Australian and New Zealand rock fishing locations. These consist of ledges, platforms or sloping headlands fronting water with a mean depth between two and ten metres. The sea bed may be composed of flat rock, reef ledges, boulders, gravel or sand.

Frequently these mixed depth locations are adjacent to or sandwiched between shallow reef areas. They may also lie in close proximity to the final rock formation category: deep-water ledges. Demarcation zones between these geographic types are often fishing 'hot spots'.

Mixed depth locations see the bulk of rock fishing effort and produce the greatest range of species. Common target species in mixed depth areas include bream, drummer, trevally, groper, salmon (kahawai), tailor, kingfish, Samson fish, mackerel, mulloway, luderick, snapper and the smaller tunas and bonito. Most of these fish bite best in mixed depth areas on rising tides around dawn and dusk, or when there is enough wave action to produce a foamy, aerated zone of white water called a 'wash'.

Deep-water ledges are less

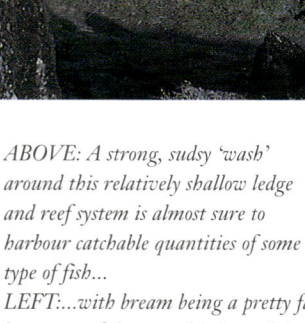

ABOVE: A strong, sudsy 'wash' around this relatively shallow ledge and reef system is almost sure to harbour catchable quantities of some type of fish...
LEFT:...with bream being a pretty fair bet as one of the more likely candidates!
ABOVE RIGHT: Deep water frontages have narrower 'wash' zones, less food and less diversity of life — however, they also offer accesss to big predators such as tuna, mackerel, kingfish and even marlin.

widespread than the first two rock types. They are typified by famous land-based gamefishing spots such as the Beecroft Peninsula in New South Wales, Steep Point in Western Australia, and Spirits Bay in New Zealand's Northland.

These areas are by flat, relatively safe and dry rock ledges fronting water with a depth range of eight to 20 metres.

Here, true deep-sea species are available to the shore-based angler. These include big yellowtail kingfish, large tuna, mackerel, sharks and even billfish such as marlin and sailfish. Many of these locations are also excellent snapper fishing spots.

Life is less abundant along the narrow inter-tidal zones on these ledges. There is less weed and fewer crabs or shellfish than in shallower, more gradually sloping areas. As a result the occurrence of desirable target species is largely dictated by currents, water temperature and the presence or otherwise of bait fish. For these reasons, true deep-water ledges tend to have clearly defined cycles of activity. When they are 'off', they produce very little angling action.

Many overlaps occur between the three classifications. A single headland may exhibit all three geographic types within a 400 metre stretch, and many mixed depth or deep-water locations are bounded on either side by areas of shallow reef. However, learning to recognise the distinct characteristics of each major class of rock formation and adapting your fishing techniques will help to make you a better and more productive rock hopper.

Beside the physical structure of the rock formation, it is important to consider the water movement generated by tides, currents, wave wash and wind drift. Australasian rock ledges and foreshores have four tide changes every 24 hours. In other words, there are two high tides and two low tides each day.

Extreme variations between high and low water range from six or eight metres in some tropical areas, to a metre or less in other regions. Tidal variation is typically in the order of two metres. In addition, tidal variations change with the lunar calendar: the greatest variations (spring tides) occurring on the full and new moon cycles, and the smallest variations (neaps) during the first and last quarter of the moon.

A period of relatively little tidal movement — called 'slack water' — often occurs around each change of the tide. This may last from several minutes to an hour. For the rest of the time, the water level is either rising or falling along the ocean rocks.

This tidal movement has a major influence on the positioning, behaviour and feeding of the rock and reef dwelling species. Tides influence water movement around rock ledges and offer fish varying degrees of access to food types. For example, luderick may use a high tide to reach succulent beds of 'sea cabbage' weed, while blue groper take advantage of the same increase in water depth to grab red crabs from a wave-washed gutter. Conversely, kingfish or tailor may wait for a falling tide to force mullet or yellowtail out of the foamy shallows into deeper water.

Reading the rocks comes down to observation and the repetition of successful patterns.

Rock fishing is a potentially dangerous sport. Most tragedies could be avoided if fishermen followed the simple expedients of never fishing alone, always watching the sea for at least 10 or 15 minutes before beginning to fish, and having a plan of action in case of emergency.

Reading the Bluewater Currents

Many anglers have a great deal of difficulty coming to grips with the vast tracts of open ocean that are the province of the bluewater sport and game fisherman. While the open ocean may not be as easily deciphered as a shallow trout stream or a tidal mangrove estuary, the same basic water reading skills and natural signposts apply in all of these aquatic environments.

Again, 'structure' is the key to fish location, although the fish-attracting and aggregating structures of the open ocean may be more subtle and difficult to detect than boulders in a creek or fallen tree trunks along an estuary shoreline.

The structures which dominate offshore fishing are the seabed topography, ocean currents, floating objects, and zones of demarcation or 'break-lines' between bodies of water with varying temperatures.

In deeper water, the best tools for detecting changes in seabed topography are an accurate set of marine charts with numerous depth soundings, and a sonar unit or depth sounder.

The seabed formations most likely to attract and hold concentrations of game and sport fish include: reef complexes, peaks, pinnacles, sudden drop-offs, undersea mountains, and so-called 'canyons' in the ocean's floor. The least productive areas are those with a relatively uniform depth and a soft bottom strata of sand, gravel or mud.

Hard seabed structure may not be enough on its own to attract large quantities of pelagic fish such as tuna, sharks and marlin. These fish also require the correct combination of current and water quality. True 'hot spots' occur only when all of these factors combine.

Currents are important to the free-wandering or pelagic fishes of the sea. They provide highways and food chains in what would otherwise be an aquatic desert. In fact, currents are sometimes referred to as 'rivers in the sea' — a very apt description of both their physical properties and their importance.

Our major tools for identifying likely fish-holding currents and eddies are keen eyes, polarised sunglasses, binoculars, water temperature gauges and satellite-generated thermal 'maps' of the ocean's surface. First of all, however, we must know what to look for!

The major ocean currents are reasonably steady and predictable in nature. Some of the most important to Australasian anglers are: the East Australian Current (which flows from north to south down the continent's east coast), the Leeuwin Current (which flows northwards along the West Australian coast), the West Wind Drift (which flows from west to east off Australia's southern shores and past New Zealand's South Island), the Tasman Current (which flows from south to north up New Zealand's west coast), and the South Pacific Current (which swirls southwards down the eastern shore of New Zealand's North Island).

Of greater day-to-day and week-to-week importance for anglers are the various offshoots and eddies which break away from these deep water, oceanic currents and swirl inshore over the shallower areas within the Continental Shelf. These inshore currents and eddies which can make or break the fishing fortunes of Australasian bluewater sport and game anglers.

Currents carry water with different properties to that found in surrounding seas. They may be warm or cool, clear or discoloured, nutrient-rich or relatively infertile. Currents flowing southwards around Australasia from the tropics are warm and relatively infertile, while northward flowing currents and the West Wind Drift are cold and loaded with nutrients. The most favourable fishing conditions occur where these different currents collide or mix, causing upwellings of cold,

nutrient rich water intermingled with swirls and eddies of warm, tropical water.

All pelagic fish have a band or zone of water temperature preferences, and although they will occasionally be encountered in warmer or cooler waters, they are much easier to find and catch within this 'comfort zone'. For example, yellowfin tuna may be caught in waters as cold as 15 degrees Celsius and as hot as 30 degrees Celsius, but are far more likely to be hooked when the water is between about 20 and 25 degrees Celsius.

Many of our more popular sport and game species — marlin, sailfish, wahoo, dolphin fish and the like — tend to be associated with warm water and southward-flowing currents. In temperate latitudes, these currents swing inshore more frequently during summer and autumn. However, it should be remembered that hot water alone does not necessarily make for great offshore fishing. Warm currents can be rather barren and sterile. It is only where they collide with colder, nutrient rich waters that they become prolific. For this reason, thermal fronts — zones of sudden temperature change — tend to be more productive than large, stable masses of warm, tropical water.

The other important feature offered by currents is water movement, which tends to concentrate both food and predators. This is especially true where current interacts with the seabed structures.

These ocean floor formations cause upwellings, bringing deep (cool) water and nutrients to the surface, where sunlight can act upon them and generate a rich food chain. Current-washed undersea mountains and islands can be viewed as boulders or snags in a river. Fish will aggregate around and over them, especially on the upcurrent side of the structural element.

Water clarity and colour are further indicators of likely offshore angling results. Clear, blue water is preferred by most game and sport species, and the best water of all for highly-prized targets such as marlin is the rich, almost purple water found at the leading edge of a warm current. The presence of brightly coloured flecks of planktonic life ('sparklers') in this purple-blue water confirms its richness and the likelihood of encountering concentrations of pelagic fish.

Floating objects such as logs, pieces of man-made flotsam and jetsam, rafts of weed, mats of pumice stone and the like can also be important keys to finding fish. These items tend to accumulate along the edges of currents and over distinct thermal fronts or breaklines. As well as signposting such structural elements as current lines, the objects themselves are attractive to pelagic fish, offering shade, cover, accumulations of food and a point of reference for navigation.

LEFT: A yellowfin tuna taken from a current edge. Note the cut up pilchard pieces and fish scraps alongside the angler. These were used for both berley and bait.
ABOVE: One of the clearest signposts in the sea! Birds wheel frantically over a splashing, foaming school of skipjack tuna. Down deeper, much larger predators hunt.
RIGHT: A lure-caught trevally hooked in the kind of cobalt blue water that game fishermen everywhere love to see.

THE COMPLETE BOOK OF AUSTRALIAN FISHING

Reading a Mangrove Stream

The family of tough, salt resistant plants and trees called mangroves are found in many parts of Australia and even the north of New Zealand. They almost always grow in very close proximity to tidal saltwater — usually along the shores of estuaries, bays and harbours. It is in tropical estuaries, north of about the 25th parallel of latitude, that mangroves become critical to the angler.

Northwards from Fraser Island in the east and Shark Bay in the west, mangroves begin to totally dominate our estuary and inshore tidal systems. Their spiky root systems, gnarled trunks and luxuriant green leaves form dense forest walls along the water's edge in almost every estuary, bay or inlet.

The functions of mangroves are manifold. They hold soft, muddy banks together and allow tidal channels to be formed. They filter the water to remove sediment and other suspended matter, and provide shade, shelter and a home for many forms of life. And, perhaps most important of all, their falling leaves decay to provide the nutrients which form the very basis of the inshore food chain in tropical and sub-tropical seas. These fallen leaves feed the shrimps, prawns, crabs, garfish, herring and mullet which will ultimately be eaten by larger and larger marine predators.

Mangrove estuaries are also their breeding grounds and nurseries. Many species of fish spend their entire lives within a mangrove estuary, but even those that don't rely on the mangroves for at least a part of their life cycle before moving upstream into freshwater or offshore.

With this teeming abundance of life, mangrove estuaries offer some of our finest tropical angling opportunities, fish are not evenly spread throughout every mangrove system.

As in all other habitat types, concentration zones exist. Special features or structures must be identified to enjoy consistent sport.

The structural elements within a mangrove estuary can be

TOP: Sunset in the tropical mangroves — a time when many fish come out to hunt, particularly if the tide is right. ABOVE: One such change-of-light food hunter is the barramundi. This one came from the stretch of mangroves and oysters shown above.

broken into various types. The most obvious is the shore-line itself, which is charact-erised by a 'picket line' of man-grove tree trunks and root systems.

In areas with maximum tidal variations of two or three metres, these picket lines are nearly always partially in the water, even if it is only lapping at their feet. In contrast, regions with larger tidal variations (three to nine metres) may see the mangrove roots high and dry at the bottom of the tide, and completely inundated at high water. These tides play a vital role in reading the mangroves.

Mangrove roots are home to an abundance of invertebrate life forms such as shellfish, crabs, worms, shrimps and prawns. Because of this, and the cover they offer to prey and predators alike, they will always attract at least some catchable fish. However, there may be hundreds of kilometres of almost identical picket fence shoreline in a tropical estuary. Fishing it all would take weeks, and may produce only mediocre fishing results. To maximise chances, we need to identify important secondary structural features.

The most obvious secondary structure types are 'snags' form-ed by fallen mangrove trees or timber washed downriver by floods or big tides. Snags are one of the most prolific producers of fish within a mangrove estuary.

Other important items of secondary structure include boulders, rock outcrops and rock bars. These are especially im-portant in areas where the dominant strata is mud. Rocky outcrops in these systems are usually covered with oysters and other shellfish. They also attract quantities of invertebrate organ-isms and, in turn, predatory fish.

Creek mouths and channel inflows are another group of vital secondary structural elements and are always worthy of atten-tion from the angler, especially when the tidal flow has water moving from the smaller tribut-ary into the larger channel.

More subtle secondary elem-ents include colour and temp-erature 'breaklines'. These are the distinct lines where bodies of water with different sediment loads or temperatures butt up against each other. Tidal rips, back eddies and current shear lines are also important, and worth examination.

The tides play a critical role in reading and fishing our tropical mangrove systems. Most northern estuaries have maxi-mum (spring tide) variations of at least two or three metres, and many have far greater ranges. In areas of the Northern Territory and the north west of Western Australia, tidal variation may run to seven metres or more!

You should try to examine and fish your chosen estuary at the very bottom of a major low tide. This will allow you to identify and map the channel system, find holes, rock bars and mid-stream snags. These elements may well be hidden when the water is deeper, and knowing where they are can be vital to your results.

Realise that most mangrove estuary sport fish such as barra-mundi, mangrove jacks, finger-mark bream and estuary cod are quite mobile, and will use the tides to feed and seek shelter. On the top of a very high tide, these fish may move well back into the flooded mangrove forest and be almost unreachable with conven-tional angling techniques. Low tide may concentrate such fish in small holes and pockets, making them easier to find.

In particular, look for snags, rock bars and other secondary structural elements that are vertically oriented and span a great deal of the tidal range. These features are much more likely to hold quantities of fish throughout a tide cycle than a log which is only in the water at the very top of the tide, or a boulder that is only exposed at the very bottom.

Look also for 'leading edges' and front lines where a run-in or run-out tide flows into and splits to pass around an obstacle such as a mid-stream snag, rock bar or island. These can be almost guaranteed producers of fish.

Reading a mangrove estuary is never dull. Some are so rich in structural elements it becomes confusing to decide which to work first. Others have so few that those you find are almost sure to harbour good quantities of fish. Either way, you will need to use your eyes, your polarised glasses, your powers of observ-ation and possibly tools such as a depth sounder and temperature gauge to crack the code and decipher the message.

ABOVE: The beautiful and distinctive giant threadfin salmon or king salmon is one of the most exciting sport fish to be found in our mangrove estuaries. This species particularly favours areas of demarcation between turbid, muddy water and clearer currents. Here, it hunts prawns, shrimp and tiny fish, rounding them up with its whiskers.

Reading a Trout Stream

In many ways, trout streams are the easiest of all waterways for the angler to read. Currents are defined, structural elements are often visible and the fish themselves tend to adopt predictable 'lies' or holding stations. Indeed, many of the basic rules we apply to reading trout streams form a valuable foundation for all the other waterways we attempt to decode — in both the freshwater and marine environments.

Trout streams themselves vary from tiny brooks and mountain creeks that an energetic angler could easily jump across, through to large and powerful rivers. Each is different, yet a set of basic ground rules applies to them all.

The features most good trout streams have in common are: reasonably cool water with a relatively high level of dissolved oxygen, at least a few areas of gravel bottom strata, a regular flow, and a diversity of invertebrate stream-borne life forms (insect nymphs, larvae, shrimps, crayfish and so on).

The very best and most productive trout streams are also somewhat alkaline in their pH — often as a result of flowing through limestone country or deposits of similarly alkaline minerals, such as chalk. They may also be spring-fed, assuring reasonably stable flow rates and temperatures. Such spring-fed, limestone streams are characterised by relatively heavy in-stream weed growth, especially during the summer months. They also have an abundance of invertebrate life. As a result, trout grow fast and are typically in excellent condition. Add reasonable beds of pea- to marble-size gravel and you are also looking at a prime spawning stream for trout — one likely to support a large population of so-called 'wild' fish, and requiring very little or no re-stocking.

In reality, many streams in Australasia — particularly on the Australian mainland — fall well short of such ideals. A lot of them could best be described as 'marginal'. This means that they require regular planting of hatchery-bred fish in order to sustain reasonable fishing pressure, and that drought cycles may well decimate their trout stocks. Even in the more favourable areas — such as Tasmania and New Zealand's South Island — very dry years, heat waves, bushfires and other natural phenomena can place serious strains on localised trout population, necessitating re-stocking by government fisheries, clubs or private individuals.

One of the first tricks to reading trout water lies in establishing the suitability of the stream. If the creek or river in question is less than ideal or even marginal, it is important to find out how frequently, how heavily and with which trout species it is stocked. These details can provide valuable clues to the 'where', 'how' and 'when' of catching trout in such waters.

After establishing the credentials of your chosen trout stream — from ideal to marginal — and gaining an insight into the likely population density and size range of the fish, it is time to begin assessing the physical attributes of the creek or river.

Most flowing waterways are composed of two types of stream configuration: pools and riffles. These are also known as pools and rapids, holes and bars, or even runs and riffles, depending on the precise nature of the stream. Regardless of the actual terminology used, these labels are intended to differentiate between the deeper, relatively slow flowing areas of the stream (pools) and the shallower, faster stretches (riffles).

In a typical stream, pools and riffles alternate with at least some pattern, although the length and depth of a pool or the speed of

flow through a riffle may be very different between, for example, the headwaters and lower reaches of any given watercourse. We can further break up these two major stream configurations by talking about secondary features within them — such as pockets, glides and pressure waves in a riffle, or the head and tail-out areas of a pool.

Generally speaking, all of the trout within a stream will choose a lie facing directly upstream, into the current. Furthermore, they will choose a holding station close to relatively fast moving water, but just slightly out of it. Finally, they will also opt for cover of some sort, be it broken white water, depth, an undercut bank, or the shadow of a tree, high bank or boulder.

Just how good a lie each trout finds will depend on its size, aggression and place within the 'pecking order'. Big, bold fish tend to secure the best lies. However, just to add a little uncertainty to the issue, it should also be remembered that trout do not remain 'at station' all the time. They will cruise around a pool, drop back or move up through a riffle and even adopt different lies at different times of the day and night as cover and feeding conditions change. The system is dynamic and fluid.

Bearing all this in mind, we'll examine the more productive areas of typical riffles and pools.

To begin with, shallow, quick moving rapids will not hold many worthwhile sized fish for long periods unless there are relatively quiet pockets or significant pressure waves and/or eddies in front of and behind boulders or logs. In other words, it is relatively easy to choose the slots within a riffle that might hold good fish simply look for those areas where a fish need not work so hard in order to maintain its position. The major exception to this rule occurs during times of very hot weather or reduced stream flow, when stressed trout seek the more agitated, oxygenated water found in fast moving chutes and rapids.

For most of the season, one of the prime areas in a stream lies at the transition zone between the riffle and the head of the pool. Here the current rapidly loses force and back eddies may occur along each bank as the water becomes deeper and more slow moving. Often there is a circular or oval patch of almost motionless water — sometimes two such patches — within this transition zone called 'eyes' are very productive fish-holding areas.

As well as eyes, one is also likely to find 'shear lines' in the current just downstream of the transition zone. These are quite clearly defined longitudinal breaks between fast and slow moving water. Fish will hold along these, keeping just within the slower body of water.

The middle or belly of the pool is often surprisingly unproductive on a trout stream, although good fish will cruise and rise here in the mornings and evenings, especially if an insect hatch is in progress.

Finally, there is the tail-out — another very productive area, where the water begins to shallow and speed up before rushing away into the next riffle. This feature will hold fish most of the year — especially at dawn and dusk — but is particularly productive early and late in the season when the fish are preparing to spawn, spawning or recovering from spawning.

As well as thinking about the horizontal or longitudinal arrangement of trout through a stream, you should also consider their vertical positioning within the water column. Here it is necessary to understand that the current is slowest right on the stream bed and at the surface, and usually strongest just above mid-depth. For these reasons, trout usually hold very close to the bottom or, more rarely, just under the surface.

Combine these guidelines with your own observations and you will quickly begin to identify prime fish-holding areas within a stream, thus optimising your angling results.

FAR LEFT: Spinning the 'eye' of a pool, where good fish often hold. CENTRE: This brown trout picked up a free-drifted white jig. Trout take much of their food on the bottom. BELOW: Shadows and back eddies around trees are also hot spots.

Reading an Outback River

Reading or decoding the fish-holding secrets of Australia's outback rivers is a little more difficult than understanding a shallow, clear trout stream. These western rivers tend to be deeper and much more turbid than their alpine and sub-alpine counterparts. In addition, the native freshwater species of the outback are somewhat less predictable in their behaviour than the introduced salmonids.

Despite the differences between a relatively slowflowing, muddy outback river and a lively, quickmoving trout stream, remember that the basic rules of stream mechanics still apply. Even the Murray and Darling rivers feature the alternating 'riffle and pool' structure previously discussed under the heading of 'Reading A Trout Stream'.

Nearly all flowing waterways are composed of these two types of stream configuration: pools and riffles. They are also known as pools and rapids, holes and bars, or even runs and riffles, depending on the precise nature of the stream. Regardless of the actual terminology used, such labels are intended to differentiate between the deeper, relatively slowflowing areas of the river (pools) and the shallower, faster stretches (riffles).

In a typical outback river, pools and riffles (or holes and bars) alternate with at least a vague pattern, although the length and depth of a pool, or the speed of flow over a bar, may vary considerably at different points along the river. We can break down the two major stream configurations and examine secondary features within them — such as pockets, glides and pressure waves in the faster water over a bar, or the head and tail-out areas of a pool.

Generally, all the fish within the flowing part of a river will choose to hold position facing directly upstream, into the current. Furthermore, they will select a holding station quite close to faster moving water, but not right in it. Finally, they will also opt for cover of some sort, be it depth, a fallen tree, an undercut bank, or the shadow of bankside vegetation, a high bank or boulder.

The quality of the holding position or 'station' each fish ends up with will depend on its size, aggression and place within the 'pecking order'. Big, bold fish such as mature Murray cod tend to secure the best territory. However, just to add uncertainty to the picture, it should also be remembered that fish do not remain 'at station' all the time. They will cruise around a pool, drop back or move up through a shallower run, and even adopt different territories at different times of the day and night as cover and feeding conditions change. Naturally, this behaviour

LEFT: The presence of food, like this succulent yabby, is a good indicator of the likelihood of catching fish.
ABOVE: Releasing a nice Murray cod taken just as night fell — a time when many natives become active.
RIGHT: The broad and turbid rivers of the outback are not always easy to read. This is the Darling, near Bourke.

varies with the size and type of fish under discussion.

The main angling species present in our inland rivers include: Murray cod, golden perch (yellowbelly), silver perch and eel-tailed catfish. Several introduced species are also found in many areas. These include European carp, English perch (redfin) and tench.

Our native freshwater fish tend to be strongly 'structure-oriented' — particularly the two largest species, the Murray cod and golden perch. These heavyweights often become rather solitary in nature as they grow in size, although golden perch will form loose schools of varying sizes, especially around spawning time (spring).

Cod and goldens will usually be found near fallen timber, undercut banks, exposed tree roots or rock bars. They favour the deeper parts of the pools, especially during daylight hours, and in faster flowing water they will seek the sanctuary and still water offered by a large obstruction such as a tree trunk, bridge pylon or boulder.

Silver perch and redfin are schooling, open-water species which often feed in the quicker moving areas of our outback river systems, while catfish and carp will utilise nearly every part of the river, including shallow backwaters, swampy margins and isolated ox-bow lagoons.

The prime structures of interest to inland anglers pursuing our larger natives are large fallen trees or tangles of trees, rock bars and steep, current-scoured banks. If these structures lie in, or very close to, the deepest parts of a pool or hole, so much the better.

Man-made structures can also be of great importance. The most significant are weirs, which are commonplace on big, outback rivers like the Murray and Darling. Fishing is often at its best just downstream of these barriers, where fish attempting to migrate upriver 'stack up' and compete for food. The kilometre or so of river just downstream of a weir is a great place to start prospecting on a new stretch of outback river, particularly if good snag-piles of fallen timber or rock bars are present.

Variations in water flow, volume and depth are also critically important to outback fish and the anglers who pursue them. Before the coming of white man and his weirs, these seasonal swings between high and low water, and the longer term cycles of drought and flood, were the biological clocks by which all life in the western rivers was organised. Even now, after two centuries of detrimental modification by man, floods or 'freshes' have a major impact on inland angling.

The arrival of a 'fresh' tends to send native fish into a frenzy of activity and feeding. This typically begins a day or two before the advancing flood front arrives, and may continue for a few more days as the water level rises and the river muddies. Outback anglers can keep one jump ahead of the flood waters and enjoy sensational action, especially if they take the effects of weirs into consideration.

At the opposite end of the scale, periods of stable and relatively low river heights can lead to a partial clearing of the water. This is the time to break out lures and try spinning or trolling for native fish. Should such clear water occur in the spring or early summer, action is almost assured.

Perhaps the best of both worlds is an advancing fresh or flood front encroaching on a stretch of low, clear water during late September, October or November.

Reading a Freshwater Lake

Australia is one of the driest continents on earth. As a result, the mainland is not overly endowed with natural, freshwater lakes. Lake George, near Canberra, is one of the largest, but even it becomes almost completely dry on regular occasions. Others, like South Australia's vast Lake Eyre, are dry salt pans more often than inland seas.

Tasmania has more natural lakes than the mainland, and there are quite a number in New Zealand. Both areas, however, are still rather dry in comparison with countries like Canada, which boasts in excess of one million natural lakes!

Australasia's lack of freshwater lakes has been partially compensated by the construction of man-made waterways variously known as dams, reservoirs or impoundments. Man-made impoundments are built for various purposes, the most important of which are the generation of hydro-electricity, storage of water for urban and rural consumption, flood mitigation and recreational activities.

For the purposes of this book, we will look at natural lakes and man-made impoundments together, as there are many similarities from the angling point of view. However, it should be remembered that water level fluctuations are more common in man-made dams, and that many of our man-made impoundments also feature deeper water than natural lakes.

From the fishing point of view, Australasian lakes and dams tend to fall into three broad groupings: salmonid (trout and salmon) fisheries, 'mixed' fisheries and warm water fisheries.

Almost all of the lakes and impoundments in Tasmania and New Zealand fall into the first (salmonid) grouping. In the southern half of the Australian mainland, lakes and dams in alpine and sub-alpine regions (above about 700 metres elevation) also tend to be primarily salmonid habitats, while those at lower altitudes are more likely to contain 'mixed' fish populations, with some salmonids and some warm water species present. In the outback and the north of the country, lakes and impoundments are warm water habitats.

Lakes and impoundments are arguably the most difficult of all freshwater environments for the angler to 'read' and understand. These difficulties are magnified in low altitude, mixed and warm water fisheries, which typically feature large areas of shallow, turbid water and few distinctive shoreline features. However, by applying the basic rules of fish location and behaviour and being keenly observant, an angler can begin to crack the 'code' of apparently barren water.

Fortunately, not all lakes and impoundments are featureless. Many of those at higher elevations (salmonid and 'mixed' fisheries) lie in deep valleys and are surrounded by steep hills and ridges. More often than not, the contours evident along the shoreline continue beneath the surface, so that a ridge top will form an underwater reef, while an inflowing creek gully will most likely continue beneath the surface as a submerged gutter. Similarly, shorelines characterised by grassy flats, paddocks or swampy marshes typically lie alongside areas of shallow water with a relatively uniform depth.

Submerged or partially submerged standing trees — common in newer man-made impoundments — are also valuable indicators of water depth and bottom contour. By comparing them with similar trees on the shore, it is possible to make very accurate assumptions about the shape of the lake bed.

Relating shoreline topogr-

READING THE WATER

LEFT: Big, freshwater lakes and impoundments are nowhere near as easy to decipher as trout streams. However, careful study of the shoreline topography is a good place to start.
TOP: Sunset on a freshwater reservoir and an angler cleans her catch. Note the flooded timber.
ABOVE: European perch or redfin are just one species which hang around flooded trees.
RIGHT: Another is the Macquarie perch.

aphy and vegetation to structures beneath the water's surface is the most basic and important of all lake-reading skills. Indeed, for the shore-based angler, it may be the only skill needed. Boat fishermen, however, require a little more knowledge of what is going on beneath the surface. They are also in a better position to use water reading tools such as depth sounders, temperature gauges, pH meters and dissolved oxygen probes.

As in all the other environment types discussed in this chapter, consistent lake angling results will only come to those who can identify the correct combination of structural elements, water quality and food supply most attractive to their target species. Obviously, these requirements vary between fish, and the ideal habitat for a rainbow trout would be completely unsuited to a Murray cod, eel-tailed catfish or sooty grunter. It is up to the angler to learn as much as he or she can about their chosen target species and apply this knowledge to reading the water and assessing likely hot spots.

Despite these variations from one species to another, certain broad parameters apply to nearly all lake and impoundment fish. They all require cover (from predators such as eagles and cormorants), a food supply, and water with enough dissolved oxygen to sustain life. Beyond these three basic requirements, factors such as preferred temperature zones and acidity (pH) come into play.

In most cases, cover is provided by water depth, water discolouration, or structure such as submerged timber, rock outcrops and weed beds. Food supply will most likely be related to the same structures, as well as to creek and river inflows. Rising water levels inundate new ground and greatly increase the availability of food.

Water quality itself is a slightly more complex and dynamic subject.

One of the things we must remember about relatively still bodies of water such as larger lakes and dams is that they become 'stratified'. In other words, layers of water with different temperatures, dissolved oxygen levels and acidity (pH) form over time, and change with the seasons and prevailing weather conditions.

In Australasian lakes and dams, three distinct layers are common. These are the epilimnion, the thermocline and the hypolimnion.

The epilimnion forms at the surface and may extend down many metres. It is relatively warm (hot in lower altitude lakes during summer), contains reasonably high levels of dissolved oxygen and holds large quantities of food.

The thermocline is a much narrower zone or layer of sudden change between the warm, oxygen-rich epilimnion and the cold, oxygen-depleted hypolimnion. At times, the thermocline may be almost a distinct line. On other occasions, it is a layer several metres thick. Its depth beneath the surface varies from a few metres (as in a salmonid or 'mixed' fishery in spring), down to significant depths (as in a warm water impoundment during late summer).

The hypolimnion is the deepest zone, characterised by still, cool to cold and relatively oxygen-depleted water with very little food supply. In extreme cases, the hypolimnion becomes so oxygen-depleted that it cannot sustain aerobic (oxygen-breathing) life of any type.

Fishing for warm water species is typically best in the epilimnion and on top of the thermocline. Cold-water trout and salmon usually bite best in and just below the thermocline. Remember, however, that these layers change in depth and intensity with the seasons, and that strong winds may cause them to mix, especially in shallow or very broad lakes.

Fishing Locations

New South Wales

FAR NORTH COAST

TWEED RIVER-TWEED HEADS
This area is mecca for anglers from northern New South Wales, southern Queensland and further afield. For that reason it can become rather crowded during school holidays.

The rocky headlands and breakwalls adjacent to the entrance of the Tweed are renowned autumn and winter tailor haunts and produce big numbers of these fish, especially for anglers casting and retrieving gang-hooked pilchards and garfish during the early morning or late afternoon. Tailor hot spots include Kirra Point, Grenwell Point, Snapper Rocks and the North and South Walls.

These same headlands, along with the beaches in between, also have a good record of producing mid-size to large mulloway (jewfish). Concentrate on this heavyweight species while the sea or 'bully' mullet are making their annual run, and also when the tailor are at their thickest.

The lower Tweed itself is renowned for fine breaming, and also produces flathead, whiting and mulloway. The Blue Hole and Nussex Wall are proven estuary locations. Tides at the entrance of the Tweed are about 15 minutes behind times listed for Port Jackson (Sydney Harbour).

UPPER TWEED RIVER
Further upriver, towards Murwillumbah and beyond, there is some excellent estuary angling to be enjoyed, although navigation is made difficult in places by the relatively shallow water.

Night fishing is popular along this stretch of river, especially during holiday times when the daytime water ski traffic can be rather heavy. However, be extra careful of the shallows and of working dredges in the darkness. Try the pylons around the bridge below Lillies Island with live baits for mangrove jack, school jew and big flathead.

Further upstream there are some very productive whiting, bream and luderick (blackfish) locations, particularly around the Tumblegum area, the Sugar Hole (just downstream of the sugar mill at Condong) and the Weir. These stretches are at their best when there is not too much 'fresh' in the system.

TWEED HEADS TO KINGSCLIFFE
This is a great stretch of coastline for the experienced and adventurous beach angler and rockhopper. Generally there are good beach formations (gutters etc.), or fish activity close to headlands, to be found somewhere along this stretch during every week of the year; however, the autumn and winter tailor run is particularly noteworthy.

More exposed and prominent headlands in this area also produce mulloway and are well worth a try with live and dead baits or lures for Spanish mackerel, cobia and longtail (northern bluefin) tuna, particularly during the first half of the year. Longtails become so thick at times off this far northern section of the New South Wales coast that the locals regard them as a pest!

Beaches along this stretch produce the usual fare of bream, whiting, dart, tailor and the occasional mulloway.

OFFSHORE
Excellent bottom fishing, pilchard tossing and lure casting and trolling is available for trailer boat fishermen working out of the Tweed, Kingscliff or Brunswick Heads. Snapper, pearl perch, samson fish, cod, yellowtail kingfish, Spanish and spotted mackerel, cobia, dolphin fish, tuna and mulloway are just a few of the desirable species available on and over the inshore reefs and around headlands and bomboras. Further out, marlin, large tuna and even sailfish are seasonally abundant.

Black Rocks, south of Hastings Point, is a boat fishing hot spot, but it is rather a long run from any of the safer launching spots.

BRUNSWICK HEADS TO BYRON BAY
Brunswick Heads, at the mouth of the Brunswick River, lies in the middle of a long expanse of beach stretching away towards Pottsville and Kingscliffe in the north and Byron Bay to the south. These beaches fish well at times, especially when productive formations such as holes and gutters can be located.

The Brunswick River fishes well for

all the usual estuarine species up as far as Mullumbimby and beyond. Pay particular attention to the North Arm, Boat Harbour and around the pylons of the Highway Bridge.

Byron Bay is famous as the most easterly point on the Australian mainland. As one would expect of a headland which juts so far out into the ocean, it is a prime 'fish intersection' for pelagic and semi-pelagic species such as Spanish and spotted mackerel, tuna of several types, cobia, tailor and sharks. The Cape also offers superb bream and mulloway (jewfish) action at times.

Tallow Beach, just south of Cape Byron, attracts a big following among dedicated beachcasters who take some great hauls of tailor, as well as bream and the occasional mulloway. There's also plenty of bait to be had here in the form of beach worms and pipis.

OFFSHORE

Offshore of cape Byron is an excellent stretch of boat water, with similar species to those described for the Tweed area. The offshore hot spot around Byron Bay is Lulian Rocks, about four kilometres north west of Cape Byron. This red hot area is a state marine park, and anglers are restricted to one line and one hook each within a kilometre of the rocks.

BYRON BAY TO BALLINA

The stretch of rugged coast between Cape Byron and Lennox Head has much to offer the rockhopper and beachcaster, particularly in the form of tailor, bream, whiting and mulloway, but pelagics such as mackerel and tuna are always a chance from the more exposed headlands.

Lennox Headland itself, along with sweeping Seven Mile Beach to the north, offers superb tailor runs, particularly in autumn and through the winter months, while the Iron Peg, to the south, is a famous (if somewhat dangerous) rock fishing locale.

The Ballina area is another tourist magnet, drawing anglers from southern Queensland as well as from all over New South Wales. As with the Tweed Heads region, it can become a little crowded during holiday time.

The Richmond River estuary at Ballina is full of surprises, with even the fenced-off swimming area of Shaws Bay producing outside fish at times. Recently a massive 11 kilo mangrove jack was taken from this estuary by an angler soaking a live pink nipper on his bream gear! Apart from such oddball catches, the Lower Richmond offers all the usual estuarine species.

Richmond River hot spots include the Bream Hole, off the Apex boat ramp, the Porpoise Wall and, further upstream, Pimlico Island.

OFFSHORE

The conditions are similar to the areas described above. The local hot spot is around north and south Riordan Reefs, which lie south of Ballina and some three kilometres offshore (seek local advice on precise marks).

BALLINA TO EVANS HEAD

More good to excellent beach fishing country is to be found along this extensive stretch, with Airforce Beach (just north of Evans Head) being particularly noteworthy for its bumper bream, hot tailor bite and big jewie runs.

Evans Head has abundant estuary fishing on tap in the lower Evans River, as well as some productive headlands and beaches very close to town. Hot spots include Half Tide Rock, Joggily Point, the Piano Rocks and the exposed and rather dangerous Snapper Rock.

YAMBA TO ILUKA

More fine fishing territory lies along the stretch of coast between Evans Head and Iluka, but access can be a problem. For this reason, anglers tend to concentrate on the Yamba area itself.

The lower Clarence is one of the best estuary systems on the far north coast, with superlative bream, flathead, whiting and blackfish angling for those willing to invest a little time and effort. Hot spots here include the Middle Wall, Browns Rock, Palmers Island and Sleeper Island.

The upper Clarence, between Maclean and Grafton, also has some great fishing territory. Much further upstream this system is renowned for its freshwater bass, although these are unfortunately not as prolific as they once were. Also found in this system is the east coast cod (a close relative of the Murray cod) however, it is so close to extinction that it is now totally protected.

SANDON RIVER TO MINNIE WATERS

This pocket of coastline between Yamba and Woolgoolga is often overlooked by travelling anglers because it is somewhat off the beaten track and not as well serviced as the more popular tourist destinations. Perhaps because of this, the area offers some fantastic fishing. Sandon River, in particular, is a beautiful and 'fishy' location, with great whiting, flathead, bream and trevally inside and some hot Spaniard action outside in season.

Further south, Wooli and the Wooli River are a little better known and harder fished, but still offer good returns. Offshore fishing from here is particularly rewarding, but beware of the notorious bar at the entrance!

WOOLGOOLA TO COFFS HARBOUR

This is another popular holidaying and fishing area, with plenty of opportunities for beach, rock, estuary and off shore hopefuls. The 'Wash', wide of Woolgoolga, is particularly renowned for producing big tailor, mackerel, cobia and kings.

Offshore from this stretch of coast lie the Solitary Islands, with lots of excellent opportunities for boat anglers chasing snapper, pearl perch, mulloway, mackerel, tuna, and kings.

Coffs Harbour is a real fisherman's mecca, with many potential hot spots close to town. Especially good areas are Boambee Beach (tailor, bream, whiting and school jew), the Bream Hole south of the East Wall, the Walls themselves and Muttonbird Island, which is a rock fishing hot spot producing everything including big mackerel and longtail tuna.

South of Coffs, Bonville Creek is

recognised as one of the more southerly locales capable of producing good mangrove jack action at times.

URUNGA TO NAMBUCCA HEADS

Urunga has estuary fishing in the lower Bellingen River (a fine bass stream higher up) and access to excellent beach and rock positions.

Further south, Valla and Deep Creek are also productive at times, with Deep Creek occasionally yielding unusually large mangrove jack.

Just north of the mouth of the Nambucca River lies the aptly named Jew or Jewie Hole, a rock spot with a reputation for mulloway, as well as consistent tailor and bream. Inside the Nambucca River itself, the estuary angling is prolific in season, with an abundance of all the north coast estuarine species.

NAMBUCCA HEADS TO SMOKY CAPE

Scotts Head, Grassy Head and the Jail Wall at South West Rocks are all headlands with a well-earned reputation for producing big bags of both the 'bread-and-butter' species (bream, drummer, tailor, etc.) as well as pelagics like mackerel, cobia and tuna.

The Macleay River estuary is renowned for its big flathead, stud bream, prolific whiting and luderick (blackfish). The breakwalls there regularly produce monster flatties and jew for live baiters, as well as the occasional mangrove jack. Hot spots further upstream include the Clybucca Mouth, the Broadwater and Kemps Corner.

OFFSHORE

What a variety of options this region offers. One can fish floaters in a berley trail for excellent snapper, plumb the bottom for more snapper, pearl perch, Venus Tusk fish, teraglin and jew, or troll and live bait for mackerel, cobia, kings, tuna and marlin.

Access to the sea along this stretch of coast is either out through South West Rocks or the creek at Hat Head. Both approaches can be a little difficult in heavy weather.

HAT HEAD TO PORT MACQUARIE

This area offers more fine rock, beach, estuary and offshore fishing. The lovely little township of Hat Head and nearby Korongoro Point are particularly well known for great fishing. Point Plomer is a little less famous, but nonetheless productive, with drummer, groper, bream, tailor, jew and the pelagic species in season.

In many ways Port Macquarie itself marks the southern limits of the Far North Coast, and also the limit of southerly movement (in any numbers, at least) of some of the more tropical species such as Spanish mackerel and mangrove jacks.

Port Macquarie has great estuary fishing in the Hastings, Maria and Wilson Rivers. There are also many good rock, beach and breakwall positions, along with access to an exciting offshore scene.

NEW SOUTH WALES NORTH COAST

CAMDEN HAVEN

There are three small, peaceful villages around the Camden Haven River, and all are popular with anglers — particularly those who enjoy small boat estuary fishing for bream, flathead, whiting and luderick (blackfish). Hot spots include the North Haven Wall, Camden Point (blackfish), Hanleys Point, Grassy Island, the Long Arm (flathead) and the Logs.

TAREE TO MANNING RIVER

Crowdy Head, north of Harrington and the Manning River mouth, is a fine exposed rock headland. Harrington itself offers access to the good estuary fishing available in the lower Manning, between its mouth and Taree. Hot spots are the buoy downstream of Jones Island, Cundle Bridge, Peters Pipe (mullet and blackfish), Bohnock Bridge and the Old Bar.

FORSTER TO TUNCURRY

These twin towns, which lie at the entrance to Wallis Lake, are very tourist and angler orientated. Fine estuary fishing is available here, though many older locals lament that it is not nearly as good as it once was. Places worth trying include the Paddock (particularly for bream), Tuncurry Breakwall (mulloway), Fish Co-Op Wharf (bream), Hells Gate (flathead), Breckenridge Channel and the Step.

Tide changes at the entrance of Wallis Lake are about 20 minutes behind Sydney Harbour.

SEAL ROCKS TO TEA GARDENS

As well as offering much in the way of fine rock and beach fishing (the Gibber being a particularly renowned beach location), this stretch of coast is very popular with offshore anglers, especially those chasing snapper and other table fish around Broughton Island.

PORT STEPHENS

The picturesque estuary of Port Stephens draws tourists from all over New South Wales and even further afield, particularly during the summer holiday months. This deep, usually clean and tidal scoured inlet has some great fishing for bream, flathead, whiting, mulloway (jewfish) and luderick (blackfish), as well as playing host each spring and early summer to runs of oceanic pelagics such as mackerel tuna, striped tuna and longtail tuna, some of which travel far up beyond Soldiers Point.

The inspiring headlands that guard the entrance to Port Stephens — Yacaaba to the north and Tomaree to the south — also provide excellent general rock fishing, though Tomaree is even more famous as a land-based hot spot for big longtail tuna, mackerel tuna, bonito, sharks and even the occasional cobia.

OFFSHORE

Besides excellent snapper grounds, this area boasts some fine gamefishing in season — the annual gamefishing competitions held out of Port Stephens producing world-class marlin, shark and tuna action.

NEWCASTLE

This northern steel city of New South Wales is blessed with some quite good fishing on its doorstep. The Nobby Breakwall at Port Hunter produces snapper, tailor, bream, jewfish and even pelagics, while further back, towards Stoney Point, there is excellent sport with blackfish at times.

The harbour itself is fished hard, but despite this pressure and the degradation brought about by pollution, continues to produce reasonable estuarine action for all the common species. In recent years, the autumn and winter run of hairtail, in particular, has been prodigious.

NEW SOUTH WALES CENTRAL COAST

SWANSEA/LAKE MACQUARIE

Swansea Channel is justifiably famous for its large and prolific flathead. These fish are particularly fond of lures and live baits. The Channel also has bream, whiting and other estuarine species; and the occasional 'invasions' of big, tackle-breaking yellowtail kingfish keep things very interesting indeed!

Lake Macquarie offers a host of potential fishing spots for the boat or bank angler, but those of special note are the artificial reefs off Warners Bay, on the south side of Coal Point, at Wangi, and off The Pelican. The hot water outlets at the Eraring Power Station are another popular spot, and occasionally produce such exotic species as giant herring. The same is true, to an extent, further south in Lake Munmorah.

FRASER PARK TO TERRIGAL

Fraser Park features a headland with a good reputation for all kinds of rock fishing, including live baiting for big kingfish and the occasional tuna. Wybung Head offers similar fishing, and good spinning for smaller pelagics.

Norah Head features safe launching for some excellent offshore action on snapper and all sorts of other reef and pelagic species, as well as good rockhopping for drummer, groper, bream and so forth.

North Entrance Beach, which runs from south of Norah Head to the famous and much-frequented Entrance, produces respectable bags of tailor, bream, whiting and the occasional mulloway (jewfish).

The Entrance itself marks the opening to the sea of Tuggerah Lake, which is another fine estuary fishing locale, with the emphasis usually on bream and flathead.

Further south, Forresters Beach is well worth a try after heavy seas, as some big snapper have been taken from the shore here. It's also a good spot for big whiting, but live worms are a must.

Good bream and tailor are taken from the point at Terrigal Haven, particularly after southerly weather, while further around the front, bream, snapper, drummer, groper and the like are landed Further down the coast again, The Skillion is a rock location well known for bonito, striped tuna, mackerel tuna and kingfish, especially for spinmen throwing metal lures off high speed reels.

AVOCA TO BOX HEAD

These are more great rock positions in this stretch, although some are rather dangerous in a swell. As one moves closer to Box Head, the effects of run-out from the massive Hawkesbury River system become more influential to the fishing. These are the headlands which produce so many large mulloway or jewfish at floodtime, with fish falling both to conventional live and dead baiting methods, and to lures such as red and white feathers, 'chair leg' poppers and big sonic plugs.

BROKEN BAY-LOWER HAWKESBURY

Lying right on the northern doorstep of Sydney, this waterway is extremely popular for all kinds of recreational uses. Despite the pressures placed on it, the entire Hawkesbury system continues to produce excellent results for anglers.

Brisbane Waters is a particularly productive piece of estuary, and possibly the hottest spot is the channel joining it to the main body of Broken Bay, from Saratoga down to Ettalong. Here a veritable picket line of boats take superb bream, whiting, flathead and even school jew for much of the year, as well as delicious blue swimmer crabs in summer. On the southern side, Pittwater has similar, if a little less consistent, fishing.

Out in Broken Bay itself, we often find open ocean species such as snapper, teraglin, salmon and even the smaller tunas, ranging well beyond Lion Island, where they overlap with the more conventional estuarine species such as bream, flathead, whiting, flounder, mulloway and hairtail.

A little further up the Hawkesbury, hot spots include the Patonga area, the deep water off Juno Point and Flint and Steel (mulloway, big flathead and bream), the mouth of Cowan Creek, Dangar Island and the stretch of river between the bridges (the railway and road bridges).

UPPER HAWKESBURY

Fishing in this stretch of the river is largely tied to the seasonal abundance of prawns, which are at their best from early spring right through the summer months. These tasty crustaceans attract bream, flathead, school jew, estuary perch, bass and a host of other fish.

Hot spots in the upper Hawkesbury include the tributaries such as Mangrove and Webbs Creek, the Colo River (bass further up) and the MacDonald (also bass). The salt and tidal influence reach all the way to Lower Portland, but often estuarine species extend even further, overlapping with the range of bass and freshwater mullet.

Lower down on the Hawkesbury two other major arms branch off —Cowan and Berowra Creeks. Both of these also offer excellent fishing, particularly for the elusive hairtail in their deeper holes during winter.

Offshore Broken Bay offers easy boat access to the sea and to some great inshore and offshore angling for a huge range of species. Apart from the usual reef fishermen, this port is home to a strong gamefishing contingent who fish on the Continental Shelf wide of Broken Bay for massive tiger sharks, marlin and tuna.

SYDNEY

NORTHERN BEACHES
From Barrenjoey Lighthouse to North Head runs a series of beautiful beaches and headlands, each of which attracts its own band of devoted anglers. All produce fish, but particularly noteworthy are Newport Reef (tailor), Warriewood (mulloway and snapper), Long Reef (snapper, tailor, bream, groper, etc.), Avoca (bottom and surface fish) and North Head itself for a wide range of reef and pelagic species.

SYDNEY HARBOUR
Sydney's famous harbour, with its breathtaking views, its Bridge and its Opera House, is also one of our most popular fishing waterways. While many hopefuls may return empty handed or with meagre catches after a day on the Harbour, those willing to apply a little extra effort to secure fresh or live bait and to fish early and late or during the week still take some surprisingly good hauls from this much-exploited body of water.

For the fisherman's purposes, the Harbour may be broken into two sections: the Lower Harbour (up as far as the Bridge) and the Upper Harbour (west of the Bridge).

LOWER SYDNEY HARBOUR
There are some fine rock fishing locations around both sides of the Harbour entrance, particularly around Inner North Head and, on the southern side, between The Gap and Lady Jane Beach.

Of all the boat fishing locations in the Lower Harbour, none is more famous than the highly productive Sow and Pigs, with its bumper hauls of tailor, trevally, bream and so on. This position is best fished at night on a making to full moon.

Further up the Harbour, other boating hot spots include: Shark Island and Rose Bay (troll for chopper tailor), Bottle and Glass, Clarke Island (the same as Shark), Clifton Gardens, the Kirribilli Dolphins (trevally, bream and tailor at night), and under the Bridge itself (blackfish).

Shore bound anglers can enjoy reasonable sport off any number of vantage points, but favourites include: Watsons Bay Wharf and Baths, Point Piper, and any of the ferry wharves, particularly Taronga Park and Manly.

Up in Middle Harbour some of the quieter backwaters offer some surprisingly good sport with bream, flathead, school jew and so forth. Spots to try here include the following: the Spit Marina, Pearl Bay, Beauty Point, Inkerman Street Wharf, Primrose Park Bay, Long Folly Point, Northbridge Marina and Fig Tree Point. Most of these fish best from dusk until well after dark.

UPPER HARBOUR
West of the Bridge, spots with proven reputations include: Dawes Point, No. 13 Wharf at Pyrmont, Luna Park (blackfish), McMahons Point (good general fishing), Balmain Baths (big trevally), Wolseley Street Wharf (good general fishing) and around the Gladesville Bridge.

SOUTHERN BEACHES
Between South Head and La Perouse are another string of beaches and headlands not unlike those found on the northern side of the Harbour. Again, these offer a variety of fishing for those anglers willing to put in the time and learn the ropes. The emphasis here is on rock fishing for luderick (blackfish), bream, drummer, the occasional snapper and tailor in season. Beaches here provide generally scarce fishing, but good runs of whiting are experienced during some summers.

The sewerage outfalls at Bondi and Malabar are famous—or rather infamous—locations which produce a great many fish, but also claim lives because of the low and very slippery rock ledges. These places may well see a downturn in popularity with the completion of the offshore sewerage outfall pipes.

BOTANY BAY
This is another popular city-side fishing spot, but one which really has succumbed to the ravages of over-exploitation and environmental damage. Fish are still taken—and good hauls at times — but mainly by the very keen and very knowledgeable. For the novice, the schools of chopper tailor which range widely across the Bay at times, and the trevally which are occasionally prolific around the Container Terminal retaining walls, are probably the easiest fishing.

CRONULLA-PORT HACKING
Rock and beach fishing generally improves from Kurnell down towards Cronulla as one moves away from the heaviest of the city influences. The Kurnell rocks, in particular, produce good hauls of bream, drummer, blackfish and trevally, as well as tailor in season.

Port Hacking is to southern Sydney what Broken Bay and the Hawkesbury are to the north — a dividing line between the city and the 'bush' and a wonderful area of escape from city pressures.

Fishing in Port Hacking produces all of the usual estuarine species, and some of the better places to try are: Bonnie Vale, The Basin, Maianbar, Ship Rock, Dolans Bay, the Ballast Heap, South West Arm, Lilli Pilli and Yowie Bay.

Outside Port Hacking, Jibbon Bombora provides on excellent sport at times with kingfish, snapper, tailor and small tuna. Port Hacking is also a popular stepping-off point for fishing the Peak, wide of Maroubra, which is Sydney's most productive southern offshore mark for gamefish such as kingies, tuna, marlin, wahoo and so on.

NEW SOUTH WALES SOUTH COAST

PORT HACKING TO STANWELL PARK

This stretch of ruggedly attractive coastline includes the Royal National Park—our oldest and best known national parkland—and the coast here provides some tremendous rock-hopping for bream, drummer, blackfish, snapper, groper, salmon, tailor and pelagics such as tuna and kingfish. Hot spots in the Park include the Gulf and Curracurrang.

The first beaches at the south end of this rocky stretch—Garie and Stanwell Park — also offer much better beach fishing than that generally encountered further north nearer to the city.

STANWELL PARK TO WOLLONGONG

There are some great beaches and headlands along this stretch of coast, although the rock ledges tend to be rather low and wave-affected. Exercise extreme caution during heavy swells. These rocks produce good hauls of luderick (blackfish), drummer, bream, leatherjackets and so on, as well some excellent snapper for the specialist willing to put in the time. There are also runs of tailor, salmon and bonito at times. The beaches have their share of whiting in summer, as well as bream and tailor a little later in the year. Look for better formations such as holes, gutters and sandbank drop-offs.

WOLLONGONG TO LAKE ILLAWARRA

Between the Little Lighthouse and Wollongong Head some fine luderick (blackfish) are taken, particularly in heavier seas, while to the south, along Coniston Beach, tailor, salmon and the occasional mulloway turn up in the better holes and gutters.

The area of Port Kembla Harbour, although heavily industrialised, produces some excellent results for the many local anglers who fish there. The North Wall is particularly productive, yielding tailor, salmon, bream and mulloway (particularly school jew). There is even a good hairtail run here some years. This spot fishes best at dawn and dusk.

Inside Port Kembla Harbour, many anglers fish for yellowtail and, at times, for slimy mackerel to use elsewhere as bait. No. 6 wharf is one of the better bait catching locations. However, it also produces splendid John dory, school jew and even kingfish at times, so don't take all your live baits to other places! Numbers of bream are also found around this wharf area in numbers after dark and when shipping traffic isn't too heavy.

The South Breakwall can also be productive, though it doesn't seem to receive the same attention as the North Wall. Similar species are available.

The rocky headland running south east from the base of the South Wall to Red Point offers good general rockhopping, but be particularly wary at its south eastern tip, known as Dead Man's Hole due to the number of anglers washed in and drowned over the years.

South Beach runs on down to the entrance of Lake Illawarra and offers reasonable to very good beachcasting at times, particularly for bream closer to the lake mouth. Windang Beach, at the mouth, is a jewie hot spot.

The Lake itself is a prolific fishing and prawning ground, despite its shallowness and a degree of water pollution from the city. Hot spots include the lower reaches of Mullet Creek and Macquarie Rivulet, which run into the back of the Lake (both are top bream locations), around Tallawarra Power House and Kanahooka Point. The entrance channel also attracts big crowds and produces hauls of blackfish, flathead and bream at times.

OFFSHORE

The Five Island Group off Wollongong/Port Kembla is renowned as a small boat ground for great catches of tailor, bream, snapper, mulloway and so on, particularly in the washes around Pig and Tom Thumb Islands. Toothbrush Island, closer in to Red Point, is a hot spot for boat anglers chasing big blue groper and drummer.

Further out off this stretch of coastline lie some excellent deep grounds for snapper, morwong and teraglin, while Bandit Reef is known for its big kingfish and monster yellowfin tuna, the latter being at their best from late March until early June.

WINDANG TO KIAMA

Windang Island is a great bream spot, and also produces snapper, tailor, drummer and groper from the front. Warilla Beach, to the south, fishes well in summer when currents push run-out water from the Lake onto it.

Barrack Point has reasonable bream and luderick, plus the occasional snapper and a run of tailor at times.

Shell Harbour is an attractive port offering good boat access to the sea. Its harbour is also prolific with blackfish after a big sea. The Church Grounds, down towards Bass Point, are a very popular offshore destination, and are particularly good for kingfish of all sizes, from 'rats' to 'hoodlums'.

Bass Point offers an extensive area of excellent rock fishing territory and, among other things, has a reputation for producing the biggest tailor on the south coast, with the occasional seven-kilo-plus fish coming in. Probably the most productive area is towards the eastern extremity of the point, particularly around the bombora. Note that Bushrangers Bay on the south eastern corner is a Marine Sanctuary and is totally closed to fishing.

The Minnamurra River mouth area and Stack Island or 'Rangoon' can be a red hot area at times for tailor, snapper, bream, salmon and the like. Tailor are particularly good a few hundred metres offshore during autumn. This area also produces its share of big mulloway and snapper.

To the south, Boyds Beach has whiting in summer and the Boneyard—a famous surfboard riding location—is a real fish producer in a big southerly sea. Further south again, Bombo Beach is always full of fish-holding formations, and produces good catches for those who put in the time.

Kiama Harbour is a fine bait catching ground and also has John dory and, after a blow, blackfish and bream. Ramps here offer safe access to the sea and some good reef and surface fishing offshore.

KIAMA TO GERROA
Kiama Head, famous for its Blow Hole, juts well out into deep water and has many top rockfishing ledges, though the entire point is characterised by rather sporadic fishing. Along with the usual rock species, some big kingfish and tuna, particularly longtails, are often taken from the eastern and south eastern points.

To the south, Kendalls and Bubbly are rock ledges with good reputations for snapper, kingfish, big trevally, bream and drummer.

Marsdens Head offers fairly deep water, good snapper and a great run of trevally in the cooler months. Lure casters do well here at times for bonito, salmon, small tuna and kingfish. The stretch of rock from Marsdens south past the Little Blow Hole to Easts Beach is similar, and Easts High, south of the beach, has groper, snapper, trevally, drummer and so forth, but as the ledge is high off the water, a cliff gaff may be necessary.

Further south again, MacClennans, or 'Mac's' as it is locally known, is a very productive ledge for all the usual rock species, especially blackfish, tailor and snapper. Be warned though — it is a low, wet rock and the walk out is a back-breaker!

The rocks just north of Werri Beach offer good to very good live baiting for kingfish, as well as spinning for salmon and tailor and general activity on drummer, bream, groper etc., while Werri Beach itself often holds good formations and has been known to produce surprises in the form of big snapper after a blow.

The rocks from South Werri around to Boat Harbour offer a range of low ledges and washes with bream, luderick, drummer and groper, while sheltered Boat Harbour itself has launching facilities for small to medium boats in reasonable seas and produces bream, drummer and luderick after a heavy surge.

The point to the south and Big Rock offer reasonable rock action on all sorts of species, with good snapper from the front if the sea isn't too big. From here south to Black Head at Gerroa there are a few good little rock positions, but most are hard to get to and often not worth the effort. Walkers Beach should not be overlooked, though, as it has produced some enormous mulloway and big snapper.

Black Head is a popular rock spot for all the usual species, and the deeper water at its eastern end produces good kingfish on live baits at times. The bomboras south west of the point are a boat fishing hot spot, with prolific small to medium snapper, good trevally, tailor, mulloway and teraglin at times.

GERROA TO CURRARONG
Seven Mile Beach fishes very well on occasions, with mulloway concentrated at both ends and tailor, bream and whiting all the way along. Shoalhaven Heads, at the usually-closed or very shallow mouth of the Shoalhaven River, offers access to beach fishing, estuary activity and good bait-pumping flats.

Comerong Island (which is actually not an island when the river is closed) has fine beach fishing and the old Coal Wharf at its southern end is a hot spot for big bream, luderick, tailor and mulloway.

The Shoalhaven River is a fine, big estuary which fishes well up to Nowra and beyond, although since the completion of Tallowa Dam further upstream, fishing in the higher reaches has suffered. Hot spots include the Reef, near Nowra, the Horlicks Factory (mullet and blackfish), the Milk Factory (mullet and blackfish), Broughton Creek (general estuary species) and the Canal (blackfish, bream and flathead).

Greenwell Point, at the confluence of the Canal from the Shoalhaven and the short but healthy Crookhaven River, is a famous oyster growing centre and also offers fine estuary fishing. The drop-offs directly east of the town are excellent dusky flathead drifts, and the Cannon has fine luderick fishing.

Crookhaven Heads offers rock fishing, and Culburra Beach to the south is active when Lake Wollumboola (a fine prawning location) breaks through to the sea. Culburra Head has fair, if rather shallow rock fishing.

Currarong is a popular tourist and fishing village, offering road and walking track access to many of Jervis Bay's renowned rock ledges, as well as small to medium boat launching facilities for offshore work.

OFFSHORE
The most famous boat grounds here are the Banks, off Greenwell Point and north east of Currarong. This reef complex is widely known for its superb game and sport fishing for big yellowtail kingfish, tuna, sharks and marlin. It also has excellent bottom fishing for snapper, morwong and trevally etc..

JERVIS BAY
Two long headlands enclose this massive body of water and provide a myriad of rock, beach and estuary-style fishing locations too numerous to list. Rock hot spots with reputations for big fish such as kings, tuna and even marlin include: Big Beecroft, Drum and Drumsticks-Neverfail, Devils Gorge, the Outer Tubes and the Docks.

Some of the better general rock-hopping and beach fishing lies around Target Beach on the northern side and between Bowen Island and Steamers Beach on the southern peninsula.

A boat fishing mark worthy of attention is Middle Ground, between the heads, while the bombies off Long Nose Point work very well in a sea.

SUSSEX INLET TO ULLADULLA
Sussex Inlet lies at the mouth of St Georges Basin, an extensive, if rather shallow, estuary system. Sussex itself often sees superlative estuarine fishing.

The many low, rocky headlands and beaches between Sussex Inlet and Ulladulla produce excellent tailor, salmon, bream, drummer and blackfish for those anglers willing to move around and chase concentrations of fish.

Ulladulla itself has fine general rock

fishing from Bannister, Warden and Racecourse Heads, with drummer, bream, groper and blackfish predominating.

Lake Conjolla, to the north of Ulladulla, is one of the best estuaries in the district, with a reputation for crocodile-size flathead, particularly from its Steps and Berringer Lake areas.

ULLADULLA TO BATEMANS BAY

Top estuaries in this stretch include Burrill Lake, Lake Tabourie, Durras Lake and the lower Clyde River at Batemans itself.

Great rock fishing is to be enjoyed at Snapper Point, near Merry and Pretty Beaches. This headland lives up to its name with great snapper fishing for those who can throw long casts, and some fine live baiting and spinning for kingfish, tuna, salmon, tailor and the like. All the rocky ledges along this stretch also offer drummer, bream and blackfish, particularly if berley is used.

The best beaches include Racecourse, Kioloa, Pretty and Merry, all of which have excellent whiting in summer, and general angling for bream, tailor, salmon and the very occasional mulloway year round.

Batemans Bay is a large and well-serviced tourist centre which caters for a huge influx of tourists at holiday time. As well as being popular with New South Wales residents, this stretch of coast is the number one seaside destination for Canberra's holidaymakers.

Batemans has superb estuary fishing in the lower Clyde, with flathead, bream and mulloway being particularly popular targets. Further upstream, above Shallow Crossing, excellent bass are available in summer.

Offshore This entire stretch of coast has much to offer the boat angler, from excellent inshore and wash fishing for snapper, bream, tailor and the like around Brush Island, Durras and Batemans Bay's Tollgate Islands, to wider bottom bouncing for reds, mowies and flathead, plus gamefishing for all sorts of pelagics.

NEW SOUTH WALES FAR SOUTH COAST

BATEMANS BAY TO BERMAGUI

South of Batemans the stretch of rocky shoreline to Burrewarra or 'Burre' Point offers many great ledges for casting for snapper, tailor, salmon, bream, groper and drummer. Further south again the Moruya River has fine estuary fishing and access to offshore drifting grounds known for their big hauls of sand flathead, morwong and snapper.

The Tuross Lake System, east of the cheese-making township of Bodalla, is another extensive estuary system with all the usual southern inshore species, and Wagonga Inlet at Narooma is particularly famous for its clean, blue-green water, big whiting, over-size flathead and prolific bream.

Narooma also offers boat access to the sea over its bar which, although rather notorious, is safe enough in flat to moderate conditions. The favourite offshore destination here is Montague Island, with its seal colony and top class fishing for kingfish, snapper, bonito and a wide range of pelagics including marlin and some of the largest yellowfin tuna in Australian waters.

The rocks, beaches, lakes and inlets south towards the fishing village of Bermagui are all active at times, particularly for salmon, tailor and bream, with drummer and groper readily available for those who wish to specifically seek them.

Bermagui—a rather sleepy little port for much of the year—comes alive for a string of hard-fished game competitions between late January and early June each year, for this is the historic home of Australian gamefishing and still offers some of the best marlin, tuna and shark fishing on the coast out over its prolific Four Mile, Six Mile and Twelve Mile Reef systems. Many boats also make the run from here up to Montague Island or the Kink area of the Shelf to avoid Narooma's bar.

Of course, Bermagui doesn't only have gamefishing. Estuary angling in the Bermagui River itself and Wallaga Lake, a little to the north, is very good at times, and Wallaga, in particular, has a record for producing big dusky flathead.

BERMAGUI TO PAMBULA

The stretch of coast south of Bermagui features several relatively small estuary systems which offer surprisingly good fishing, especially for flathead, bream, whiting and blackfish. The best of these are Cuttagee, Murrah and Wapengo Lakes, although Tanja Lagoon and Nelson Lake also feature sometimes.

The lower Bega River, north of Tathra, is a large and productive estuary, with great flathead and bream, in particular, for those willing to chase the hot spots. This river once produced exceptional bass and estuary perch, but silting of its upper reaches has greatly reduced the number, extent and size of these fine fish.

Tathra Beach is long and often filled with fine formations. It experiences excellent salmon runs at times and has big bream and the occasional mulloway in the better holes.

Tathra Wharf, on the northern side of Tathra Head, is a historic structure more than a century old, and also a superb and much-frequented fishing platform, allowing anglers access to abundant baitfish, good luderick, leatherjackets, pike, trevally, salmon, tailor and the like, as well as deeper water species such as snapper, kingfish, tuna and big sharks.

Tathra Head has a host of fishable rock ledges and is particularly good for drummer, groper, blackfish and salmon. Longtail tuna and kingfish may also be live baited and spun from the more exposed points at times.

Sheltered Kianinny Bay, just south of Tathra, offers small and medium boat access to the many reef and drifting grounds wide of this pretty port.

The rugged stretch of shoreline between Tathra Head and Merimbula is not fished excessively and offers excellent opportunities for southern rock species. Tura Head, north of Merimbula, is a particular hot spot.

Merimbula is yet another popular tourist destination, particularly among Victorian anglers, and offers a wide variety of fishing opportunities. Merimbula Lake has prolific flathead, and the Merimbula Wharf is similar to the structure at Tathra, offering shore-bound anglers access to exciting live baiting for kingfish and tuna, as well as leatherjackets, trevally and so forth.

Pambula Lake is similar to Merimbula Lake, but doesn't seem to produce quite as many flathead on such a regular basis.

PAMBULA TO THE BORDER

Toalla Point, Haycock Rock and the nearby offshore bomboras called Hunter Rock all offer very exciting angling opportunities for the boat and rock fisherman. This area has big drummer, snapper, kingfish, salmon, bream, luderick and—at times—tuna.

Further south, the channel inside Lennards Island offers some of the biggest sweep on the south coast, along with prolific leatherjackets and some drummer and bream.

Twofold Bay and the fishing/timber-milling town of Eden provide another tourist mecca, although not generally attracting quite the crowds that flock to Merimbula and Pambula. Twofold Bay and its several wharves offer excellent family fishing, with abundant yellowtail, slimy mackerel, trevally, tailor, leatherjackets, pike and so forth. The Bay has many fine boat marks, and the big mooring buoys off the oil terminal produce particularly big six-spine leatherjackets in abundance.

Further south, Green Cape is a real rockhoppers paradise, offering numerous ledges and almost unlimited fishing potential.

The very south eastern extremity of Green Cape boasts ledges which offer land based gamefishing that sometimes rivals that of Jervis Bay to the north. Big longtail and yellowfin tuna, along with kingfish and prolific bonito and striped tuna, are taken here in the late summer and early autumn months.

Just south of Green Cape lies Disaster Bay and Wonboyn Lake and River — a superb estuary system with a reputation for abundant and large southern bream as well as flathead, whiting, estuary perch and the like. Drifting in Disaster Bay itself can yield fish boxes full of delicious sand flathead in suitable weather.

The rugged coast between Disaster Bay and the Victorian-New South Wales border at Cape Howe or Hicks is largely inaccessible, but offers some potentially exciting rock ledges, headlands and beaches for the adventurous. The little Nadgee River and nearby Nadgee Inlet also promise virtually untouched estuary angling, but are rarely visited by tourists.

Queensland

THE GULF COUNTRY

MORNINGTON ISLAND TO BURKETOWN

A fishing lodge exists on the Aboriginal-controlled Mornington Island, and from here anglers may boat or shore fish for saltwater barramundi, cod of several species, mangrove jacks, giant herring, mackerel, queenies, prolific numbers of trevally and a variety of reef species.

The Gregory, Nicholson and Alexandra River systems run to sea in the Gulf of Carpentaria through a complex series of deltas near Burketown. Further up these rivers, especially in the upper Gregory and the O'Shannassey, whose headwaters rise very close to those of the southward-flowing Georgina system, sooty grunter, catfish, archer fish and freshwater long tom are prolific. Some areas also hold saratoga.

Lower down, barramundi take over as the prime target species, while closer to the sea, mangrove jack, estuary cod, threadfin salmon and small queenfish are more abundant, along with the ever-present trevallies.

As with most of the Top End and Gulf, access to and travel within this area is very difficult during the Wet (usually November through April or even May).

BURKETOWN TO KARUMBA

The Gulf is famous for its prawns, and the commercial fishery for these succulent crustacea attracts a big fleet of domestic and foreign trawlers. The prawns also attract vast numbers of fish to the area.

Rivers such as the Flinders, Norman, Saxby and Carron all offer good barramundi fishing in their lower and middle reaches, with sooty grunter (black bream), catfish and pockets of saratoga further upstream.

Karumba, on the coast, and Normanton, further inland, both offer ideal bases for visiting anglers fishing these rivers.

Trolling with minnow-style lures and bait fishing with live prawns, shrimp or small baitfish are popular ways of taking barramundi in this region. A boat of some sort is almost essential for good fishing.

CAPE YORK

KARUMBA TO WEIPA

A very isolated stretch of coast, but one with exciting fishing for those who can gain access. The Mitchell River system, in particular, offers diverse and profuse fishing, with sooty grunter (black bream), catfish, tarpon, archer fish, long tom and some saratoga higher up, while the lower estuary carries healthy barramundi stocks big forktail catfish, mangrove jack etc..

Similar conditions exist in the Staaten River, south of the Mitchell, and the Coleman, Edward, Holroyd and Archer Rivers to the north.

Weipa and adjacent Albatross Bay has superb shallow water inshore angling for barramundi, mangrove jacks, estuary cod, flathead, trevally, queenfish and even the occasional giant herring. Schools of feeding bonefish have been sighted here on occasion, but getting a bait or lure to them through the abundant trevally and small to mid-size queenfish usually proves to be an impossible task.

WEIPA TO THURSDAY ISLAND

The Wenlock River, north of Weipa, is another superb barramundi stream, particularly around its mouth near Cullen Point and up into the tidal stretches. Higher up there are sooty grunter, catfish, archers and smaller barramundi.

Bamaga, right at the tip of Cape York, is an isolated community offering access to the nearby Jardine River, with its excellent barramundi and saratoga, as well as all the usual estuarine and freshwater species. This is the easternmost range of the northern saratoga species, but is a primary river for them, a fact recognised in the scientific name of that species; *Scleropages jardini*.

Bamaga also offers access to offshore reef and bombie fishing for heavyweight trevally, big cod and — at times — prolific shoals of mackerel, longtail tuna, mackerel tuna, queenfish and barracuda. Small billfish—sails and marlin—are also sighted here at times.

Across at Thursday Island and the nearby Prince of Wales, Horn and Hammond Islands, the emphasis is on offshore lure casting and trolling for all the pelagics mentioned above, as well as bait fishing the reef complexes for all manner of tasty, hard-pulling target species, from red emperor to coral trout to cod of all types.

THURSDAY ISLAND TO COOKTOWN

This attractive and largely pristine stretch of coastline runs parallel to the very northernmost section of the famous Great Barrier Reef, a coral atoll and reef system which stretches from here some 2 000 kilometres south to Lady Elliott Island off Bundaberg.

The section of coastline from the tip of Cape York southwards to Cape Melville, east of Princess Charlotte Bay, consists of a procession of rocky headlands or capes with beaches and relatively short, mangrove-lined estuaries in between.

The headlands offer very good boat and shore-based fishing for big mangrove jack, trevally, queenfish, saltwater barramundi and—when the water is clean—coral trout. The estuaries and flats adjacent to their mouths are dominated by mangrove jacks, estuary cod, pikey bream, flathead, javelin fish, fingermark, barracuda, trevally and, at times, barramundi.

Princess Charlotte Bay is a particularly well-rated angling environment, with several large rivers emptying into the relatively shallow waters of the bay. These rivers, particularly the Normanby, offer visiting anglers their very best chance of taking a barramundi on the eastern seaboard, though even here the silver king cannot be regarded as a 'sure thing', such has been the decline in barramundi stocks over recent decades.

Cape Melville is an exposed, rocky headland with superb prospects for spinning trevally, queenies, jacks and even mackerel. The occasional big saltie barramundi will also be spun or live baited here.

Offshore, Lizard Island offers an exclusive lodge for the well-heeled and a primitive camping area for the not-so-wealthy. Camping is by permission of the Great Barrier Reef Marine Parks Authority (GBRMPA) in Townsville, and a written permit is essential.

Lizard Island is justifiably famous for its angling, both as a base for the springtime giant marlin fishery outside the reef (blacks in excess of 500 kilos are taken each year) and as a light and medium tackle paradise for coral trout, big trevally, mackerel, cobia and so on.

Access to the island is by plane from Cairns or Cooktown or by private boat, with a good southerly weather anchorage in Watsons Bay.

Back on the coast, Cape Flattery and Bedford offer long, rocky headlands with spinning and bait fishing for big fingermark, mangrove jack, trevally of all sizes, queenfish, mackerel and occasional feeding sprees by saltwater barramundi. When clean water pushes inshore, big coral trout also haunt these ledges.

A wreck just inside the northern side of Cape Bedford is a fingermark bream hotspot, with live herring being the number one bait.

The many small islands, reefs and bombies out from this area offer exceptional fishing, especially in the shallower areas not often worked over by bottom bashers and professionals. Egret Reef, off Cooktown, is a lure tosser's and live baiter's paradise, with magnum, mangrove jack, red emperor, coral trout and good trevally over the shallow bombies.

Cooktown and the Endeavour River are often used as starting points for trips further afield, but there is some good fishing to be had right on the doorstep of the town. Live baiting with mullet and herring off the town wharf will turn up school mackerel, queenies, mangrove jack, fingermark and even the occasional barramundi, particularly from June until November. Leperosy Creek has a reasonable population of kilo-class jacks, and the main river offers occasional barramundi and very good fingermark holes on some of the deeper corners upstream.

Rock ledges just south of town boast sparodic bursts of intense activity for the shore-based lure caster and bait soaker.

FAR NORTH QUEENSLAND

COOKTOWN TO CAIRNS

The Cooktown to Cairns road is rather rough, but it is certainly passable in the family car during the Dry. Just south of Cooktown it crosses several rivers, including the Annan, which have sooty grunter, tarpon, catties and some small to middling barramundi.

The Daintree River, Mossman and, further south, Port Douglas areas all offer shore-based, estuarine and offshore fishing of a high standard. As explained earlier, barramundi fishing down the eastern seaboard, especially south of Princess Charlotte Bay, has deteriorated in recent years, but the mangrove-lined streams on this part of the coast certainly offer the chance of a barramundi or two for the keen (and lucky!) visitor. Fortunately, in between barramundi there are plenty of splendid mangrove jack, estuary cod, pikey bream, bar-tail flathead, fingermark, javelin fish, trevally, barracuda and archer fish to be caught—to name just a few of the more common types.

Cairns is a big, cosmopolitan city and the capital of the far north in every way. It has an international airport, top class hotels and motels and all the services a visitor could possibly require, either for a prolonged stay in the area or as a staging point for more adventurous trips northwards.

As may be expected of an area as heavily settled and hard-fished as Cairns, the angling is not up to past standards. However, Trinity Inlet still produces its share of exceptional fish, including fingermark bream to more than 10 kilos and barramundi twice that big. Most of these are taken by a dedicated band of local live baiters using lively king prawns or herring around the snags. Visiting 'danglers' more often come home with sunburn or a few catfish, small sharks or rays for their efforts!

Offshore from Cairns the situation changes, with some great reef and bombie fishing still existing, particularly in shallow, rough-bottomed areas. Michealmas Cay is one spot renowned for its lure-eating coral trout, red bass, cod, trevally and mackerel.

Game and sportfishing wide of Cairns produce good mackerel at times, as well as tuna of several species, big trevally or 'turrum', queenfish and— outside the reef—wahoo, dolphin fish and marlin.

During the months from the end of September until the middle of November or a little later, giant black marlin are taken wide off Cairns, with several 'granders' (fish over the old 1 000 pound mark) being weighed each season. However, marlin fishing emphasis has moved from here north to Cooktown and Lizard Island during the last decade or so, and today fewer boats make the four hour run out from Cairns Harbour.

As a final note, anglers are well advised to visit the aquarium near the Marlin Jetty on the Cairns waterfront in order to see the excellent specimens of popular northern angling species. That way, even if you don't catch a barramundi on your northern sojourn, you can at least take photos of some great specimens in excess of 15 kilos!

CAIRNS TO TOWNSVILLE

This area is a very popular one, both with visiting anglers and residents of the two big northern cities. It offers a diversity of estuarine, freshwater, shore-based and offshore opportunities, with a great deal of the focus being placed on the Hinchinbrook Island area.

Hinchinbrook, or 'Hinch', is a big, impressive lump of land, running parallel with the coast from Cardwell in the north to Point Lucinda in the south and boasting the highest mountain peaks of any eastern seaboard island in Australia.

The complex mangrove estuary system on the western or 'back' side of 'Hinch' creates a vast angling paradise for fishermen chasing bream, fingermark, javelin, flathead, whiting, estuary cod, mangrove jack, trevally and barracuda—always, of course, with the outside chance of a silver-plated jackpot in the form of a saltwater barramundi.

The eastern shore of the island is visited less often, but if anything presents more angling opportunities than the western side. Zoe Bay, in particular, is an excellent location with rock, estuary and inshore angling for a myriad of species.

On the freshwater front the Tully River, back on the mainland, has reasonable sooty grunter, with tarpon, catfish and mangrove jacks for variety, while some of the smaller, more remote jungle streams still have populations of the overfished jungle perch. Not surprisingly, locals who know such hot spots are not always willing to share them with visitors unless a pledge is made to release all fish unharmed.

OFFSHORE

There is more great reef fishing along this section of coast, with bottom bouncing for coral trout, sweetlip and emperor, casting and jigging for the same species and light to medium tackle trolling for mackerel, tuna, barracuda, trevally, sailfish and small marlin, particularly around Dunk. Some reef areas have been rather hard hit, and anglers may need to look further afield than they once did.

Before working any of the offshore reefs by boat, check with the Great Barrier Reef Marine Parks Authority (GBRMPA) in Townsville and obtain a map showing the designated zoning of the reef. Some areas are completely closed to fishing, others may only be trolled over and in some, anchoring is prohibited.

NORTH QUEENSLAND

TOWNSVILLE-MAGNETIC ISLAND

Townsville is another big, well-developed city with an international airport and world standard accommodation and services.

Magnetic Island—a pleasant ferry ride off the coast—has some fine rock platforms for the shore-based angler, with queenfish, trevally, mackerel and occasionally tuna.

The Townsville Harbour and breakwall complex has its share of devotees who baitfish and spin for trevally, mangrove jack, fingermark, school mackerel and the odd (sometimes very large) saltwater barramundi.

Mackerel and even cobia are also taken at times by boat anglers working around the Harbour lead lights, though generally Townsville Harbour sees vessels departing for greener pastures further afield — particularly the fingermark, trevally and queenfish bombies around Cape Cleveland and the red hot sailfish and mackerel grounds off Cape Bowling Green. In fact, so productive has Bowling Green been for sails over recent years that it is today regarded as one of the best Pacific sailfish locations in the world! Peak times for these slender aerialists occur between June and October, but the occasional patch is encountered near bait schools year round.

CAPE CLEVELAND TO MACKAY

Capes Cleveland and Upstart both offer shore-based opportunities for mackerel, queenfish, trevally, tuna and mangrove jack, as well as great near-shore fishing around the numerous bombies and drop-offs for those species and more. Big fingermark are often prevalent off these points around Christmas and the New Year.

Bowen has Cape Edgecumbe, the prolific 'Mackerel Patches', Southern Cross Reef and Innaminka Rocks, as well as the Don and Gregory River, with reasonable to good estuary action. Threadfin salmon are a particularly popular target species in this area, which is hardly surprising when one considers their sporting prowess and eating qualities.

The Whitsunday Islands, off Airlie Beach, present a multitude of fishing prospects for the boat angler, whether he operates his own trailer boat from the mainland or charters one of those available in the area. All the usual inshore and offshore species inter-mix in the channels and reef areas around these beautiful islands, and there is also some fine sailfishing and mackerel trolling at times. Proserpine offers another ideal stepping-off point for fishing the Whitsundays and has a thriving bare-boat charter fleet. The mackerel run wide of this port hits its peak between August and October each year. The tidal range here is extensive and should always be taken into account when planning trips.

Mackay also has huge tides, and these dictate the standard of fishing and best locations, especially in the estuaries and inshore reef areas. As well as all the usual tropical species, flathead, whiting and bream feature heavily in the bags of shore and near-shore anglers around Mackay.

CAPRICORN COAST

MACKAY TO YEPPOON

The Hay Point and Cape Palmerston areas offer much potential to shore-based anglers, with mackerel and tuna passing by close to the rocks at times, as well as the usual resident species such as cod, mangrove jack and the very occasional barramundi.

The Broad Sound and Shoalwater Bay region offers some of the best inshore and estuarine fishing on the Central Queensland or Capricorn Coasts, and is perhaps the best place to try for a barramundi south of Princess Charlotte. However, access is limited, as the Australian Army controls large tracts of the land and sea, and the big tides of the Mackay district also prevail here. This is not an easy area to fish, but well worth it if possible.

Cape Mansfield offers mackerel, queenfish, black jew and grunter for the land-based and near-shore boat operator, while the nearby Flat Island reef complex is a hot spot for boat owners chasing mackerel, other pelagics and reef dwellers such as coral trout and various cods.

Corio Bay is another inshore, estuarine complex with good javelin (grunter), some black jew, mangrove jack, lots of bream, whiting and flathead, as well as few barramundi for those who persevere. Conical Rocks, Outer Rock, Man and Wife Rocks and the Keppel Islands all offer superb boat fishing opportunities for those using Rosslyn Bay, near Yeppoon, as a base.

There is a good Spanish mackerel run through this region of the Capricorn Coast in late winter and spring, as well as tuna, queenfish, cobia (black kingfish) and black jew, plus all the common tropical reef species. This part of the coast also marks the usual northern boundary of the southern snapper, and some very big hauls of outsize reds are taken here during the cooler months of the year. Check with locals for the precise timing of the run, as it is often short and intense.

Rosslyn Bay itself has good land-based and small boat fishing for grunter, bream, whiting, flathead, threadfin salmon and the occasional black jew, while Causeway Lake to the south is an excellent estuary with a mix of southern and northern species. Trevally and even a few barramundi run in here on a big making tide.

ROCKHAMPTON-FITZROY RIVER

The Fitzroy at Rockhampton once had good barramundi fishing, but this is now largely a thing of the past, due to over-exploitation and habitat destruction or modification, particularly the construction of weirs or barrages. A few knowledgeable locals still take good barramundi at times, but most visitors end up with, at best, catfish and small tarpon (ox-eye herring).

Further upstream, in the freshwater, the Fitzroy/Dawson System is home to the southern species of saratoga, as well as sooty grunter, spangled perch, numerous catfish, tarpon and even golden perch. Fishing here isn't up to past standards, but there is still good sport to be had in better preserved pockets.

YEPPOON TO BUNDABERG

Emu Park and its many offshore islands, rocks and reefs havesimilar fishing to that described for the more northerly parts of the Capricorn Coast. Again, boat access is by way of Rosslyn Bay.

Coorooman Creek is one of the better estuary systems in the region and, as well as prolific whiting, bream, flathead and grunter etc., offers mangrove jack and at least the chance of a barramundi. Nearby Keppel Sands has similar fishing and is a favourite with light tackle anglers after bags of whiting, bream and flatties.

The long, sheltered strait, called the Narrows, between Curtis Island and the mainland, provides a wealth of estuarine angling for shore-based and small boat fishermen. Here great hauls of bream, whiting, flathead, grunter, trevally and mud crabs are taken. Hot spots include the channels around Balaclava Island to the north, Kangaroo Island in the middle of the Narrows and near the Calliope River and Gladstone itself at the southern end. One particularly noteworthy hot spot (in every sense of the term) is the warm water discharge at Gladstone. Here mangrove jack, queenfish and even barramundi are taken along with the usual estuarine species.

The outside of Curtis Island has bluewater trolling and bottom fishing, with the deep water adjacent to Cape Capricorn offering some excellent mackerel fishing in late winter, spring and early summer.

Tannum Sands, south of Gladstone, and the Boyne River, have reasonable to very good estuary action at times, with bream, flathead, whiting, mangrove jacks, black jew, queenfish, mud crabs and a few barramundi. This fishing extends on down the inside of Wild Cattle Island and around Hummock Hill Island.

The township of 1770 and adjacent Round Hill Head and Rocky Point areas provide a range of fine estuary, beach, rock headland and inshore options for anglers. Because of 1770's relative isolation, a high standard of fishing remains, especially for flathead, mangrove jack and even barramundi, though the latter are by no means common.

Bame Creek, Miara Park, the Kolan River and Moore Park offer more good estuary and shallow flats fishing. Here the favoured approach is to cast lightly-weighted baits of live yabbies (nippers) pumped from the abundant flats to catch bream, whiting, flathead and grunter. More adventurous anglers may wish to cast lures for flathead, mangrove jack, threadfin salmon, trevally and the faint possibility of a barramundi.

The Burnett estuary at Bundaberg has fishing similar to that described above, with the emphasis again on bream, flathead and whiting, though salmon are very popular when they run. The situation is the same around Elliot Heads and the Burrum Heads-Gregory River area to the south.

OFFSHORE

Mackerel on the troll or with drifted live and dead baits, and sweetlip, cod and snapper from the reefs predominate among offshore catches between Yeppoon and Bundaberg-Burrum heads. Along this stretch some of the more tropical species such as queenfish begin to lose dominance as they approach the southern limits of their range and are replaced by fish such as yellowtail kings and snapper

SOUTHERN QUEENSLAND

BUNDABERG TO DOUBLE ISLAND POINT

Hervey Bay, inside Fraser Island, represents an extensive area of fishing ground. Here the major emphasis is on offshore boat angling for snapper and 'squire' (immature snapper), school mackerel, cod, sweetlip, mulloway, tailor and so forth. Closer to shore and in the shallows there are plentiful bream, whiting, flathead and some healthy stocks of mangrove jack.

Hot spots include: Moon Ledge (snapper and reef fish), Woody Island Beacons (reef fishing), the Black Buoy (good reef fish), the Artificial Reef (big cod and general reef species) the Outer Banks (yellowtail kings and mackerel, Picnic Island (tailor, bream, etc.), Mary River Heads (whiting and bait pumping), McKenzies (reef fish and mulloway), German Creek (superlative estuarine angling) and Ungowa/Deep Creek (reef fishing in deeper water, great bream, whiting and flatties in the shallows).

Urangan Pier is a shore angler's paradise, with mackerel, cobia, tuna and so on brought within reach of those without a boat.

Fraser Island itself is famous as being the largest sand island in the world and is a favourite destination for adventurous anglers from all over southern Queensland, New South Wales and even further afield.

Beach fishing is what brings most people to Fraser Island, and undoubtedly it offers some of the best beach casting opportunities in the country. However, anglers should not forget the excellent mangrove estuaries along the inside of Fraser, with their big whiting, prolific bream, flathead, mangrove jacks, crabs and so forth; nor the rocky headlands such as Waddy Point, Middle Rocks and Indian Head with their tailor, bream, mackerel and sharks.

Beach fishing along the ocean side of Fraser produces bream, whiting, dart, 'oyster crackers' (snub-nose dart or permit), golden trevally, mulloway, sharks and even the occasional bonefish. But one species above all others brings visitors to Fraser — and that species is the tailor.

Lying close to the northern end of the fish's range, Fraser offers some of the best and most prolific tailor fishing in the country. The run over recent years has not been up to the standards of a decade or so ago, but it is still good, with lots of big tailor between one and five kilos or more being beached between July and October.

The proven method of beach fishing on Fraser is to drive along the top of the beach in a four wheel drive vehicle until good formations, wheeling birds or gatherings of anglers with bent rods are sighted. One then joins in casting gang-hooked pilchards or—more rarely—garfish at the ravenous 'choppers'.

Tin Can Bay, south of Fraser, is another top estuary/inshore complex, and has whiting, bream, flathead, dart, mangrove jacks, lots of great crabbing and some reef fishing over the deeper rock and gravel patches. Hot spots include the Pannikin Island Banks (whiting), Teebah Creek (jacks and estuary fish), the Parrot Hole (parrot fish, flathead, cod, etc.) and Poverty Point (estuary fish and crabs).

Double Island Point is a long, exposed headland with some shore-based opportunities as well as excellent boat-fishing for mackerel, yellowtail kingfish, cobia and tuna.

SUNSHINE COAST

NOOSA-NOOSA RIVER
A hard-fished and popular region which still offers flathead, whiting, bream and tailor in good numbers, as well as the occasional mangrove jack.

Hot spots in the Noosa river include: Noosa Bar (bream), the Lagoon (bream and flathead), the Snags (top bream hole), Munna Point (general fshing), Elis (whiting and bream) and the Old Fish Board Landing (big bream). Anglers chasing mangrove jacks should try lures and live baits around the Old Bridge, on the way up to Lake Weyba.

Further upstream the Noosa still has good bass fishing, with live prawns and lures fished around sunken snags yielding best results.

OFFSHORE
Sunshine, North and Chardons Reef, as well as the Barwon Banks, are the major offshore grounds here, with fine snapper, cod, sweetlip, parrot fish, venus tusk fish, mulloway, mackerel, cobia, tuna and yellowtail kings being taken. Most boat fishermen work out of Noosa Heads.

NOOSA NATIONAL PARK
This area offers some of the finest rock fishing in southern Queensland, with Dolphin Point, the Fairy Pools, Noosa Head, Hells Gate, Oyster Rock, Lion Rock and Paradise Cave all producing bream, tailor, mulloway (jewfish), sweetlip and even the occasional mackerel for live baiters and spinmen. Luderick and drummer are also found here, but they are not much fished for.

NOOSA HEADS TO BRIBIE ISLAND
Sunshine, Marcus, Peregian, Coolum, Yaroomba, Marcoola and Mudjimba Beaches all offer fair to excellent fishing in the better formations for whiting, bream, tailor, dart and mulloway (jewfish).

The Maroochy River contains all the usual southern Queensland estuarine species, as well as some good pockets of mangrove jacks. Hot spots worthy of attention on this river include: Pincushion Island (tailor and estuary species), Goat Island (general), Channel Island (luderick—which are often called black bream in this area), Chambers Island (flathead, etc.) Cod Hole (jew, bream and some estuary cod, Eudlo Creek (flathead and mud crabs), Petrie Creek (flathead, bream, whiting and some jacks) and the Bli Bli Bridge (school jew, whiting, flathead and crabs).

Further south, the Mooloolah River has a similar type of fishing, although it is somewhat more built-up and developed than the Maroochy. Here, places to try are: the Mouth (school mackerel, jew, tailor and bream), the Highway Bridge (general) and the Reserve (general estuary fishing).

Point Cartwright, south of the Mooloolah Mouth, has good rockhopping for school mackerel, mulloway (jewfish), bream and the occasional sweetlip.

Currimindi and Dickey Beach, down towards Caloundra Head, offer reasonable to good tailor, whiting and bream fishing in among the numerous sufboard riders, and there are a few big mulloway (jew) to be baited after dark.

Caloundra Head has good tailor fishing as well as bream, reef fish and the occasional jew.

Pumicestone Passage, down the western side of Bribie, has excellent flathead in places, as well as bream, whiting, cod and some mulloway. The ocean beaches on the eastern side of Bribie offer a high general standard of beach fishing and there is some superb flathead spinning around the Island.

MORETON BAY

MORETON BAY
Lying right on Brisbane's eastern doorstep, this vast expanse of relatively shallow water is fished hard, but still offers good fishing in most categories, from estuary and inshore action on bream, whiting, etc. to reef fishing, plus trolling and spinning for mackerel (Spanish and school), tuna, yellowtail kings and cobia. Just outside the Bay, around the corner of Cape Moreton, lies some of the best sailfish and small marlin water in the country, if not the world.

For those with even greater aspirations, some monster tiger sharks and white pointers also cruise the deeper channels, particularly around Peel Island, and the Bay boasts several Australian and World records for these (mainly caught in the l950s and '60s).

Anglers fishing close in to the western shore of Moreton Island do well with bream, tailor, whiting, flathead and reef fish. Hot spots are: Kianga Channel (mulloway and bream), Bulwer Wrecks (snapper, parrot, baitfish and sometimes cobia), Cowan Cowan (general), Laguna Bay (excellent flathead), the Sandhills and Blue Hole (prime winter or 'diver' whiting) and Mays Hole (general).

South Passage, between Moreton and North Stradbroke Islands, is an area of strong currents and changing sandbars. Caution is needed, but the fishing for estuary and inshore species can be very rewarding, especially around Sandy Point Reach, Browns Gutter and Days Gutter.

WARNING: Moreton Bay is generally quite shallow and chops up badly in moderate to strong winds. Small boat operators should exercise extreme caution at all times.

BRISBANE RIVER
The lower Brisbane River sometimes produces quite good angling for a range of species, especially bream, whiting, flathead and school jew (small mulloway). Some of the better spots include the walls at Doboy, Lytton, Pinkenba and Hamilton, as well as the tanker and cargo terminal, Luggage Point and Bishop Island. Some tropical species are also occasionally caught around these areas, most notably tarpon (ox-eye herring), javelin fish and mangrove jacks. Some big mulloway (jew) come out of the deeper holes.

The Pine River/Hayes Inlet area, north of the Brisbane River, offers similar, and in fact slightly superior, angling opportunities.

JUMPINPIN

Perhaps the most popular fishing and boating area in all southern Queensland, Jumpinpin is an extensive area of mangrove-lined channels, islands and holes inside the hazardous bar between North and South Stradbroke Islands.

Jumpinpin is particularly renowned for its prolific winter bream fishery, but the area also boasts abundant flathead, whiting, mulloway (jew) and crabs.

Hot spots within the Jumpinpin System include: the Breakthrough at the end of Tipplers Passage (tailor and bream), Kalinga Bank (whiting and bream, as well as excellent flathead in summer), Caniapa Passage (bream and flathead), Crusoe Island (flathead and bream), Greenbank (excellent luderick and bream), Squire Island (big flathead), the Mud Clump (bream), Short Island (a prime bream location) and the downstream end of Short Island for mulloway.

THE BROADWATER

Southport Broadwater is connected to Jumpinpin by way of Tipplers Passage. The Broadwater is another immensely popular stretch of fishing and boating water, with its much-improved access to the open sea through the newly rebuilt Southport Bar.

If bream are the number one drawcard in Jumpinpin, then that position is taken by whiting inside the Broadwater area, as some fantastic bags of these tasty little fish are taken here. However, there are also some great spots for bream, flathead, dart, trevally, mulloway and crabs within the Broadwater, and as a result of the deepened bar, offshore visitors like yellowtail kings and cobia, or exotics such as tarpon and giant trevally also come inside.

The Bonanza stretch, the Goalposts, Crab Island, Little Crab Island and the new Wave Break Island are all top spots within this estuary.

The entire area is in a state of change at the moment due to the extensive re-developments. Some interesting alterations have occurred, including the 'invasion' of open ocean species as described above, and the arrival of 'new' species such as hairtail. In the short term, whiting fishing may have suffered, but this has been compensated by slight improvements in catches of bream and flathead. In the longer term, most observers believe the remodelling of the Broadwater will result in better fishing.

OFFSHORE

The much safer new bar out of the Broadwater offers access to some great offshore angling, with good runs of mackerel, longtail tuna and—wider out—yellowfin, as well as sailfish and marlin. Reef anglers fish the deeper water for an interesting mix of northern and southern species: snapper, cod, parrot fish, venus tusk fish, emperor, pearl perch, samson, cobia and rosy jobfish (king snapper) to name just a few.

THE GOLD COAST

BURLEIGH HEADS TO TUGUN

Burleigh Head has rockhopping for some big tailor catches, bream and the occasional mulloway (jew), while the Groyne on the southern side of Tallebudgerah Creek is a good location for more tailor, bream, jew and flathead. The creek itself fishes well for bream, whiting, flathead, trevally and crabs, with good bait pumping flats around the aptly named Yabbie Island.

Even the man-made canals to the south have reasonable fishing, with bream, whiting, flathead and the rare mangrove jack.

Palm Beach usually has good formations of holes and gutters which hold tailor and a few jew, while the shallower banks have whiting, bream and dart.

The Groynes at 21st and 11th Avenues, along the beachfront, provide land-based anglers with reasonable sport for tailor, bream, whiting, mulloway and school mackerel when these pelagics run in close. Currumbin Groyne, to the south, is a tailor hot spot.

Currumbin Creek has flathead, bream, whiting, trevally and some quite good pockets of mangrove jack fishing, particularly upstream of Marlin Waters.

Currumbin Rock, to the south, offers tailor, bream, luderick and some mackerel at times, but Currumbin Beach is often too crowded with surfers for good fishing. Elephant Rock is a better choice than the beach, with tailor and bream on a rising tide.

Flat Rock, at Tugun, is dangerous in any sort of sea, but also produces excellent tailor bags at times, with bream and a rare jewie for variety. Tugun Beach, to the south, changes its formations frequently, but holds tailor, bream and whiting when conditions are right and surfers aren't too numerous.

OFFSHORE

The Close Reef off Palm Beach and the Gravel Patch, a little wider out, both present excellent bottom fishing for snapper, parrot fish, jew, teraglin and cod, while mackerel—Spanish and school—are trolled and baited here in summer and early autumn.

SURFERS PARADISE-TWEED HEADS

Although often crowded with swimmers and surfers, these beaches produce at least a few tailor year-round, as well as whiting and bream.

Snapper Rocks, just north of the Tweed, can be a red hot location for tailor, bream and jew, as well as occasionally producing school and Spanish mackerel. Even sailfish have been hooked here!

Victoria

EAST GIPPSLAND

MALLACOOTA

Mallacoota Inlet forms the entrance to two lake systems connected by a channel. The entire estuarine area is renowned for great southern bream fishing, particularly in late winter and spring, but also provides some excellent flathead angling, with some real monster 'lizards' in evidence.

The mouth of the inlet offers access to the sea, but it is shallow, breaks badly in a sea and is rather dangerous to all but experienced boat operators. Talk to and watch the local abalone divers crossing the bar first.

Besides bream and flathead, Mallacoota has luderick, flounder and mulloway inside; salmon, gummy sharks and the occasional mulloway along the beaches; and snapper, barracouta, pike, morwong and the like further offshore.

MARLO-SNOWY RIVER
The township of Marlo lies at the mouth of the Snowy River, and although often overlooked by travelling anglers, offers some top class estuary, beach and offshore action.

The lower Snowy provides excellent bream fishing, especially for anglers using live shrimps or sandworms. Estuary perch are also in abundance, and catches regularly include both these species. Further upstream, bass mix in with, and eventually take over from, the bream and perch and provide excellent sport on live prawns or lures around the many sunken snags.

BEMM RIVER
Justifiably renowned as one of Victoria's best bream estuaries, the Bemm and Sydenham Inlets also provide abundant fat luderick, mullet, estuary perch, flathead and flounder. Salmon are available near the entrance and salmon, gummy sharks and mulloway may be taken in numbers from the surf itself.

LAKES ENTRANCE-NINETY MILE BEACH
The fishing port of Lakes Entrance marks the beginning of the extensive and very productive Gippsland Lakes area, as well as being an excellent starting point for offshore work and beachcasting along the extensive and aptly named Ninety Mile Beach. Top spots include Golden, Paradise and Delroy Beaches.

Ninety Mile Beach offers gummy sharks, salmon, mulloway and — for those who are interested — large whaler sharks and tackle-destroying rays and skate.

The Narrows at Lakes Entrance offer good sport for bream, flathead and even snapper at times, while barracouta, salmon, tailor and silver trevally also venture inside through this channel.

GIPPSLAND LAKES

THE LAKES
This extensive and complex area of interconnected lakes, channels and rivers is home to the country's best and most popular southern bream fishing. Particular hot spots for these delicious and sporty fish are the 'Big Three' rivers: the Nicholson, the Mitchell and the Tambo. These fish are at their best from about late winter until the beginning of summer, but some can be caught all year, especially by anglers using live sandworms, shrimp and fresh local prawns.

Bream are also caught throughout the lakes themselves, as well as in all the other feeder streams and connecting channels. Here you will also find flathead, flounder, luderick, small salmon, estuary perch and the occasional mulloway.

Hot spots in the lake system include: the Paynesville-Raymond Island area, Lake Victoria, McClennans Straight and the mouth and lower reaches of the Latrobe River, at the back of Lake Wellington.

PORT WELSHPOOL-CORNER INLET
Ports Albert and Welshpool played an important role in the early settlement of the Gippsland region, and today are important to anglers, giving access to the vast and interesting fishing territory represented by Corner Inlet and its many islands and channels.

Around November each year snapper, including some very large fish, move inside this area and begin to feed in the deep water of the entrance, near Snake and Clonmell Islands.

Whiting and flathead are prolific throughout the inside waters of Corner Inlet, particularly around Sunday Island. Top baits for these fish are live nippers or bass yabbies (called 'clickers' by the locals in this area).

SOUTH EASTERN VICTORIA

WILSONS PROMONTORY
This rugged headland is the most southerly point on the Australian mainland, jutting far out into the cool, windswept waters of Bass Strait. Fishing around the Prom' is excellent when the weather permits, although boat anglers are forced to make a fairly long run to the best areas from either Corner Inlet to the north or Waratah Bay in the south.

Rock fishing from ledges around the Prom' can be extremely dangerous in any sort of weather, but anglers who pick their days can take sweep, pike, parrot fish, salmon and garfish etc. in good numbers.

WARATAH BAY
There is excellent year-round whiting fishing in the Bay itself, as well as snook, parrot fish, barracouta and salmon on and over the nearby reefs. In good years southern bluefin tuna are available not too far out off Wilsons Promontory and Cape Liptrap.

WONTHAGGI TO PHILLIP ISLAND
Here is more good territory often overlooked by the traveller, although like much of the exposed coast of southern Victoria, weather can be a real problem. All the usual southern rock and beach species are found, plus good schools of salmon and barracouta close to shore and, in some years, southern bluefin tuna and even yellowtail kingfish offshore.

WESTERNPORT BAY
George Bass charted this bay in 1798,

FISHING LOCATIONS

at which time it was also being used by whalers and sealers to escape the wrath of Bass Strait. Today it is home to many keen snapper and King George whiting specialists, who operate out of ports such as San Remo in the east and Hastings in the west. Tides run much harder here than in Port Phillip Bay, so heavier sinkers and sturdier tackle may be required.

For anglers with greater aspirations, sharks of several kinds including giant white pointers are sometimes available around the Nobbies and West Head, while bluefin tuna pass not too far out in good years.

Around the corner to the west lies Cape Schanck and a stretch of rocky coastline which offers excellent fishing for sweep, parrot fish, pike, snook, garfish, salmon and even luderick. Once again, weather conditions are a major consideration here, as the area is very exposed to prevailing southerly and westerly winds and seas.

PORT PHILLIP BAY

LOWER PORT PHILLIP BAY

The infamous Rip is the narrow, turbulent channel through which the waters of Port Phillip Bay rush during tidal ebb and flow. A very dangerous area for small boats and inexperienced seamen, the Rip is nonetheless a popular fishing spot, especially for large yellowtail kingfish. Salmon, snapper, big King George whiting, snook, barracouta and sharks of various types are taken here as well, and in the past bluefin tuna made forays through these straits. Bluefin visits became rare or unknown during the drastic decline in that fish's numbers during the 1970s and early '80s, but as their numbers increase with better management over coming years, it is likely that schools of bluefin will again be encountered around the Lonsdale and Rip region.

There are many fine snapper and whiting grounds around the lower end of Port Phillip Bay. King George whiting can be taken in the shallows along the Bay side of the Mornington Peninsula, as well as on the other side of the Rip in Swan Bay. Other whiting grounds — which mainly consist of sand patches among the weed beds in relatively shallow water—lie around Mud Island.

Snapper are caught over the artificial reef off Dromana as well as through Corio Bay on the western side of the Bay, towards Geelong. Another artificial reef off Portalington also produces fish.

UPPER PORT PHILLIP BAY

This end of the Bay is particularly popular with boat anglers chasing snapper from October to April each year. These fish tend to move around a great deal, and some hot spots will be active whilst others go dead.

Well known snapper locations around the top of the Bay include Point Wilson, Kirk Point, Point Cook, Altona Bay, St. Kilda, Ricketts Point, Mordialloc and Carrum.

Fine King George whiting are also taken around the top of the Bay at times, particularly in the shallows from Kirk Point to Point Cook and down the eastern shore towards Mornington.

Out in the open, central sections of the Bay, snapper are also taken, particularly over reefs, ballast heaps and other foul grounds. A depth sounder is invaluable in finding such structures.

Schools of salmon, barracouta, mullet and garfish also frequent the upper Bay, as do sharks of several species and even the occasional patch of yellowtail kingfish.

YARRA-MARIBYRNONG

The lower end of this river system produces good southern bream fishing, particularly in the months between late September and early January.

A particularly popular spot on the lower Yarra for anglers seeking bream, tailor, mullet and even mulloway is the hot water outlet at the Newport Power station. This location is widely known as 'the Hotties'.

Further up the Yarra, trout, Macquarie perch, freshwater blackfish and eels are taken by freshwater anglers, particularly around the township of Launching Place.

BARWON HEADS

This estuary lies west of Port Phillip Bay, with its mouth near Point Flinders. The lower end, around Barwon Heads, produces bream, luderick, whiting, snapper and trevally. This is also one of Victoria's best mulloway waters.

THE OTWAYS

LORNE TO APOLLO BAY

This is a lovely section of the Victorian coastline which unaccountably, as it has some superb fishing to offer, is often overlooked by anglers.

For the shore-based angler, salmon are the major target, with quantities of these high jumping sport fish to be found along the beaches and around the rocks. Trevally, sweep, big garfish, parrot fish and gummy sharks are also available to the beach and rock fisherman.

The Apollo Bay region is particularly attractive to trailer boat anglers, with excellent salmon, snook, barracouta, trevally, warehou and pike on offer along Marengo Beach, Wild Dog Beach and particularly over the reef systems close in to Haleys Point.

CAPE OTWAY TO PORT CAMBELL

This is another expanse of rugged, rocky coastline thrusting out into the wild and unpredictable wastes of Bass Strait. Excellent rock fishing for sea sweep, pike, garfish, parrot fish and salmon when the wind and weather allow.

The Gellibrand River offers access to the ocean for small boats as well as estuary fishing for all the usual southern estuary species.

Clifftop fishing is also popular around Port Cambell and the rough Otway Coast.

WESTERN VICTORIA

CURDIES RIVER TO WARRNAMBOOL

Like most of these western Victorian estuaries, the lower Curdies offers bream, whiting, mullet, estuary perch and the chance of a mulloway.

The coast here has many rocky ledges which may be fished for big sea sweep, whiting, parrot fish, salmon and so on. Warrnambool is a popular summer time tourist spot, offering snook and barracouta. From February until June or July southern bluefin tuna schools of varying sizes pass this port.

WARRNAMBOOL TO PORTLAND

The Hopkins River at Warrnambool has fine estuary fishing as well as redfin and trout further upstream.

In the nearby Merri River, trout move right down into the brackish water, being caught in good numbers below the Bromfield Street Weir. Here they overlap with bream, mullet and other more traditional estuarine species.

Port Fairy is an attractive harbour village with a strong professional fleet and access to the sea for amateur boat anglers who go out to chase salmon, barracouta, snook, pike, tuna, warehou, snapper and parrot fish, as well as tuna in season.

Narrawong Beach, running around the back of Portland Bay, offers a wide range of beach fishing spots where anglers can hope to catch salmon, mullet, gummy sharks, rays and even snapper and mulloway at times. Hot spots include the mouth of the Fitzroy River, east of the Surrey River mouth and the Narrawong road.

Portland, Melbourne's oldest settlement and a town steeped in history, is a pleasant and attractive port. Anglers can choose between fishing the beaches, jetties, breakwalls, rock headlands and offshore areas. Boat access to the sea is very good, with a wide concrete ramp inside the big safe harbour. Unfortunately conditions are often much rougher outside the harbour!

Lady Julia Percy Island, towards Port Fairy, offers very good offshore fishing as does the sea around Lawrence Rocks, at Portland, when the wind and swell permit.

Between March and July each year, schools of bluefin tuna weighing between six and 25 kilos (sometimes bigger) swim past this port—often less than a kilometre offshore. Mako and blue sharks are also abundant in these bait-rich waters.

Discovery Bay, to the west, runs through to the South Australian water and offers good fishing during those rare spells of good weather.

The Glenelg River, which flows into the ocean just east of the border, is definitely the region's best mulloway water. Hot spots for this species—which occasionally reaches 35 kilos here, but averages two to eight kilos—are mainly between the mouth and the Nelson Bridge

Tasmania

NORTH COAST

Estuary fishing for big southern bream is particularly good along this stretch of coastline facing Bass Strait. Top rivers are the Mersey and the Tamar. Higher up, both rivers contain good trout, and a small percentage of these run down the estuaries towards the sea. Flathead, small salmon, flounder and mullet also frequent these northern estuaries.

Offshore anglers chase salmon, barracouta, cod, flathead, trevally, warehou, pike and snook.

WEST AND SOUTH WEST COAST

The entire west and south west coast of Tasmania is extremely rugged, windswept and, for a large part, difficult to reach. Estuaries here also contain bream flathead, flounder, mullet and salmon trout (immature salmon), as well as playing host to annual runs of sea trout — sea-run brown trout moving down and back from the fresh.

Offshore are barracouta, big salmon schools, warehou, cod, flathead, trumpeter, snook and the like.

EAST COAST

The stretch of coast from approximately St Helens in the north to Tasman Island in the south sees the heaviest concentration of saltwater anglers in the Apple Island — a state dominated by freshwater fishing.

Good offshore fishing is available down this eastern shoreline for cod, flathead, barracouta, trumpeter, snook, pike, salmon, trevally and, on rare occasions, yellowtail kingfish.

From about the end of January, warm water currents from the north begin to lick the east coast of Tasmania, bringing with them pelagic fishes of the temperate seas. First to arrive are prolific schools of striped tuna and albacore. Most of the stripeys weigh between two and four kilos, while the albacore average a little heavier, but sometimes run to 15 and 20 kilos. Most of these fish are taken on trolled lures.

Later, towards the end of February, the first bluefin tuna arrive. These are mainly 'schoolies' from 10 to 20 kilos, but there is likely to be the occasional 'bottle fish' (over 45 kilos) mixed in.

The chances of a bottle or 'two bottle' (90 kilo-plus) tuna increase as the season progresses through March and early April. Indeed, southern bluefin over 150 kilos in weight have been taken off areas such as Bicheno and Eagle Hawk Neck at this time of year.

In good seasons tuna may still be caught in May, but by the end of that month it is too bitter and cold for most amateurs to think about going to sea. Blue sharks, makos and the odd white pointer are encountered offshore, along with a few striped marlin and broadbill.

There are also fine estuary, jetty and rock fishing opportunities existing down the eastern shore of Tasmania, with big sweep, salmon, ling, cod, flathead, parrot fish, barracouta, pike and snook to be caught, along with seasonal runs of warehou. There are also some as yet almost untouched fisheries for luderick and rock blackfish (drummer) of sizes that would be regarded as extremely impressive on the mainland.

Unfortunately Tasmanian saltwater anglers are few in number and seem to prefer the use of nets (legal for amateurs in this state) to hook and line fishing. Until more Tasmanians decide to abandon their mesh for a rod and reel, the potential of marine angling around the picturesque coast will remain a largely unknown quantity.

FRESHWATER

Tasmania's freshwater fishing is justifiably famous the world over, and in contrast to the saltwater scene, practically every Tasmanian wets a line in the freshwater at some time during his or her life.

Although there are a few pockets of estuary perch on the north coast, grayling along the north and east, and freshwater blackfish in the north—as well as whitebait runs for the gourmet—it is trout for which Tasmania is renowned.

Superb river, stream and lake fishing for trout exists all over the state, and there are even sea run populations of these fish—especially browns—in many rivers, including the much-polluted Derwent.

Some of the better known and more productive trout waters include: Lake Pedder (over-size browns and some rainbows), Great Lake, Lake Sorell, Lake Leake, Arthurs Lake, Lake Echo, Lake St Clair, Lake Crescent, Bradys Lake, Dee Lagoon, Lake King William, Little Pine Lagoon, Penstock Lagoon, Bronte Lagoon and Little Pine Lagoon.

Top rivers and streams include: the Macquarie, St Patricks, North and South Esk, Tamar, Brumbys Creek (and weirs), the Isis, Liffey, Meander, Lake and Elizabeth, the Break-o-Day, St Patricks and St Pauls, the Coal and Huon, the Plenty, Styx, Russel and Ouse, the Scamander and George and, over in the rugged west, the Inglis, Flowerdale, Leven, Forth, Upper Mersey, Gordon and Pieman.

South Australia

MOUNT GAMBIER TO THE COORONG

The south eastern corner of the Festival State is one often overlooked by Adelaide anglers, but this area offers some excellent fishing, particularly during the summer months.

Rockhopping is fair to good along this stretch, with the emphasis on snapper, sea sweep, tommy ruff, parrot fish and garfish.

Beach fishing opportunities are excellent, with some of the best salmon in the country, as well as gummy sharks, mullet, rays and the occasional mulloway. Many amateurs in this area also pot for the numerous crayfish which are found very close in along the rocky foreshore.

The Coorong is a delightful and extensive estuary, offering over 130 kilometres of superb fishing for mullet, bream, small salmon, flounder and mulloway.

VICTOR HARBOUR

A popular and picturesque seaside resort with access to fine offshore, beach, jetty and rock angling for salmon, snook, King George whiting, silver trevally, sharks and even yellowtail kingfish and bluefin tuna at times. Hot spots include Granite Island, the Bluff, Kings Beach and Waitpinga Beach. Big tailor and the occasional mulloway also turn up in these areas at times.

The Hindmarsh and Inman Rivers have good southern bream fishing, as well as mullet, flounder and small salmon (salmon trout).

KANGAROO ISLAND

A very popular destination for more adventurous anglers, Kangaroo Island has some of the best sea fishing in South Australia, with massive schools of salmon at times (October to November in the west, February to June along the southern coast), abundant King George whiting, parrot fish, sweep, snook and the like. Land based hotspots for these species include: Penneshaw, Vivonne Bay, Cape du Couedic, Snug Cove and Harveys Return.

The Island also has some of the biggest and most prolific King George whiting grounds, particularly around American River. For the bream specialists, Cygnet, Middle and Harriet Rivers are well worth investigating.

CAPE JERVIS TO NOARLUNGA

Cape Jervis is well known for its winter salmon run, tommy ruff, trevally and squid. Yellowtail kingfish are also taken at times and schools of southern bluefin tuna sometimes run through Backstairs Passage between the mainland and Kangaroo Island.

Port Noarlunga and the Onkaparinga River provide a variety of fishing opportunities, with small to medium salmon, trevally, mullet and, in the river, superb bream, with trout further upstream.

ADELAIDE AND ST VINCENTS GULF

South Australia's capital is within easy striking distance of first rate fishing. Jetty fishing is particularly popular and produces salmon, tommy ruff, garfish, mullet, trevally, flathead, and squid. Some of the best jetties are at Port Noarlunga, Brighton, Glenelg, Grange, Henley, Semaphore and Largs Bay.

Boat anglers off the metropolitan stretch concentrate on snapper, both little 'ruggers' and the big specimens up to 10 kilos and more. There are also salmon, flathead, trevally and excellent King George and yellowfin whiting. Sharks—from schoolies and hammerheads to big whites — can be either a problem or a bonus, depending on your attitudes and ambitions.

The Outer Harbour and Port River are known for their big mulloway, with fish to 30 kilos and more being taken by specialists using live or fresh dead squid, live fish, garfish and even lures.

The Murray Mouth is another top mulloway location, with plenty of schoolies and also the occasional heavyweight. This is another place where the species is taken on lures.

YORKE PENINSULA
The jetties at Edithburgh, Stansbury, Pine Point, Port Giles, Ardossan and Wool Bay offer garfish, whiting, tommy ruff, snook, salmon and some excellent snapper at times. As with much of this southern coastline, weather conditions can be a problem, particularly in winter.

Brown Beach and Hillocks Drive are especially well known for good sport when the black-back salmon schools move in.

CORNER POINT TO PORT PIRIE, SPENCER GULF
This is top fishing water for snapper and smaller fare. Hot spots include Point Turton, Hardwicke Bay, Port Victoria and Wardang Island. Jetty anglers frequent the structures at Port Hughes, Moonta and Wallaroo for all the usual shore and pier-based species, particularly gar and tommy ruff.

PORT PIRIE TO WHYALLA
This end of Spencer Gulf produces perhaps the biggest snapper in Australia, with 10, 12 and even the occasional 14 kilo fish being taken by boat and, more rarely, shore-based anglers. There are more than enough sharks here—including white pointers to a tonne or more—to satisfy game anglers too.

WHYALLA TO PORT LINCOLN
The red hot snapper fishing of the upper Gulf extends well down this western shore, with the Sir Joseph Banks Group of islands, Tumby Bay and Dangerous Reef providing some of the best opportunities. Lipsons Cove, just north of Tumby Bay, is recognised as a great location for land-based fishermen seeking a big snapper or two.

This stretch of coast and its adjacent island also provide excellent opportunities for tangling with a record-size white shark.

PORT LINCOLN TO CEDUNA
White beaches, rugged headlands, high cliffs and a relative lack of people characterise this extensive sweep of coastline.

Excellent rock and beach fishing exists here for big blue groper, salmon, trevally, snook, sea sweep, garfish, tommy ruff and sharks. Where boats can be safely launched, the same species plus tuna and yellowtail kingfish are readily available. Beaches on this coastline sometimes produce enormous mulloway. Streaky Bay is the site from which famous game fisherman Alf Dean launched his assaults on the monstrous white pointer sharks that frequent the area. These predators still swim in these waters, and some are at least as big as the records Dean set many years ago.

CEDUNA TO THE BORDER
With the wastes of the desert inland and cliffs along much of the coast, this can be a rather inhospitable tract of territory, but where access to the sea is possible, there is some very good fishing to be had. Here are found massive blue groper, dense schools of salmon, King George whiting, prolific tommy ruff and garfish, sea sweep, snook, snapper and mulloway. Tailor are caught here at times also.

The offshore waters contain most of the species described above as well as a variety of sharks up to and including big whites. There is also the chance of a yellowtail king or samson fish and, in better years, migrating schools of bluefin tuna in various sizes.

Western Australia

SOUTH EASTERN WESTERN AUSTRALIA

THE BORDER TO ESPERANCE
This isolated tract of coast has much in common with that described in the last South Australian entry — rugged shorelines, widely spaced townships and a generally inhospitable geography. However, where access can be obtained, good fishing is to be had. As one travels westwards along this coast, more and more Western Australian species such as samson fish, big blue groper and even Westralian jewfish are encountered.

ESPERANCE TO CAPE LEEUWIN
These fish are found — salmon, snapper, big blue groper, sharks, tailor, sweep and tommy ruff, with samson fish, Westralian jewies and tuna offshore. The many islands off this coast are particularly worthy of attention for their big samson fish, which occasionally top 40 kilos in weight. For those with ambitions aimed more at providing a succulent meal than a tackle-busting battle, this is also extremely good King George whiting country.

SOUTHERN WESTERN AUSTRALIA

CAPE LEEUWIN TO FREMANTLE
This is a delightful stretch of coastline and one which attracts plenty of attention from Perth anglers as well as locals.

Cape Naturaliste offers excellent rock fishing at the end of a three kilometre walking track. Species available include samson fish, salmon, trevally, herring (tommy ruff), sharks and sweep. Geographe Bay has many fine boat fishing grounds and some prime rock and beach locations.

To the north, the long jetty at Busselton is very popular with anglers chasing herring (tommy ruff), leatherjackets, salmon, tailor, trevally (skippies) and so on. The area is also a good one for squidding and crabbing.

Cockburn Sound is renowned for its large to very large snapper (caught almost exclusively by boat fishermen), as well as samson fish, King George whiting and other species.

METROPOLITAN PERTH

Perth and Fremantle metropolitan anglers have the choice of a wide range of beach, rock, estuary, breakwall (groyne), jetty and inshore boat fishing right on the doorstep of this western capital.

The most popular species of angling fish in the area are tailor, salmon, herring, trevally (skippies), mulloway, flathead and southern or 'black' bream. With the exception of bream, each of these species is available at one size range or another in every one of the environments mentioned. Bream are confined to the estuary, with the Swan being a particularly fine stretch of bream water.

Breaming hot spots in the Swan include Mosmans and Claremont, which usually begin activity in early spring and reach their peak by the start of summer, Applecross and Nedlands—which start a little later—and then the upper reaches of the river through the heat of summer. The fish move back downstream with the winter rains. Whitebait and prawns are favourite offerings for these bream.

The Swan estuary also produces excellent mulloway fishing most years from November through until at least March or early April, with the Narrows Bridge area being a hot spot. These big, hard-fighting and delicious fish are mainly taken on live yellowtail or gang-hook rigged mulies (pilchards to easterners). Dusk, dawn and through the night is the best fishing time.

Along the metropolitan beaches, surf casters mainly throw mulies or whitebait in search of salmon, tailor and mulloway. The salmon runs are not what they once were, due to over-exploitation of the stocks, but the size of the average run has improved slightly each season for the past few years.

On the jetties and rock ledges, a unique breed of anglers use the 'blob-and-maggot' system for catching the abundant and tasty herring (tommy ruff). This involves rigging a large, wooden float with a cavity that is filled with berley a metre or so above one or more small hooks, each carrying a fat, juicy maggot or 'gentle'. Most herring specialists breed their own maggots at home for this purpose.

Other jetty, rock and groyne anglers chase skippies—two very closely related species of silver trevally.

The North and South Moles of Fremantle Harbour are perhaps the most popular of all such land-based spots, and besides all the usual species, these walls sometimes see a good run of bonito during the warmer months, particularly for the early morning lure casters.

ROTTNEST ISLAND

Lying some 20 kilometres off the Western Australian coast, wide of Fremantle, Rottnest or 'Rotto' is a favourite holiday spot for Perth residents and becomes very busy and crowded during school holidays, particularly in the warmer months. One of the major attractions of this picturesque island is its excellent and diverse fishing.

All of the species available to mainland metropolitan anglers may be taken here, but usually in better numbers and at larger sizes. Herring fishing is particularly good here, with May being a peak month and the beginning of a run which sees tens of thousands of these little fish landed.

Trevally (skippies) bite best in late winter and early spring, while salmon are sometimes taken year around. Yellowtail kingfish and samsons occur mainly in the warmer months, as do the big King George or spotted whiting. Other target species for land-based anglers on the island include blue groper, sweep, tailor, mulloway, pike and cobbler (catfish). Westralian jewfish are also a possibility.

Some shore-based hot spots on the island include: West End (yellowtail kingfish, salmon and samson), Natural Jetty (tailor and salmon), Salmon Bay (mulloway and salmon), Ricey Beach, Mary Cove and Radar Reef (all good salmon spots), Parker Point (big whiting) and Thompson Bay (cobbler, pike and skippies).

Boat anglers work the reef waters around Rottnest for all these fish, but particularly for Westralian jewfish, samson and snapper. Spanish and shark mackerel also run in the warm currents off West End and Parker Point at times, mainly late in summer or autumn.

Further out, game boats work the Rottnest Trench area of the Continental Shelf for big blue marlin, dolphin fish, tuna and sharks of many types.

FREMANTLE TO GERALDTON

Many Perth anglers drive straight past this section of coast on their annual pilgrimages to the Murchison and points north; however, there is a good deal of fine fishing available along this stretch. Moore River and Jwien Bay are two of the better locations.

Species along this stretch are much the same as further south. Tailor, mulloway and salmon dominate beach fishing while groper, samson, tailor, salmon and skippies are available from the rocks. There are bream, tarwhine, flounder and flathead in the estuaries, and boat anglers mainly concentrate on Westralian jew, breaksea cod and samson.

CENTRAL WESTERN AUSTRALIA

GERALDTON-TO-KALBARRI

Offshore from Geraldton lie the numerous islands of the Houtman Abrolhos, often just called 'the Abrolhos'. This 70 kilometre string of islands, lying just inside the Continental Shelf, is a haven for bluewater boat anglers seeking a mix of northern and southern reef and pelagic species. Mackerel, tuna, marlin and sharks are particularly prolific around the Abrolhos at times, while the succulent baldchin groper is a very popular bottom fishing target.

Kalbarri, at the mouth of the Murchison River, is a very popular and exciting base for fishing of all kinds. On the estuary front there are bream, tarwhine, flathead, flounder and so on to be caught, while beach anglers mainly pursue mulloway and monster tailor to five kilos and more. Rockhoppers spin and bait-fish for tailor, and chase mulloway, snapper, baldchin, sharks and even Spanish mackerel at times. Boat owners go after Spanish, sharkies, big tailor, tuna, baldchin, jewfish, snapper and mulloway.

Hot spots around Kalbarri include: Oyster Reef and Chinaman Rock (tailors), Frustration Rock (mulloway and mackerel), Bluff Point and Beach (tailor and mulloway), Lucky Bay, Halfway Bay, Northampton, Horrocks Beach and Port Gregory.

Excellent trolling for pelagics is to be enjoyed by boat operators working the stretch of ocean between Lucky Bay and the mouth of the Murchison.

SHARK BAY

The vast and fishy expanse of Shark Bay not only marks the most westerly point of the Australian mainland, it also serves as a fascinating intersection between tropical waters to the north and sub-tropic and temperate waters to the south. Here tailor mix with Spanish mackerel, samson fish overlap with cobia, and mulloway and pink snapper are caught alongside baldchin and nor'westers (spangled emperor).

Steep Point, south of the Bay and facing Dirk Hartog Island, is one of the most famous and productive rock fishing locations. Here the sky is the limit for rockhoppers, with marlin and sailfish being hooked from the shore, as well as thrilling ballooning for big mackerel, cobia and sharks, spinning for mackerel and sharkies, baiting for mulloway, pink snapper, nor'westers and so on.

South Passage and Useless Loop are famous for their big runs of oversize pink snapper. These are taken by boaties and, to a lesser extent, shore and jetty anglers. Monkey Mia has abundant snapper, mulloway, trevally, barracuda and cobia, while similar action is available around Denham on the Peron Peninsula. Out wider, Bernier and Dorre Islands have superb mackerel fishing and almost untapped potential for marlin, sharks, cobia, wahoo and the like.

Shark Bay is famous for its monster tailor, and many of these are caught in the shallows right back in the Bay. Line class world records, including tailor over seven and eight kilos, have been taken here by the dedicated few who chase the isolated schools of monsters.

Carnarvon, north of the Bay, offers jetty fishing for over-abundant mulloway ('kingies'), mackerel, queenfish, big trevally, tailor, and sharks etc.. Offshore there are all those species and more, as well as pink snapper occasionally approaching plague proportions!

Carnarvon also provides the perfect stepping-off point for adventurous shore-based and small boat anglers keen to explore the awe-inspiring stretch of coast which lies to the north, stretching from Point Quobba to North West Cape.

THE NOR'WEST

CARNARVON TO ONSLOW

The rock ledges of Quobba, Cuvier, Garths Rock, High Rock and Point Maud are famous all over the country for their superb shore-based opportunities. Here Spanish mackerel, shark mackerel, longtail tuna, mackerel tuna, and yellowfin tuna, tropical trevally of half a dozen species (including 40 kilo-plus giants), cobia, isolated monster tailor, nor'west snapper, queenfish, baldchin, 212 groper, sailfish and marlin are all available to the rockhopper, to name less than half the potential species in the area!

These rocks are rugged, isolated and unserviced. The roads are long and rough and camping facilities practically unknown. But for those who are keen enough, the rewards are many.

WARNING The entire stretch of coast between the Murchison River and North West Cape is infamous for its rock fishing fatalities. This is the land of the 'king' or 'killer' wave, as well as huge ground swells and violent storm seas. Be especially careful when fishing the shore anywhere in this stretch. Talk to the locals, watch the sea for at least half an hour before fishing, never fish alone and always carry some form of safety flotation device which can be thrown to an angler in the water.

NORTH WEST CAPE-EXMOUTH

Exmouth services the United States Navy base on the tip of North West Cape and also offers a great base for fishermen, with several lodges in the town catering specifically to the needs of anglers.

Emphasis in this area is mainly on boat-based, offshore fishing, although there is some great shore fishing for big trevally, queenfish, mangrove jacks and so forth, particularly down the inside of the Exmouth Gulf. Coral Bay is also one of the few places on the Australian mainland with a reasonably consistent record for producing the elusive and highly-prized bonefish for shallow water bait anglers. While waiting for a bone, the angler is sure to catch small to medium threadfin salmon, trevally of several species, dart, sharks and the like.

Boat fishing out of Exmouth starts with party boat reef bashing for prolific nor'westers, emperor (red, long nosed and others), cod, baldchin, trevally and a host of other species. There is also light and medium tackle trolling, spinning and live baiting for mackerel, cobia, big trevally, etc. and heavy tackle gamefishing for marlin and sharks. Marlin fishing here is excellent at times, with very good numbers of mid-range blue and black marlin between 100 and 300 kilos striking baits and lures out towards the Continental Shelf (which comes very close to the shore west of the Cape).

EXMOUTH TO BROOME

The numerous islands which lie off this extensive sweep of coast provide thrilling fishing for big trevally, record-size cobia, tuna of several species, mackerel, sailfish and small to mid-range marlin. Over the reefs are abundant emperor, cod, baldchin, wrasse and the like.

The Ashburton River and Onslow area mark the southernmost range of the barramundi, although this mighty fish is far from common through this region. Not until north of Eighty Mile Beach—which extends up towards Broome—do barramundi become reasonably widespread.

The Dampier Archipelago, off Dampier, offers some of the finest sail-fishing in the world. These spindle-beaked gamesters are at their best during the second half of the year, from the end of June until late October or November. All the other light and medium tackle pelagics are abundant here, too, as are tropical reef fish.

Point Samson, near Roebourne, has a long jetty which puts the shore-bound angler in contact with pelagics such as mackerel and queenies.

Port Hedland is a reasonable-sized centre serving as a base for a variety of shore, jetty and trailer boat fishing for all the species previously described.

The Eighty Mile Beach stretch of coast between the De Grey River and Broome is desolate, isolated and not often fished, but there is some fascinating territory in there for shore-based fishing. Queenfish, trevally, barracuda and other tropical species predominate, and there is always the chance of a bonefish or a giant herring.

BROOME TO THE TERRITORY

The Kimberley Coast offers a myriad of exciting angling opportunities, with Broome as its southern base and Wyndham offering a stepping-off point for the even more remote far nor'western corner of the state near the border with the Northern Territory.

Broome, a diverse and historic port with a background based on pearling, has tremendous jetty fishing and provides boat access to sometimes wild fishing for big 'bumper' trevally, mackerel, cobia, sailfish, tuna of half a dozen types and a huge variety of reef fish. Broome Jetty is as good a starting point as any for visiting anglers. Here queenfish, trevally and mackerel may be caught, with sharks, big cod and groper available for the more adventurous.

The Fitzroy River and its tributaries—north of Broome—offer good to excellent barramundi for those willing to track down the hot spots and talk to the locals.

Dampier Land, the knob of country between Broome and King Bay, is rough and largely inaccessible, especially for visiting anglers with limited time. Big tides and strong winds can also make it hazardous country, but there is certainly no shortage of fishing rewards for the adventurous.

The many rivers between the Fitzroy and the Ord — including the Meda, Isdell, Charnley, Regent, Durack, Carson and Drysdale—all offer bountiful barramundi fishing at times, along with mangrove jack, fingermark, cod, tarpon, big forktail catfish and, higher upstream, sooty grunter and chanda perch.

The mighty Ord is another good barramundi stream in season, with fish running right up towards the wall of the big dam. Here too are monster catfish, tarpon or ox-eye herring, sooties and mangrove jack.

Offshore, the racing tidal waters are home to chopping schools of queenies, mackerel, longtail tuna and mackerel tuna, not to mention prolific reef species — cod, groper, wrasse, emperor, fingermark bream and so forth.

The Northern Territory

THE WEST

BORDER TO DARWIN

The extensive Victoria River estuary system is wild and hard-to-get-to country, but offers exceptional barramundi angling for those who strike it at the right time and have four wheel drive vehicles and outboard powered boats. This is a place of heat, big tides, mud and crocodiles; it is not for everyone, but a truly exciting piece of fishing territory, all the same.

Between the Victoria and the next big river system— the Daly —lies some fantastic but very hard to reach fishing. The Moyle and Little Moyle river systems in particular have superb barramundi, countless mangrove jacks, fingermark, queenfish (skinnies), threadfin salmon, tarpon, catfish and a host of other species. For much of the year, the only sure access to this productive stretch of coast is by way of boat from Darwin.

The Daly system sees a great deal of fishing from Territorians and visitors alike, and rightly so. It regularly produces the biggest barramundi west of Darwin, with 10, 15, 20 and even the very occasional 25 kilo specimens being taken, particularly by anglers trolling lures in the snag-lined holes downstream of Browns Creek.

The Point Blaze region has big schools of queenfish, mackerel and tuna, and these often extend well across the prawning grounds of Fogg Bay towards the wide entrance of Darwin Harbour.

DARWIN HARBOUR.

Darwin Harbour has prolific and varied fishing. The creeks which feed it fish well for barramundi, particularly during the build-up to the Wet, early Wet and again in April or May after the big rains are gone. Threadfin salmon work the colour changes and tide lines through the Harbour shallows and up the Middle Arm, while queenfish range wider and, when slightly cleaner water pushes in from the sea on a making tide during the Dry, mackerel often run well up past Port Darwin.

Darwin Harbour, especially around East and Lee Points, offers chances for the land-based angler as well as the boat owner—a fairly rare situation in the Territory, where a craft of some sort is almost mandatory for good fishing. By fishing the wrecks and reefs in the Harbour, directly off the Port and also across towards Mandorah, boat anglers take succulent fingermark (golden snapper), cod, mangrove jack and, best of all, very large black jew to 20 kilos and more. These hard-pulling, wreck-loving cousins of the southern mulloway look great and eat better than most other fish — at least matching the table qualities of saltwater barramundi.

THE CENTRAL TOP END

DARWIN TO THE EAST ALLIGATOR

This region of the Top End accounts for a lion's share of the barramundi fishing done by locals and visitors and produces some great fishing. While the barramundi aren't always as big as those trolled from the Daly, they are often more prolific and better fun to catch, with casting and retrieving lines frequently replacing trolling as the number one technique.

Top rivers in this area include: the Finnis, Adelaide, Mary, South Alligator and East Alligator.

The crossing into Arnhem Land on the East Alligator, towards Oenpelli, offers a rare opportunity for shore-bound fishermen to cast lures into good barramundi water, but watch the crocodiles and remember, entry into Arnhem Land is by permit only.

Most of this country fishes best for barramundi in the weeks immediately following the end of the Wet season, when the roads dry sufficiently to allow access, but muddy water continues to pour off the floodplains and into the rivers. Fish these run-off points for some intense action at this time.

Fish can also be taken right through the Dry, though there are some quiet spells in the relatively cool conditions of July, August and early September. Billabongs and holes may offer the best alternatives at such times, and of course there are always saratoga, sooty grunter, tarpon and catfish for those who can tear themselves away from the quest for the mighty barramundi.

Shady Camp and Corroberee Billabong, on the Mary, offer fine fishing at times, mainly for small, dark, barramundi, but also with the occasional 10 and 12 kilo fish.

Yellow Waters and Nourlangie, beyond the South Alligator, offer some of the best-known billabong and lagoon barramundi action in the Top End. These waters are extremely exciting to fish at night with 'noise-maker' lures such as poppers and fizzers, but again — be careful of crocodiles.

ARNHEM LAND

ARNHEM LAND

This is superb and largely untouched fishing country, but as explained earlier, access is by permit only.

NHULUNBUY (GOVE)

Situated on the north eastern corner of Arnhem Land, Nhulunbuy or Gove offers an ideal base camp for estuary and inshore fishing for all the favourite Territory species, including barramundi. Gove is also a growing centre for offshore boat fishing, with abundant Spanish mackerel, queenfish, tuna, sailfish and small to mid-range marlin.

The tides here are much smaller than around Darwin, with a range more like that found around the southern capitals (two metres or so).

ROPER RIVER

This is another very large river system like the Daly, but it is not fished to the same extent because of the difficult access and a lack of service towns and facilities. There is one camping site, near the Roper Bar police station at the upper limits of the tidal movement. From here boat anglers can travel up or downstream to fish, but as the river forms the south eastern boundary of Arnhem Land, going ashore on the northern bank is prohibited without a permit. Check at the Police Station before travelling too far afield.

Freshwater

NEW SOUTH WALES

BASS WATERS

Bass and the closely-related estuary perch are caught in varying numbers in nearly all of New South Wales' coastal streams, upriver to at least the first impassable barrier (waterfall, weir, dam, etc). A few dams and lakes have also been stocked.

The state's most famous bass regions include the big northern rivers, such as the Richmond and Clarence, and some of the larger southern systems including the Shoalhaven, Clyde and Bega Rivers. These days, however, better fishing is often found in smaller creeks or tributaries of the big rivers.

As well as these rivers, bass have been stocked with varying levels of success in lakes such as Clarrie Hall, Glenbawn, Fitzroy Falls and Brogo Dam.

NATIVE FISH WATERS

Native species including Murray cod, golden perch (yellowbelly), silver perch, Macquarie perch and eel-tailed catfish are found throughout the inland, western flowing rivers of New South Wales, as well as in many low altitude lakes, dams and impoundments, and the headwaters of at least a few eastern streams. In most regions, these native fish are joined by introduced pests such as European carp, goldfish, redfin perch and tench. The Murray/Darling system and its major tributaries, including the Murrumbidgee, Lachlan, Macquarie, Namoi, Gwydir and Paroo are the traditional strongholds of our native fish. Today, however, some of the best angling is found in man-made reservoirs on these rivers.

Productive native fish impoundments include (roughly from north to south) Pindari, Copeton, Keepit, Glenbawn, Windamere, Burrendong, Burrinjuck, Wyangala, Googong and Hume.

TROUT WATERS

The most famous and productive trout fishing districts in New South Wales lie along the Great Dividing Range at altitudes above about 500 metres.

The New England District, centred around Armidale, represents Australia's northernmost trout water. Productive rivers include the Styx, Guy Fawkes, Severn and upper Gwydir.

Further south, the Barrington Tops region also contains some fine little trout rivers and creeks.

West of Sydney is a superb and largely under-utilised trout fishing region which takes in the Blue Mountains and Oberon districts. Top rivers here include the Coxs, Kowmung, Hollanders, Fish, Duckmaloi, Abercrombie and Wollindilly. Warragamba Dam (Lake Burragorang) contains world-class trout stocks, but as Sydney's water supply, it is strictly off-limits to anglers — a situation that may eventually be relaxed. Oberon Dam and Lake Lyell, however, are open and provide great fishing.

Further south again, there is some excellent, if rather seasonal, fishing around Crookwell, Laggan and Taralga, on the South Western Slopes, north of Goulburn. Best rivers here include the Bolong, Crookwell, Abercrombie, Lost, Phils and Wheeo. Lakes in this districts which hold good trout stocks are Pejar, Crookwell (Redground) and Fitzroy Falls.

The real stronghold of trout in New South Wales is the Monaro and Snowy Mountains district, stretching from Canberra in the north to the Victorian border in the south, and westwards to Yass and Albury. Within this vast block of high country lie the giant lakes of the Snowy Mountains' Scheme (Eucumbene, Jindabyne, Tantangara, Blowering, Guthega, etc) as well as hundreds of rivers, streams and creeks. All of this water contains trout, both browns and rainbows, and would take a lifetime to thoroughly explore. Famous waterways here include the dams previously named, as well as rivers like the upper Murrumbidgee, Eucumbene, Snowy, Thredbo, upper Murray, Indi, Gungarlin, Delegate and many others.

QUEENSLAND

TROPICAL FRESHWATER

The tropical coastal streams of north Queensland hold several fish species of great interest to sport fishermen. Foremost among these are barramundi, mangrove jack, sooty grunter, jungle perch and tarpon (ox-eye herring). Less significant but nonetheless interesting are freshwater long tom, archer fish, catfish and the snake-headed gudgeon or 'mud cod'.

Fishing for this mix of species tends to improve as one moves northwards from Rockhampton, with the best action these days occuring in lightly-fished waters well off the beaten track. Long hikes or canoe trips into rugged gorge country back in the tablelands is often necessary to find quantities of good-sized fish.

Some of the better river systems include the Fitzroy and Dawson (which contain golden perch and saratoga), the Burdekin, Herbert, Tully, Normanby and Jardine. Less accessible rivers on the western (Gulf) side of Cape York, such as the Wenlock, Mission, Staaten and Norman, also offer some superb opportunities for the adventurous.

SOUTHERN COASTAL RIVERS

South of the Mary River, from Bundaberg to Coolangatta, Australian bass and catfish become the most important freshwater species in coastal river systems, along with some tarpon and introduced stocks of saratoga, golden perch and silver perch.

Southern Queensland's best bass waters include the Noosa, behind the famous Sunshine Coast. Some bass are still caught in the Brisbane River, too, although many keen Brisbane bass anglers now travel south of the border into New South Wales to pursue this species.

OUTBACK RIVERS

Queensland's western-flowing, outback rivers are part of either the Coopers Creek drainage, which ultimately flows towards Lake Eyre in South Australia, or tributaries of the Murray/Darling system. Most contain stocks of silver, golden and spangled perch, various catfish species, bony bream or herring, plus less well-known fish such as Welch's grunter. A few also contain Murray cod.

Most of these rivers are hot and turbid. Their discoloured waters discourage most lure fishermen, but often provide good sport for bait soakers. Some of the best angling in this vast tract of outback Queensland occurs in the many large, man-made impoundments.

LAKES AND DAMS

The past few decades have seen an intensive period of dam building on Queensland's rivers — both eastern and western flowing. Most of these dams have now been stocked with fish, ranging from barramundi and sooty grunter in tropical latitudes to golden perch, Murray cod and silver perch further south. Small pockets of stocked saratoga also exist, and experimental work is being undertaken with the likes of Welch's and Barcoo grunter. Most impoundments also contain spangled perch and catfish.

The best-known Queensland dams include: Lake Tinarro, west of Cairns (sooty grunter and barra), Fairbairn, near Emerald (cod and goldens), Cania, near Monto (cod, goldens, etc), Boondooma and Bjelke Peterson, near Kingaroy (cod, goldens, etc), Wivenhoe, Leslie and Glenlyon, west of Brisbane (cod, goldens, etc), Borumba, near Gympie and McDonald, near Noosa(saratoga, silver perch, etc) and Beardmore, near St George (cod, goldens, etc).

SOUTH AUSTRALIA

TROUT WATERS

The Light, Broughton, Wakefield, Rocky and Hutt Rivers all carry nice trout, and although the climate in the State's northern areas is often harsh, many of these rivers are deep enough to enable trout to escape the summer heat. Both browns and rainbows are stocked in northern streams, which during the warmer months are still and clear, making fishing quite challenging.

The Onkaparinga, Finniss and Hindmarsh are probably the most productive southern streams, with the Onkaparinga being the most popular.

The Onkaparinga varies along its length from a deep, still waterway to a narrow, fast-flowing torrent. It is broken roughly in two by the Mount Bold Reservoir, and carries both trout species, as well as some very large redfin. State records for both rainbows and browns have come from this river. The creeks south of the capital also support trout populations, and there are countless private farm dams liberally stocked with both browns and rainbows.

Just about all the recognised trout fishing techniques are employed on South Australian streams, including fly fishing, lure casting and bait fishing. All can be effective, but there is little doubt that the knowledgeable fly fisherman will tend to consistently catch bigger trout than his or her counterparts using lures or bait.

As there are very few natural insect hatches on South Australian streams, most fly fishing is done with nymphs, or with streamers such as Matukas, and similar wet flies. There will be an occasional rise when atmospheric conditions are suitable.

As a lot of fishable water flows through private property, access to river banks is often restricted by property owners. While many farmers don't mind angling visitors, provided they are extended the courtesy of being asked, some refuse to allow anyone onto their land except members of the Fly Fishing Association.

Scotch thistles and blackberries are the curse of the South Australian trout fisher. Almost all of the northern waters are lined with dense thistles, which invariably leave their mark on the angler after a day's fishing. Blackberries take over on the southern streams, making fishing painful in some areas and impossible in others.

THE MURRAY RIVER

The Murray River is the only South Australian inland waterway to carry native fish of any angling significance. In the past two decades, there has been a gradual decline in the State's native fish stocks.

Years ago, when the Murray ran relatively clean and clear, golden perch, cod, congolies, silver perch and the occasional tench or redfin were regular captures. The latter two varieties were the only imports, and neither proved too much of a problem.

The introduction of European carp has really turned the river's ecosystem upside down. Carp are among the most efficient and destructive feeders in the piscine world. As their numbers escalated, they quickly began to take control, endangering the native species.

For a few years it was predicted that the carp would take over altogether, wiping out the indigenous species in the Murray. Thankfully, this hasn't happened.

Golden perch, in particular, seem to be on the way back. Fishing live shrimps or small yabbies around the snags appears to pay dividends on goldens (known locally as callop), but a bunch of tiger worms will also have the desired effect if there are no carp in the vicinity. The average weight of the callop taken in South Australia would be a little better than a kilogram, although a few fish of three times that figure are taken annually.

Once abundant around Mannum, Morgan and other popular Murray ports, cod are rare these days, particularly the bigger specimens. An occasional big fellow will sometimes create excitement among regular river specialists, but the incidence of cod captures is definitely on an unfortunate decline. In recognition of this fact, a total ban on the taking of Murray cod in South Australian waters came into force during 1990. This moratorium was expected to last for at least two years, so check with local authorities before angling for this species.

Redfin perch, while no longer common in the Murray, have become established in good numbers in many of the other rivers throughout the State.

As mentioned, European carp are now a fact of life in the Murray and some other South Australian waters. Although they are considered a nuisance by most, some anglers scale down their tackle and actually fish for them exclusively. One thing the carp definitely has going for it is its massive growth potential. No one was really sure just how big they would grow here in the early years after their introduction, but specimens of over 10 kilograms rarely raise an eyebrow these days.

South Australian legislation stipulates that it is an offense to return carp to the water alive. However, only by some quirk of nature will carp ever vanish from South Australia. Meanwhile, anglers have little choice other than to learn to live with them.

TASMANIA

THE LAKES

Lake Sorell is probably Tasmania's most productive and heavily fished lake. Every year trout are taken from this location weighing in excess of three kilograms. Anglers fishing this water for more than a few days are almost guaranteed a result.

The majority of trout taken here are browns, although rainbows make their presence felt at times. Lake Sorell is a lure and fly-fishing area only, fishing with bait can bring a heavy fine and confiscation of tackle.

There is a launching ramp at Lake Sorell. As with most Tasmanian waters, keep an eye on the weather here because due to the lake's shallowness it can become quite rough in a very short time. Many anglers prefer to troll, covering great distances, and this method produces the heaviest bags. Each boat is allowed to troll only one rod per person.

Lake Sorell offers good fly-fishing. The majority of fishing is wet fly-fishing. Fly patterns such as black and red Matuka, Mrs. Simpson, Yetti and Jumbuck are all successful.

Most anglers prefer to fish blind, covering as much area as possible. During spring, trout can be seen foraging in the shallow, vegetated areas of the lake. They can be spotted easily as their tails often protrude from the water, it is then a matter of putting the fly a foot or two in front of the fish. This will result in the take or refusal, more often the latter.

Lake Pedder is primarily trolling water Fish taken here in recent years are nowhere near the size of those taken from this water during the 1970s, when monster browns regularly ran to six, seven and eight kilograms. Nonetheless, Pedder still provides reasonable fishing. Nowadays, the average fish weighs between one and two kilograms.

The lake has good launching facilities and there is also a boat hire service.

The best time to fish is around Christmas, when there is often a hatch of mudeyes (the larval stage of dragonflies), which create an interest among the fish. The best time to fish an imitation is just on dark, when the fish start to move in on the mudeyes.

One of Lake Pedder's only drawbacks is the every-changing weather, which is often atrocious. Great care should be exercised when boating on this waterway.

Great Lake is one of Tasmania's most central lakes and provides good fishing. It holds rainbow and brown trout, and more recently there have been liberations of Atlantic salmon. Great Lake's waters are very clear, and this can be a disadvantage, as it makes the fish very wary and unapproachable.

Along with lure fishing, this water is also a bait fishery. Best results are often achieved by those fishing with wattle grubs. Although this method may not be as interesting as using a lure, it is certainly the most productive, especially after dark. Most anglers, after baiting up with their grub, cast it out and leave the rod set on the shore. Usually the line is placed on a stick or bottle and this is used as a strike indicator.

The Great Lake has good launching facilities and accommodation. Local knowledge is a big advantage, as many fish congregate over hidden weedbeds. When trolling, deep-diving lures are helpful. Popular lures include the X4 Flatfish, Tassie Devils, Cobra Wobblers and various spoons. Deep trolling with downriggers, lead core or wire line can be extremely effective at times.

Trolling large wet flies is particularly successful in weeded areas, as the flies do not tend to snag the way lures do. Large fur-bodied flies and Matukas are a good choice. Dark streamer flies, bucktails and marabous are also very successful.

Great Lake also offers good fly-fishing in clear water. Working around the lakes' margins is a productive method to catch some of the lake's larger specimens, but care must be taken to keep out of sight, as once a trout has noticed your presence, it will ignore your offerings and continue along the shore, or spook into deeper water. During summer, there will be hatches of insects and good sport can be had pursuing the rising fish with dry flies.

Lake Crescent yields some of Tasmania's largest brown trout. There are ample launching facilities available, and trolling and bait fishing are the two most popular methods employed.

Fly-fishing is often rewarded with only marginal success because of the generally murky water. The biggest fish in this lake are taken withbaits of small, native fish called galaxias or minnows. Slightly heavier tackle is required due to the snaggy area and the size of the fish. Use lures similar as those recommended for Lake Sorell

Lagoon of Islands is primarily fly-fishing water, with rainbow trout predominant. Fish average around three kilograms, and reports of five or six kilogram fish are not uncommon.

Lake Arthur, Tasmania's second most heavily fished lake, has good launching facilities and camping areas. Although the fish are generally smaller, they make up for this with their abundance. Bait fishing, spinning and fly fishing are all acceptable methods of capture here.

During summer, this area offers exceptional fly fishing, with large rises. Flies such as Highland Duns are especially productive.

Lake Leake is fast growing into a very reliable fishery. Brown trout predominate over rainbows, and the area offers good fly fishing and spinning. Boat anglers have an advantage as access to some locations is difficult. The area has good launching facilities and the local anglers are happy to assist with advice.

TROUT RIVERS AND CREEKS

Tasmania is blessed with many accessible freshwater rivers and creeks which contain good trout fishing. The majority of locations have stocks of fish and can be reached by a short walk from the roadside. If in any doubt about crossing property, it is best to ask permission.

Early in the season, the freshwater rivers and creeks are usually in flood, due to snow melt and excessive rainfall. Fishing the flooded backwaters can be highly successful.

Later in the season, as the water clears, insect life becomes more prevalent, and the fish feed on the insects that are emerging, laying eggs, or are blown on to the water. At these times, lures only work in the faster waters, whereas the fly fisherman comes into his own on the longer reaches and pools. Successful dry fly patterns include the Red Spinner, Highland Dun, Black Spinner, Royal Coachman and Grey Duster.

Other species encountered in Tasmanian freshwater rivers and creeks are eels, cucumber herring (Australian grayling), redfin perch, tench, and freshwater blackfish.

Anglers visiting during spring or early season may encounter sea-run trout, which have worked their way up from the mouth of rivers. These large fish can provide an unusual surprise in some of the smaller waterways. Methods used to take them are the same as those used for the resident trout. You are able to tell a sea-run trout by its silvery appearance, and characteristic dark-red flesh, which is highly prized on the table.

In the northern half of Tasmania, small rivers and creeks predominate. Although good fishing water can be reached in the south within 30 minutes of Hobart, the choice of location is more limited than in the north.

The Tyenna and North-West Bay River (at Margate) hold large populations of small trout, which will readily accept baits and lures.

The North Esk and Huon Rivers contain fewer, larger fish, which are better 'educated' and may prove exceptionally difficult to approach and hook.

Saint Patrick's River, South Esk and Brumby's Creek (at Cressy) are excellent trout fisheries, although once again, some experience and a good deal of caution around the water are required.

The township of Perth, in the north of the state, is a great venue for northern trout fishermen. The township lies on the South Esk River which holds large numbers of smaller fish from half a kilo to a kilo. Any method of capture may be employed.

Hadspen picnic grounds is another popular northern trout fishery. It is a safe and productive angling location for fishermen of all ages and capabilities.

In southern Tasmania, easily accessible waters include the upper Derwent River, Huon River, Brown's River, and the Styx River.

The Derwent River is the most accessible river from Hobart. It frequently harbours large numbers of fish in its upper reaches. Derwent Bridge and Plenty are among some of the most popular locations visited during the season.

VICTORIA

NATIVE FISH WATERS

There are abundant native fishing prospects in Victoria. Lakes and rivers all over the state hold good stocks of Murray cod, golden perch (yellowbelly), Macquarie perch, silver perch and freshwater blackfish.

Techniques required to catch native fish in Victoria are similar to those used in other states, however, the use of bait is more popular. Nonetheless, the exciting sport of lure fishing is increasing in popularity.

The upsurge in stocks of native fish in Victorian waters has been the result of the combined effects of Fisheries stocking the waterways and the diminishing carp population.

Lake Dartmouth is one of the last strongholds of the hard-fighting and delicious Macquarie perch. The fishery for this species at Dartmouth is excellent.

To catch Macquarie perch, worms or mudeyes presented with the aid of a sinker are required. Macquarie perch will rarely take lures. Best time is usually in spring and early summer.

Dartmouth also holds some Murray cod and perhaps a few trout cod, although these species are rarely encountered.

Lake Eildon has stocks (both natural and introduced) of Murray cod in the Delatite Arm of the Lake. The cod respond to deep diving cod lures and baits over the summer months.

Lake Mulwala, on the Murray River at Yarrawonga, has some of the best stocks of Murray cod in Victoria. They are very responsive to lures and trolled deep divers regularly produce cod between two and six kilograms. Old river beds are the best areas, with lures being most productive when worked right down near the bottom.

The western district known as the Wimmera contains many fine native fish waters, mostly centered around the town of Horsham. Lake Charlegrark, in particular, offers superb cod fishing, whilst others such as Green Lake have yellowbelly and other natives. This region also offers fine yabby fishing, while the Wimmera River itself is quite good for yellowbelly, freshwater blackfish and the occasional Murray cod.

The most productive fishing time in these areas is in October and November and through the late summer until mid-April.

The Murray River has made a come-back in recent years, especially with Murray cod and yellowbelly stocks. The best method is with bait during the early winter months of May and June when the water clears and lures are very successful.

The middle reaches of Melbourne's Yarra River offer improving sport for native fish. The main species is the Macquarie perch, first transplanted here in the 1920s and '30s by local angling clubs, and recently re-stocked by the active Melbourne branch of Native Fish Australia. The fishing is best from October to December.

There are also limited stocks of Murray cod in some sections of the Yarra's middle reaches.

The Goulburn River, below Lake Nagambie, has excellent stocks of silver perch, Murray cod and yellowbelly. From Nagambie to Shepparton and on to Echuca, there are many, many kilometres of river to explore.

The best action occurs during the summer months, with bait fishing favoured. However, when the water clears up a little, lures come into their own.

TROUT STREAMS

The Goulburn River, along with its tributaries, the Acheron and Rubicon Rivers are amongst Victoria's most popular trout waters. This system is close to Melbourne and drains Lake Eildon. It is good for rainbow and brown trout all year round, but is best in spring and autumn, when all techniques — lure, fly and bait — produce fish.

Best areas include the Breakaway, Gilmours Bridge and the junction of the Goulburn and Rubicon Rivers.

The north-east High Country offers some challenging and spectacular fishing. The Mitta River between the township of Mitta Mitta and where it flows into the upper arm of the Hume Weir is great for big brown trout using lure casting. It is accessible from the Omeo Highway.

Other streams of the north-east that are excellent fly and lure waters include the Ovens, King and Alpine Creeks. The townships of Porpenkah and Dartmouth are excellent bases. Fishing these high country streams is excellent in late spring and summer. Fly-fishing and compact lure casting with spinner blade lures or light jigs are preferred.

The Victorian alpine country extends westward from these areas. On its western edge one finds the rivers and streams that flow into Lake Eildon. The Big River, the Delatite, the Goulburn and the Howqua are just a few that offer excellent fishing at the right time of year.

Again, spring and summer are top times and as there is a strong run of fish out of the lake and up these rivers in winter, the prospects are good in May and June.

In the central area of the State there are a number of rivers that hold good stocks of trout and provide excellent fishing. The area around Ballarat is the starting point and the best rivers are the Mt. Emu Creek, some reaches of the Loddon, Caliban and Avoca, as well as the many small creeks in the area.

To the west, there are two famous rivers that hold the largest river run browns in the State, the Merri at Warrnambool and the Gelibrand in the Otways.

The lower reaches of the Merri runs right through the township of Warrnambool and, in stark contrast, the Gellibrand runs through the isolated rugged Otway Ranges.

Both, however, are reasonably accessible by road and both are best approached with lure casting techniques. The lower sections of each river are large enough to launch a boat and actually troll for trout.

TROUT LAKES

There are many fine trout lakes and dams in Victoria. Some of the more famous include Lakes Eildon, Dartmouth, Rocklands, Purrumbete and Bullen Merri. The last two named, which lie in the Western Districts, also contain land-locked stocks of chinook or 'quinnat' salmon, which provide exciting action at times.

All of these larger waters are fished regularly and heavily by anglers using the full range of impoundment trout techniques; from shore-based bait fishing to lure casting, fly fishing, flat-line trolling and downrigging.

Less well known, but just as exciting are some of the smaller, shallower lakes, such as Murdeduke, near Winchelsea, Toolondo, near Horsham and Glenmaggie, near Heyfield. These waters tend to exhibit considerable fluctuations in fish stocks and angling returns, so up-to-date local knowledge is vital.

WESTERN AUSTRALIA

TROPICAL FRESHWATER

In tropical Western Australia, the Pilbara and Kimberley regions offer little permanent freshwater fishing. There are several lagoons that hold barramundi year round, but even the mightiest of rivers can virtually dry up within a couple of months of the end of Wet season rains.

There are a few hardy, native species that can tolerate this changing environment. Sooty grunter, tarpon, long tom, archer fish and catfish survive in the fresh water, while barramundi and mangrove jack move with tidal influence in the lower reaches of the rivers.

The Kimberleys contain the largest body of fresh water in Australia, the man-made Lake Argyle which holds commercial quantities of huge catfish, and some sooty grunter and long tom. Ivanhow Crossing or the Diversion Dam gates, a short trip from Wyndham, are hotspots for barramundi during the Wet season.

Further down the Ord River are the Dry season locations, although a quarantine area encompassing the tidal reaches restricts access. Charter operations out of Kununurra have special permission to enter the area. Carlton Crossing and Sandy Beach are in the freshwater stretch, and can be reached by four-wheel drive.

There are also helicopter and floatplane charters which reach the otherwise virtually inaccessible rivers and Wet season coastal creeks across the top end of Western Australia.

Wyndham has little freshwater fishing close to town, as it is situated amongst tidal mudflats. The Penetecost River crossing, which is influenced by the ocean tides, is a good location for barramundi. Other river locations are accessible by four-wheel drive.

From Wyndham and Cambridge Gulf to Derby, access is a major problem. Cruising yachts and adventurous off-roaders are at an advantage, as there is no way for an average tourist to reach the Mitchell, Prince Regent or Sale Rivers, or Walcott Inlet with its feeder rivers, Calder, Charnley and Isdell. This entire area is a largely untouched natural sanctuary for barramundi.

Derby, although also situated among tidal mudflats, has the distinction of being built at the mouth of the Fitzroy River. Willare Bridge, Yeeda and Langi Crossing are not far from town and offer good barramundi fishing, while upstream pools also offer tarpon and catfish. The river is dammed at Camballin. The larger sooty grunter and catfish are upstream from the dam, while the barramundi reach hundreds of kilometres inland to Geikie Gorge.

May River is a small river also accessible from town via the Bigg River road. It is a good barramundi spot, with threadfin salmon also available.

Live pop-eye mullet, caught with a cast net, are the best bait for barramundi throughout the Kimberleys.

Although barramundi and tarpon are caught as far south as Onslow, there are few freshwater creeks south of Fitzroy that hold fish all year.

SOUTHERN FRESHWATER

The far south-west corner of this dry State has a wealth of streams, rivers and impoundments, many of which contain introduced stocks of trout and redfin perch. Rivers meander through huge jarrah and karri forests, leaving a succession of deep pools to attract both the fly fisherman and the spinman.

Though not as highly rated as trout, redfin offer the freshwater angler the opportunity of a large catch.

Small lures, such as the Rapala Mini Fat Rap, 8 gram Nilsmaster, and small Halco Laser or Combat work on both trout and redfin. Many of the south-west's rivers are heavily overgrown, limiting opportunities for fly fisherman.

Warren River and Lefroy Brook are the best natural waterways in which to catch quantities of large rainbow and brown trout. Autumn and spring are favoured times. The Warren River drains the wettest part of the State and trout are taken right at the mouth, where it reaches the sea.

Lefroy Brook has excellent lure and fly-fishing water, and some reasonably accessible bank, unlike the inhospitable Warren which can only be fished from a few deep, long pools.

Bedelup Park has been developed as a tourist complex near Beedelup Dam. Trout and marron (crayfish) chasing are favoured sports with visitors to this superb, thickly forested countryside.

Samson Dam, Logue Brook, the Upper Blackwood River, and Waroona Dam are other top trout waters, although redfin have diminished trout numbers in the latter. An excellent caravan park is situated at Waroona Dam, which is also a marron or crayfish lurk.

Blackwood River holds many marron in its upper reaches and also some large trout, sometimes caught in farm waters open to the public.

As in all Western Australian freshwater fishing, summer temperatures cause the fish to seek deep cooler waters. Rivers like the Blackwood and Warren have only a trickle of water then and fish seek refuge in perennial pools among the karri forests around Pemberton.

Around Perth there is less freshwater action, as water supply dams are off-limits to anglers. Lake Leschenaultia has a limited season on introduced stock, and a farm at Lesmurdie a private hatchery.

The Murray River is superb, especially for redfin, with fine trout in lesser-fished water. Near Dwellingup is best, and many fine rocky pools exist near the Baden Powell waterspout. Right down near Pinjarra big fish have come from some surprising water quite close to the estuary.

Drakesbrook Reservoir, below Waroona Dam, has a large population of redfin, and quiet stretches of river can house big marron. A strictly controlled season exists on the vulnerable marron stock.

At Harvey Weir, trout are best pursued in spring to early summer, while many Harvey locals use baits and lures year round for redfin.

In Stirling Dam, lures are suited to the expansive, easily accessible waters. Marron are keenly pursued.

Wellington Dam fishes well for redfin, and is a very popular venue for marron fishing.

Index

A

Adelaide 207
Adelaide River 212
Airlie Beach 200
Albacore 78 206
Alexander River 197
Amberjack 156
Anchovies 64
Apollo Bay 205
Archer fish 197 198 199
Archer river 197
Arnhem Land 212
Ashburton River 211
Avoca, NSW 192 193

B

Bait 53-75
    bream 165
    estuary, harbour and beach 54 55 *54 *55
    freshwater 62 63 *62 *63
    offshore and deep-sea 58 59 *58 *59
Baitcaster reels 16 17 *16 *17
Baitcaster rods 30-32 *30 *32
Balaclava Island 201
Balling 190
Bamaga 198
Barracouta 64 66 78 156 *169 204 205 206 207
Barracuda 79 *141 198 199 210 211
Barramundi 25 28 65 69 80 163 167 *180 181 197 198 199 200 201 211
Barwon Heads 205
Bass 15 17 65 81 162 163 167 167 192 196 199 204
Bass Point 194
Bateman's Bay 196
Beecroft Peninsula 177
Bega River 196
Bemm River 204

Berley 60 61 *60 *61 158 159 160
Bermagui 196
Billfish 28 177 198
Black Rocks 189
Blackfish   See Luderick
Blue swimmer crabs 192
Bluewater trolling 152
Boat Harbour 195
Body baits 69
Bondi 193
Bonefish 198 201 210 211
Bonito 64 66 82 176 191 192 194 195 196 197 209
Bonville Creek 190
Botany Bay 193
Bottom bouncing 160 199
Bowen 200
Box Head 192
Boyd's Beach 194
Bream 15 *82 83 *83 *159 164-5 *165 *172 *173 176 189 190 191 192 193 194 195 196 197 199 200 201 202 203 204 205 206 207 209 210
    fingermark bream *59 90 181 198 199 200 211
Bribie Island 202
Brisbane River 202
Brisbane Waters 192
Broome 211
Brunswick Heads 189
Brunswick River 189
Brush Island 196
Bundaberg 2000 201
Burketown 197
Burleigh Heads 203
Burrewara 196
Byron Bay 189 190

C

Cairns 198 199
Calliope Island 201
Caloundra Head 202

Camden Haven 191
Cape Bedford 198
Cape Bowling Green 200
Cape Capricorn 201
Cape Cleveland 200
Cape Flattery 198
Cape Hicks 197
Cape Howe 197
Cape Jervis 207
Cape Leeuwin 208
Cape Liptrap 204
Cape Mansfield 200
Cape Melville 198
Cape Otway 205
Cape Palmerston 200
Cape Upstart 200
Cape Schanck 205
Cape Yorke 197
Capricorn Coast 200-1
Carnarvon 210
Carp 84 163 167 185
Carron River 197
Catfish 15 163 185 197 198 199 200 209 210 211 212
Ceduna 208
Centrepin reels 22 23
Chairfishing rods 35
Chardon's Reef 202
Clarence River 190
Closed-face reels 14 15 *14 *15
Cobia 156 189 190 191 198 199 200 201 203 210 211
Cod 86 160 181 189 197 198 199 200 201 202 206 207 210 211 212
Coff's Harbour 190
Coleman River 197
Comerong Island 195
Connections 44 *45
Cooktown 198
Coorong River 207
Coral trout 87 160 198 199 200
Corio Bay 200
Corner Inlet 204
Corner Point 208
Crabs 201 203 209

219

Crayfish 207
Cronulla 193
Crookhaven Heads 195
Curdie's river 206
Currarong 195
Currents 178-9
Currimindi 202
Currumbin Creek 203
      Groyne 203
      Rock 203
Curtis Island 201
Cuttagee Lake 196

D

Daintree River 198
Daly River 211
Dampier Archipelago 211
Dampier Land 211
Darling River 185
Dart 88 189 201 202 203
Darwin 211
Deepwater bottom bouncing 160
Depth sound 50 51
Dickey Beach 202
Disaster Bay 197
Discovery Bay 206
Distance casting 146 147 *146 *147
Dolphin fish 28 66 *67 88 189 199 209
Double Island Point 201
Double-handed spinning rod 28 29 *28 *29
Downriggers 143 162
Drummers 89 *149 176 191 192 193 194 195 196 197 202 207
Dunk Island 199

E

East Alligator River 212
Eden 197
Edward River 197
Egret Reef 198
Eighty Mile Beach 211
Emperore, Red 90 198 199 203 210 211
      spangled 90 210
      long-nosed 210
Emu Park 200
Endeavour River 198
Epilimnion 187
Esperance 208

Estuary systems 172-3
Evans Head 190
Exmouth 210

F

Finnis River 211
Fish anatomy 76-7
Fishing electronics 50-2
Fishing lines 36 37 *36 *37
Fitzroy River 200 211
Five Island Group 194
Flat Island 200
Flathead 15 17 *24 64 92 *93 160 189 191 192 193 194 195 196 197 198 199 200 201 202 203 204 206 207 208 209 210
Flinders River 197
Floaters 158 *159 160
Floats 46 *46
Flounder 93 192 204 206 207 210
Fly casting 167
Fly fishing freshwater 166-7
      saltwater 168-70
Fly lines 167
Fly reels 24 25
Fly tying 73
Forrester's Beach 192
Forster 191
Fraser Island 201
Fraser Park 192
Fremantle 208 209
Freshwater blackfish 206 207
Freshwater flies 70-71 *70 *71 166 *166
Freshwater lures 68 69
Freshwater rigs 142-3
      bubble float 142
      deep trolling 142
      downriggers 143
      fixed quill float 142
      fly casting 143
      lure trolling 142
Freshwater trolling 162-3

G

Gaffs 48 *48
Game fishing, land-based 150
      baits 150 151
      best venues 150
      rock fishing 150
      tackle 151

Game reel 18
Game rod *29
Garfish 94 189 201 204 205 207 208
Gellibrand River 205
Georgina River 197
Geraldton 209
Gerroa 195
Gippsland Lakes 204
Gladstone 201
Glenelg River 206
Gold Coast 203
Golden Perch 17 69 162 163 167 185
Gove (Nhulumbuy) 212
Graph sounders 50
Grayling 207
Green Cape 197
Greenwell Point 195
Gregory River 197
Groper, Blue *23 *57 95 176 191 192 193 194 195 196 208 209 211
      baldchin 210 211
Gulf of Carpentaria 193
Gurnard 160

H

Hairtail 95 192 194
Hammond Island 198
Harrington 201
Hastings 205
Hat Head 191
Hawkesbury River 192
Hay Point 200
Herring (giant) 192 197
Hinchinbrook Island 199
Holroyd River 197
Hooks 38 *39 144
Hopkin's River 208
Horn Island 198
Hypolymnion 187

I

Iluka 190
Iron-style lures 64

J

Jardine River 198
Javelin fish 96 198 199 200 202

INDEX

Jervis Bay 195
Jewfish see Mulloway
    black 200 212
    school 193
    Westralian 96 208 209
Jig rods 35
Jigging 156
John Dory 97 194 195
Jumpinpin 203

K

Kalbarri 209
Kangaroo Island 207
Karumba 197
Keppel Islands 200
Kiama 194
Kianinny Bay 196
Kingfish 10 11 17 19 *19 25 28 64 98 156 159 176 177 189 190 191 192 193 194 195 196 197 201 202 204 205 206 207 208
Kingscliffe 189
Kirra Point 189
Konahead lures 67 152
Knots 130-3
    basic 130-1
    advanced 132-3

L

Lake Conjolla 196
Lake Illawarra 194
Lake Macquarie 192
Lake Taupo 162
Lake Wollumboola 195
Lakes Entrance 204
Landing tackle 48 *48
Leaders 40 *40
Lead-head jigs 64-5
Leatherjackets 99 160 194 196 197 209
Lennox Head 190
Light tackle spinning and plug casting 144
Ling 207
Liquid crystal displays (LCD) 50
Lizard Island 198
Long Reef 193
Long Tom 197
Lorne 205
Luderick 98 149 176 189 191 192 193 194 195 196 197 202 203 204 205 207
Lure casting 149

Lures, freshwater 68 69 *69
    saltwater 64-5 *65 *65
    saltwater trolling 66-7 *66 *67

M

Mac Clennans 195
Mackay 200
Mackerel 10 11 17 19 28 64 66 100 101 156 176 177 189 190 191 192 194 197 198 199 200 201 202 203 209 210 211 212
Macleay River 191
Magnetic Island 199
Malabar 193
Malacoota 203 204
Mangrove jack 17 *17 64 102 *135 181 189 191 197 198 199 200 201 202 203 210 211
Mangrove streams 180-1
Manning River 191
Maribynong 205
Marlin 28 66 103 *152 176 177 189 191 193 195 196 198 199 202 203 209 210 211 212
Marlo 204
Maroochy River 202
Marsden's Head 195
Mary River 212
Merimbula 197
Merri River 206
Minamurra River 194
Minnie Water 190
Minnow (lures) 64 66 *67 69 162 163
Mitchell River 197 204
Mooloolah River 202
Moreton Bay 202
Moreton Island 202
Mornington Island 197
Moruya River 196
Morwong 105 160 194 195 196 204
Mossman 198
Mount Gambier 207
Mud crabs 201 202
Mullet 105 176 189 192 195 204 205 206 207
Mulloway 19 *31 *59 104 159 176 189 190 191 192 193 195 196 201 202 203 204 205 206 207 208 209 210
Mullumbimby 190

Murchison River 210
Murrah River 186
Murray cod 17 69 106 162 163 167 *184 185
Murray River 185
Murwillumbah 189
Muttonbird Island 190

N

Nadjee Inlet 197
Nadjee River 197
Nambucca Heads 191
Nannygai 106 160
Narooma 196
Nelson Lake 196
Nets 48 *48
Newcastle 192
Newport Reef 193
Nhulumbuy 212
Nicholson River 197 204
Noalunga 207
Noosa Heads 202
Noosa National Park 202
Noosa River 202
Norah Head 192
Norman River 197
Normanby River 198
Normanton 197
North Entrance Beach 192
North Head 193
North Reef 202
North-west Cape 210

O

Oenpelli 212
Onslow 210
Ord River 211
O'Shanassey River 197
Overhead casting reel 18-19
Overhead casting rods 32
Oysters 195

P

Palm Beach 203
Pambula 196-7
Paper chart sounders 50
Parrot fish 202 203 204 205 206 207
Perch 15 109 163 see also Golden perch

English 108 163 185 206
 estuary 162 192 196 197 204 206 207
 Macquarie *163 163 *187
 pearl 107 189 190 191 203
 redfin 163 *187
 silver 163 185
 spangled 200
Phillip Island 204
Picker's Doom 165
Pike 110 196 197 204 205 206 207 209
Pikey bream 198 199
Pilchards 64 189 204
Pine River- Hayes Island 202
Pittwater 192
Plug casting 144
Plug rods (see Baitcaster rods)
Plugs (lures) 65 69 162 163
Point Cartwright 202
Point Plomer 191
Point Samson 211
Poppers 64 73 156
Port Albert 204
Port Campbell 205
Port Fairy 206
Port Hacking 193 194
Port Hedland 193 194
Port Kembla 194
Port Lincoln 208
Port Macquarie 191
Port Phillip Bay 205
Port Pyrie 208
Port Stephens 191
Port Welshpool 200
Portland 206
Prawns 192 195 197
Prince of Wales Island 198
Princess Charlotte Bay 199
Proserpine 200
Pumicestone Passage 202
Pushers 67

Q

Queenfish 25 64 110 156 197 198 199 200 201 211 212

R

Radar 51
Rattlebaits 69
Ray 204 206 207
Redfin see Perch, English

Reels Baitcaster 16-7 *16
 centre-pin 22-3
 closed-face 14 *14
 fixed-spool 10
 fly 24 *24 25 *25
 game 18 20
 side-cast 22 *22
 spinning 10
 trolling 20
Richmond River 190
Rigs 134-43
 balanced 137
 beach, rock, jetty 136
 bluewater trolling lure 139
 bobby cork 141
 casting lure or jig 139 140
 deep sea 135
 estuary and harbour 134-5
 fixed pencil float 135
 fixed quill float 142
 freshwater 142
 game 140
 ganged hook 136 138 140-1
 lightweight 164
 lure trolling 142
 no-sinker 134
 no-sinker and swivel 135
 Paternoster dropper 135 137 139
 running bobby 137
 running sinker 134 136 138 164
 running sinker and swivel 135 136
 skirted trolling lures 141
 specialised 141
 spoon sinker 137
 sport 140
Rings 44 45 *45
Rivers, outback 184-5
Rock fishing 150 176-9
Rockhampton 200
Rocky beaches 176-9
Rods 26-35
 baitcaster 30 *30 144
 beach 32-3
 breakwall 32-3
 chair 35
 double-handed spinning 28 *28 29
 game 29 *29 34 *34 35 *35
 jig 35 light 26 *26
 make your own 31
 overhead casting 32
 rock 32-3
 sport 34
 ultralight 26 *26
Roper River 212
Rosslyn Bay 200
Rosy jobfish 203
Rottnest Island 209

S

St. Vincent's Gulf 207
Sailfish *20 28 66 111 177 189 198 199 200 202 203 210 211 212
Salmon (kahawai) 15 17 25 64 66 156 159
 Australian 112 192 194 195 196 204 205 206 207 203 209
 freshwater 113 162 187
 threadfin 113 *181 197 200 201 211 212
Saltwater casting lures 64 65 *64 *65
Saltwater flies 72-3 168 *169
Saltwater trolling lures 66 *66 67 *67
Samson fish 114 156 176 189 203 208 209 210
San Remo 205
Sandon River 192
Saratoga 15 69 114 167 197 198 200 212
Satellite navigational systems 51
Saxby River 197
Seal Rocks 191
Seven Mile Beach 195 177 201
Shark Bay 210
Sharks 19 116 154 *154 190 191 195 196 201 205 206 208 209 210
 gummy 115 204 205 206 207
 hammerhead 151
 offshore fishing of 154
 whaler 204
 white pointer 202 205 206
 white tiger 202
Shell Harbour 194
Shoalhaven Heads 195
Shoalhaven River 195
Shoalwater Bay 200
Shore-casting rods 32-3 *33
Shot 42-3 *42-3
Side-cast reels 22 *22
Silver drummer *33

Sinkers 42-3
Skate 204
Skipjack 125 156
Smoky Cape 191
Snapper 11 17 19 25 28 118 156 159 *159 161 176 177 189 190 191 192 193 194 195 196 197 200 201 202 203 204 205 206 207 208 209 210
Snapper Bay 189
Snook 66 119 204 205 206 207 208
Snowy River 204
Solitary Islands 190
Sooty grunter 69 120 167 197 198 199 200 201 211 212
South Alligator River 212
Southport Broadwater 203
Spencer Gulf 208
Spinners 63-9
Spinning 156
Spinning reels, light and ultra-light 10 *10 11 *11
Spirits Bay, NZ 177
Spoons 64 66 68 163
Sprats 64
Squid 207 208 209
Staaten River 197
Stanwell Park 194
Steep Point 177
Stradbroke Islands 202 203
Sunday Island 204
Sunshine Reef 202
Surf beaches 174-5
Surfers' Paradise 203
Sussex Inlet 195
Swansea 192
Sweep 120 176 197 204 205 206 207 208 209
Sweetlip 121 160 199 201 202
Swivels 44 *44 *45
Sydney, Upper and lower harbour, Northern and Southern Beaches 193

T

Tackle 9-53
Tailor 15 17 25 64 66 122 156 176 189 190 191 192 193 194 195 196 197 201 202 203 204 205 207 208 209 210
Tallow Beach 190
Tambo River 204
Tanja Lagoon 196
Tannum Sands 201
Taree 191
Tarpon (ox-eye herring) 197 198 199 200 202 203 211 212
Tarwhine 209 210
Tasmania 206-7
Tasmanaian Trumpeter *160 206
Tathra 196
Tea Gardens 191
Tench 185
Terrigal 192
Terraglin 159 191 192 194 195
The Boneyard 184
The Entrance 192
The Narrows 200 201 204
The Otways 205
The Skillion 192
Thermocline 187
Threadline reels 12 *12 13 *13
Thursday Island 19
Tin Can Bay 201
Tollgate Islands 196
Tommy ruff 123 207 208 209
Top End 212
Topwater flies 73
Topwater lures 69
Topwater plugs 65
Townsville 199
Traces 40
Trevally *17 17 28 64 123 *148 156 159 *159 176 *179 193 195 196 197 198 199 200 201 203 204 205 206 207 208 209 210 211
Trolling reels 20 *20 21 *21
   bluewater lures 138 152
Trolling rods 35
Trout 15 *15 *24 *26 51 65 124 *142 160 162 *162 *167 182-3 *182 187 206 207
Trout streams 182-3
Tuggerah Lake 192
Tugun 203
Tully River 199
Tuna 10 11 17 19 25 28 *48 66 125 176 177 *178 189 190 191 192 193 194 195 196 197 198 199 200 201 203 204 206 208 209 210 211
   see also Bluefin tuna
Tuncurry 191
Tura Head 196
Tuross Lake 196
Tweed Heads 189 203
Tweed River 189
Twofold Bay 197

U

Ulladulla 195-6
Urunga 191

V

Venus tusk fish *29 191 202 203
Victor harbour 207
Video sounders 50

W

Wahoo 66 126 193 199 210
Wallaga Lake 196
Wapengo Lake 196
Waratah Bay 204
Warehou 205 206 207
Warnambool 206
Warriewood 193
Washes 148 *148 149 *176
Water, reading the 171-189
Weipa 197-8
Werri Beach 195
Westernport Bay 204-5
Whitebait 64 207
Whiting 15 126 189 191 192 194 195 196 197 199 200 201 202 203 204
   King George 205 206 207 208 209
Whitsunday Islands 200
Whyalla 208
Wilson's Promontory 204
Windang 194
Wollangong 194
Wonboyn Lake 197
Wonboyn River 197
Wonthaggi 204
Woolgoola 190
Wooli 190
Wooli River 190
Wrasse 211

Y

Yabbie Island 203
Yamba 190
Yarra 205
Yellowfish tuna *18 159 203
Yellowtail 127 156 194 197 201
Yeppoon 200 201
Yorke Peninsula 208